D0045998

COME AS YOU ARE

COME AS YOU ARE

DISCARD

THE
PEACE CORPS
STORY

COATES REDMON

HARCOURT BRACE JOVANOVICH, PUBLISHERS

SAN DIEGO · NEW YORK · LONDON

Requests for permission to make copies of any part of the work should be mailed to: Permissions, Harcourt Brace Jovanovich, Publishers, Orlando, Florida 32887.

Library of Congress Cataloging-in-Publication Data

Redmon, Coates.
    Come as you are.

    Includes index.
    1. Peace Corps (U.S.) I. Title.
HC60.5.R44—1986   361.2'6'06073   86-9791
ISBN 0-15-119435-1

Designed by Jill Casty & Company Design Unltd.
Printed in the United States of America
First edition
A B C D E

for Alfred Winslow Jones

CONTENTS

AUTHOR'S NOTE

I decided to write this book over poached salmon and a glass of white wine at the Jean-Pierre restaurant on K Street in Washington, D.C., April 1975. My luncheon companion was David Baldwin, then the public relations director for the American Medical Association. A gifted southern raconteur, Baldwin was mainly to listen that particular day. But he first regaled me with how much Washington had changed since I had moved away in 1967. The Kennedy Center had sprung up; people no longer dashed up to New York for the best theater, music, and dance. Washington had become a town of good restaurants— "and who ever thought *that* could happen?" laughed the hard-to-please New Orleans native. "And your old Peace Corps buddies," he added, "have formed a kind of 'new old-boy network.' And whoever thought that could happen, either? But they are everywhere and wielding influence. I, and many others in 1961," said Baldwin, "thought the Peace Corps was a charming idea that was doomed to failure and would drag down all of the high-minded, talented idealists associated with it. Quite the opposite has happened." Baldwin then reeled off a Hit Parade of Peace Corps names: Sargent Shriver, Bill Moyers, Jack Vaughn, Frank Mankiewicz, Charlie Peters, Warren Wiggins, Bill Haddad, Franklin Williams, Harris Wofford, Betty Harris, Bob Gale, Nan McEvoy, Don McClure, Dick Ottinger—people who had gone on, as Baldwin pointed out, to become ambassadors, nationally prominent journalists, college presidents, corporate executives, authors, high-powered political operatives, founders of controversial organizations, congressmen. I was astonished; Baldwin had kept track of my "old buddies" better than I had in my interim sojourns in Cambridge, Massachusetts, and New York City.

Baldwin was quick to qualify his "new old-boy network" theory: if all of these people had not actually stayed in Washington since their happy days in the early 1960s as Peace Corps pioneers, they had nonetheless risen, created, ruled and prospered to the extent that they reflected Washington, influenced Washington, and accordingly, was the assumption, the nation.

As the memories that Baldwin evoked flooded in on me, I began to regale *him* with some of the most riotous stories of the Peace Corps' early years. Most of them were too outrageous to have been told at the time, inside or outside the new agency. Baldwin, who always had his ear to the ground, had never heard them and he laughed and laughed and laughed. Finally I apologized for talking so much.

"*Mustn't* apologize," said Baldwin, tapping me insistently on the wrist. "You've got it."

Mystified, I asked, "Got what?"

"Got the *book*," said Baldwin.

"What book?"

"The Peace Corps book, silly darling girl. The quintessential story. Not the history. The *story*. No one else has ever written it. No one else ever will. Go home and start writing it this afternoon."

And so I did.

◆   ◆   ◆

I am grateful to David Baldwin and Albert Meisel for encouraging me to write this book and for advising me to make it not a conventional history but rather an unconventional "mood-and-flavor" account that evokes the all-too-fleeting Kennedy years—the style, the dash, the daring, the rare humor, and most of all, the hope—as it was personified by Sargent Shriver's leadership and inspiration.

Michele Slung was a gracious broker, and a pal throughout.

Mary Finch Hoyt and Dick Elwell provided canny editorial suggestions at the beginning of my work.

Those who rendered technical and research assistance were Julie Edgeworth, Alicia Hetzner, Elizabeth Hyman, and Ruth Sizer Marshall. My daughter, Skipwith, and my son, Evan, provided research assistance, too, as well as a view from the under-twenty group.

Marie Arana-Ward, my editor at Harcourt Brace Jovanovich, deserves medals for patience, wisdom, taste, humor, and a wizardly way with the blue pencil.

Loret Miller Ruppe, the present Peace Corps Director, was cordial and generous during the course of my research at my old stomping ground, the Peace Corps headquarters. Jim Hogan, the director of marketing, opened up the doors of his domain with unfailing bonhomie. The Peace Corps librarian, Rita Warphea, and her associate, Victoria Freis, were also helpful as was Jim Mayer, head of the Peace Corps Twenty-Fifth Anniversary Office. John Von Reyn did yeoman work in arranging for me to obtain evaluation reports from the early 1960s under the Freedom of Information Act. As for Anne Alvarez, the Peace Corps director of photography, I must declare her a saint.

She cheerfully tolerated my frequent binges of nostalgia as I went through the early Peace Corps photo files, and she helped me ferret out many items that had been buried for years.

COME AS YOU ARE

Bill Robinson in his front yard in Dhankuta, Nepal

"We hiked into Dhankuta having come up through thirty miles of rocky, desolate Himalayan foothills with forty-pound backpacks containing the barest possible minimum of clothes and worldly possessions we would need for two years. As we came up the trail the children ran down to greet us and danced along beside us. By the time we reached the village, all the dogs were barking; people were rushing out of their huts to stare at us. They examined every little thing—our shoes, our socks, our watches. We were welcomed as incredibly powerful, successful people. We knew enough Nepali to know that. And we could see Mount Everest from our backyard. Jim and I were literally and figuratively on an all-time high that day.

"But within forty-eight hours all of our exhilaration was just washed away by the first monsoon rain. Mud oozed into our hut, the roof leaked, there was no electricity. The fire wouldn't light. I thought: Oh, God. This is it. *Two years*. Jim lay on his bunk moaning, 'What have I done, what have I done?' Occasionally he would come out of his trance and we'd both say 'Why the hell didn't we go to Harvard Business School?' and 'Are we insane?' A week later, Jim left. We had arrived in triumph and he just snuck out. He had to go, I guess. But I couldn't go."

Robinson couldn't go because he had been personally recruited by Sargent Shriver at the University of Colorado. He had hiked with Supreme Court Justice William O. Douglas during training. His Rep, Willi Unsoeld, had climbed Everest the previous year. He himself had written a letter to *Newsweek* in gratitude for an editorial by Walter Lippmann that had praised President Kennedy for creating the Peace Corps, and *Newsweek* had published the letter. "Right after Jim walked out of Dhankuta," says Robinson, "I was dangerously close to doing it myself. But then I thought, 'I can't let all of those great people down—Kennedy, Shriver, Douglas, Unsoeld, Lippmann. Hell, I can't leave. I was quoted in *Newsweek*!'"

CHAPTER 1

THE
GENERAL('S)
IDEA

There is a plaque on the steps of the University of Michigan Student Union at Ann Arbor that reads:

> Here at 2:00 A.M. on October 14, 1960, John Fitzgerald Kennedy first defined the Peace Corps. He stood at the place marked by the medallion and was cheered by a large and enthusiastic student audience for the hope and promise his idea gave the world.

It makes no difference that this statement trifles with the truth, so pure and shimmering were the feelings that inspired it twenty-five years ago. In its very inaccuracy is a larger truth: The Peace Corps was wished and willed into existence by some ambitious, affluent, idealistic college students who were convinced that America had been lulled into a near stupor after eight years of rule by grandfather figures and organization men. They felt they were being towed by some great, ponderous ship that had lost its compass. They were joined in the sense that America was becoming increasingly fat, arrogant, and materialistic. They believed the message of the 1958 novel *The Ugly American*, that the United States was losing out to the Communists in the developing nations because of these very traits. And so, they wanted to take charge of their own lives and destinies, to set a new course for themselves, quite divergent from that of their parents. The British critic Cyril Connolly had recently noted that this mentality was taking hold "at a time when the American way, backed by American resources, has made the country into the greatest power the world has known, there has never been more doubting and questioning of the purpose of the American process; the higher up one goes [in the society] the more searching becomes the self-criticism, the deeper the thirst for a valid mystique of humanity." The plaque at Ann Arbor is a testimonial to this thirst.

◆　　　◆　　　◆

Senator John F. Kennedy was making an unannounced stop at the University of Michigan in the last month of his campaign for the presidency to rest up after his third debate with Richard Nixon. The next day he was to make a one-day campaign train tour through southern Michigan. No campaign speech at Ann Arbor had been scheduled; Kennedy had come to sleep, not to speak. But as his car pulled onto the campus and neared the Student Union, where he was to stay, it was apparent that he was not alone: ten thousand students surrounded the Union and environs, and obviously for only one purpose—to lay eyes on the youngest, handsomest, most dynamic presidential candidate in their lifetime.

The Ann Arbor crowd had been gathering, by means of word of mouth, since the middle of the evening. Deborah Bacon, the dean of women at Michigan, knew of the visit and was inspired to lift the ban that said women had to be in their dorms by midnight.

"The mood," says Mildred Jeffrey, Kennedy's Michigan coordinator, "was, see this man or else. I had to battle my way through the crowd, and I had to wonder what Kennedy was going to do with this situation. It was a serious crowd, minus the usual jumpers and screamers, and there were even some people with Nixon placards there. The Michigan faculty was at that time rather skeptical of Kennedy, by and large, but the insistence upon seeing him was something that throbbed."

It was just a few minutes before 2:00 A.M. when Kennedy got out of his car and was led up the steps to the Student Union, and according to Mildred Jeffrey and others present at that moment, Kennedy immediately sensed that the atmosphere was challenging and dicey. He thus opened with some light, teasing remarks about the late hour and the need to get to bed. This was greeted by muted giggles and hoots, suggestive whistles, a few disappointed moans, and the faintest sound of booing. Kennedy suddenly tightened his tone, raised his voice, and swung into this:

> How many of you are willing to spend ten years in Africa or Latin America or Asia working for the U.S. and working for freedom? How many of you who are going to be doctors are willing to spend your days in Ghana? Technicians or engineers, how many of you are willing to work in the foreign service and spend your lives travelling around the world? On your willingness to do that, not merely to serve one or two years in the service, but on your willingness to contribute part of your life to this country, I think, will depend the answer to whether we as a free society can compete.

The unexpected challenge came, as it was meant to—Kennedy was irritated—as something of a dressing down, and the students were quiet and thoughtful for a moment, numbed almost. Then, there was some nodding and nudging and whispering, and then warm, friendly applause. And finally, cheers.

Although Kennedy never once uttered the words "peace corps" (because they did not yet exist in his vocabulary), although he rather outlandishly suggested anything from ten years to a lifetime of selfless service in near-mythical lands, although he had really not "defined" anything at all, the peace corps idea had been launched, and it is rather doubtful that Kennedy could have thereafter turned his back on it. He had struck an exposed nerve.

"There was an almost magical interaction between Kennedy and the crowd after that," says Mildred Jeffrey. "They were suddenly crying to touch him. That moment was thirty seconds ago as far as my feelings are concerned. The students were in a state of euphoria. He had gotten to them, I thought, maybe for all time."

The next morning, Kennedy's regular entourage, which now included Mildred Jeffrey and other anointed pro-Kennedy Michiganites, boarded the campaign train to find the candidate "greatly refreshed and just full of talk about Afrikkur. At every stop—Battle Creek, Kalamazoo—" says Jeffrey, "Kennedy pressed on about Afrikkur. Those crowds couldn't have cared less about Africa, but that was all he wanted to talk about, no doubt because of the tremendous response to his remarks the night before. But of course, it wasn't Africa that had turned the students on, it was that hint of a noble anti-Communist international crusade that got to them. I'm not too sure that Kennedy really caught that. But the next day, on he went. It was Tunizhur and Algeriur and Kenyur and Ghanur the whole day. We called it our 'Afrikkur trip.' "

If someone had asked Kennedy about the new program he had proposed the night before in Ann Arbor, he would probably have wondered what they were talking about. But back at the Michigan campus, some students thought they had heard an invitation to join something exciting, new, and hopeful. Their joyful, intellectually wanton, self-induced misinterpretation soon uncorked and began to pour into the Kennedy campaign. It was the beginning of the final push behind an idea that had been kicking around for a while but still had a long way to go.

The Peace Corps grew out of some creative liberal thinking, the purist political expediency, a full moon on the rise at a passing moment of pacifistic patriotism between the cold war and the Vietnam War, the all-American drive to do good and be loved, and a lot of crazy good luck. Had even one of these elements been missing from the astonishing confluence of political event and personal need that existed in 1960–61, the Peace Corps would not have seen the light of day, or if it had, it would have almost surely fizzled or boomeranged within six months. Peace Corps enthusiasts were calling it "an idea whose time had come," and that it was, but that presumes that the peace corps idea was inevitable, which it wasn't. There is no inevitability in politics. From the time that John F. Kennedy first flirted with the idea rather tentatively late in his presidential campaign until it was marginally operational in late April of 1961, when Ghana became the first country to request Peace Corps Volunteers, the Peace Corps was usually the dispensable item on the Kennedy agenda. It almost slipped away several times during the postelection, preinaugural period due to indifference on the part of the president-elect and his principal advisors; and finally, in the first week of May 1961, at what would be its eleventh hour, the Peace Corps had to be dramatically rescued by Lyndon Johnson. A curious business for an idea whose time had come. The early Peace Corps was always locked in a behind-the-scenes struggle to exist. It was the secret soap opera of the New Frontier.

Certainly John F. Kennedy did not know exactly what he was spawning when he finally allowed himself to be persuaded that it would be politically wise to put the Peace Corps into action early in his administration. The idea of large numbers of young people going into the touchy, crucial Third World nations on his behalf and apparently with his blessing must have given him some nervous moments. How could he not worry that the likes of Holden Caulfield would be turned loose from Nigeria to Indonesia?

But the fact was, Kennedy *had* to embrace a peace corps idea, because at the time he did, there were no other available new gambits to make the New Frontier look as refreshing and innovative as it sounded, and he needed one. The peace corps idea seized him in a metaphysical grip; it defined his intentions in the Third World and his personal style as an innovative internationalist more than he knew at first, and it dogged him persistently into the Oval Office. It would not let go, no matter how many times it was brushed aside.

In its relentless pursuit of Kennedy, the peace corps idea first beckoned obliquely in the spring of 1960. One of its first and major champions, Senator Hubert Humphrey, wanted to be president, and just as Humphrey was preparing legislation for a "peace corps," the West Virginia primary contest against Kennedy intervened. (Congressman Henry Reuss of Wisconsin and Senator Richard Neuberger of Oregon had cosponsored a "Point Four Youth Corps" a few months earlier.) The Kennedy juggernaut, of course, was destined to overrun Humphrey and chase him out of the presidential race. But during the West Virginia primary, on May 1, 1960, a cruel irony manifested itself that would eclipse every other event and mangle every possibility of a presidential candidate focusing on such a cozy, innocent thing as a peace corps idea for some time to come. Theodore H. White in *The Making of the President 1960* describes it:

> While Hubert Humphrey and John F. Kennedy were rising to bounce once more over the roads of the Appalachians, a mountain boy raised in these same hills was already parachuting through the air to fall in the flat farmlands near Sverdlovsk [Russia] . . . His mishap warped both world events and the American electoral exercise for the rest of the year.
> . Francis Gary Powers . . . in a high-altitude plane called the U-2 . . . was exposed as prey to Soviet fighter craft and was to become, when shot down that afternoon, the first acknowledged American spy ever seized by the Soviet Union . . .

The U-2 flight gave the Russians an excuse to abort an imminent summit conference between Eisenhower and Khrushchev and to denounce Eisenhower (who claimed he did not order the flight) as a hypocrite and liar. Disarmament negotiations between Russia and the United States broke down, and Eisenhower's last goodwill mission (he had traveled sixty thousand miles around the world in a grand peacemaking gesture) to Japan was also aborted; the Japanese would not receive him. The nation was as shaken and as deeply embarrassed as it ever had been. As White points out: "The U-2 incident raised the matter of America's honor and prestige . . . and [it] raised the problem of Presidential command . . . If Eisenhower had not [ordered the flight]—as apparently he had not . . . [then] who exercised American authority in such crucial matters?"

Meanwhile, the Democratic National Convention.

American political conventions are generally like raging forest fires and highway disasters—dreadful but fascinating. Amid everything that is loud, cheap, and jarring is the next probable leader of the free world chosen. With few exceptions, the prevailing sentiment is "Be kind to your web-footed friend, for a duck may be somebody's mother." But at the Democratic National Convention of 1960 there was an element of high drama as well in the heartfelt intention to honor the honorable. While few Republicans could not honestly view as tragic Eisenhower's departure from public office—his time had so clearly passed—large numbers of Democrats were not at all prepared for their wise man/ hero of the past eight years, Adlai Stevenson, to be put out to pasture. Senator Eugene McCarthy of Minnesota pleaded this cause memorably: "Do not reject this man who has made us all proud to be Democrats," he exhorted the still-faithful and the recently faithful. "Do not leave this prophet without honor in his own party." Also memorable was the response to that exhortation, which was as wild and uncontrollable as it was loving. Again, Theodore White in *The Making of the President 1960*:

> The Los Angeles police called for reinforcements as the marching thousands of Stevensonians threatened to storm the Convention. Minute by minute one could detect a seepage through the barred gates, rising to flood. Observers speculated on how the Stevensonians were slipping their demonstrators into the hall, where every seat was numbered and ticketed . . . But the galleries were now wquivering with impatient Stevensonians waiting to demonstrate.
>   . . . As Eugene McCarthy concluded, the floor erupted. In from all the gates poured the demonstrators, snake-dancing, chanting, wriggling, yelling . . . the mob yelled WE WANT STEVENSON . . . As they passed the state standards . . . McCarthy pleaded for order; the Convention band attempted to blare above the shouting; the lights were turned out; and still the chant went on.

Among those who contrived the massive Stevenson demonstration were two brash young men, William F. Haddad and Tedson J. Meyers, who typified the tough but idealistic spirit of the New York Democratic reform movement, and along with many others that year, they were almost suicidally bent on pushing the levers that would accomplish the impossible: Stop Kennedy, restart Stevenson. Haddad, who in 1960 was a prize-winning investigative reporter for the *New York Post*, in 1956 had been Senator Estes Kefauver's floor manager at the Democratic National Convention, where Kefauver was seeking the vice presidential nomination. When Stevenson threw the convention open for the vice presidential nomination and the young senator from Massachusetts, John F. Kennedy, challenged Kefauver—with his younger brother, Bobby, as *his* floor manager—Haddad was instrumental in engineering Kennedy's only defeat for an office he had sought.

By 1960 the realities of the Kennedy drive, the Kennedy wealth, the Kennedy glamour, and the Kennedy primary victories—plus the Stevenson reluctance—might have caused a political realist to switch candidates while the switching was good. But Haddad was stubborn. And angrily disappointed as he noticed many trusted liberal friends rapidly switching over to Kennedy, foremost among them Arthur Schlesinger, Jr., at Harvard, who had gone so far as to suggest to the die-hard Haddad that he actually go to *work* for Kennedy because, quite simply, Kennedy could *win*. "Arthur had been so pro-Stevenson," says Haddad, "that it just amazed me. So I thought, 'Okay, the rats are desertin' the sinkin' ship. I'll just go out to Los Angeles and help Tedson get somethin' goin' for Stevenson at the convention.' "

Tedson Meyers, who was then working in the legal department of ABC, had landed in Los Angeles as a key Stevenson organizer by way of having put together a highly successful volunteer group for Stevenson in New York with friends from the reform movement and David Garth, a television producer and political image-maker.

In the flamboyant and extemporaneous fashion that was soon to become standard operating procedure at the Peace Corps, Meyers rented a Fifth Avenue bus from MGM, using the bottom part as an office and the top part as a speaker's platform from which he would organize the Stevenson demonstrators. There was one problem and it was horrendous: Because Stevenson was not a formal candidate, his supporters had been allotted fewer than fifty convention tickets from the Democratic National Committee. Meyers, Haddad, David Garth, and other key Stevenson men were outraged. So while Haddad feverishly "worked" the delegations inside the convention hall, Meyers and Garth were "inspired to acquire" thousands of Kennedy buttons from Kennedy campaign headquarters and pin them on ardent and willing Stevenson fans, whom they then lined up in regular distribution lines at the convention, thus garnering about twenty-five hundred tickets of some four thousand originally slated for Kennedy supporters. (Meanwhile, Meyers and his colleagues had managed to bargain successfully with Democratic clubs around the country for hundreds more.) In a final act of defiance, a regular guard at one of the convention doors was "induced to disappear," and an out-of-work actor replaced him in official garb. Meyers, from the top of his bus, was able to get the Stevenson demonstrators lined up at another key door, and when someone inside opened it for a last-minute check, "in we all went, screaming," exults Meyers, "just as McCarthy had placed Stevenson's name in nomination. It was like a bullfight."

Denounced at the time as "hooligans" by Florida Governor Leroy Collins, who was chairman of the convention (and who didn't know the half of it), Meyers, Haddad, and the others were content that at least their candidate had received a proper "last hurrah," if not altogether within proper limits.

Today both Haddad and Meyers are philosophical about the Stevenson demonstration. Meyers reflects: "Actually, that demonstration was very much related to the Kennedy/Peace Corps constituency, as it later got put together and labeled. The Stevenson crowds were full of idealistic young people who had fled college and their jobs, driven to Los Angeles from all over the country just for the privilege of cheering for the only political candidate they then believed could lift politics up and make government service an interesting, attractive exercise. It was a phenomenal mass gesture. Most of those in the 1960 Stevenson movement weren't much older than thirty, and some weren't even twenty, and there were many thousands of them.

"You can't tell me," continues Meyers, "that the Kennedy people didn't take note of what we had put together. They saw that day what the young were prepared to do for a candidate they really admired."

As Haddad sees it, "It's a lucky thing for Kennedy that he finally latched on to the Peace Corps, because among other benefits it brought him, it kept that youthful idealism intact. An awful lot of the first Volunteers and many of us on the Peace Corps staff had gotten our idealism stirred up by Stevenson. Kennedy and the Peace Corps staff inherited it." The Peace Corps also inherited Haddad and Meyers.

If Kennedy did not mention the Peace Corps in his acceptance speech, it later seemed to many that he had, for as always, Kennedy's rhetoric was sprinkled with New Frontier buzzwords ("challenges," "sacrifice," "pioneers"), which so neatly matched the character of the Peace Corps, as it later came to be known, that it all seemed to have been deliberately planned. Even the name, New Frontier, would seem to have been hatched from the same egg as the Peace Corps; what was the Peace Corps except a new frontier in American experience? Later on, too, when the Peace Corps borrowed some of Kennedy's language to describe itself publicly ("help people help themselves"—a phrase lifted from Kennedy's inaugural address), that only added to the impression that the Peace Corps had long been a specific plan of Kennedy's. And the following quotes from Kennedy's acceptance speech in Los Angeles still sound like a perfectly planned preamble to his inaugural address, which in turn sounds like a preamble to the Peace Corps:

> The problems are not all solved and the battles are not all won, and we stand today on the edge of a new frontier—the frontier of the 1960s, a frontier of unknown opportunities and paths, a frontier of unfulfilled hopes . . .
> The new frontier of which I speak is not a set of promises—it is a set of challenges. It sums up not what I intend to *offer* the American people, but what I intend to *ask* of them . . . It holds out the promise of more sacrifice instead of more security . . .

Bill Haddad did not wait for Kennedy's acceptance speech. When it got around that Lyndon Johnson was to be Kennedy's running mate, Democratic party liberals, including Haddad, went into shock. As they raged against the man who would soon prove more liberal than all of them, and certainly more liberal than Kennedy, words like "betrayal" and "double cross" were being bandied about. Haddad, furious at Johnson's nomination, "fled the convention in disgust. It was bad enough we hadda have Kennedy instead of Stevenson, but now we hadda take that crook, Johnson, as well."

A day after the convention was over, Haddad received a phone call from William McCormick Blair, a former law partner of Adlai Stevenson's who would become Kennedy's Ambassador to Denmark and the Philippines. Blair had agreed to help the Kennedys recruit agreeable and talented Stevenson supporters for the upcoming campaign. "Bill Blair told me that Bobby wanted to talk to me. Under the circumstances," Haddad chuckles, "I couldn't think why. But I said I'd see him."

In addition to what might be judged within the Kennedy camp as scurrilously unforgivable anti-Kennedy convention activities both in 1956 and 1960, Haddad had also written a number of pro-Stevenson pieces in the *New York Post* that had been interpreted by the Kennedys as also irascibly anti-Kennedy. A number of Haddad's acquaintances in the New York reform movement assumed that the Kennedys hired

Haddad out of sheer exasperation and frustration, to get this talented troublemaker on their side and out of harm's way.

"Bobby was sittin' on the corner of his desk when I walked in. He asked me bluntly if I'd come work for him. I said, 'I don't want to come under false colors. I have not been a fan of yours.' Bobby just said, 'That is not the question I asked.' "

Haddad took a leave of absence from the *Post* and joined the Kennedy team as Bobby Kennedy's special assistant.

During the early part of the campaign a free-floating idea for utilizing young people in some kind of overseas development program wafted by Haddad's reporter's ears for the first time; they perked up. "I thought, Wow! What's this? Where'd that come from? A *great* thing for Kennedy. Make him look more relaxed, more liberal. I didn't think he looked liberal enough, and he could afford to. No question. Get the youth vote, have a hot new program to go with." But his enthusiasm for the idea was not only unappreciated within the tough-talking, politically pragmatic Kennedy camp, it made him an occasional pariah. "Kenny O'Donnell especially hated it, just couldn't stand it. It made him sick," says Haddad. "He'd say to me, 'Oh well, Jesus, Bill, maybe it'd be okay as a campaign gimmick, but it's a kooky, liberal, reform idea,' he'd say, 'and oh, dear God, not for *real*.' " More than one Kennedy spokesman told Haddad to "knock it off," that such talk would embarrass the candidate. "I don't think Kennedy was embarrassed by the idea, but he had other things on his mind. He had the problem of facin' a two-time vice president, the problem of bein' a Catholic. He hadda keep talkin' about Quemoy and Matsu and worryin' about how he was gonna win the South. It was a tense campaign."

Kennedy didn't actually propose a "peace corps" by name or as any sort of organization, program, or movement until November 2, at the Cow Palace in San Francisco, just six days before the 1960 election—and three weeks *after* his Ann Arbor remarks. To be sure, the eager collegians from Michigan were on the march and gathering strength from campuses across the country, but it took two almost random events in the last hectic days of the campaign to convince Kennedy that he should formally welcome them into his camp.

Mildred Jeffrey, whose daughter, Sharon, was a Michigan undergraduate, followed the feverish activity of the students and helped the college movement grow. Central to the activity on the Michigan campus was a graduate student in social psychology, Alan Guskin, and his wife, Judy, a graduate student in comparative literature, who were forming the "Americans Committed to World Responsibility," which, as Jeffrey wryly puts it, "is the, er, um, terribly modest sort of thing that Kennedy inspired in students at that time." With some fellow graduate students, the Guskins composed a piece for the *Michigan Daily*, which appeared on October 21, to answer Kennedy's October 14 "challenge." And within days there were numerous petitions from all corners of the campus stating a willingness to join any Kennedy-sponsored volunteer force in the Third World. The first of thousands of letters and telegrams from the campuses began to pour in at Kennedy headquarters everywhere and into the Democratic National Committee in Washington. Within the next two weeks, several other college news-papers, moving from Midwest to West, had joined the bandwagon, and as Kennedy would reach subsequent stops, he would be greeted with even more youthful enthusiasm. But the Michigan groups must get credit for having the most political savvy and the best follow-through.

Through the urgings of the Guskins and tales of continuing campus excitement from her daughter, Sharon, Mildred Jeffrey happily agreed to pursue her candidate on this issue. "I knew," said Mildred Jeffrey, "that Kennedy was soon going to make a major foreign policy speech and that it would be in San Francisco. I made it my business, therefore, to try to get the peace corps idea into it. I talked to Mike Feldman and Ted Sorensen fairly regularly, and I pressed when I could, without, you know, sounding like a female nuisance, and the speech input was made through Mike Feldman. But then the kids, the Guskins and their 'Americans Committed to World Responsibility,' wanted more. They wanted an audience with Kennedy and they were willing to go anywhere—*anywhere*—to meet him. This I was able to arrange, with amazingly little difficulty, through Ted Sorensen. Those kids were political amateurs, but they knew where to aim—at the top—and who could help them."

Two weeks after Kennedy's Ann Arbor remarks, Judy Guskin an-swered the phone in her married-graduate-student pad. "God. It was Millie Jeffrey," she says, "telling me that Al and I and our group could actually meet Kennedy."

"I'll never forget the look on my wife's face," says Al Guskin. "She was in a state of total shock."

On November 5, 1960, three days after Kennedy's formal proposal of the Peace Corps in San Francisco, Millie Jeffrey and the "Americans Committed to World Responsibility" drove down in five carloads to Toledo, Ohio, to meet the candidate at the airport.

Al Guskin says, "We were so damned excited. We were all standing with Kennedy, about a hundred feet from the *Caroline*, which then seemed like a very glamorous plane and now seems so obsolete. And there was Judy, handing Kennedy our petitions and message. It was unreal. Kennedy joked with Judy about the petitions, saying, 'I guess you don't really want me to have them, do you?' He suspected rightly that these were our only copies of these hundreds of signatures. Then he said, 'Judy, until Tuesday [election day], we will worry about the nation, but after that, the world.' "

Millie Jeffrey, who was standing with the group, recalls that Kennedy said to Judy Guskin, "Judy, give me three more days, and then we will do it." Millie Jeffrey was hardly surprised when the Guskins went into the first Peace Corps training program for Thailand in October 1961, asking not.

General James M. Gavin was unaware of Kennedy's remarks in Ann Arbor or the programmatic fantasies they had recently stirred up in the Midwest. However, he had an interesting idea of his own, born of some rather unnerving but enlightening talks with ROTC groups at Harvard and Tufts and with the 1960 graduating class at MIT. His idea was that there should be a reasonable alternative to military service to meet the growing hostility among male college students toward the draft and "the system" in general. He decided that he would try the idea out in his next major speech, knowing all the while that it might be received with anything from disinterest to amused derision to outrage.

Gavin had retired from the army in 1957 as a major general to become president of the Arthur D. Little Co. (a prestigious industrial research and management consulting firm) in Cambridge, Massachusetts, and was much in demand as a speaker at establishment gatherings. Handsome, articulate, and possessed of a dazzling war record, he commanded respect of both liberals and conservatives. On October 27, 1960, he was keynote speaker at a conference of educators and businessmen at the Americana Hotel in Bal Harbour (Miami Beach), Florida. That conference was opaquely entitled, "Manpower Resources in the South: An Industry-Education Conference, sponsored by the Regional Advisory Council on Nuclear Energy and OCDM, Executive Office of the President, in cooperation with The Oak Ridge Institute of Nuclear Studies, Inc." His audience consisted of two hundred college presidents and two hundred heads of corporations.

After Gavin had concluded his prepared text, he launched into his favorite idea, off the cuff. No written account exists, but Gavin recalls that he said, "I think we can do better [a favorite Kennedy phrase] than to send our young men around the globe to watch over other societies in military uniform. I know many young men who would rather do something more ennobling for their country."

Gavin then described his many encounters, over a period of two years, with thousands of college students in the Boston area. Gavin pointed out that they came from all over the country but shared similar attitudes: They were strongly antimilitary, wary of possible American involvement in Southeast Asia, "outraged by our recent policies of brinkmanship and massive retaliation—really horrible ideas and horrible words—but still very patriotic, dedicated to the best democratic ideals and more than willing to serve their country in some acceptable, worthwhile, moral capacity." And most were willing to do so without pay, Gavin pointed out. Gavin then suggested that a peacetime volunteer force be started as an alternative to military service. Summarizing, Gavin proposed that the United States use available talent in this country to fill educational and technical needs in the developing nations overseas, thereby accomplishing two important objectives: channel the growing disenchantment among the young with the military services into morale-building good works among the poor, and thus more effectively compete with the Communists in the delicately balanced new nations.

From this solidly establishment and largely conservative audience, an astonished Gavin got a standing ovation. "The most applause," he says, "that I ever received in my life."

With Gavin on the dais that evening was the then-governor of South Carolina, Ernest F. (Fritz) Hollings (now a senator from South Carolina and briefly a candidate for president in 1984), who was chairman of the conference. He immediately grabbed Gavin's arm and steered him away to his room in the Americana Hotel, where he probed Gavin for more about his "peace army."

"I told Gavin," says Hollings, "that this idea of his was just great— oh, very, *very* acceptable. Secretly, I was thinking that the idea sounded like something good for Kennedy, something he would be for." They talked further and suddenly Hollings noticed that Gavin was wearing a PT-109 tie clasp. He exclaimed, "Ah! Then *you* are with *we.*" (*We* being prominent figures for Kennedy.)

At that point, Hollings excitedly suggested, "You know, this is such a fine idea, I'd hate to see the Republicans get a hold of it, and you know, there were a lot of Nixon supporters in the audience today. Let's call Kennedy *now!*"

Since both Hollings and Gavin were valued Kennedy loyalists, they had the key telephone numbers—Hyannis Port, campaign head-quarters in various locations, the homes of important campaign staff members—for just such an occasion. "I started calling. I called Kennedy, but missed him. I called Bobby and couldn't find him. Finally, at midnight, I reached Mike Feldman in Washington. I told him about Gavin's speech, about the tremendous response. Mike sounded interested. I went on to summarize Gavin's main points and pointed out that there were lots of Nixon supporters in that crowd, some fat-cat contributors, you know, and for God's sake, let's not let them beat us to this. Mike sounded *very* interested, and he said flatly, 'Fritz, Kennedy will cover it.' "

Nothing is less strange in the midst of a presidential campaign than that the right hand does not know what the left is doing. It could be assumed that Gavin was a stalking horse, that Kennedy had privately asked him to float the peace corps idea by a "difficult" audience. But that was not the case.

Gavin was unaware that there was proposed legislation along these lines already in Congress, did not know that Kennedy had already sprinkled the idea over the Michigan campus, and had not ever before discussed it with others of a similar mind in the Boston area. * Hollings had not heard of the idea before the night of Gavin's speech, October 27, nor had he realized at first that he and Gavin shared pro-Kennedy sentiments (neither man thought that the other came from a likely

*Professor Robert Bowie, Director of the Center for International Affairs at Harvard and a former head of the policy planning staff at the State Department, had testified in closed session in June 1960 before the Senate Subcommittee on National Policy Machinery (which had been holding hearings on the adequacy of the country's policy-making apparatus in the cold war) that he favored recruiting "one thousand or more seniors coming out of college each year" who could "do most anything for two or three years in one of the underdeveloped countries." This would give, said Bowie, the citizens of those countries, a chance to see educated Americans "who were not afraid of getting their hands dirty." And that in turn would give young Americans a chance to "feel they are being useful." Bowie's main point was that it was difficult to get people "to work for the government in trying jobs." And this was one of his solutions.

The New York Times on November 4, 1960—two days after Kennedy's Peace Corps proposal in San Francisco—remarked that Professor Bowie's closed-session testimony (which they were revealing for the first time) was "markedly similar to the 'peace corps' [idea]" just "advocated by Senator John F. Kennedy."

The Kennedy Administration chroniclers, Sorensen and Schlesinger, briefly acknowledged possible sources of the peace corps idea, but neither mentioned the Bowie testimony, which, because it had come in closed session, was not released even to Senate conferees; therefore, they were probably totally unaware of it.

background for such sentiments). Mike Feldman says that Hollings's midnight call to him on October 27 was the first *he* had heard of it.

Mildred Jeffrey, Kennedy's campaign coordinator in Michigan, recalls that when she had reached Mike Feldman by phone to urge the peace corps idea on him for Kennedy's foreign policy speech, Feldman remarked with some bemusement that General Gavin had just come up with a very similar idea. Feldman did not think to add that Hollings was submitting a memo on the idea to the Kennedy staff or that Gavin had talked to Kennedy personally about it.

General Gavin recalls that brief but highly significant conversation: "When I returned to Wellesley [Massachusetts] from my speech in Miami Beach, I had a phone call from Senator Kennedy. He said, 'Jim, what the hell did you say to them down there, anyway?' I told him, and he asked me to give him a one-page statement on it and to get it in the mail right away. Using my own typewriter at home, I did so." Gavin recalls that the name "Peace Corps" surfaced at a brainstorming meeting he had a few days later at Arthur D. Little Co. "Someone suggested it, but we thought at first that it had too military a ring—like Rommel's Afrika Korps of World War II. Someone else said that 'peace' was too often used in Communist propaganda." But Gavin and his colleagues could think of no better name, and he recommended it.

Kennedy and Feldman had high regard for both Hollings's and Mildred Jeffrey's political judgment (Hollings was one of the few major southern political figures to support Kennedy in 1960), and it seems clear that on or about October 30 this jumbo combination of advocacies persuaded Kennedy to commit himself to putting the Peace Corps up front in his campaign. There was Gavin in the Northeast with his unimpeachable military and business credentials and his firsthand knowledge of the mood at Harvard, Tufts, and MIT; there was Mildred Jeffrey in the Midwest with her long experience in the labor movement (UAW) and Democratic politics in Michigan (plus her intimacy with the mood and activities on the huge Michigan campus); and there was Fritz Hollings, a conservative southern Democratic governor with strong ties to the business community. Not one of them a "knee-jerk liberal" and all dedicated to a Kennedy victory.

At about the time that Millie Jeffrey was urging the peace corps idea on Mike Feldman from her vantage point in Michigan, Kennedy was phoning Gavin in Wellesley to get his recently well received views on that attractive alternative to military service. These conversations took place on October 29 and 30, 1960. On October 31, Gavin's one-page statement reached Kennedy, and two days later Kennedy proposed the Peace Corps in San Francisco, publicly giving it Gavin's blessing. (Gavin was soon to become U.S. ambassador to France.)

Of the entire Peace Corps staff in 1961 (or at any time later) only Bill Haddad knew about the important Gavin connection—not because he was made privy to it by the candidate or any others among the Kennedy inner circle, but because Fritz Hollings couldn't resist sharing this irony with him. Haddad, who could more easily than most of his Peace Corps colleagues appreciate the wild chances in politics that often turn out to be the real mothers of invention, thoroughly enjoyed the joke: Ho ho! An army general was the real magician behind the Peace Corps. Ah, but it wouldn't do, it wouldn't do at all to noise this thoroughly incompatible incongruity about, thought Haddad. Not only would it detract from the creative-cavalier image of the young president, it would throw the Peace Corps into ideological chaos. Most Peace Corps practitioners, admit it or not, preferred to imagine that the Peace Corps came down from Heaven through John F. Kennedy (with a passing nod to Saint/Senators Humphrey and Neuberger and Congressman Reuss). And given the virulent antimilitary sentiment that pervaded the Peace Corps, *no* general, not even a *good* general—as Gavin was later to be called when he spoke out against American involvement in Vietnam—was acceptable. Gavin should be given eternal credit for his restraint and modesty; a lesser man would have found a way to promote his role in the most exciting new governmental program in twenty-seven years. But Gavin demures: "I can't take credit for the Peace Corps. Yes, I certainly think that I had an influence on Kennedy, but really, no one else but Kennedy could have made it happen. No one."

And thus the Peace Corps myth. But, as B. F. Skinner, the renowned behavioral psychologist, puts it: "Myths are very important in bringing new ideas to a society . . . an important way to handle something not so easily handled." According to psychologist Rollo May, myths "are a method for finding genuine compassion and empathy." Part of the Peace Corps myth was that the program was something of a miracle that might contain a certain alchemy from which world peace could actually result. But how much better to believe that than be cynical, thought Haddad. "I liked to believe it myself. I still do," he adds.

So, in spite of Kennedy's prominent mention of Gavin in his foreign policy speech in San Francisco, where Gavin's name was obviously invoked as a means of giving the brand-new peace corps idea both respectability and panache, no one in the press or at the Peace Corps ever stopped to wonder, Why Gavin?

Donovan McClure, who would soon find himself on the New Frontier as a pioneer Peace Corps official, was at the Cow Palace on the night of November 2, not as a Peace Corps fan but as a campaign reporter for the *San Francisco Chronicle*. McClure recalls: "Nixon, who had promised to visit all fifty states, was up in Alaska that day. How's that for dull? But the word had come down from on high at the *Chonicle* that the Nixon visit was to be the banner line, whereas the big Kennedy speech right there on our doorstep was to go below the fold. Ironic, because the Cow Palace was jammed and fantastically electric, with a thousand kids outside trying to break down the doors. I'd covered Kennedy before in California—at Mills College—and witnessed the Elvis phenomenon—the jumping, shrieking girls—and I filed a story on it that made Kennedy look like Robert Redford looks now. But this was something else: pandemonium. All of the young people in the crowd, and not just the girls, were just *howling* in support of the peace corps idea. That was a bit before I had, um, got religion."

Whatever Kennedy really thought about the peace corps idea, whatever his inner reservations about the practicality of such a program, he argued for it forcefully that night. His speech was filled with crowd-pleasing facts and figures about this nation's shabby performance in foreign affairs under the previous Republican administration, facts which bore straight into the cold war anxieties of the nation:

> [We] have seen enough of warmongers. Let our great role in history be that of peacemakers [*applause*] . . . If we are successful on Tuesday, we are going to set up in the National Government a national peace agency [because] we are going to have to have the best Americans we can get to speak for our country abroad.
>
> All of us have admired what Dr. Tom Dooley has done in Laos [*applause*]. And others have been discouraged at the examples that we read of in *The Ugly American* . . . the United States is going to have to do much better in this area if we are going to defend freedom and peace in the 1960s [*applause*].

Kennedy went on to point out that the Communist countries train teachers and technicians "to spend their lives abroad in the service of world communism," and that they were well trained in the languages and customs of the countries they visited. "This can only be countered," he said, "by skill and dedication of Americans who are willing to spend their lives serving the cause of freedom [*applause*]." Kennedy listed our recent diplomatic failings: ambassadors and embassy staffs lacking compassion and language facility both in Iron Curtain countries and in the new nations. "We cannot understand what is in the minds of other people if we cannot even speak to them . . . Yet do you think it is possible for us in the most deadly struggle in which freedom has ever been engaged [a cold war tub thumper that always, then, pleased] to win if we approached it as casually as these statistics indicate that we are? [*response from audience*]."

It was a neat jump from a public shaming of our foreign service under Eisenhower to the Peace Corps proposal:

> I therefore propose that our inadequate efforts in this area be supplemented by a peace corps of talented young men and women, willing to serve their country in this fashion for three years as an alternative or as a supplement to peacetime selective service [*applause*], well qualified through rigorous standards, well trained in the language, skills, and customs they will need to know . . .
>
> We cannot discontinue training our young men as soldiers of war, but we also want them to be ambassadors of peace [*applause*]. The combat soldiers, like General Gavin, who jumped with his division in northern France, said that no young man today could serve his country with more distinction than in this struggle for peace around the world [*applause*].

Kennedy proposed that his "ambassadors of peace" be directed and paid by the "ICA Point Four Agencies." But the details were irrelevant to the young "ambassadors of peace" in the audience and around the country, whose idealism had been sufficiently whetted and whose egos had been plentifully boosted by their sudden promotion from kids to ambassadors. It could not have mattered less to them who paid them, or how much (if at all), and even less who or what would "direct" them, because, as they saw it, Kennedy would direct them personally.

Kennedy had reopened the "Ugly American" wound by documenting the Eisenhower administration's nondeeds and misdeeds in matters of foreign diplomacy and then immediately proposed a bracing alternative: the Peace Corps.

Kennedy seemed to have committed himself to the idea, and forcefully so, in a major foreign policy speech, and to an enormously receptive audience. But it was late in the day. Kennedy referred to the Peace Corps publicly only twice more before the election, once in a speech in Chicago on November 4, and finally in Boston on election eve, November 7. In the latter two instances, he joined it to the cold war struggle. In Chicago, Kennedy declared that the Peace Corps Volunteers would act "as a counter to the flood of well-trained and accomplished tacticians now helping nations with their problems that the Communists are sending out." In Boston, he replied to a question from the audience as to how he would stop the Communists by saying that through the good works of the Peace Corps, for instance, "Communism can be checked . . . [and] freedom can begin to grow back of the Communist curtain." The people loved it and desperately wanted to believe it.

It is doubtful, however, that Kennedy really believed that the Peace Corps could be a highly effective weapon against Communism. He knew the world too well. But it is clear that he firmly believed, at that point, that the Peace Corps needed to be sold with a clear anti-Communist label on it because cold war fears were still a chronic national ailment. So he turned the Peace Corps into a prescription— and just like that, the patient felt better.

Kennedy supporters, and especially the young, took the Kennedy victory on November 8 to be a sure sign of astringent change, of devoutly-to-be-wished new directions. And Kennedy's seeming commitment to the Peace Corps, understandably, was perhaps the major sign. New, young, brave, and caring. Just as the aging General Douglas MacArthur had, a decade before, exulted over the outbreak of the Korean conflict, "Mars's last gift to an old warrior!" Kennedy's young, would-be peace soldiers were savoring their fantasy mandate to sweeten up the world for democracy. High, high hopes existed on Election Day, 1960.

CHAPTER 2

PASS THE TORCH, PLEASE

But a few days after the 1960 election, the peace corps idea was as dead, gone, and forgotten as it had been lively and well reported as front-page news a week before.* The minds of the president-elect and his staff were suddenly sharply focused on only two things: rest and recuperation in some sunny clime, and who would get the top positions in the new administration, strictly in that order.

Not everybody went snorkling in Caribbean waters, however. Harris Wofford recalls, "On election day, Shriver called from Hyannis Port to say that Kennedy had asked him to head a task force—a talent search—to get nonpolitical people from the professions, universities, foundations, business, labor, into the administration. 'Get Adam Yarmolinsky and Louis Martin to help us, and let's go.' "

Working out of Democratic National Headquarters three and a half blocks from the White House, Shriver, Wofford, Yarmolinsky, Martin, and later, Tom Farmer—all lawyers with privileged contacts in every field—worked around the clock to fill the choicest posts on the New Frontier. Farmer says, "I don't recall even discussing the Peace Corps during the talent-hunt days. I was working on filling foreign policy jobs, and the Peace Corps wasn't even in the foreign policy grab bag. We were working from a huge civil service list—top government jobs we called the 'Wish Book' (now known as the 'Plum Book')—so of course the Peace Corps directorship wasn't in it. The Peace Corps didn't exist."

But the next thing Farmer knew, "Sarge was running the Peace Corps task force, doing what he does better than anyone—selling a good idea."

*Next to the larger front-page headlines relating to Eisenhower's appearance in New York in support of Nixon (which was the first time Eisenhower had lent such support— five days before election) was Kennedy's Peace Corps proposal. In smaller type but right at the top of the page it reads, "Kennedy Favors U.S. 'Peace Corps' to Work Abroad." The article beneath was written by one of the Time's most esteemed reporters, Harrison Salisbury. The article ran on for pages, and a lengthy excerpt of Kennedy's speech was also provided. Salisbury did not comment on Kennedy's mention of General Gavin; this may be because it wasn't in the version given to the press.

Once the Peace Corps was the hottest thing in town, somewhat later in 1961, and Shriver was a frequent front-page personage and fast becoming a household name, there was never any thought but that it was all inevitable, a match made in New Frontier heaven. Shriver, the dapper, quick-witted, clean-living, irrepressibly optimistic brother-in-law was perceived by outsiders to be some kind of miracle of casting: Robin Hood out of Yale, the Pied Piper from Chicago. Cary Grant turned Eagle Scout comes to Washington. (Adam Yarmolinsky says that the Shriver exuberance and super-salesmanship got on the nerves of the Irish Mafia. Unlike Kennedy, they couldn't appreciate this independent, always upbeat brother-in-law in a political sense. "They interpreted his cheerfulness as weakness," says Yarmolinsky, "and his independence as showboating. They suspected him of too much self-promotion; they didn't think he had supreme loyalty to The Man, though he did.")

Wofford recalls that Shriver called him one day after the inauguration, "when everyone else was collapsing, including me, and there he was, raring to go again, and as usual, immediately. The president had asked him to set up a task force to see if the peace corps idea really made any *sense*."

Between election and inauguration, Haddad had only one more brush with the peace corps idea, about whose chances he had become increasingly pessimistic. "There were two problems at that time," he says. "One was other priorities—staffin' up the New Frontier, all those important appointments. The Peace Corps was hardly a jumpin'-up-and-down priority. It got lost in the shuffle. The other problem was lack of interest. There was still zero seriousness about it as far as I could tell. I gave it about a 2 percent chance to survive. It was the last thing anybody wanted to think about. But I was still yellin' and screamin' about it and makin' a pain in the ass of myself. One thing I did was to push for reports from Harvard and MIT. You know, Jack always wanted to know what those people thought. So I pushed hard for a paper from Max Millikan at MIT, who was the only guy who seemed to have a handle on the idea.

"Well, down it came," says Haddad in evident scorn. "The Peace Corps. Six hundred people. Like a junior year abroad. Mostly out of the Ivy League. Jesus! No vision, no concept. *None* of it had the feeling or the rationale of Kennedy's Cow Palace speech. Millikan had translated it into 'credit overseas,' paid by the government. Shocking. I went through the roof." Haddad was always shocked when a certified, degree-laden brain, such as an MIT professor, could not tune into the elaborate liberal symphony in Haddad's head. But the melody lingered on in the academic community and would later prove harmonic.

In the preinaugural lull of early January, with the Peace Corps still no more than a rudderless probability, Haddad went back to New York with the intention to stay. He didn't want a government job: "Christ, I'm a newspaperman, I kept tellin' 'em. The bureaucracy would drive me crazy." He did not, however, rule out the Peace Corps, but was disinclined to bring up the subject again. Just after the inauguration, before the Peace Corps task force had been formally set up or announced, a funny thing happened in the "Poet's Corner" of the *New York Post* city room.

David Gelman, a *Post* writer whose desk adjoined Haddad's, answered Haddad's phone. "That's what I really did for a living," says Gelman. "I took Haddad's important phone calls." Gelman (who was later to join Haddad at the Peace Corps) remembers a mumbly New England voice asking, "Bill Haddad theah? Bob Kennedy calling."

Haddad recalls: "Bobby was in a phone booth at La Guardia. He said, 'Listen Bill, since you're the one who's so jazzed up about the Peace Corps, why don't you come down and set it up?' I told him that was the one thing in government that interested me. He told me to go down to Washington and tell Ralph Dungan, who was handling the reorganization of foreign aid programs, that I was prepared to do this."

Gelman, watching and listening in numb fascination, says that Haddad started pacing furiously around the city room, repeating over and over, "I got it, I got it! I got the Peace Corps!" Gelman asked, "Bill, what do you *mean* you got the Peace Corps?"

"The Peace Corps," said Haddad breathlessly, "is the only fuckin' thing I wanted, and I got it."

Gelman says, "It seemed to be a fact. Bill ran back into Weschler's cubicle (James Weschler was the *Post*'s editor) and Weschler was congratulating him. It had to be a fact. "He called his wife, Kate. He talked to Dorothy Schiff (the *Post*'s owner). That's how they interpreted the call, too. We all assumed that since Bobby had said he wanted me to set it up, that meant he also wanted me to run it. The *Post* gave me a six-month leave of absence, and Weschler told me to go right down and get Ralph Dungan to give me a desk."

One of Haddad's former campaign colleagues got wind of the Kennedy offer. He was incredulous. "There are few people more talented than Bill Haddad," he says, "but I couldn't believe that those cool-cat Kennedys were prepared to turn a government agency over to someone so volatile and outspoken. I wondered at the time—was Bobby Kennedy really speaking for that whole bunch? Had this been thoroughly checked out?"

Apparently it had not been checked out, and when Haddad sailed into Ralph Dungan's office, volubly seeking an instant desk, Dungan bristled: "Who the hell do you think you are?"

Haddad was embarrassed; Dungan was mad. Haddad sought to explain. He received this call from none other than Bobby Kennedy; Bobby had asked him to "come down and set up the Peace Corps" and to tell Dungan that he was prepared to do so. And here he was. "I conveyed my own feeling to Ralph. I had always been interested in the Peace Corps; *nothin'* else could ever get me into government. I realized I wasn't an administrator, and while I had the confidence to set the thing up, I really didn't have the confidence to run it. I told him I couldn't *really* believe that the whole Kennedy team wanted that, either, or would back me up ultimately."

Oddly enough, Haddad does not believe Bobby Kennedy led him up the garden path. He merely thinks that he misunderstood Bobby Kennedy's more limited intention for him. Kate Haddad, who at the time had the absolute conviction that Bobby Kennedy's offer to her husband included the stewardship of the Peace Corps, later said, "I think we have to write it off to imprecise language and sheer impulse on Bobby's part."

Fritz Hollings remembers other curious gestures of that period. Sometimes, it would seem, between the first of the year and the inauguration on January 20, 1961, the Kennedy staff was "running the Peace Corps by a lot of people. They were still uncertain about it, I think, and wanted feedback and reassurance from all kinds of different people. Well, in a way, I have to say, I got the impression they simply wanted someone to take it off their hands, relieve them of it. They obviously didn't have a clear picture of what they wanted it to be. Why, they even ran it by Herbert Hoover. I know that for a fact. Nooooo. *Not* Herbert Hoover's *son*. Her-bert . . . Hoover . . . him-self!" (Hoover, then approaching ninety, presumably felt it wise to decline to be the spearhead of a youth movement.)

"Hell," chortles Hollings, "they even ran it by *me*. I said, well fine, if you really think it's a smart idea to send a white, supposedly segregationist southern governor to Africa."

Hollings, of course, went back to South Carolina and Haddad "stuck around."

There has never been a grander American show to stick around for than the occasion of the Kennedy inaugural address and swearing in. Even the weather had complied magnificently: The snow sparkled, the air was crystal, the hat-hating young president-elect rode with a look of Rooseveltian delight in an open car in a top hat, his chic, fragile wife at his side. Jackie, with her mink pillbox hat and matching muff, was to become that day the Instant Glamour Queen of the World. The bands played; the float containing the surviving crew of PT-109 passed the reviewing stand. There was the aged, faltering poet Robert Frost, trying to read an original poem in the blinding sunlight, the smoking lectern under Cardinal Cushing matching his fire-and-brimstone rhetoric, face, and voice. There were all those Kennedy women, profuse of hair and teeth, the triumphant Boston-Irish patriarch, and the quizzical, dignified old general symbolizing the passing of an era.

Kennedy did not miss the opportunity to underscore just that, for in the opening seconds of his address he ringingly declared, "Let the word go forth from this time and place to friend and foe alike that the torch has been passed to a new generation of Americans, born in this century, tempered by war, disciplined by a harsh and bitter peace . . ."

The imagery was Olympic, a paean to youthful "vigah." Kennedy had become the first Peace Corps recruiter.

Kennedy's inaugural address was, as *Time* magazine put it days later, "destined to be famous within minutes of its delivery."

Soon after the inauguration, Harris Wofford was splitting his time between consulting on civil rights at the White House and assisting Shriver with Peace Corps task force work; he was finding to his surprise that the peace corps idea had already caused a lot of "busy work" and serious contemplation outside the administration. The major proposals that Wofford and Shriver had before them, as they commenced the task force on February 2, 1961, were these: The Reuss-Neuberger and Humphrey legislation, the report from Max Millikan of MIT, a report from Professor Samuel Hayes of the University of Michigan that Kennedy had called for earlier, and a summary of Reuss's meeting on Capitol Hill in December 1960, to which he had invited a variety of opinion. From Colorado State University they had a preliminary report of their studies of Reuss's proposal.

Shriver and Wofford soon lit on three uninteresting similarities among the proposals: First, none favored a big, open-ended Peace Corps. Second, none suggested a wholly independent government agency, or even an agency that would be tucked under the president's personal wing in the Executive Branch. (Some thought it should be attached to the United Nations, others thought it belonged in among other foreign assistance programs, to be administered by one of them, and in addition, should have its overseas projects prepared and administered by private agencies, the universities, and in some cases the UN as well.) And third, all but one favored a cautious start, with low-profile pilot projects. Really, except for Humphrey's proposal for five thousand young men immediately, no sense of excitement or urgency—at least on paper—existed.

As Shriver and Wofford saw it, there was a righteous sameness, a strained tentativeness about it all. Those writing before Kennedy's Cow Palace proposal and those writing after the fact suffered equally from political naiveté: Where was the zinger? What would make it different, special? What would make it sell? After four eighteen-hour days of reading what the "experts" had to say—the experts in privately sponsored American programs overseas, the experts in government service overseas, the experts in academia—Shriver and Wofford were bored. If they were bored, they reasoned, Kennedy would only be more so.

The bell finally rang, and loudly, in the still of the night, as the story goes, when at 2:00 A.M. on February 6, 1961, Shriver began to read his last paper of the "day." It was thirty pages long and thunderously entitled, "The Towering Task." Its author, Warren Wiggins, was a faceless bureaucrat in the International Cooperation Administration (ICA). But Shriver read it and, as the story further goes, seized the phone at 3:00 A.M. and sent a telegram to Wiggins in suburban Virginia, urging him to be present at a task force meeting seven hours later, at 10:00 A.M. Wiggins appeared on the dot, and what to his wondering eyes did appear but mimeographed copies of "The Towering Task" set out neatly at each task force member's place, as if elves had been at work.

Wiggins now says with a wry chuckle, "That's Sarge's version. Maybe it was all a bit less dramatic than that. But it's a lovely version, and why change it now?"

Since Shriver's versions of everything concerning the Peace Corps were usually a bit better than the reality, as will become increasingly apparent, Wiggins is right: Let it stand. For in time, even the Peace Corps' recurrent human nightmare, the late Representative Otto Passman, the dyspeptic chairman of the House Appropriations Committee from whom all blessings flowed or failed to flow, himself came 'round to this view, albeit with weary sarcasm: "Ah *know* the Peace Corps is a success, Mr. Shrivuh, and Ah know *whah* it is a success. It is a success because yew say it is, sooo often."

What was the magic of the "towering task?"

Start immediately and start big, wrote Wiggins in effect. He noted that previous advice had been timid and cautionary, which would have the effect of causing "limited political, economic, and psychological impact. This cautious approach," Wiggins wrote, "is proposed by many because of the clear possibility of a fiasco." But, Wiggins pointed out, if a Peace Corps did not come on strong, it would give short shrift to nations in need and only create nuisance for American ambassadors in developing nations. Further, a small Peace Corps would be more likely to fizzle than a big one because no one, politically or institutionally, would be inclined to enthusiastically support just one more do-good pilot project. Also, a small Peace Corps would not address its only possible motivations: Train young people for future foreign service, make the developing nations more aware of American culture and ideals, redirect youth from private profit motivations into the public service mentality, and provide trained middle-level manpower where needed. Wiggins was quick to see that the motivations of young Americans wanting to serve were many and complicated but that, taken together, they would constitute a national motive. But again, as to size, Kennedy would get no credit, and perhaps ignominy, for sending in a warm puppy dog to meet a hungry bear.

The two most interesting suggestions of Wiggins's "Towering Task" were these: Go immediately into the Philippines with five thousand volunteer English teachers. In a nation of seventy-five linguistic groups, English had become nonetheless the medium of instruction in the public schools and the official language of the government and commerce. English was a unity-building factor; English teachers were in short supply, and the impact of five thousand young teachers from the United States (who would need only minimum preparation) would be considerable, if not enormous. (Wiggins knew the Philippines, having served there as an economic adviser for ICA in the 1950s.)

The other original suggestion was the executive order. Wiggins gives full credit for this persuasive stroke to a colleague from ICA, William Josephson, a brilliant twenty-five-year-old lawyer. Josephson had researched the possibility of the executive order, knowing that it had been created for use at times of national emergency. The country was in neither war nor economic depression, but it seemed to Josephson there was reason enough to use it to get the Peace Corps launched immediately. The power existed within the Mutual Security Act of 1954 (on which Reuss had based his Point Four Youth Corps). Since there was now widespread demonstrated interest in such a program, since a congressional hassle over it could take months (which would dilute the psychological urgency that then existed and destroy the essential spontaneous nature of it), and since the president could reap maximum benefit by causing lightning to flash early in his administration, Josephson proposed that the president take advantage of his rightful powers and bring it into existence right away, temporarily bypassing the need for congressional approval. The combination of "big" and "fast" and "bold" appealed greatly to Shriver and Wofford; furthermore, the drama of it had been backed up by persuasive facts, figures, and rationale. Then too, this plan had been composed by two men experienced in foreign assistance programs—bureaucrats, true, but clearly, highly intelligent and creative ones.

But the fact that Wiggins and Josephson came out of the regular bureaucracy had been a considerable hindrance to them earlier. Wiggins explains their dilemma: "Bill Josephson and I wanted very much to be part of the Kennedy administration. We therefore wrote a few papers on how to run foreign aid, which we knew something about, and we sent them through various channels. George Ball, for one, was involved in screening ideas and people in the field of foreign aid. But he and other Kennedy people didn't want to listen to anybody on the inside of government. The insinuation was that bureaucrats could not possibly have fresh, new ideas. Says Wiggins, "I thought this was so wrong a way to go about things; you *have* to listen to people on the inside. But there was this stone wall.

"So," Wiggins continues, "Josephson and I decided that if they didn't want to hear what we were writing about, we'd have to write about something they wanted to hear. Which seemed at that time to be the Peace Corps. We could see, too, that it had the promise of becoming something quite important if done right, and that is the level at which we made our connection. We started writing 'The Towering Task' in December 1960, and we sent it over to Shriver in early February of 1961." (Josephson says, "Warren and I made a secret pact: The Volunteers must *never* do anything but teach English. Warren was even lukewarm to that at first. He couldn't believe that kids could be trusted to carry out foreign assistance program objectives at any level. Frankly, we did not think much of the whole idea when we began writing, but we went ahead with it in order to gain attention.")

Shriver said of Wiggins in that first task force meeting to which Wiggins had been summoned at 3:00 A.M. the night before, "I never met this man until this morning, but I have read his paper and it comes the closest to representing what I believe should happen."

From that day, Wiggins technically never went back to ICA, although Shriver appropriated three rooms on the sixth floor of 806 Connecticut Avenue, the Maiatico Building, where Wiggins and Josephson already worked. There, they feverishly commenced a report to the president.

There was another now-or-never aspect that Shriver could argue in attempting to win the president over to an executive action: the class of 1961. It would be graduating in three months, and it was the crucial "Peace Corps class." If attention was to be paid by its members, advantage must be taken immediately. Further, during the summer months the campuses would be free to take on training programs into which could be poured the seniors who had been most vigorously activated by Kennedy's Peace Corps proposal. Shriver later said, "A year's delay might well have proved fatal to a baby whose birth was being celebrated with hoots of derision" in many establishment quarters. Eisenhower called the Peace Corps a juvenile experiment; Nixon, a haven for draft dodgers; columnist Robert Ruark, "Kennedy's Kiddie Korps." The DAR denounced it. Even the usually circumspect *Wall Street Journal* fumed: "Who but the very young themselves can really believe that an Africa aflame with violence will have its fires quenched because some Harvard boy or Vassar girl lives in a mud hut and speaks Swahili?" Indeed, pockets of the news media could at first find no love in their hearts. "There is nothing so irresistible," cracked veteran CBS commentator Eric Sevareid, "as pure intentions backed up by pure publicity."

On March 1, 1961, "the news hit us like a thunderclap," says Wiggins. "The president had issued the executive order immediately. We had been prepared to wait a few days, possibly longer for the announcement. Shriver, of course, knew Kennedy was prepared to go the executive-order route, but no one guessed it would happen so fast. Talk about morale—we were sky-high."

The Peace Corps, however, would *not* send in a high-impact team of five thousand Volunteers to a single country as Wiggins had suggested, but rather spread that number over a few countries initially. A large Philippines teaching project would be an early priority, but not *the* priority, as positive rumblings were coming in from Africa, Asia, and Latin America, as well. The Peace Corps' first rule, as represented in the president's executive order: Go only where invited, but *go* where invited.

The objectives of the Peace Corps, according to the report were these:

- To contribute to the development of critical countries and regions.
- To promote international cooperation and good will toward America.
- To contribute to the education of America and to more intelligent participation in the world.

The word was simply this: The Peace Corps would "help people help themselves," and in selling the Peace Corps to Congress and the Third World in subsequent months, Shriver hammered away at that idea. No high-priced technical assistance, no involvement with the intelligence community whatsoever. The Peace Corps would be strictly a "people to people" program.

The *New York Times*, which from the first had been a champion of the peace corps idea, now went into high gear extolling and explaining it to the public. The *Times* gave the Peace Corps more than thorough coverage; it doted in obvious delight on its every move. Peter Braestrup, one of its top reporters of that period (and now the editor of the *Wilson Quarterly*), tells why:

The *Times* loved the Peace Corps. The *Times* loved college kids, glamour, Shriver, Kennedy. They'd happily put the Peace Corps on page one. The *Times* liked Kennedy's style and rhetoric, felt a psychological closeness to the campus. The liberal establishment viewpoint and feeling. The *Wall Street Journal* didn't like the Peace Corps, didn't like the New Frontier—too much razzmatazz—didn't like it stylistically, ideologically. They didn't like Schlesinger and Galbraith, thought they were snobs. The *Journal* didn't like people who understood things. Vermont Royster isn't from Vermont, but he might as well be. "We'll believe it when we see it kind of thing." That was their attitude. All the stuff that the *Journal* didn't like, the *Times* loved. The *Times* was liberal, liked liberals, liked the Third World, the Chester Bowles approach.

The *Times* loved Galbraith and Schlesinger, loved the rhetoric because it was their kind of rhetoric. The difference in attitude between the *Times* and the *Journal* created interesting interlocking circles for the Peace Corps. It created a dialogue.

What Kennedy had done was to tap into the upper-middle-class and give them a role in government, in the New Frontier. It was elitist, and I know that wasn't the intention, but that's how it turned out that first year. And that's what the *Times* liked. And there is no doubt that the *Times* had a great influence on the public's acceptance of the Peace Corps.

Braestrup believes that he himself was objective:

> I thought the Peace Corps was *terrific*, but I was a fussy, critical friend. No one was watching it every day the way I was. It was very interesting. The way it behaved and how it used the environment. The regular bureaucracy didn't like the Peace Corps. Shriver was the brother-in-law of the president, which scared other bureaucrats. They couldn't lean on him as if he had been just another guy. That relationship to the White House was essential to the start of the Peace Corps. You had to have a license to steal to get it going—not to steal unlimitedly, but to steal. Staff it up with your own kind of person, get an instant audience with every member of Congress, put a high priority on the program, get maximum publicity.

Braestrup says that the Peace Corps' openness, which made the regular bureaucracy nervous and carried with it great potential risk, was one of its main strengths.

> It was a conscious strategy on Shriver's part; you could see it. He was saying out loud, "We are going to have problems, we are going to make mistakes. Better let us find out about them first; we'll let you know, we'll explain them to you." There were no secrets at the early Peace Corps. Everyone talked. Period. How much smarter to do things that way than to pretend everything was fine and then let the press find out differently and you get yourself jumped on. Shriver played it exactly right. Made the Peace Corps' problems *your* problems. Very adroit. I did favorable pieces on the Peace Corps, but I wasn't a patsy. Shriver didn't encourage patsies. He

was enough in the catbird seat. He took what he needed to get it off the ground. To get an agency going takes others two or more years. Shriver did it in six weeks.

Braestrup liked the Peace Corps because, among other things,

> almost everybody running it was my age—in their early thirties. Bill Haddad was helping run it. I had been best man at his wedding. Tony Schulte was in it; he was a classmate of mine at Yale. (Schulte is now vice president of Random House.) It was like the Marine Corps—the fantastic spirit—and yet it was like the city room of a big metropolitan newspaper. That flavor—work like hell but don't take yourself too seriously. I was fascinated as a journalist that a government agency could manage to work this way. Shriver seemed to adhere naturally to Henry Luce's theory: You need a couple of wild men and a couple of rocks at the top. Shriver and Haddad were the wild men; Wiggins was the rock. Wiggins kept the agency out of trouble; he taught Shriver and Haddad how the bureaucracy worked.

Haddad sees it the same way: "Shriver had that invaluable White House connection, I had the freedom to say what I thought because everyone knew I wasn't about to stay around and build some goddamned little bureaucratic empire, and Wiggins—well, Wiggins was the rock on which Peace Corps was built. We did a lot of fightin' and hollerin' among ourselves but the best interests of the Peace Corps always came first."

Shriver announced some of his first staff activity on March 2, 1961. It was reported in detail by the *New York Times* on the front page. David Halberstam, under the headline "Recruits Flocking to Join Corps," led off with: "Rafer Johnson, the Olympic decathlon champion, has volunteered to join the Peace Corps . . . Forest Evashevski, former football coach at the University of Iowa and once a noted blocking back at the University of Michigan, will soon take a job [at Peace Corps headquarters] . . . Sally Bowles, daughter of Undersecretary of State Chester Bowles, and Nancy Gore, daughter of Senator Albert Gore of Tennessee, are already at work at corps headquarters."

The instant response to the Peace Corps' existence, Halberstam continued, "caused the switchboard at Peace Corps headquarters to jangle endlessly; it could not handle the thousands of calls from volunteers and inquirers."

Mitzi Mallina, a graduate of the University of Wisconsin and a recent veteran of "Crossroads Africa," and the first Peace Corps employee, says, "Kennedy's announcement turned on a tap. It opened and it would not stop. I was the only one answering the phones at first, and people would call in at all hours to say they wanted to help if they couldn't actually join. One man called at 8:15 on a Saturday morning, saying that he had heard we were in temporary quarters and had no office furniture, which was absolutely true. He was offering us free desks, free typewriters, whatever we needed. It was always like that. What can I say? We were *adored*!"

And also not adored. In some quarters, bitterly resented—even detested. "But," says Peace Corps Employee Number One, "we were adored by the people who could help us most, and the people who just couldn't stand us—like the DAR, who kept denouncing us—we didn't want or need as friends, anyway."

On the same front page as Halberstam's "recruiting" article was a piece by Peter Braestrup, who reported on Kennedy's Peace Corps message to Congress on March 1, 1961, noting that "negotiations are under way with . . . Brazil, Colombia, Nigeria, Pakistan, and the Philippines . . . The Administration will prohibit any use of the Peace Corps for religious missionary purposes. Nor will the Central Intelligence Agency be involved."

Back on the front page of the *Times* again on March 5, Peter Braestrup reported on Shriver's formal nomination as Peace Corps director and fourteen new staff appointments. (Often, prominent people would announce to the press that they *wanted* to join the Peace Corps, or they would simply show up and go to work, thus making accurate reporting extremely difficult. *Personages* would drop by to see "the new thing," get caught up in the excitement, and start opening mail. Nancy Gore and Sally Bowles told David Halberstam that no, they didn't know what they were being paid, or even *if* they were being paid. It was irrelevant. The volunteer spirit was total. Shriver himself worked as a dollar-a-year man. He once went to his personnel director, Dorothy Jacobsen, to inquire how he should go about getting government health insurance. "You can't, Sarge," she replied. "You don't make enough money."

The lead editorial in the Sunday *Times* of March 5 declared that the Peace Corps was based on William James's essay "The Moral Equivalent of War": "William James' conception of 'the moral equivalent' lingers with us in sort of an afterglow. Some thought that [Roosevelt's] Civilian Conservation Corps took its inspiration from James.

Perhaps it did, but now we have a more imminent vision in [Kennedy's] proposal for a permanent Peace Corps."

As shiny as it all seemed for the newly minted Peace Corps in March 1961, one crucial roadblock loomed. Peace Corps officials did not speak of it publicly, but it was a knot in the stomach that was being smiled through in public, gloomed over in private. And it was to turn one of Kennedy's most able, trusted, and likable aides into a temporary unwilling villain by Peace Corps standards. Kennedy had charged Ralph Dungan to oversee the difficult reorganization of foreign aid programs that were scattered inefficiently throughout government and to bring them all under one new, more efficient and manageable umbrella, the Agency for International Development (AID). And there was the Peace Corps, the Kennedy contribution to foreign assistance and at the same time a completely original, separate-seeming entity. Dungan and most others in Kennedy's court did not share the *New York Times*'s reverence for it nor the public's delight.

Naturally, the possibility of the Peace Corps being absorbed was totally unacceptable to Shriver. Wiggins, the smart and sensible bureaucrat out of the foreign aid program, no less than Haddad, the fiery antibureaucrat out of politics and newspapering, was in horror that Dungan might carry the day with Kennedy and send the sparkly new Peace Corps into bureaucratic purdah. Shriver, now thoroughly enjoying his place in the sun, fought the prospect with Kennedy's aides but was careful not to go over their heads to Kennedy. The main guessing game at the Peace Corps was this: Where does Kennedy himself stand on this issue?

"None of the men around Kennedy, and therefore I assumed Kennedy himself, wanted the Peace Corps to be a separate agency," says Wiggins.

"I could understand that," says Haddad, not usually so forgiving of bureaucratic intentions. "Dungan had been directed by Kennedy to get all foreign assistance programs herded into the same corral, and there's the Peace Corps, the stray lamb that won't come along. He hadda try to herd it in with the rest. But," he adds, "we woulda been hind tit on a hog under AID. Nowhere. The last priority, as usual. I knew Shriver wasn't gonna stand for that."

"Ralph Dungan," says Wiggins, "had been with Kennedy for a long time, and when he said to me over the phone in late April that the Peace Corps *must* go under AID, I supposed that he spoke for the president. And he was using, um, quite strong language to get his message across."

"Ralph had a terrible job, doing that foreign aid reorganization," says Bureaucratic Enemy Number One, Haddad, "so you could sympathize. But on the other hand, Ralph was missin' the political point—what the Peace Corps, independent, could do for Kennedy's image."

Arthur Schlesinger pointed out that with two such strong advocates as Shriver and Lyndon Johnson, the Peace Corps would have been unlikely to go under. Schlesinger thought they would not have permitted it "to vanish into the opaque depths of AID," adding that "Kennedy himself held the Rooseveltian view that there were things in life more important than the symmetry of organization charts." Kennedy no doubt held this view, but it was Shriver who lived by it absolutely.

Those in favor of the Peace Corps' independence included everyone at the tiny, feisty Peace Corps at that time (around thirty people), plus, it would seem, Schlesinger, who was not directly involved in the controversy, and, as it happened, Peter Braestrup of the *New York Times*, a close friend of Bill Haddad's. Persuasively against were primarily Ralph Dungan, Henry Labouisse (then head of ICA), and David Bell (soon to be head of AID), with the president abstaining but leaning, obviously, in Dungan's direction. At White House meetings, Shriver was the lone proindependence vote, which, as Haddad points out, "should have carried more weight than it did, since he was the agency's director, but in those days the Kennedy people didn't have the respect for Sarge that later developed in Washington."

Haddad knew that Shriver was about to take off for a long trip into the developing nations to sell the Peace Corps and would have to leave, perhaps, before the controversy was resolved. "That scared me," says Haddad. "Warren Wiggins was scarin' me more. He knew the bureaucracy and was sayin' that the Peace Corps would be *finished* if it went under AID."

Haddad had the dangerous notion that if the Peace Corps controversy could be surfaced in print before Shriver left the country, a quicker and more favorable resolution might result. His friend, Peter Braestrup of the *Times*, dropped hints in print that a difference of opinion existed as to the Peace Corps' fate.*

But it was not until Shriver had been away for two weeks that the confrontation seemed imminent. Wiggins was called to the White

*The White House, upon reading the apparently leaked information, would call Haddad accusingly. Haddad would say, "Who, me?" "Listen," his callers would say, "don't give us that. We know Braestrup was best man in your wedding; we know he lives next door to you; we know he hangs around the Peace Corps; we know . . ."

House to discuss the situation with Kennedy and Dungan. Moyers urged Johnson to attend and bolster Wiggins's case. (Johnson was then, in addition to performing his relatively dreary ceremonial duties as vice president, heading the Peace Corps Advisory Council, so the arrangement did not seem unnatural.) "There we stood," says Wiggins, "outside the Oval Office, waiting. Johnson suddenly started taking Dungan on about foreign aid. I was amazed to hear Johnson—here I was, having been in it for years, thought I knew something about it—and there was Johnson, who hadn't, just giving *hell* to Dungan. Johnson said in effect that you ought to run foreign aid like he, Johnson, politicked in Texas. I mean, he'd say, you make a program *work*, you get people on your side, you do whatever you have to do to make it work—he didn't say 'Buy votes,' but that was the gist of it. At one point, he backed Dungan up against the wall right outside the Oval Office, yelling down at him about what was wrong with foreign aid. It was incredible. And then somebody came out and said the meeting was canceled. God, what a letdown."

The battle for the tiny agency's life was not over. The two fellows from Texas, Moyers and Johnson, went back into a huddle. Moyers begged Johnson to try again, this time alone, if possible. Johnson agreed.

Wiggins says, "I think Johnson did it as a favor to Moyers. I think he did it because he honestly liked the Peace Corps, but I think he also did it because the Kennedy people liked to keep Johnson in his place, and it's certain Johnson enjoyed taking them on at any opportunity. Moyers and I had drafted a very long, vehemently worded cable to Shriver, who was then on his way to India to negotiate with Nehru to open up the Peace Corps there, telling him what was happening, how terrible it was, what the Kennedy people were trying to do to us. I let Dungan know I was sending a very strong cable to Shriver, and he just snapped, 'Oh, go ahead and send it.' I knew he thought, 'This schoolboy Moyers and this unknown bureaucrat Wiggins—having the nerve to talk back to *me*.'

"Moyers showed our cable to Johnson and he got a big kick out of it, the way we'd taken on the Kennedy people. He liked the way we, as underdogs, were kind of trying to kick the shit out of them. And of course Shriver was encouraging us all along the way."

Moyers was not present when Johnson confronted Kennedy man to man but gleaned the following: "Johnson told Kennedy that the Peace Corps would be destroyed if it went under AID. Johnson said that the AID people would take the Peace Corps over for themselves and run it in an entirely different way than we intended or that Johnson thought was right or that Johnson believed that Kennedy would ultimately think was right. Johnson made the point that Roosevelt had benefited from the high visibility and relative autonomy of his New Deal program, such as CCC (the Civilian Conservation Corps).

"I'm sure," says Moyers, "that Johnson was on his best behavior on that occasion, but Kennedy may not have been prepared to put up much opposition anyway. He didn't want to alienate Lyndon. How much he cared about the Peace Corps I really don't know. I do know that all of those around him constantly mocked it, treated it as a joke, a plaything. Who knows? Maybe Kennedy gave in to Johnson just to be done with the subject."*

Moyers ran into Dungan shortly after the heady victory and was greeted with a wry smile: "Well, you sons of bitches won." But, undoubtedly, Dungan little enjoyed Peter Braestrup's evident delight in reporting the underdogs' victory on page one of the *New York Times* a few days later on May 4, 1961, under the headline, "Peace Corps Wins Fight For Autonomy":

> President Kennedy has decided that the Peace Corps will not be merged with the nation's other foreign aid programs . . . The President's decision followed a two-month tug-of-war within the Administration. For Peace Corps officials, it was an important victory. These officials had contended that without a special identity of its own, the new agency would attract few recruits, get snarled in red tape and lose its effectiveness abroad. Mr. Kennedy made his decision after consulting with Vice President Johnson who had pressed the Peace Corps cause.

*Even before Kennedy issued the executive order to create the Peace Corps, Moyers began actively chafing to get into it. Johnson dug in his heels. "Finally," says Moyers, "he gave in. He was in kind of a blue funk one day and he was feeling nibbled away by me. He said, 'Your heart's not here anymore. I guess you should go on over there.' " Kennedy, too, wanted Moyers to stay where he was, with Johnson, because Moyers had been invaluable during the campaign in keeping lines of communication open between the staffs of the two men. Kennedy told Moyers, "Bill, we need you here to talk to because, you know, working with Lyndon is not the easiest thing in the world. But if you are determined, I don't see how I can stop you."

Johnson was probably really thinking, "If I'm ever going to get that boy back, I'd better let him go now." And Kennedy, probably this: "He's very useful heah, but he might be even more useful theah."

Before going on an overseas trip last month, R. Sargent Shriver, the President's brother-in-law and Peace Corps Director, argued his case at the White House staff level but deliberately refrained from going to the President in person . . . The President's decision putting the Peace Corps under the State Department also called for Mr. Shriver to seek separate legislative authority and appropriations from Congress. Mr. Shriver would have Assistant Secretary of State status, reporting directly to Dean Rusk.

A new public career had begun, a monument marked, a torch truly passed.

CHAPTER 3

COME
AS
YOU ARE

Shriver had to set up a fully operating agency of the federal government within a matter of weeks, had to recruit, winnow, and train several hundred Volunteers and get a hefty number of them into the field, working hard, living humbly, and behaving themselves, before the first leaf of autumn 1961, fell in Lafayette Park. This challenge had no precedent but it had to be met for three reasons: one, because Shriver had publicly proclaimed that it would be done; two, because most of the first Volunteers were bound to come out of the class of 1961 and would be assigned to training programs on college campuses that could only accommodate such operations during the summer months; and three, because Congress was slated to debate and vote on the Peace Corps bill in September of 1961, and thus, there simply had to *be* a Peace Corps. Shriver was not about to go up to the Hill with a lick and a promise, under which circumstances he would surely be pelted with taunts of "It won't work," or "Nice idea, but where are the Volunteers?"

For Shriver, failure was unthinkable. Indeed, failure *had* to be unthinkable. One may permit one's mind to hover around the spectre of failure when one is faced with a difficult but doable task; such a negative mental exercise only adds more luster to the victory when it predictably comes. But in the case of something that has never been done before—where the obstacles are multiple and formidable, where there are no guidelines or "book" to go by—one must simply summon up a vision of success that is impenetrable. Fortunately, Shriver was and is a man who has success written all over him; he radiates optimism and pulsates with robust mental and physical health. People wanted to believe in him and did. But he also needed people he could believe in; he also needed inspiration for the "towering task" ahead. While Shriver was a very conventional man in many ways, and while he had proved himself a capable executive in managing Chicago's enormous Merchandise Mart for his father-in-law, he saw almost immediately that conventional behavior and conventional management techniques would not work in putting the Peace Corps together. In his last nod to convention for some time, Shriver brought over Jack Young, who had been serving at NASA, another new agency, as director of management analysis. Young had also worked at McKinsey and Company, management consultants. Even the Peace Corps had to start with an organization chart, and the first one that Shriver and Young came up with included the five associate directorships under the director and deputy director that dictated the basic structure of the Peace Corps throughout the tenures of both Shriver and his successor, Jack Vaughn. Young became the Peace Corps' first associate director for management, and he piped the Peace Corps' charter staff members on board before leaving to return to NASA.

"That had to be quite an experience for someone like Young, who came out of both corporate world and government," says Warren Wiggins. "Here was Young's nice, orderly organization chart, and suddenly Sarge flings open the doors and starts hiring at incredible speed and with great flamboyance a whole slew of people, some of whom came running to us and few of whom Sarge had to pry out of budding, even spectacular, careers in law, medicine, academia, journalism. Sarge made no pretense that this was an orderly or predictable affair. He was grabbing at talent, period. He was looking for certain skills and certain kinds of personalities—people who could understand a volunteer movement, could relate to exciting adventurous young people and who could fit together as a unit that would have spiritual force *and* generate great publicity."

Since Shriver possessed moral authority and an uncanny knack for public relations himself, he saw no conflict in the two qualities coexisting in others or within an entire staff. "It really didn't matter what you were—a lawyer, a fisherman, a preacher, a government bureaucrat," says Wiggins. Shriver was in a hurry. Shriver created the Peace Corps in twenty-one days (from February 7, 1961, when he lit on Wiggins's blueprint, "The Towering Task," to March 1, 1961, when the executive order, Bill Josephson's contribution to the creation, was signed by President Kennedy). "That's a record for a government agency," says Wiggins. "Something like a year or two is usually the case. But he got it together that fast; he created its laws, its principles, and he staffed it up."

When you staff up that fast, Wiggins points out, you are going to get people who by their nature are gamblers—very ambitious people, people who are willing to drop everything to try something new. "Shriver couldn't wait three months for a guy; he had to come at once. So, the first priority was talent and the second was availability. If he found somebody he thought had unusual talent, he'd think of a job for him to do, or let the person create one if there wasn't something on the organization chart that suggested itself. This is the complete reverse of the way things are normally done." But Shriver knew that he had to have the most dazzling staff in Washington, and he used the bait of excitement and job flexibility to assemble it.

"Look," says Wiggins, "Government agencies just don't go out *looking* for guys like Tom Mathews."

TOM MATHEWS

The sun was setting behind the mountains in the ski resort of Alta, Utah, and a night chill was building. Tom Mathews was making his last exhilarating run of the day, looking forward to a hot toddy in the lodge, a hearty dinner, and, tomorrow, another perfect day of late-spring skiing. He had reached the euphoric point where he had forgotten all about his job at the *San Francisco Chronicle* and the strain of daily deadlines.

Seating himself at the lodge's bar, he ordered his toddy and glanced around idly to see if he could spot a familiar face. He spotted instead the newly famous figure of Secretary of Defense Robert Strange McNamara, also in ski clothes, having a drink at the other end of the bar. Mathews mused on the oddness of McNamara's presence at that time and place: The New Frontier was known to be notoriously workaholic, so what was President Kennedy's top guy at the Pentagon doing on a ski holiday just two months after inauguration? The bartender then arrived with Mathews's toddy, bantering with this Utah native and Alta regular.

The telephone behind the bar rang; the bartender answered it casually, then began nodding earnestly, suddenly turning and announcing, "*Washington* is calling." McNamara rose immediately and reached across the bar to take the call.

"No, I'm sorry, Mr. Secretary," explained the bartender. "It's not for you. It's for Tom."

Tom Mathews took the phone, as baffled as if the call were coming from Mars. "Yes. This is Tom Mathews."

A voice crackling with purpose and high spirits came through: "Tom, this is Sarge Shriver calling from the Peace Corps in Washington. I've heard a lot of great things about you from Pierre Salinger and Fred Dutton, and I want you to come work with us and help put this new thing together. How soon can you get here? What about tomorrow?"

"Well," began the utterly flummoxed Mathews, "I'm on vacation and I have nothing but ski clothes and bad sunburn."

"That's fine, Tom. Come as you are. See ya tomorrow." Click.

Tom Mathews, then thirty-nine, had been happy in his job at the *San Francisco Chronicle* and had planned to spend the rest of his life working and skiing in the West. He had never "thought East" or "thought federal government." But in the space of a few moments, he had talked to the brother-in-law of the president of the United States and had been offered a job in the already near-mythic precincts of the New Frontier. The message was, put your life on "hold" and get East fast. And funnily enough, he knew he was going to do it. He grabbed his shaving kit, jumped into his car, and careened into the Salt Lake City airport in time to board a flight for Chicago, which would connect with another flight bound for Washington, D.C.

The following evening, when most office workers are turning off their lights and going home, Mathews arrived at Peace Corps head-quarters at 806 Connecticut Avenue to find the slice-of-pie-shaped twelve-story building ablaze with lights and its inhabitants scurrying about with an energy level that one usually associates with the morning hours. Bill Haddad, associate director of the Peace Corps for Planning, Evaluation and Research was leaving his fifth floor office when the elevator doors opened, revealing what Haddad describes as "an apparition—a short round guy in ski clothes, ski boots, a fur cap, and a crimson face on which was fixed the grin of a man who was in on a fabulous joke."

Haddad approached the apparition: "Jesus Christ. Who are you, anyway?"

"I'm Tom Mathews of the *San Francisco Chronicle* and I'm looking for Sarge Shriver. He's expecting me."

"Okay, Tom," said Haddad. "I think I believe you. Come with me. I'm going into a meeting with Sarge right now."

Haddad began to shake with silent laughter and Mathews just kept grinning. Haddad opened the conference room door and announced to the assembled group: "Hey, you guys, I think I've just met a new staff member. Here he is—Tom Mathews of the *San Francisco Chronicle*. Am I right, Sarge?"

"When I walked into that room," recalls Mathews, "Sarge jumped up and yelled, 'That's my man! T'rrfic!' And the rest of them, oh God, they just went crazy, laughing and screaming and pounding the table." When the hilarity abated, Shriver explained that he had just twenty-four hours earlier summoned Mathews off a mountain in Utah and said "Come as you are, and as you see, he has." Shriver needn't have explained; the early staff was used to sudden, startling happenings and hirings and had immediately put two and two together in Mathews's case. It was a foregone conclusion that Mathews would be hired, having come highly recommended by two influential men at the White House, Pierre Salinger and Fred Dutton, plus the fact of the panache of his arrival.

Mathews spent the night at the quaint little Claridge Hotel a few doors away and the next day being briefed by the Peace Corps staff. By the end of the day, Shriver and Haddad formally popped the question: Would Mathews be deputy director of public information under Ed Bayley (a newspaperman and former aide to Governor Gaylord Nelson of Wisconsin), hired five weeks earlier? Mathews immediately called his wife, Bonnie, in San Francisco, and told her the astonishing news—that he'd be moving East and starting this new job immediately and that she should follow as soon as possible. "She was stoic," says Mathews. "She said she felt like a squaw. Pack up the pots and pans and the teepee and move on."

Mathews then called his nineteen-year-old son and namesake at Princeton (now a senior editor at *Newsweek*), "a Peace Corps type if ever there was one," says Mathews. "Hi, Tom. I'm in Washington."

"Hey Dad," said young Mathews excitedly. "What are you doing here in the East?"

"I've joined the Peace Corps. How do you like that?"

After a pause, young Mathews issued a long, admiring whistle. "Nooooo shit!"

That was in late March 1961. The Peace Corps was one month old on April 1.

FRANK MANKIEWICZ

In May 1961, Frank Mankiewicz was living in Los Angeles and practicing law. He had come to the conclusion that this was not an appropriate role for a young man of thirty-six who had worked for a Kennedy victory and who was now very much aware of the high excitement and social change that was bubbling up in Washington. "It just didn't seem to me, as I guess it didn't seem to thousands of people at that time, that worrying about things like whether Burt Lancaster's earnings might be shielded in Lichtenstein or Tangiers should be all that important. To hell with it.

"So I wrote to some people who had already gone to work in the Kennedy administration, such as Adam Yarmolinsky, with whom I had worked years before on a loyalty security study for the Ford Foundation. At that time, in May, 1961, I also wrote to Franklin Williams, an old friend from early civil rights days in Los Angeles. Franklin had been the director of the California NAACP while I was working for the antidefamation league, and Holly (Mankiewicz's wife) worked for Franklin, whom she considered maybe the most handsome man who ever lived. "He had those kind of languid, Ivy League good looks, only he was black. I used to kid him and say, 'Franklin, you look like Alger Hiss with a tan.' "

Since 1958, Franklin Williams had been assistant attorney general of California in charge of civil rights, and he was the first friend of Mankiewicz's to head east after Kennedy's inauguration. Williams was being courted by Shriver for an important Peace Corps job and by others who wanted him to run the Civil Rights Commission.

But he soon wound up with Sarge, as almost everyone who met Sarge in those days did. So I wrote Franklin and some others, such as Adam, and said, here's my background, here I am, use me. I don't know what I can do, but I know something about politics and God knows I'm a Democrat and I gave about fifty speeches for Kennedy during the campaign. (I was not for Kennedy originally, and I got into his campaign for what I then thought were the wrong reasons. My heart was really with Adlai, but I knew that Stevenson was Nixon's natural prey. Everything in nature has a natural prey, and I thought Nixon would just eat Stevenson alive. I liked Kennedy—it wasn't exactly as if I was picking some enemy.)

My feeling was, well, now's the time and it might never come again. I was perfectly willing to be secretary of state or third assistant examiner at Bureau of Mines. I didn't care. I just wanted *in*. My first response came from Adam Yarmolinsky, one of McNamara's "whiz kids" at the Pentagon. I'd always thought that Adam was one of the smartest people in the whole world and not much has happened since to make me change my mind. But when Adam introduced me to Bob McNamara, I realized that Adam was no better than the second smartest man in the world. I was dazzled by those guys—McNamara, Charlie Hitch, his assistant secretary and comptroller (formerly a member of the Policy Council of the Rand Corporation in Santa Monica and future president of the University of California), and Adam. They were doing all this "roles and missions" business, and Adam gave me a paper that Hitch had drawn up on the way to prepare a defense budget. I read it and thought—look, I speak English; I have a good mastery of the language, and there is no word in this paper that is not an English word. But what the hell are they talking about? Why is it that I cannot penetrate it at any point? Huh?

But Yarmolinsky, unaware of Mankiewicz's befuddlement over Hitch's paper, offered him a job, on the spot. Mankiewicz as much as he wanted *in* on the New Frontier, did not immediately jump at the flattering offer. He hedged; he said he'd have to talk it over with Holly. He'd need some time to think it through.

"My interview with Adam ended at 3:00 P.M., and I was booked on a plane back to Los Angeles in the early evening. I called my office in Beverly Hills to see if someone had to pay $800,000 because somebody had filed some paper—the usual stuff of my law practice—and my secretary said, 'Glenn Ferguson of the Peace Corps in Washington called you here. Franklin Williams prompted the call. Here's Mr. Ferguson's number.' "

Mankiewicz jotted it down with a strange premonition. "I won't be home tonight," he told his secretary in Beverly Hills. "I'll take an early morning flight instead."

"I was thinking on the surface, 'Oh, what the hell, I'm here, so why not?' I had no conscious interest in the Peace Corps. I vaguely viewed it at the time as a bunch of guitar-plucking wastrels. But when I called Ferguson, he was so full of enthusiasm that I was swayed. He said, 'Frank Williams says you're keen for a job in this administration, that you're very highly qualified in any number of ways, that you would fit in perfectly at the Peace Corps. Could you come over here right away? Is that possibe?' "

Mankiewicz said sure, he could come by for an hour or two. Ferguson said, "Oh no, we need you for a whole day—tonight, and then all day tomorrow."

Mankiewicz rejoined, "Well, jeez, I've been at the Pentagon all day and I'm scheduled on a 7:00 A.M. flight tomorrow to Los Angeles, where I've got six appointments."

Ferguson said, "Okay, come over now and we'll talk and you can meet some of the staff." Mankiewicz met Glenn Ferguson, head of recruiting (many early staff members were head of recruiting for a while—Ferguson later became Rep in Thailand and later became president of Lincoln Center), who spoke with fervor about training and placing hundreds of Peace Corps Volunteers in Ghana, Colombia, Tanganyika, and the Philippines by late summer of 1961. It was now May. Mankiewicz was skeptical but nonetheless fascinated. Ferguson introduced Mankiewicz to Joe Wheeler, acting director of the Near East/South Asia (PDO/NESA in office parlance) Regional Office, who rapidly described credible plans to put Volunteers in countries from Tunisia to Borneo in the following year. "Then," says Mankiewicz, "I met Bill Haddad. Anyone who had any interest in investigative reporting—which, as a former journalist, I certainly did—had heard of Haddad, who had won dozens of prizes for his work at the *New York Post*. And you could see why. He was bursting with energy, opinions, ideas. Very ungovernmental, very irreverent, very colorful language. And very political, which I liked. I figured, Jesus, if this guy is working here and this is the way it's going to be, then this is where I belong."

Then Mankiewicz met Derek Singer, acting director of the Latin America Regional Office (PDO/LA), and, only incidentally, Ted Sorensen's brother-in-law. Singer said, "I don't suppose you speak Spanish. But, ah, do you?"

"Yeah, I do speak Spanish." So, to prove that he did, Mankiewicz conversed with Singer in Spanish for a few minutes. "Singer looked very pleasantly surprised. He said, 'Okay, Frank. Pick a country in Latin America. Where would you like to go?'

"I said, 'What do you mean, pick a country?' Singer said, 'We'd like for you to direct a Peace Corps program in Peru, Ecuador, Costa Rica . . .' "

Mankiewicz claims he was not exactly sure of the location of these countries and had never been to Latin America. But he was caught up in the mad excitement that then existed at Peace Corps headquarters and he recalled that an old friend of his from his ADA (Americans for Democratic Action) days in the late 1940s, Jim Loeb, had just been appointed ambassador to Peru. "So I said, okay, fine—I'll take Peru."

Singer stood up, shook Mankiewicz's hand vigorously, and smiling the blinding smile of conquest, said, "Great! That's it!" Mankiewicz, suddenly weak in the knees from such a rapid bestowment, asked with uncharacteristic meekness, "But what happens now?" Singer replied, "Damned if I know. But you have to see Shriver before you can be officially appointed. He has to approve every staff person we take on."

Then came another jolt. Ralph Dungan was calling from the White House for Mr. Frank Mankiewicz. It was 9:00 P.M. Dungan wanted to know if Mankiewicz could come over to the White House immediately for some serious talk about being a country director for AID. What man who wanted an interesting job in the Kennedy administration would say no to a White House invitation, no matter how awkward the timing? Mankiewicz thus bade farewell to his new Peace Corps pals and trekked the two and a half blocks to the White House.

On that balmy spring night, Mankiewicz sought to create a state of mind that told him that the events of this day in Washington were business-as-usual for any slightly bored, thirty-six-year-old West Coast tax lawyer whose political muse had whispered that it was time to go East. He had boarded a plane that morning in Los Angeles with modest expectations. He had come to the nation's capital with no specific goal and no foolish fantasies, and yet he had spent the day being assiduously wooed by key operatives of the Kennedy administration. He now had two solid job offers from two of the most vital and remarked-upon areas of the administration: the genius corner of the mighty Pentagon and Sarge Shriver's idealistic crusaders at the Peace Corps. War and Peace. Not a bad story to take back to Beverly Hills. But now, he was about to top it. He was about to enter "the palace" to talk about yet another job.

Dungan came right to the point: "I imagine they've already made you an offer at the Peace Corps. I've heard enough about you to know that they'd find you appealing over there, and vice versa. [How had Dungan heard about him, wondered Mankiewicz?] I know that McNamara's inner circle is 'high' on you. [And how did Dungan know that, too?] But if you want to, you could also be an AID country director because, you know, if you're head of an AID mission in some reasonably sized Latin American country, you'd have a budget of two or three million dollars. [How did Dungan know Mankiewicz would be interested in Latin America?] On the other hand, I have a feeling that what Sarge is building over there is going to be really something. Very exciting. But it's a gamble. It could turn out to be, you know, obnoxious kids making trouble."

"I thanked Dungan," says Mankiewicz, "and said I would think about AID seriously, in spite of being pretty taken with the Peace Corps and tacitly committed to it. Well, I mean, *of course* I'd think about AID seriously."

Two days after Mankiewicz was back in Los Angeles, the phone started to ring both at home and at the office. Washington was calling. "Adam was pressing me for a decision. And Sarge, whom I had yet to meet, was calling every couple of days with preposterous suggestions such as, 'Can you come to dinner tonight?' I'd say, 'You mean, in *Washington?*' He'd say, 'Sure. You could catch a plane and be here around dinner time.' I'd say, 'Well . . . I have a dinner engagement tonight and I have to be in court tomorrow morning.' He'd say, 'Well, okay, then sometime next week. I wanna see ya.' "

Dungan called once to ask if Mankiewicz was close to making a decision. Mankiewicz found this odd, since he had come to assume that Dungan was clairvoyant and surely therefore must know that Mankiewicz was in an agony of indecision. "Finally, I knew I had to get away and go to the mountains in order to clear my head. I rented a cabin up in Squaw Valley—it was July 1961—and the only way anyone could reach you was to call the ranger, and the ranger would leave a note tacked to your door. The only person I left the ranger's number with was my mother in Los Angeles. I told my office that if a call sounded *really* important, they were to call my mother and she'd know where to find me.

"One day I returned from a hike and there was this note on my cabin door saying, 'Mr. Mankiewicz: Please call Robert McNamara, and Sargent Shriver, or your mother.'

"Oh Christ," I thought, "here it comes. I got to a phone and called my mother. And she said that someone from McNamara's office had called once, and I figured it must be Adam Yarmolinsky. She said that Shriver had called three times and made it sound terribly urgent. Sarge had all along been the most persistent, and so I made the fateful decision. I called Sarge first. He was in El Paso presiding over the first graduation of Peace Corps trainees, and he was ecstatic. He now had a *product.* The Peace Corps was actually about to *happen.*" (This first training group to graduate was headed for Tanganyika, soon to become Tanzania, the twenty-second African nation to gain independence since World War II. The group, consisting of thirty-five engineers, surveyors, and geologists, speaking passable Swahili, were about to leave for Washington, where they would meet President Kennedy, and from there to New York and the United Nations, where they would meet Secretary General Adlai Stevenson. They would then fly to Puerto Rico to become the first trainees ever to confront the Peace Corps' Outward Bound camp in Arecibo.) Shriver said to Mankiewicz: "I've come over halfway to California, so you've got to come here now. Tomorrow morning." "And of course I was there," says Mankiewicz. "I hooked up with Sarge in some motel room in El Paso. Fletcher Knebel was there. Bill Haddad was there. Everyone was totally charged up. Shriver and Haddad closed in on me: 'You're going to Peru—right?' And finally I said it: 'Yeah.' After a lot of whooping and back-slapping and shouts of 't'rrfic,' Sarge turned to me as he was leaving and asked, 'Hey, don't you want to know what the job pays?' "

Somewhat embarrassed, Mankiewicz replied, "Wellll, yeah, I guess so. I mean, sure. How much does it pay?"

"I haven't the foggiest idea," said Shriver with a great cackle.

A month later, in September 1961, Mankiewicz joined Shriver in Lima, Peru, on the first leg of Shriver's first sweep through Latin America to put Peace Corps programs in place. (Maryann Orlando had called Mankiewicz on the previous Thursday and told him to be in Lima by Saturday.) Also traveling with Shriver were Jack Vaughn, now the first full-fledged Director of the Latin America Regional Office; Dick Ottinger, who was overseeing Peace Corps programs in western Latin America for Vaughn; and Bill Haddad. For Shriver, Haddad, and Mankiewicz, it was their first trip ever to Latin America. Jack Vaughn had come to the Peace Corps with considerable experience with the foreign aid program in Latin America. He had also been a serious amateur boxer, having once won the Golden Gloves feather-weight championship in Michigan. He had worked his way through the University of Michigan to a degree in Latin American studies with a job as university boxing coach. He had come out of World War II a decorated Marine captain, having seen grisly combat duty on Eni-wetok, Guam, and Okinawa. He then went for a master's degree in Latin American studies and subsequently taught at the University of Michigan, University of Pennsylvania, and Johns Hopkins School of International Studies. He was to prove a valuable companion on the Peace Corps' first foray into the immense American continent to the south. Vaughn spoke Spanish fluently. He knew Latin America in-timately. At first glance, Vaughn seemed not in the New Frontier mold. Of barely medium height, slight of build, with ginger-colored hair and a 1940s moustache to match, quietly spoken and careful of gesture, he initially seemed "out of synch" with his far more assertive, impulsive traveling companions. But Vaughn was very soon to surprise them all with his physical stamina, disarming sangfroid, and a marked inclination toward gallows humor.

"The fun had begun," says Mankiewicz with an ominous chuckle. "We went down to Arequipa, Peru's second city, at six thousand feet, which is attractive at its core but which, like Lima, was surrounded by some of the worst slums that any of us had ever seen. They were massive, endless. From there, we traveled by jeep up to Puno, which is at Lake Titicaca at fourteen thousand feet. You took oxygen along. You *used* oxygen. At one point, we approached a suspension bridge. To get to Lake Titicaca, we had to cross it, period. From a distance, it seemed to be made of leaves, vines, and branches a couple of centuries before the advent of the jeep, and it was swinging back and forth over a great chasm. Jack Vaughn seemed unperturbed; he had been there before. Sarge is fearless, but I don't think he liked the looks of it any more than I did. He asked Vaughn as casually as possible, 'Uh, Jack. What's the story on this, uh, thing? This bridge. Can it, uh, does it have a name?' 'Sarge,' said Vaughn, in a very even, bedside-manner tone, 'they call this "The Bridge of San Luis Rey." ' "

Later the group launched on a trip to one of the great shrines of the Andes, Machu Picchu, at thirteen thousand feet. But this time the travel arrangements seemed less perilous. An efficient and safe train would take them up, they were told by Peruvian officials. "But, ah, the train was just a tiny four-passenger railroad car," Mankiewicz went on. "One car. One track. Single gauge. After climbing for hours, all of us gulping oxygen increasingly, Sarge at one point seemed about to *succumb*. We told him he simply could not succumb, because none of the rest of us were Catholics and couldn't do the proper thing, you know? And then, the engine just stopped. Griiiiind, and stop. We had another half hour to go to Machu Picchu. It was 5:30 P.M. Sarge asked, between deep intakes of oxygen, 'Jack, are there any other trains coming this way tonight?'

"Jack seemed to be pondering the question. Finally he said, 'Only the Express.' "

♦   ♦   ♦

As Mankiewicz flew back to Washington after his high-altitude perils in Peru, he wondered if this final stint at Peace Corps headquarters might not seem suddenly too tame for a man who had crossed "The

Bridge of San Luis Rey" and lived to tell the tale. He needn't have worried. Peace Corps headquarters was in a frenzy. The president was coming! Well, no, not in the next half hour, but soon—just after Shriver returned from his long trip through Latin America.

Tom Mathews, deputy director of Public Information, had meanwhile decided that the best possible public relations ploy at that point was to get Mankiewicz on television. Mankiewicz had natural charm, a sure wit, a famous name, and a face that was beguiling in its curious, mercurial mixture of handsomeness and homeliness. He had seen a corner of the future and concluded it might work. Based on conversations with Mankiewicz about the drama of his trip to Peru with Shriver and his talks with Peruvian officials about "honest work" for the soon-to-arrive Volunteers, Mathews scheduled Mankiewicz into a slot on what was then known as "Mike Wallace's Tonight Show," the most useful place to be seen and heard. (The term *talk show* had yet to be invented.) Shortly thereafter, having rated Mankiewicz's TV performance A-plus, Shriver tapped Mankiewicz to "warm up" the crowd during the Kennedy-Shriver "walkover" from the White House to the chamber of commerce building directly across the street from Peace Corps headquarters at Connecticut and H. Up on the stage was a lectern emblazoned with the presidential seal, behind which Mankiewicz, Shriver's most articulate white executive, and Franklin Williams, Shriver's most articulate black executive, held forth in a bantering buildup before the two "royals" arrived. (Mankiewicz and Williams were both native New Yorkers turned Californians turned Washingtonians, and both were old friends.) "When Kennedy and Shriver entered the chamber of commerce auditorium with about a dozen Secret Service guys in lockstep, the place erupted," says Mankiewicz. "Pandemonium. Hundreds of flashbulbs went off, TV cameras were whirring, the crowd was on its feet cheering and stamping. When Kennedy and Shriver came up on stage, you couldn't hear anything but the bedlam. But Shriver brought the president right over to Frank Williams and me and introduced us. Of course, Sarge had to shout and I figured Kennedy didn't hear a word. But as I shook his hand, he stepped back, pointed at me and shouted, 'I know you. I've seen you before. You were on the Mike Wallace show last week.' "

More delightful days were coming. "Gretchen Handwerger, director of the eastern region of Latin America (and later deputy director and acting director of the Peace Corps during the Carter administration) would pull out folders on Peace Corps applicants and would say things like, 'Hey Frank, could you use a beautician in Cuzco?' And I'd say, 'Sounds interesting.' And she'd say, 'Married to a funeral director?' And I'd say, 'Why not?' "

By midfall of 1961, three groups bound for Peru had begun training. One group was at Cornell and two were at the Peace Corps' training camp in Arecibo, Puerto Rico. Mankiewicz thought that the camp sounded a bit too "macho" before he arrived, but when he got there, he was appalled:

It was bad form to criticize the place but I have to say that I didn't like it at all. It was ultra-tough-guy, let's-see-if-you-can-take-it. I wanted people who cared about the social structure and language of Peru; I didn't give a damn whether they could rappel down a dam or not. But they were doing it, males and females of all ages, and it was expected that visiting Peace Corps staff would do it, too. Well, I wasn't going to do it. And I didn't. I jogged, and I went over the goddam obstacle course, but I wouldn't go into that goddamn grubby pool where you were required to float with your hands and legs tied. I think it was called "drownproofing." I mean, I was not going to risk my life. To hell with it. The Reverend William Sloane Coffin was running the place, and he was a terrific guy, but there were plenty of rigid jocks down there, too. I got one of them fired—this Georgia redneck swimming coach—because he insulted some of the black trainees by telling them, "You colored boys will have trouble doing it because colored boys don't float good." Jesus. I said to him, "Is it something about the long muscle in the heel?" I told Sarge about that, and shortly thereafter the guy was gone.

But as it turned out, the kids came out of that experience pretty well trained in the language and anthropology. Most of them had liked the super-summer-camp aspects of it and they were all fired up and ready to go.

◆　◆　◆

Peru! At last!

Well, almost.

Just as Mankiewicz was about to leave the country, Shriver invited him to spend a weekend afternoon at Timberlawn, Shriver's estate in Rockville, Maryland. Timberlawn was a handsome spread, much on the order of Hickory Hill where the Robert Kennedys lived in McLean,

Virginia. Each estate boasted a swimming pool, a tennis court, stables, paddocks, and a backyard big enough to accommodate two thousand people without undue crowding. At Timberlawn, as at Hickory Hill, the New Favorites joined the Old Favorites; longtime Kennedy advisers and hangers-on and squadrons of Kennedy cousins engaged in extremely spirited games of touch football and softball. Mankiewicz could hold his own with the fiercely competitive Kennedy clan, but he also knew that you did not necessarily have to excel at sports; you merely had to get in there and fling yourself around with a lot of enthusiasm. Mankiewicz knew, too, the unspoken rule that you did not intercept passes thrown by Kennedys or Kennedy in-laws, and you did not catch fly balls hit by young Kennedy batters. But on this particular occasion in the late summer of 1962, with his bags packed for his long-awaited pilgrimage to Peru, Mankiewicz "got carried away. I hit the ball hard and figured I had a double for sure. I raced around first base and slid into second, knocking down the second baseman, seven-year-old Maria Shriver (now an anchor for "CBS Morning News"). I just lay there. And I could see Eunice heading over, and I thought, 'Oh God, it's British Honduras—if I'm lucky.' But Eunice just said, 'Gosh, Frank, that was a good slide.'"

Peru! At last!

DAVID GELMAN

In early 1962, David Gelman, a writer of extraordinary talent, was, at thirty-seven, a burned-out nineteen-year fixture of the *New York Post* city room. He was existentially bored, spiritually immobilized, and not just a little envious of the manic happiness of two former *Post* colleagues, Bill Haddad and Ben Schiff, who were writing ecstatic letters to him from their new desks at Peace Corps headquarters in Washington. The three men had had neighboring desks in what was called the "Poet's Corner" of the *New York Post*. Gelman had been the one to answer Haddad's telephone when the call came from Bobby Kennedy from a telephone booth at La Guardia Airport, apparently offering the Peace Corps directorship to Haddad during the transition period between the 1960 election and the 1961 inauguration.

Gelman had also been the one to answer Bill Haddad's telephone at the *Post* a hundred times previously, by Gelman's account, when the callers had been "governors of states and girls with hyphenated names," and later, from a silvery voiced young woman named Kate Roosevelt—a granddaughter of FDR, daughter of James Roosevelt and Betsy Cushing Roosevelt Whitney, and the adopted daughter of John Hay Whitney—who subsequently became Bill Haddad's wife.

Haddad really did lead the life that his telephone messages indicated. He really had been instrumental in managing Kefauver's vice presidential nomination in 1956—over JFK—and he really had been the 1960 campaign liaison between the two Kennedy brothers. For proof, there were published pictures of him kneeling at Jack's side at Hyannis Port while they were watching the election returns. Bobby Kennedy had certainly offered him *something* big at the Peace Corps. And God knows, he had had a meteoric career at the *Post*; he whirled in and he whirled out, and he impressed the hell out of everybody. He won every goddamn award for investigative reporting in New York City in a very short time. And whatever Bobby Kennedy had actually offered him during the interregnum period, Haddad did, in fact, wind up near the top at the Peace Corps, and at the very beginning. And I didn't doubt that he was making waves and exerting great influence again. But Haddad had also told me how embarrassing the Bobby Kennedy incident had been. Haddad's father-in-law, Jock Whitney (the socially impeccable, multimillionaire publisher of the *New York Herald Tribune*) had taken to introducing him at social gatherings as the new head of the Peace Corps for John F. Kennedy—and suddenly, well, it wasn't quite so.

Still, Haddad had landed within shouting distance of the center of power. He had recruited Ben Schiff from the *Post*'s "Poet's Corner," and now the two of them were trying to recruit Gelman.

As despondent and near-hysteric as I was in the winter of 1961–62, I was influenced by a letter from Ben which said, "You gotta come down here"—and he knew what my condition was, too, because he'd been in it. He wrote that he'd never been happier in his life, the Peace Corps was absolutely the greatest place, he'd never met so many talented or amusing people, that he'd never been treated better, never been so challenged, never had so much fun. Given the fact that, like me, he'd been at the *Post* all his life—I mean, the frame of comparison was somewhat narrow. But he was crazy about Tom Mathews, his boss in Public Information at the Peace Corps. He was crazy about everybody at the Peace Corps. He had turned into a true believer.

So I wrote Haddad a very cynical, negative letter—the only kind I was capable of writing, saying that I didn't believe in working for the enemy (Gelman had been staunchly for Stevenson), but I am willing to listen. I was asking him for a job.

Haddad wrote back immediately saying that he had set up a series of appointments for Gelman at Peace Corps headquarters.

Unfortunately, one of them was a former *New York Post* guy, sort of a hustler and an operator who had left the *Post* to go to USIA, but he had pulled some stunts there, and they had bounced him out, and Haddad wound up rescuing him. Haddad likes to save his friends. But Haddad rescued this guy much to everyone's regret at the Peace Corps, because it didn't work out there, either. Later, he landed on Nelson Rockefeller's staff. But I had to sit there with him at the Peace Corps while he intoned, "Ah, Davy, this is not for you, not for Gelman. You're too soft. You're a poet. They need hard guys here, go-getters, guys who can charge around the world, make deals. Ah, it's not for you, Davy." I could have killed him, the son of a bitch, because I really wanted to leave the *Post*.

Despite the hustler's admonitions, Haddad assigned Gelman to do several Peace Corps training evaluations on a consultant basis. Gelman thus took leave from the *Post* in March 1962, to observe the training program for Somalia I at New York University. "It was disastrous," says Gelman. "One female trainee in the program was psychotic and had to be let go, which in turn prompted some of the 'experts' at NYU to call in a bunch of psychologists, who were in turn using the trainees as guinea pigs—they just couldn't wait to get their hands on this new breed. In just three days at NYU, I saw the 'consultant syndrome' take root—all these parasites latching on to the Peace Corps, to get grants, to get overseas trips. I objected to this practice, this syndrome, and I objected to the trainees being picked over and patronized by people who only meant to advance their own careers. And it all had made the trainees miserable."

Gelman next traveled to the Peace Corps' Outward Bound camp in Puerto Rico, where he found an atmosphere and spirit among the staff and trainees that was the opposite of the Somalia I group. "I was very impressed, and I wrote one of those very rapturous, very believing evaluations that evaluators were apt to write in the early days when they encountered a group whose morale was high and whose motivation to succeed for the Peace Corps was so tremendous. I didn't provide many insights as to *why* these trainees were so happy; I hadn't been around long enough to know. But at NYU I knew in a matter of hours why that group was so wretched."

Throughout the spring of 1962, Gelman evaluated training programs at the University of Indiana for Tunisia II and at San Francisco State for Liberia III, and in July, at Berkeley for Ghana III.

I was only in Berkeley a day or two when I got a fateful call from Haddad in Washington. He told me to drop everything, big things were happening. It was just—here are your instructions, and this tape will self-destruct.

I was to fly back to New York immediately, forget anything else, rent a car at the airport, drive to Southbury, Connecticut, where I was to meet Sargent and Eunice Shriver at a training school for the mentally retarded. Haddad had told Shriver that I was the foremost magazine writer in the country. It seemed that Haddad had committed me to help Eunice Shriver write magazine articles. Well, I had never written a magazine piece in my life; in fact, I had never written for anybody but the *New York Post*. Haddad told me that I was not to worry about such details, as he was many times to tell me whenever I got hysterical at the Peace Corps in later years. I was now off the Peace Corps payroll and onto Shriver's personal payroll.

The only thing that took the edge off my terror and permitted me to go through with this caper was that I had met Sarge at Peace Corps headquarters when I was first being interviewed. We were immediately on a first-name basis. He was calling me "Dave" and all but slapping me on the back. By contrast, it took me nineteen years to meet Dorothy Schiff at the *Post*. I met her only when I asked for the leave of absence to do training evaluations for the Peace Corps. Yet I had met Shriver half an hour after I got to the Peace Corps, and that suggested that the spirit of the Peace Corps would be very, very different. Ben Schiff had not been exaggerating. While I was talking to Shriver and Haddad, Bill Atwood dropped in. He was then Kennedy's ambassador to Guinea, and later, to Kenya. That's the way it was in Haddad's office—people just dropping in to banter, and a snappy group it always was.

Gelman arrived late in Southbury "due to Haddad's very cavalier instructions." Shriver greeted him "as if we were old war buddies." But Eunice was annoyed. "You're late," she snapped, without prior or further comment. "They whisked me into their car. We did some touring of the facility, with the two of them bantering nonstop in their terse, staccato styles, the pitch of their conversation rising to meet my own sense of inner hysteria about being where I was, doing what I was doing, with whom I was doing it. Suddenly, we were in a helicopter, all scrunched together, lifting off from the grounds of the school, and down there were all of these mentally retarded children and school officials waving good-bye to us. I was sitting on the outside, next to an open door. I was terrified. It was my first helicopter."

"Is it good form to close the door?" Gelman inquired of Shriver.

"No," replied Shriver merrily. "It is good form to do *this*." Whereupon Shriver leaned across Gelman and waved. Eunice leaned across both Shriver and Gelman and waved. Finally, Gelman got in the spirit and started waving, "even though I was the one in maximum jeopardy."

"*Now?*" asked Gelman, as the people below began to recede into specks.

"Fine," said Shriver, and Gelman, with profound gratitude, closed the door.

"And so we were off. But to where? I had no idea, and I didn't dare ask," says Gelman.

The helicopter landed at a small airport "somewhere in New England," where a small private plane awaited. The Shrivers began chattering casually about the need to thank so-and-so for the use of his plane. "They talked as if it were the same thing as getting a lift into town in a neighbor's pickup truck," says Gelman. "But it was *my* first private airplane."

Shriver glanced around the small craft and remarked to Eunice, "Hey, Eunie, this is even nicer than Dad's [meaning Ambassador Joseph P. Kennedy's plane]."

With both incredulity and irritation, Eunice replied, "Whaaaat?"

Gelman recalls his stupefaction:

Well, it was a *lovely* plane. And I hate all planes. But this one had stuffed armchairs on swivels, writing tables, plush carpeting, even a bar. It took my mind temporarily off the fact that I was thoroughly intimidated by Eunice Kennedy Shriver and that I still didn't know where we were going, or what, exactly, they expected of me. But then Sarge and Eunice resumed their overwrought conversation about the school in Southbury. I began to see the master plan. The Kennedy family was embarking for the first time on a public discussion of Rosemary, the retarded Kennedy sister, who was in an institution. Eunice was gathering material on progressive and enlightened ways of dealing with retarded children. Southbury, apparently, was one of the more enlightened approaches. Eunice was very excited about it. It seemed that I was to write articles on the subject for the *Saturday Evening Post* and *Glamour* magazine, while she fed me material and suggestions. It seemed she had boxes full of research material. Somewhere. But she never addressed me directly. The only thing she had said to me all day was "You're late." So I just kept quiet, waiting for the next clue.

The plane started to make its descent at 4:00 P.M. "I guess it's dinner at Dad's tonight," mused Eunice, peering out a window.

"So there it was, finally," says Gelman, with just a trace of a shudder two decades later. "I was being more or less kidnapped to the Kennedy compound in Hyannis Port. It was crazy, unreal. 'Damn Bill Haddad,' I thought. 'All I wanted was out of the "Poet's Corner." But not this; this is too much.' "

"This," said Shriver casually, "is Jack's," as they pulled up to a large, white clapboard house.

"I put my bag down in the front hall of that house. All around were Jackie's little watercolors, those Grandma Moses–style paintings. I was led upstairs by Sarge, who showed me into a frilly, little-girl's bedroom. 'It has to be Caroline's,' I thought, 'but, oh God, this is impossible.' "

"I figured Sarge would now disappear and give me time to unpack. Instead, he said with a great whoop, 'Hey Dave, c'mon! Let's take a swim before it gets dark! That water's t'rffic at this time of day.' "

It happens that David Gelman's list of things most despised and feared were, in this order: (1) air travel, (2) driving a rental car in alien territory, and (3) frigid, choppy salt water, even at high noon on a hot day. He had already been seduced into the first two dreaded activities and was now being lured into the third, and near sundown.

"I don't have a bathing suit with me," attempted Gelman, even as he knew what Shriver was bound to say next: "Oh, no problem, Dave. I'll find you a suit."

Within minutes, Shriver returned triumphantly with a pair of bathing trunks, which, Gelman considered vaguely, might well be the property of JFK himself, who was five inches taller and forty pounds heavier than Gelman.

"It was a huge suit; I had to hold it up with one hand. And I can't swim very well, but I didn't tell Sarge. We went down to the beach with his young son Bobby (Robert Sargent Shriver III), and I just said, 'Oh, you two go on ahead; I'll catch up.' "

Shriver and his son dove into the icy salt water of Nantucket Sound and with enormous strokes, "headed for Portugal," while Gelman "clung to a wooden piling, trying not to drown. When they swam back," continues Gelman, "I came out of the water with them as if I'd had quite a swim myself, and Sarge said, 'That was absolutely great, wasn't it?' And I said, 'Yeah, great.' "

Walking back toward the house with Shriver and his son, Gelman noticed a solitary Gatsby-like figure strolling across the lawn, silhouetted against a blazing orange sun that would set in seconds. He shielded his eyes with his one free arm, trying to identify the lonely figure. "Ah!" piped Shriver, with evident delight. "*El Presidente!*" Gelman felt faint. "Wouldja like to meet the president?"

"*Well,*" says Gelman with a heavy sigh and a ghoulish chuckle,

this was the moment of total unreality for me. I had been insulating myself against shocks of all kinds, all day, starting with Haddad's wild phone call to me in Berkeley. None of it—*none* of it—had any precedent in my life, and I was just accepting, sort of once-removed . . . accepting . . . absolutely . . . *anything,* anything at all . . . by now . . . that could come along.

The notion of being in the High Lamasery was dreamlike to begin with, and nothing was really registering. And now I was going to meet the president, shivering and wet, and I shook his hand, and I only recall that he looked all orange in the last rays of the sun and that I was in a disgraceful condition, holding up an oversized, dripping bathing suit with my left hand and saying, "Nice to meet you," between chattering teeth.

President Kennedy motioned the three swimmers toward the house—
"Jack's." Entering the living room, Kennedy and Shriver separated
from Gelman and Bobby Shriver as abruptly as if a heavy curtain had
suddenly dropped. As Gelman "drifted away," he heard Kennedy say,
"Sahge, we announced the Celebreeze appointment today. What do
you think?"*

Dinner that night was indeed "at Dad's." "As I groped around the
compound in the dark for the maximum source of light, several Secret
Service men began appearing out of nowhere, eyeing me, I thought,
as if I were an anarchist. They asked me where I was going. I tried to
stay calm and cool. I said I was a guest of the Shrivers' and was going
to Ambassador Kennedy's house for dinner. They must have been told
about me, knew I was legitimately on the premises. Otherwise, they
would have pounced on me and drawn their guns. I began to realize
they were just having some fun with me, and I suddenly spotted a
house with a lot of light and a flagpole, and I said with mock confidence, 'Oh sure, there it is.' "

Shriver bounded over to Gelman and drew him into the intimidating midst, introducing him enthusiastically as ("Oh boy, here it
comes," thought Gelman, and it did) "the foremost magazine writer
in America, who is going to help Eunie write articles about Rosemary
and the whole subject of care for the mentally retarded." The Kennedys
are always exceptionally keen to meet the "best" or the "most" in any
field, and therefore Gelman was greeted warmly, appreciatively as a
"foremost" who would be therapeutically involved in a project of great
concern to them. But Gelman, then and later, was constantly amazed
that they did not press him for more details about his career; he found
it bizarre that these Kennedys, who were said to be voracious readers
and up on everything, didn't find it strange that they had yet to read
a magazine piece by the "foremost" writer of the genre. Gelman finally
concluded that even the sharper-than-sharp Kennedys, just like everyone else, believed what they wanted to believe. Haddad—whom the
family knew to be a "most" in the field of investigative reporting, who
had been an insider on the 1960 campaign, who had a high post at

*Anthony Celebreeze, former governor of Ohio, had been appointed by Kennedy to
replace Abraham Ribicoff, former governor of Connecticut, as secretary of the Department of Health, Education and Welfare. Ribicoff was preparing to run for the
Senate as Shriver and others had fully expected him to do as early as December 1960,
during the New Frontier "talent search" period.

the Peace Corps, and who was married to a lady who belonged to an elegant, famous, and influential family—had to know what he was talking about.

The Ambassador sat at the head of the dinner table, flanked by Eunice and Bobby, who were obviously the family delegates to their father. Jack, uh, the president, sat next to Eunice. Most of them were there. Jackie was not, and she was never mentioned. I sat next to Joan, but I didn't know who she was. I asked her if she was an actress. Sarge sat across from me. We were at the other end of the table, physically and figuratively below the salt. I came to see that that was Sarge's place in the family; they treated him in the exasperated way a lot of large, close-knit, clannish families treat the good-natured brother-in-law who is married to the dominant senior sister.

But Sarge didn't seem to mind at all; he accepted Eunice's role without resentment. There was tremendous deference to "Old Joe" Kennedy. A far cry from the tough, unsentimental image they projected to the public. Old Joe had had a stroke which had left him speechless and partially paralyzed, as had been the case of my own father. The way those grown Kennedy offspring behaved toward Joe reminded me a lot of my own large family. He was included in a lot of joking and kidding, more so because he couldn't respond. It gave that gathering a particular poignancy, although there was the very real sense, and all of them had it, that this was an extraordinary family.

Meanwhile, Shriver and Gelman were having their own brand of fun below the salt. The two had gotten along from the first, and Gelman realized that to the extent he was making it in that awesome midst, he was making it due to his rapport with Shriver. "I discovered he liked my jokes, and he kept setting me up for irreverent one-liners. He was a great audience; he had this infectious laugh, sort of like a duck quacking, and it kept me going. The main thing was to keep talking and joking and look for an opening in the primary conversation at the other end of the table. At some point, either Bobby or Eunice mentioned John Glenn, who Bobby had apparently latched on to, and who was coming to Hyannis Port the following weekend. They all got quite excited about this." (Glenn was, of course, the ultimate all-American hero of the time, having just orbited the earth alone in the spacecraft *Friendship 7*. And he was *the* new Kennedy conquest.)

"I said, 'Oh, Glenn is too Boy Scout for me.' And Sarge immediately picked up on that theme. He enjoyed deflating them, shocking them with an opposing opinion that they hadn't expected. And it helped, obviously, if he had a sidekick, like me. That Sarge and I weren't gushing over John Glenn—their idea of the best catch possible—got their attention. It really bothered them, why we weren't taking it seriously and could actually make jokes about this big-deal astronaut. So they were willing and even eager to banter with us briefly."

◆   ◆   ◆

On warm, dry days, Gelman would sit at a typewriter on the wide, sweeping porches at "Dad's," or "Jack's." On foggy, wet, cool days, the foremost magazine writer in America would work inside "Dad's" or "Jack's" with Eunice and her endless array of boxes full of clippings and reports on care for the mentally retarded. Gelman would be "allowed" to visit his family in New York occasionally and would be "allowed" to install them in a motel in Dennis on Cape Cod, where the Gelmans had often taken their vacations. But he was required to work at the compound and was usually summoned early in the morning. "The owner of the motel got a huge kick out of announcing over the loudspeaker system, 'Mr. Gelman, Mr. Gelman, Sargent Shriver is here for you.' Well, usually, it was a car and a driver sent by Sarge or Eunice, but sometimes Sarge came himself and we would discuss my work in progress, or the value of Peace Corps evaluation reports, or whatever was on his mind. But the motel owner always made the same announcement. It made him feel important, and I'm sure it was good for business."

Joining Gelman in his endeavors that summer in Hyannis Port was a psychologist from Georgia who was on a fellowship for the Joseph P. Kennedy Foundation. He knew a lot about mental retardation and he was brought to the compound to contribute scientific wisdom and to authenticate what Gelman was writing.

I was glad to have the company and the technical help. We were both captives in this exotic setting, to which I never really made a full adjustment. But my psychologist cohort not only could not adjust to it *at all*, it was a summer of terror for him. He was petrified of Eunice, he was awed by all of them. When he'd see Eunice coming, he'd cower behind me.

At one point, the psychologist—let's call him Sid—and I shared a bedroom at "Bobby's." The first night there, we were trying to figure out whose room it was. Sid looked under his pillow for a clue. He found a nightgown with the name "Kathleen" embroidered on it. I lifted my pillow and found one with "Courtney" embroidered on it. We got slightly hysterical. We began calling each other Kathleen and Courtney, but we had no idea where they were in Bobby and Ethel's lineup of kids. If I woke up first, I'd say, "Time to get up, Kathleen," and he'd answer sleepily, "Ah, Courtney, top of the mornin' to ya."

Ultimately, Gelman was installed in a study at "Dad's," and Sid returned gratefully to Georgia. It was late September 1962, and the winds off Nantucket Sound were a bit too chilling now for working on the porch. "I missed the porch scene, though, in a masochistic kind of way," says Gelman.

I'd be sitting on "Dad's" or "Jack's" porch, sometimes gazing out to sea for inspiration or just to avoid writing, and I'd hear a voice, all too unmistakable: "Eune? Eune?" And he'd open the door, come out on the porch, calling "Hey, Eune, where are you? It's time to go sailing. Eune?" And then the president would notice me. "Is my sistah heah? Have you seen Eune?" And I'd say, "No, Mr. President, I haven't seen her this morning," or "Yes, Mr. President, she went that way." One morning, near lunchtime, Pat Lawford came out on the porch looking distraught and confused and just wandered off across the lawn. Soon thereafter, Eunice appeared on the porch, looking worried, "Have you seen Pat?" I said, "She went that way." Eunice then said, "Poor Pat, she had terrible news today. Marilyn Monroe killed herself last night. Marilyn was a friend of Pat's. Pat feels just awful." Then Eunice disappeared in search of Pat.

That's how it was—this calliope of Kennedys, in and out of compound doors, inquiring as to each other's whereabouts. Gelman was the nameless sentry.

At the very end of September, Gelman had completed a long, technically precise, heart-rending article for the *Saturday Evening Post*, his first as the foremost magazine writer in America.

Eunice and Sarge read it and told me that they really liked it. They were satisfied; it had everything. But now, they said, "Jack will have to see it."

So there I was, one overcast fall day at "Dad's," sitting with Eunice and Sarge on an alcove seat by a bay window, waiting. Eunice and Sarge were on the very edge of the seat, terribly anxious. In came the president with my manuscript. He sat down, scanned it, shook it, and then let it rest on his lap. He addressed me by name for the first time: "Mr. Gelman." He started off by talking about the *New York Post* and how much he enjoyed its editorials. He liked its briefness, he liked the larger typeface used by the *Post*, as compared with the much smaller typeface of the *New York Times*. Finally, he shook my manuscript again, said he liked it, approved of it, hoped it would be published exactly as it was. I could only think, "Thank God, it's over. Escape!"

For Gelman, the terrible test was over. It was farewell—farewell to the Kennedy compound, the subject of mental retardation, Eunice Shriver's blue pencil, Shriver's watch-dogging, this strange command-performance life in exotic exile under "house arrest," life as Courtney—or was it Kathleen?

FRANKLIN WILLIAMS

"I've had the most logical career of anyone that I know, every step in it being clearly based on the step before," says Franklin Williams.

I never went out and grabbed at anything on my own. I never did anything startling or out of character in terms of my career. This will surprise many people who were around in the early days of the Peace Corps, who perceived me, I realize, as aggressive and even intimidating. I was the first black man at the Peace Corps to hold a very high position at headquarters and the first black that most of the top white officials had ever met socially. And the designation in 1961 wasn't "black"; it was still "negro." I wasn't a "token" black, or negro; Shriver wanted to make a point by hiring me. The Peace Corps, according to Shriver's wishes, was to be a *fully* integrated government agency—the first—and I was a credible person to start with.

I was born and grew up in New York City. Poor. Middle class. Black. My grandfather had been a valet, which made us middle class. My father was a musician and an alcoholic. Nevertheless, we were middle class. Middle class values. Middle class morality. The sense that you worked your way up, step by step, through the system. Went to college. I went to Lincoln College in Pennsylvania, where many other ambitious, middle class blacks went. My ambition was to go to law school, go into politics, and become the first, or one of the first, black judges in America. That was it. But in those days, that was also a lot.

Williams got into Fordham Law School, an institution that was, in the 1940s, 99 percent Catholic. "I could go there because it was in New York and I didn't have to board. Logical. I could live with my brother at the time. I had thousands of relatives in the city."

Williams was, however, drafted at the end of the first half of his freshman year at Fordham, eleven days before his final exams, into the Ninety-third Infantry Division of the U.S. Army.

"That began the career of Franklin Williams, Rebel. I won't go into what happened to me in the Ninety-third Division. But I think it's enough to say that I went in a buck private and came out twenty months later a buck private, never having been recommended for Private First. And after that experience, I was determined to fight the white man. Because, if I didn't fight the white man, I'd go into the nut house."

Williams came out of the army, returned to Fordham Law School, and graduated a year early, passing the New York Bar exam before graduating. He was hired immediately by Thurgood Marshall, now a Supreme Court justice, then a special counsel to the NAACP (National Association for the Advancement of Colored People).

In five years, 1945 to 1950, I handled all the criminal cases for the NAACP which took place in the South, even though the NAACP offices were in New York. But I couldn't get along with Thurgood for a whole range of reasons, one of which was the fact that a lot of black leaders of the day wanted nobody on their staffs to have any kind of independent personality. So, I went to the West Coast in 1950 to work for Walter White, and from 1950 to 1959 we built the most effective and successful civil rights structure in any part of the country: We built it in Oregon, Washington, Idaho, California, Arizona, Utah, Alaska, even Hawaii. We had support from people like Cesar Chavez. And by that time, in 1959, I thought we had done it. I thought that the civil rights movement was over, as far as achieving the statutes and breaking segregation. We had gotten laws passed; we had had sit-ins, marches. We had achieved so much.

But then, a new attorney general was named in California. Stanley Mosk. He asked me to come in and set up the first constitutional rights section of any Department of Justice in the country. I joined the attorney general's staff thinking, now I can bring the power of the state behind the issues I'd been concerned about. I did battle with the Real Estate Division of the Department of Education. I did battle with the governor's office and made a lot of enemies in the process, including Fred Dutton, who later worked in the Kennedy White House.

Williams said that after Kennedy's election, and after eleven years in California, he had the urge to return to the East. Just as Frank Mankiewicz was lured to Washington in the spring of 1961 by Williams, Williams was lured to Washington in late February of 1961 by Harris Wofford. During the 1960 campaign, when he was assistant attorney general of California, Williams had met Harris Wofford, fresh from a law professorship at Notre Dame and about to join Shriver on the civil rights section of the campaign. Wofford had asked Williams to give a lecture series at Notre Dame on "The Changing Legal Status of the Negro in America." "I did this, and Harris was grateful; he was impressed. He didn't forget. I made some speeches for Kennedy on the campaign and I ran the voter registration drive. Harris didn't forget that either. So, when Harris became special assistant to President Kennedy for civil rights, he called me, and I was ready to go."

But after two days in Washington, Williams was discouraged and ready to go back to California. Job offers from the Civil Rights Commission and the State Department had bored him. Not challenging enough; foggy as to exact content. He broke the news to Wofford over lunch in the White House mess. Louis Martin, a black newspaperman from Chicago, who had become deputy director of the Democratic National Committee, was there, and he urged Williams not to leave town without touching base with Shriver. It was March 1, 1961. President Kennedy had just signed the executive order creating the Peace Corps, and Shriver had announced it.

"I didn't want to see Sarge particularly," Williams recalls,

and I said so. And Harris knew why. He'd taken me to see Sarge during the campaign when Sarge was running minority affairs. There he was, up in this big hotel suite with all these blacks and Chicanos. That turned me off. Special segregated treatment was not my style.

But I figured, what the hell, I'm here. Might as well see where Sarge is at *now*. Well, he was at the barricades. And boy! He began pounding his desk and saying, "*This* is where the action is. You gotta come with me!" He made it sound so damn exciting. I said, "Like when?" He said, "Oh, *now*. Today. Well, how about to-morrow?" I saw he wasn't kidding. I said, "But Sarge, I can't leave the attorney general's office just like that."

Sarge said, "Yes you can." And he picked up the phone and called Stanley Mosk in California. He said, "Stanley, we gotta have your assistant, Williams."

Done. But now what? Shriver, enormously pleased with himself at having acquired the skilled and glamorous Williams in a three-minute, coast-to-coast telephone call with the hard-bargaining attorney general of California, pondered Williams's immediate role at the Peace Corps.

Shriver suggested to Williams that perhaps the best title would be Special Assistant to the Director. "That way," said Shriver, "you can get involved in a whole range of activity. Help me build my staff with the best people there are out there. Speech ideas. Our relationship with international organizations. University relations. The works. You can then carve out a more permanent role, find a chunk of the operations you'd like to run. You know a lot about institution building. You know a lot about the psychology of institutions. I can see you playing an active role in how we are going to work with the U.N., if, in fact, we actually are."

All of this sounded tantalizing to Williams. Shriver suggested that Williams immediately see Warren Wiggins, now the associate director for Program Development Overseas, just a notch below Shriver, and an architect of the Peace Corps. Shriver indicated that Wiggins had already established a formidable power base. But Shriver stressed that Williams should approach Wiggins with the message that he, Williams, had carte blanche to choose the area or areas that most appealed to him.

> I walked into Wiggins's office, and there he was, with an organization chart. Wiggins was clearly the guy putting together the Peace Corps' structure. At the top of the chart there was "Director" in a center box. Out to one side, all by itself, connected with a line from the Director's box, was "Division of Private Organizations." Out to the other side, same arrangement, was "Division of University Relations." The two most independent divisions, apparently, in the agency. And two very prestigious people were going to take over in these divisions: Gordon Boyce, the head of the Experiment for International Living, for Private Organizations; and Albert Sims, an executive of the Institute of International Education, for University Relations.
>
> Well, so much for those jobs. They were taken. Who wanted to play second fiddle? But Wiggins explained that he had, under him, under Program Development and Operations (known as PDO), a Division of International Organizations. That was Wiggins's territory. This would include dealing with the U.N., which Sarge had mentioned, and it was a fairly attractive idea to me.

Williams was staying in Washington with his Lincoln College roommate, Charlie Nelson, who was about to join Wiggins in PDO. Nelson, like Wiggins, was a veteran of ICA, which under Kennedy was called the Agency for International Development. That evening, Warren Wiggins and John Alexander, another former ICA official who had joined the Wiggins group, invited Williams and Nelson to dinner. "Ah, the Wiggins team," thought Williams. "I am being rushed." Something told Williams to be coy. The offer came: Would Williams take the Division of International Organizations within the bailiwick of PDO?

"Oh, you know, I'm not completely sure about the Peace Corps. Who knows? Maybe I'll end up deciding to take one of those jobs at the State Department, or for that matter, just go back and stay in California, where, after all, I have it made."

Wiggins then played his trump card. "Frank, you really ought to think seriously about coming with us, because *we* will *control* it." Williams was astounded. It had been his very distinct impression that Sargent Shriver, alone, controlled it.

Wiggins explained that money was what he was talking about. PDO controlled the size and types of programs overseas—therefore, money; and PDO controlled the matter of overseas travel—therefore, also money.

"I pretended to go along with this," says Williams. "But I was a bit disturbed by the atmosphere. I went back to California, uncertain as to my next step."

Williams's problem was solved almost immediately by Ed Bayley, the director of public information at the Peace Corps, who called Williams in California at Shriver's urging. "Sarge wanted to get out a press release on me fast, nail me down, identify me with the agency publicly. No fool, Sarge. Ed asked me what my title was. I hesitated. Finally, I said, 'Ed, just say I'm special assistant to the director.' "

No fool, Franklin Williams.

PAT KENNEDY

Padraic Kennedy was twenty-eight and a teaching fellow at the University of Wisconsin in Madison when he heard about John F. Kennedy's late-night challenge to the students at the University of Michigan. His first thought was "Wow! I've just got to get in on this." Pat Kennedy (who is not related to JFK) started out lucky; he had a direct line, in effect, to the new administration in the person of Lemoyne Billings, one of John F. Kennedy's closest friends, whom Pat had met while campaigning for Kennedy in Wisconsin.

In December 1960, Pat Kennedy and his wife, Ellen, drove east for Christmas in New York City.

We made a date with Lem Billings to go hear George Shearing at the Embers, and I told him I was really interested in the Peace Corps. As luck would have it, Lem was going down to Palm Beach the next day to be with the president-elect. He scared me, though. He said he really didn't know for sure whether or not JFK had used the peace corps idea as campaign bait or whether he was really interested in it seriously—whether it was actually going to be part of his administration. Then I thought to myself, "Now, don't be ridiculous. The man proposed it in a major foreign policy speech. Surely he couldn't renege on it."

I didn't hear anything from Lem for about a month, and then one night after grading blue books until 2:00 A.M., I fell into bed. It was twenty below zero outside. I was almost asleep when the phone rang. It was so cold I almost didn't get up, but you wonder about phone calls at that hour, so I got up and answered it. A woman said, "Mr. Kennedy? The White House is calling." In a second, there was Lem Billings on the phone saying cheerily, "Guess where I am."

I said, "Are you at the White House by any chance?"

"I'm not only at the White House," said Billings. "I'm in the Lincoln bed. Are you still interested in the Peace Corps?"

"Damn right!"

"Well, I've talked to Sarge Shriver and he'd like you to come to Washington for an interview immediately. How soon can you get here?"

I said, "I'll be there in twenty-four hours."

Kennedy was driving east with wings on his wheels when he heard on the car radio that President Kennedy had just signed something called an executive order creating the Peace Corps. It was March 1, 1961.

In Washington, Shriver told Pat Kennedy that the Peace Corps was like a rocket. It was sitting on the launching pad and no one knew where it was going to go or what it was going to do. And he invited Pat Kennedy to help him get it launched. The interview lasted into the dinner hour and Shriver asked Kennedy to join him at Paul Young's. "He was talking about how the Peace Corps should be organized. To emphasize how flexible the Peace Corps could be, he pulled out his pen and drew an organization chart on the tablecloth. I sat there terrified. I expected a scene. I expected the owner to come barging in, order him to stop, ask us to leave. But no, the waiters just stood around beaming. They were so proud to have the president's brother-in-law drawing on their tablecloth."

Shriver wanted Pat Kennedy to come on board, and, as usual, immediately.

He didn't offer me a specific job for the simple reason that there were no jobs. There were only about twelve people there in early March 1961: Sarge, Maryann Orlando, Sally Bowles, Nancy Gore, Mitzi Mallina. Warren Wiggins, Charlie Nelson, and George Carter were there, as were Gordon Boyce and Al Sims. Sims hired Al Meisel. Ed Bayley was there as Sarge's delegate to the press. Moyers hadn't come over from Lyndon Johnson's office yet. Franklin Williams was about to arrive. And Harris Wofford was there, dividing his time between the Peace Corps and the White House civil rights office. Wofford interviewed me, and he kept yawning. I knew he was important; I'd heard about him on the campaign. He was close to Shriver. And I thought, "Oh my God, I've had it. I'm boring him to death."

Each time Wofford would go into another cavernous yawn, he would apologize. "He kept saying, 'Oh, I'm so sorry. It's not you, I promise.' " And it wasn't. Wofford was working eighteen-hour days in two demanding jobs.

To solve the problem of office equipment, "of which there was none," says Kennedy,

we would go "midnight requisitioning," which meant raiding the AID offices in the same building in the middle of the night. It wasn't difficult. The AID people always left at 5:00 P.M., whereas we were working half the night.

I did what everyone else did, answered letters. There were thousands of them stacked up by the time I arrived. There were crazy stories, most of them true, and many of them were published, such as the one about Albert Sims, vice president of the Institute of International Education, and Gordon Boyce, head of the Experiment in International Living, who had only one desk and one chair between them. When one had an appointment, the other would have to sit on the floor in the next room. These were distinguished men. But they didn't mind, nobody minded. It was exciting, it was fun, and boy, did the press love it. I remember that when Sarge got William Saltonstall, headmaster of Exeter and a Republican, to say he'd be the second Peace Corps Rep in Nigeria, James Reston wrote a whole column on it in the *New York Times*. There was a sense of astonishment and respect that

Sarge was making it a truly bipartisan organization and that outstanding people were attracted to it.

Pat Kennedy knew that he would not be answering letters forever. In April 1961, Larry Dennis, a native Iowan, musician, journalist, and provost and vice president of Penn State under Dr. Milton Eisenhower, joined the staff as first associate director of the Office of Peace Corps Volunteers. Within the Office of Peace Corps Volunteers were the divisions of Training and Selection. One of the most critical problems for Shriver would be to convince the leaders of the Third World countries—especially the leaders of the newly independent, supersensitive African nations of Ghana and Nigeria—that the as yet nonexistent Peace Corps Volunteers from America would be qualified to live and teach in totally unfamiliar cultures. Therefore, where would they be trained and by whom and for how long? "The divisions of Training and Selection were unstaffed," says Kennedy, "and in Shriver's mind training was associated, logically enough, with the universities, and I was also associated in his mind with the universities. I simply *became* Training. I was charged with ferreting out the African experts, the "Africanists" who were conducting area studies at the major colleges and universities. I was to immerse myself in Africa generally and Ghana specifically."

Kennedy had never been to Africa, nor had anyone else on the earliest skeletal senior staff of the Peace Corps. Neither Kennedy nor any of them knew anything about Africa. Kennedy was as unsure of the exact geographical location of Ghana and Nigeria as Mankiewicz had been about Peru when he accepted the offer to be the Rep there. But these inadequacies did not get Pat Kennedy down. Sargent Shriver was handing out adrenalin and autonomy and everyone was grabbing it. Kennedy identified the "Africanists" on the American campuses. "I told them frankly that I was a 'beginner on Africa,' and far from being put off by my admission of ignorance, they warmed to it. I was a guy who craved to learn, who needed them, and they were the guys who knew it all but had never been so needed or so assiduously courted—by the U.S. government, by their own institutions, by publishers, by anyone. They were grateful for the attention and the chance to be used wisely. Area studies was small potatoes on the campuses at that time. Those guys were sitting in ignored corners of universities, with all of their vast knowedge, and no one was paying much attention. Africa was of small concern compared, say, to European studies or to Russian studies."

Pat Kennedy brought the distinguished professors of African studies to Washington for a week of brainstorming. There was David Apter from the University of California at Berkeley, author of *Gold Coast in Transition*, an expert on Ghana; Gray Cowan from Columbia University, an expert on Nigeria; sociologist Sinclair Drake from Roosevelt University in Chicago (and a former professor at the University of Ghana); and Robert Lystad from Johns Hopkins University, an anthropologist and author of *The Ashanti: A Proud People*. The group ultimately coalesced to design and direct the Ghana I training program at Berkeley, with Pat Kennedy as training officer, in June 1961. The four Africanists, says Kennedy, "worked so hard, they worked around the clock. They were there the whole time. It was not like a speeded-up six-week Berlitz course. It was not a heavy drill in geography and customs of the country. It was real immersion—the most intensive kind of training imaginable."

Seven weeks later, in mid-August 1961, Ghana I was ready for Ghana. (Nobody was more pleasantly surprised that the Africanists, who at the outset had believed that it would take nearly two years to prepare the Volunteers adequately, given the fact of their youth, inexperience, Kennedy connection, and accompanying media hype. Too much, it was felt, hung on their performance.) The Ghana I group, numbering fifty, had become "one"; there was an unspoken sense of being special due to their having been so closely associated with America's top four people in African studies and the ever-attentive point man from Washington headquarters, Pat Kennedy. They hadn't paused to absorb the daunting fact that they would be absolutely *the first* *Volunteers* (Tanganyika I had started and finished its training program earlier but would trail Ghana I to Africa by a few days). But there were celebrations nonetheless. John Demos, a 1959 graduate of Harvard who had done graduate work at Berkeley before entering the Ghana training group there (and who is now a professor of history at Yale), recalls that at the graduation party, "many libations were poured and the program faculty accepted cigarette lighters inscribed with the heaviest pun of the year: 'Here today, Ghana tomorrow.' " As Demos puts it, "We were set down in Accra [the capital of Ghana] on the afternoon of September 1, 1961."

Pat Kennedy remembers the group's (and his own) thrill at being wished well personally by President Kennedy at the White House, at which point it fully sank in that they were the *first*, and he remembers the subsequent happy send-off at the Ghanian Embassy in Washington on August 31. He remembers thinking that it was all quite miraculous.

And he remembers the heat. Late August in Washington, D.C. A steam bath. "Perspiration was just pouring off all of us. An official of the Ghanian Embassy said to us as we left, 'I can promise you, it will be much cooler in Africa.' "

The flight to Accra, Ghana, took twenty-one hours by a propellor-driven DC-7. The voyage was deemed of sufficient historical importance by Pan American World Airways that *Peace Corps Clipper* was painted on the fuselage. David Apter had told the group that the first impression would be extremely important. Thus, the trip to Africa turned into what Pat Kennedy called "a twenty-one-hour rehearsal." The Volunteers had been taught the Ghanian national anthem in Twi, the primary dialect of Ghana. They practiced it obsessively on the plane. "While one group would practice the song, another group would be practicing what to say in case they were interviewed. Others were practicing the highlife, the bouncy national dance of Ghana, in the back of the plane. The rehearsal paid off. There was a formal greeting party at the airport that included the minister of education, the local council, the American ambassador, and an assemblage of local chiefs." The Volunteers sang the anthem in Twi to the pop-eyed amazement of the Ghanians on the tarmac. Then Kenneth Baer, a well-groomed, scholarly looking young man, stepped to the microphone. (Baer, from Beverly Hills, had his B.A. from Yale and his M.A. in history from Berkeley. He now practices law in Atlanta.) The core of his message—in Twi—immediately found its way into Peace Corps lore: "We have to come to learn as well as to teach."

Pat Kennedy, the shepherd and cosculptor of Ghana I, stood there watching the scarcely imaginable unfold. To him, it was better than any fantasy could have fashioned. "Radio Ghana was there, recording the whole thing. I was thinking, 'Isn't life strange? Just two and a half months ago our Africanists were saying, "It can't be done in seven weeks; it will take two years." And just six and a half months ago, Lem Billings was calling me in Wisconsin from the Lincoln bed and the Peace Corps didn't even exist.' "

Two nights later, Pat Kennedy took his fifty Volunteers to the Lido, an open-air dance hall in Accra. Suddenly there were nearly fifty American college students out on the floor, dancing the highlife for all they were worth. "To say that the Ghanians were utterly astonished—well, it was like a revolution. A contest was then announced, and I thought, 'Okay, Volunteers, get off the floor. This is the national dance.' But the Volunteers stayed with it. In the end, two of them—John McGinn and Laura Damon—were awarded a dual second prize. I and everyone else viewed it purely as a courtesy prize, but still I thought, 'Sarge will go *nuts* when he hears this.' "

Pat Kennedy today, as President and CEO of The Columbia Association in Columbia, Maryland, says that there was no better job than being a training officer—especially the first one—in the agency's early days. "It was the best job you could have—the total Peace Corps job. You were in on everything, you did everything. You had total contact with the Volunteers, total contact with the area specialists, total contact with Sarge, total contact with the universities who were doing the training, contact with the embassies in Washington, contact with the host country officials. You were the center of all activity."

Kennedy soon became director of the Division of Volunteer Support, which in office code was labeled PCV/DVS and which fell within the purview of the Office of Peace Corps Volunteers. "But in this job, I could still be a training officer. I could still build a training program from scratch. I had the power to designate who would be the escort officers, and that was a job that an awful lot of people wanted. Foreign travel. Arrival ceremonies. Big Daddy to the Volunteers. I had the best patronage job since Mayor Daley!"

DONOVAN McCLURE

In 1961, Donovan McClure was not a likely prospect for the Peace Corps. He had managed, in the late 1950s, to get what he had most passionately wanted—a job on the *San Francisco Chronicle*. He and his wife, Maggie, were in love with the fabled, glistening city of hills and breathtaking views of the bay. Don McClure loved his job, and it had taken him an entire year to convince Abe Mellincoff, managing editor of the *Chronicle*, to hire him; westerners were reticent about hiring people from the East. Now that McClure was ensconced at the *Chronicle*, he was not about to budge. God knows, he would never return to the *Akron Beacon Journal* from whence he came, via his native West Virginia.

However, since that formerly unbudgeable westerner, Tom Mathews, had jumped ship and gone East to join Shriver—and seemed bent on emptying the *Chronicle* newsroom of his favorite former colleagues and collecting them around him at the Peace Corps—the bait was set. Mathews was persuasive, and Mathews was calling. He seemed to be offering McClure a job in the Peace Corps' Public Information Office.

> The last thing on earth I wanted to do was to leave San Francisco. The last. I had been an active Stevenson supporter, and the Peace Corps seemed so much a creature of Kennedy. I had covered Kennedy's Cow Palace speech when he proposed the Peace Corps, and even though the young people in that audience went wild for the idea, I had been skeptical. But I respected Tom's judgment, and if he was so crazy about the place, then maybe I ought to think about it. Finally, what propelled me into actually going East and checking it out, which Tom was urging me to do, was the somewhat disturbing thought that not one of us in the *Chronicle* newsroom knew one goddamn thing about the federal government—I mean, to the point where we didn't even know how to negotiate a call to, say, HEW. Didn't know exactly what it did, whom to ask for, how to phrase a question. Didn't have the vocabulary or mentality for it.

The *Chronicle* was famous for putting juicy local scandal before national news, which made it a highly colorful, readable, and beloved paper. San Francisco social gossip took precedence over some important nuclear test. When the opera season opened, the reader had to turn to page seventeen for world or national news. "Everybody loved the *Chronicle* the way it was," says McClure. "But I honestly thought that at least one of us ought to know how our government worked, so why not me? Why not give it a whirl for a year? I figured that after a year at the center of things—and working for the president's brother-in-law had to mean that you were at the center of things—I would come back to the *Chronicle* very conversant with the ways of Washington, which would be useful to me and useful to the paper."

McClure had not grasped the fact, until he arrived at Peace Corps headquarters, that he had not actually been hired. "God, I had never expected that I would have to be interviewed by eight people, and then be checked out by Shriver, and then maybe, just maybe, I'd be hired. I was appalled. But Tom got the number of interviews reduced to two. In effect, Tom was saying to these guys at the Peace Corps, 'Look, this guy is my friend, he is with me, I can vouch for him,' and Tom was very good at this, and obviously, his opinion was highly valued, so I got let off the hook for a lot of that ritual. But the Sarge scene was something else."

McClure was to see Shriver at 10:00 the next morning. He was told that Mr. Shriver was tied up, but please to hang on. At noon, Mr. Shriver was still tied up, but would see McClure very soon. By 4:00 P.M., alas, Mr. Shriver was just as tied up as ever. Perhaps Mr. McClure would prefer to return the following morning, when Mr. Shriver would *not* be so tied up. "I was furious. I charged back into Tom's office and said, 'This is too much, you know? I mean, I don't want to work here so badly that I'll put up with this. So, forget it, Tom. It's not your fault. I've enjoyed the trip, but I'm going home now.' "

Mathews jumped up from his desk, cajoled McClure into staying put for ten minutes, and raced for the elevators. "He was back in five," laughs McClure, "just beaming."

"Don," said Mathews, "you and Sarge and I are going to dinner." And, as usual, Shriver cast his magic spell.

I could instantly see what it was all about. It was all about Sarge. He was just enormously impressive. All the clichés fit: tall, dark, and handsome. Fit as a college athlete at forty-five. He was warm and friendly and funny—was interested in everything, full of anec- dotes. He knew as much about sports as he did about politics and as much about the civil rights movement as he did about theology. The three of us were having a great time, bantering and telling stories, but no job offer. Suddenly Sarge said, "I agree with Tom— you'd be just great here at the Peace Corps. But Don, we've got all of these *Californians*, you see"—and he and Tom had a huge laugh over that. I said, "Sarge, I'm really not a Californian; I'm from West Virginia."

And that really opened it up. The Kennedy clan had just a very special feeling for West Virginia, which had been a crucial primary state for Jack, and Sarge had spent several weeks in Huntington on the 1960 campaign.

In August 1961, Donovan McClure was installed at a desk in the Peace Corps' Public Information Office. Tom Mathews was the director, having replaced Ed Bayley, who had gone to the State Department.

Another Californian, Tim Adams, who had been lured away from the *San Francisco Examiner* newsroom, was at the next desk.

McClure got the usual assignments that were handed to the newest public information officer: He wrote press releases, he planted stories in newspapers and magazines, he met the press, he monitored his constantly changing new environment. "This was no glory job," says McClure, "but I was having fun with it, and it was a perfect place to learn how the Peace Corps worked, how Shriver operated. One of the first things I did was to write press releases about the first Peace Corps Reps. Sarge adored his Reps, and he insisted that all the stops be pulled out to describe them. Sarge also adored the Volunteers, thought they were God's gift, but he always went into raptures when he had conned a really hard-to-get guy who had a lot of status in one field or another, and he wanted that guy to be announced with all the flourishes. But that wasn't hard on me; it was nothing but fun." For instance, McClure noted, it was clear that Sarge doted on Frank Mankiewicz, and Mankiewicz *was* a good story: He really had left a lucrative, celebrity-studded law practice in Beverly Hills to be the first Peace Corps Rep in Peru, which was bound to be pretty rugged duty. His father really had written the screenplays for *Citizen Kane* and *The Pride of the Yankees*. His uncle really had directed *All About Eve*. Orson Welles had inhabited his childhood.

"But there was one Rep I was writing about that I couldn't quite figure out," says McClure.

I mean, his motives. That was Walter Carrington, who was a prominent black civil rights lawyer in Boston, very well respected in the Movement, excellent credentials. Harvard and Harvard Law School. He had signed on as Peace Corps Rep in Sierra Leone on the west coast of Africa. I wondered: Why would he join the Peace Corps and go overseas just as the civil rights movement was revving up and he was in a perfect position to take a big leadership role in that? Well, of course, the answer had to be that Sarge had charmed him into it, and boy, that must have taken some doing. I had never heard of Sierra Leone before, and plenty of others at the Peace Corps hadn't either. I mean, most of us had never heard of most of the places where the Peace Corps was going. The irony is, I replaced Walter Carrington as Rep in Sierra Leone, ultimately, which was about as curious a thing for me to do as it was for Walter. But that's Sarge for you.

McClure enjoyed watching Shriver pull in a big catch, and he was often invited to watch because McClure was the chronicler of the big catches, and Shriver wanted him to be in on the drama as it was unfolding. Further, the presence of a "biographer" or "publicist" in the same room was inevitably flattering to whomever Shriver was wooing.

"One day Sarge called me, very excited, saying to come to his office right away because he was about to interview Bob Bates, the president of the American Alpine Club. He wanted to get Bates as Rep in Nepal. You have to get a man that the host country is going to really respect, he said, and nothing is more respected in Nepal than a hotshot mountaineer. Bates had climbed K-2 and most of the other major peaks."

McClure went directly to Shriver's office and was introduced to Bates, whom McClure suspected had not been kept waiting very long, if at all. "Man, Sarge was eager for this one." Apparently, Bates had tacitly agreed to be Rep in Nepal, and as McClure was taking notes, he thought he detected closure, that Shriver was just polishing it off.

"Bob," said Shriver earnestly, "who would you like as your deputy in Nepal?"

Without a moment's hesitation, Bates replied, "Willi Unsoeld."

"Willi Unsoeld? Tell me about him, Bob. Where is he now?"

"Willi Unsoeld is now teaching religion and philosophy at some college in Oregon. He's a beloved cult figure out there. A hero in the mountain-climbing community. Tough as they come, physically, but very spiritual, too. Sarge, let me be most specific: Willi Unsoeld is one of the great mountain climbers of all time."

McClure, writing furiously, dared to look up from his notepad for one split second "because I just had to see the look on Sarge's face. It was one of transported joy. You know, the jackpot look."

Sarge handed his telephone to Bates. "Call him now!"

"Bates pulled out his little black book and dialed. I thought, Oh God, this is going to be The Moment. Unsoeld answered. Bates just sort of started shooting the breeze with him, mentioning mountains such as Nanda Devi and K-2. Then Bates started talking about Mount Everest. It seemed that some very well funded American expedition was imminent and that Unsoeld was going to be part of it. Bates then said, 'Willi, when can you come East? We have a lot to talk about.' Unsoeld said he couldn't come East for six weeks, but he would definitely come."

Bates hung up. "He'll come."

Shriver, now very stirred up, shouted, "But Bob! You never even mentioned the Peace Corps."

"Don't worry," said Bates. "He'll be my deputy and he'll climb Everest, too."

CHARLES HOUSTON

Charles Houston, M.D. A mountain-climbing cardiologist author. A skier, hiker, teacher, inventor, archivist, devoted family man. A graduate of Harvard and Columbia Medical School. A pioneer in the development of the artificial heart. An expert on high-altitude sickness. A man who had scaled Mount Foraker in Alaska (first ascent); K-2 in northwest Pakistan (the world's second highest mountain); Nanda Devi, the highest peak in India; and several peaks in the Alps of greater difficulty than the Matterhorn. Had once walked, yes *walked*, out of India, across Afghanistan, and through Iran. A man who, along with his father, had done reconnaissance on the south side of Mount Everest in 1950—the first outsiders to receive permission to do so. The perfect Peace Corps Rep for India. Shriver was euphorically convinced of it.

When Robert Bates, the president of the American Alpine Club and Houston's fellow climber of K-2—whom Shriver had tapped to be the first Peace Corps Rep in Nepal—told Shriver about Charlie Houston (pronounced *house*-ton), Shriver pounced: "Gotta have him. Bob, go get him."

Houston recalls that during the 1960 presidential campaign he had heard "vague rumors" about the idea of a Peace Corps. Although nominally a Republican, he had voted for Kennedy, believing that Kennedy's personal charisma and sophisticated education and background bespoke true leadership ability. Houston had heard that the Peace Corps seedling had actually burst into bloom in March 1961. "But to be honest, I initially scoffed at it. I thought it was a public relations ploy. It did not seem possible. It was the very last thing on earth that I could have ever expected to find myself involved in."

In early 1962, Houston received that Shriver-prompted call from his old friend and fellow mountaineer, Bob Bates. Bates was bubbling over with enthusiasm, as people are apt to be after an encounter with Shriver. Shriver had appointed him as the first Peace Corps Rep in Nepal. Nepal! The land of dreams for all mountain men. Would

Houston roll around in his mind the idea of being Peace Corps Rep in India? Bates and Houston had coauthored two books about their ascent of K-2 in northwest Pakistan: *Five Miles High* and *K-2: The Savage Mountain*. Their many shared experiences indicated to Bates that Houston might find the prospect irresistible, given his adventurous nature and in spite of his challenging and brilliant medical career. Bates pressed the prospect on Houston with a will, remembering Shriver's command: "Gotta have him. Bob, go get him."

"I was deeply involved in making an artificial heart at the time and felt that I was coming close," says Houston. "I was also deeply involved in my clinic in Aspen, Colorado, and my general practice in cardiology and general medicine. I had children who were approaching college age. I had financial responsibility for my sister's two children. I was not really earning enough money to carry all of these responsibilities, I felt, but my practice was exciting and demanding, as was my research. But Bob Bates knew that I was fascinated by India, so he had me there. He knew that I was an incurable idealist, and he had me there, too. Still, it was absurd for me to think about chucking it all and going out to India as a Peace Corps Rep. Absurd. Impossible. Out of the question. I shut the thought out."

Houston had yet to get the "Shriver treatment." As much as he had shut out the thought of being Peace Corps Rep in India, he was unprepared for the telephonic Shriver persona. "Sometime in the late spring of 1962, I got a telephone call from Shriver asking me to join the Peace Corps as Rep in India, saying that I was the *ideal* person for this job. I'd never met Sarge before, didn't know much about him, but he overwhelmed me on the phone. He insisted. He prodded and cajoled. He was all jived up and he got me kind of jived up."

Shriver called Houston "repeatedly during the next month. I explained to him over and over why I could not be Peace Corps Rep in India, much as the idea attracted me. Too many financial problems. Too many professional demands. Too many kids. Just bought a new house. Settled, finally. Can't move; not now. Really can't."

But Shriver continued to call, "would act as if he understood, would act as if he saw I just wasn't going to budge, but then he would call back in a few days and resume with more arguments to overcome me. I couldn't help but be flattered," says Houston.

Nobody had ever wooed me so hard, and my objections began to crumble. He persuaded me to come to Washington, just to *talk*. In person. And so I went. July 1, 1962.

I have to say that I had a marvelous time. The atmosphere was electric. Everyone who entered the Peace Corps building during the Kennedy years felt that electricity immediately, and it stayed with you. I was interviewed by John D. Rockefeller IV. Six feet and six inches of a dynamic, dedicated, serious young man. He was no stranger to me; I had known him at Exeter in the early 1950s when I was practicing medicine there. And I met so many others. All of them impressive and delightful. And young, so young. Bill Josephson, the deputy general counsel, a brilliant young man in his midtwenties, gave me a lot of good advice as to handling my finances. I was fifty at the time! Bill Delano, the Peace Corps' general counsel at that time, made useful suggestions about how to organize my life in order to be able to take the India job. He urged me on. And of course, Shriver in person totally bowled me over.

Houston returned to Aspen, Colorado, his clinic, his practice, and his family

with my head in a whirl, exhausted, confused. It was the Fourth of July, 1962. I talked it all over with Dorcas [his wife] in great detail. We decided that *no*, I would not go to India for the Peace Corps, no matter what, in spite of all temptation. I communicated that final decision to Sarge.

But he kept calling. By mid-August of 1962, I sent him a telegram saying, in effect, *Absolutely no, and please leave me alone.* And that, I thought, was that. And was relieved to have resolved my quandary.

But a few nights later, my three children, knowing how torn I had been, came into my bedroom, sat down on the bed, and talked to me till very late into the night. They felt I should go to India. It was clear to me that the kids knew how conflicted I had been. But they had decided, together, that we should just all go to India.

In addition to that impetus, Shriver had urged me to call Chester Bowles and discuss the matter with him. I knew, of course, that Chet had been a very successful and enthusiastic ambassador to India in the 1950s. So now, I finally called him. He said, "Do it!"

"Chet's daughter, Sally, who was in her twenties, worked at a fairly high level at Peace Corps headquarters," says Houston. "I also talked to her at length. She urgently advised me to sign on for India. She obviously loved India, but she supposed her father loved it more. 'Old Chet's 'round the bend on India,' she said with misty eyes. She told me that I just had to go, that I was the kind of American that Indians would respect, and how terribly important that was.

"I finally said the word out loud. *Yes*. At the moment of this decision, I went into my clinic office in Aspen, put my head in my hands, and moaned, 'What, oh what, have I done to my career?' "

At the end of September, Houston reported to Peace Corps headquarters at 8:00 A.M. and had a series of one-hour appointments, ending at 6:00 P.M., that were meant to edify him as to his new duties. "But the only thing that I remember now, or remembered then, ten minutes later, was something very vague—to the effect that you can transfer funds in this direction, but not in that direction."

Houston's last appointment was with the Peace Corps' general counsel, Bill Delano, whom he had met on his first exploratory trip to Washington. Unlike many other Peace Corps officials of the time, Delano did not act as if he expected to be summoned to the Oval Office to brief the president at any moment. He took time with Houston, realizing that this man was sacrificing a unique medical practice and giving up a supremely agreeable way of life to join a not completely proven experiment in its earliest stages and to go to live in a country twelve thousand miles away, where the temperature hovers around one hundred degrees five months of the year, and where more languages are spoken than in all of Europe.

At this timely moment, Brent Ashabranner showed up at Peace Corps headquarters. Ashabranner had been both Acting and Deputy Rep in Nigeria for seventeen months, and he had come to Washington to explore with Shriver the possibility of a home-based job. An Oklahoma native, Ashabranner had written several westerns and biographies of American Indians in his time and had later become an African specialist as an education official with ICA. ICA had assigned him to be Shriver's escort in Nigeria on the latter's first globe-girding, invitation-seeking trip in April and May of 1961. Shriver had been so impressed with his knowledge—not only of the country, but also of the continent—his calm manner, and his familiarity with bureaucratic systems and mentalities that he commandeered Ashabranner into instant Peace Corps service, putting him in charge of negotiations with the Nigerian government as plans for the first Peace Corps program in Nigeria evolved. But Ashabranner was keen to bring his wife and two daughters back to America after many years abroad. Further, he felt free to do so now that Shriver had found Dr. Samuel Dewitt Proctor, an imposing, likeable black minister and president of North Carolina State College for the Rep's slot in Nigeria.

Ashabranner was looking not only at the Peace Corps, but at other government agencies as well, including AID (his former employer), USIA, and HEW, but they seemed to him "almost tomblike by comparison" to the Peace Corps, which Ashabranner found "in a lather of activity and excitement." Ashabranner fully expected Shriver to wade into the deep waters of development problems in Africa, Ashabranner's longtime stomping ground and the auspices under which he had first met Shriver in 1961. He thought Shriver understood his very real intention to deal with these problems, but only as a tax-paying citizen of the Washington metropolitan area. Instead, Shriver turned his thoughts and remarks eastward:

> He started talking about India and its importance and how he felt the Peace Corps might do some of its best work there. I wondered if Sarge had got me mixed up with someone else. Then he told me that after a long search and breaking down a great deal of resistance on the person's part, he had finally got the man he wanted to be the first Peace Corps Representative in India. The man's name was Charles Houston. He was a medical doctor; he had done pioneer work on the development of a mechanical heart; he was a well-known mountain climber who had been in the assault party on the mighty Himalayan peak K-2. Houston had written a stirring account of the climb . . . in *K-2: The Savage Mountain*.
>
> Sarge's eyes glowed as he described what was obviously his vision of the perfect Peace Corps Rep for a major country: a man of proven professional ability, a man with a questing scientific mind, a man of adventurous spirit, an articulate man.*

But as Shriver spewed forth the superlatives about Houston to Ashabranner, he suddenly stopped, frowned, and added, "But he doesn't know item one about government or administration. He says so himself. That's why I want you to go to India with him and be his deputy."

Ashabranner was stunned. "I tried to tell Sarge about our plans to buy a place in Washington and get to know the country again, but he

*Brent Ashabranner, A Moment in History: The First Ten Years of the Peace Corps (New York: Doubleday, 1971), 115–16.

kept talking about India." Shriver spoke of Nehru's early interest in the Peace Corps—which, while not overwhelmingly enthusiastic by any means, was a crucial imprimatur that had caused many other Third World doors to open with far more ease than might have been the case otherwise (just as Kwame Nkrumah's acceptance of the Peace Corps idea in Ghana in 1961 had melted ice in the emerging nations). But India, Shriver stressed, being the most influential neutralist government in the world, deserved and must absolutely have the best possible programs that the Peace Corps could devise. And yet it had had quite the opposite. Shriver bemoaned the fact that the tiny Peace Corps contingent in India, as of September 1962, had had no full-time Rep, no permanent staff members, and paltry cooperation from the host government. By mid-October of 1962, another fifty Volunteers would arrive in India. There had to be a stellar, take-charge staff in place. The first twenty-five Volunteers needed their morale boosted. Shriver thought that Houston and Ashabranner would make a perfect team. (Shriver hinted vaguely that it was his own fault that the administration of Peace Corps/India had been so spotty; he had been too much the perfectionist in seeking outstanding leadership there; he had been, perhaps, too hard to please. As was stated in a Peace Corps brochure of the time: "India has been the home of high civilizations for at least four thousand years and for all its economic problems contains elements of the greatest sophistication. The search for the right man to head the Peace Corps in India developed into the most frustrating assignment ever handed the Talent Search.")

Ashabranner, certain that he would be rescued from caving in to Shriver's arm-twisting by dint of a resounding *no* from his wife, was amazed when he called her minutes after his meeting with Shriver: "She was silent a moment and then said, 'I haven't even unpacked. If you want to go, I'm ready.' "

The next day, Brent Ashabranner and Charlie Houston met for the first time over lunch. Houston was leaving within days to take up his post in India. Provided the two men did not hate each other at first sight, Ashabranner would be following him within weeks. They were joined by colleagues from the regional office, NESA (Near East/South Asia). Inevitably, they all compared notes on Shriver's powers of persuasion. Houston told of how he had just bought his dream house in Aspen. A foundation had recently given him additional funds for his work on a mechanical heart. But Shriver had won out. The conversation turned to mountain climbing and the Himalayas, and someone at the table asked Houston if he thought the Abominable Snowman really existed.

"I *know* he does," said Houston with heavy resignation. "He lives in Washington and his name is Shriver."

Houston's departure-date blues notwithstanding, Shriver, perhaps sensing Houston's lingering ambivalence, was ready with a head-spinning send-off: "You have the rank of ambassador as far as I'm concerned, although of course you aren't an ambassador, and you are not to frequent the embassy. You don't work for the American ambassador. You work for me. You work for the Peace Corps. You must not have any contact with the CIA under any circumstances. Hello and good-bye to those fellows. If they try to contact you, approach you, report it to me directly. And you should also work independently of the AID mission. That's big money technical assistance; they have different priorities. As for Ambassador [John Kenneth] Galbraith, he is a very talented, brilliant, charming man, but he is a very strong person. He'll tend to dominate you. If you have any trouble on that score, just stand up to him. Get in touch with me at once, and I'll back your position and authority all the way."

Shriver patted Houston on the back.

It was amazing how Sarge could convey encouragement and strength. Looking back, I should have been suspicious about the mad urgency surrounding my appointment as Peace Corps Rep in India, the first full-time director since the first Volunteers arrived nine months before. But as I left, I had the feeling that I would somehow make it, that this was going to be a great new adventure in my life. I had flown up to Idlewild Airport and taken that famous old Pan Am flight that left at 8:00 P.M. and arrived in New Delhi twenty-seven hours later. On that plane, I sat in the seat that became well known to all Peace Corps travelers to India. It was the seat in front of the emergency exit, which therefore had no seat in front of it, and there was room to stretch out. I was planning on doing some reading and napping, but I got into a conversation with a couple across from me who were extremely nice and all enthused about going to India as sightseers. They spoke of their trip as a lark. It suddenly occurred to me that I was going into God knows what. This conversation threw me back into a certain amount of conflict and despair. It washed over me afresh that I had abandoned my medical practice, my medical research. I wept. I despised my weeping. Which made me weep more. Which made me despise my weeping even more. God, what a trip.

BETTY HARRIS

Elizabeth Forsling Harris was a chic, thirty-nine-year-old political organizer and a public relations executive in the politically potent city of Dallas, Texas, in 1961. She had been a pioneering print and broadcast journalist and executive in New York before women had such jobs. And she was going through a cantankerous divorce from Leon Harris, the son of the founder of A. Harris, a department store in Dallas that perennially played an unconcerned second to the break-away fashion-and-opulence model of Neiman-Marcus. Indeed, Betty Harris always looked as if she had been dressed and coiffed by the masters at Neiman-Marcus. And she drove into town in a sleek gray Mercedes-Benz.

Betty Harris had known Sargent Shriver longer than anyone else at the Peace Corps. They had both worked at *Newsweek* in the late 1940s. In 1956, when she was assistant manager of the Democratic National Convention in Chicago, the Shrivers had extended themselves to make her three-month effort as comfortable as possible. "Sarge always stood out from the crowd, no matter who was in the crowd," Harris recalls. "In the pre-Eunice days," she says, "every affluent, socially ambitious Catholic—or for that matter, Protestant—family in New York was after Sarge as a potential husband for their darling daughter. He was considered a great catch. He was incredibly handsome, athletic, bright, well-educated, well-born, amusing, and polite. With all of this going for him, the fact that he had no money didn't matter. He was invited everywhere. And in the late 1950s, he was a rising influence in Chicago politics, a likely candidate for governor, when his political career there was cut short on account of the minor matter of his brother-in-law having been elected president."

At the time the Peace Corps was formed, Betty Harris didn't hear any bells ring. "I was in the midst of divorce proceedings and I was very much involved in Texas politics. The Peace Corps sounded good and I was delighted that Sarge was running it, because it seemed natural to his personality and instincts. But for me, at that time, there was no thought of rushing to Washington and getting involved."

However, Betty Harris did come to Washington on business in the summer of 1961. At dinner at the family home of Walter Jenkins, a key member of Vice President Lyndon Johnson's staff, she pressed Jenkins on behalf of a judgeship for Irving Goldberg, a mutual Dallas friend. "I wish we could do something for Irving," said Jenkins. "But we've gone as far as we can go. Now it's up to Kennedy, and we can't push any harder."

Buoyed up by a few salty dogs, Harris said, "Well, I can," and forthwith dialed the Peace Corps. It was 9:00 P.M. To her astonishment, Shriver answered. Harris told Shriver that she wanted to do everything for someone who would be a fine judge. Saying he was going to Hyannis Port that weekend, Shriver asked Harris to bring Goldberg's resume by his office and he'd see what he could do. (Goldberg was subsequently appointed to the Fifth Circuit Court in Dallas.)

"The next morning," says Harris, "I wrote out Irving's qualifications on a piece of Mayflower Hotel stationery and walked the four blocks to the Peace Corps. I ran right into Sarge as he was coming back from lunch."

Shriver queried Harris: "How's your husband?"

"Well, he isn't, Sarge. I mean, we're getting a divorce."

"Fine, so why don't you come to work for the Peace Corps?"

"But Sarge, I live in Dallas, and I'm going back tomorrow, and life is too complicated in the first place."

"Let's talk about this over dinner tonight, Betty. And we'll see."

Sargent Shriver and Betty Harris went out to dinner at *La Salle du Bois*, a big campily decorated barn of a place on Connecticut Avenue, one of the few so-called elegant French restaurants in Washington at the time.

Sarge talked Peace Corps, Peace Corps, Peace Corps. He convinced me this was the greatest thing going. And the next day, he set up a lunch for me and Larry Dennis, who was the first associate director of the Office of Peace Corps Volunteers. Presumably, I was to lead a women's division under Dennis at the Peace Corps. It doesn't sound odd now, but it sure did then. A women's division of a federal agency? In 1961? Unheard of. Naturally, I said I'd do it.

I went back to Dallas to get packed up. But then, oh God, no word from Washington. I sat and I waited. I sat and sat and sat. Larry Dennis had told me to get in touch with a young woman named Sally Bowles, but I couldn't track her down. No Sally Bowles, no travel orders, no confirmation of job or job title, no salary set. I was frantic. Finally, I called Sarge. I told him, "You tell me to come to Washington, you tell me to disrupt my life, you convince me that your operation is the best operation on the face of the earth, and I believe you, and I am ready to come, but I get no word. I've burnt all my bridges, but I can't even get ahold of anyone at the Peace Corps. What's going on?"

Shriver apologized, said he knew nothing about the mix-up, and told Harris to try Larry Dennis again. Dennis told Harris that Sally Bowles had been laid low with an ulcer but was now okay. "Come to Washington, Betty. You have a job."

But it was not to head a women's division. Instead, Harris was given a desk and told to read up on early Peace Corps documents until some duties could be defined. She was disappointed; her appetite had been whetted to deal with women's issues in an agency dominated by men who didn't want to deal with them at all.

"Then I heard that when Sarge told Paul Geren, his first and short-lived deputy director, whom I had known in Dallas, that he was thinking of bringing me up from Texas to deal with women's issues, Geren had replied—or so the story went—'Betty Harris? That's like putting Marilyn Monroe in charge of the Boy Scouts!' Apparently, Paul thought I was too wild for his type of southern Baptist upbringing, and his objection had short-circuited my appointment. But I thought the comparison to Marilyn Monroe was the best compliment I'd ever had."

Meanwhile, at Shriver's request and with the help of Sally Bowles, Harris started a newsletter for the Volunteers overseas, *Peace Corps Volunteer*. Any female with a background in journalism would have jumped at that chance, so difficult was it to get a foot in the door at the early Peace Corps, let alone a position with visibility and autonomy. But the job of editor of the newsletter (it soon became a magazine) seemed like make-work to the impatient Harris. Shriver assured her that ultimately she could write her own ticket and asked her to be thinking of other useful functions. That was the way many things in the early Peace Corps evolved: People were given the chance to invent, inaugurate, and implement. Rarely have such exciting opportunities been given to a staff as were given to the founding Peace Corps staff. Harris, for her part, conceived the need for a Volunteer advocacy office at headquarters, an office that would be concerned with and fight for the welfare of the Volunteers overseas. Within weeks of Harris's memo to Shriver on the subject, the Division of Volunteer Support (DVS) was formed, and Harris pushed Pat Kennedy as director and Sally Bowles as his deputy. Harris herself soon became deputy associate director of the Office of Peace Corps Volunteers, which oversaw the divisions of Training and Selection, as well.

And then there was the matter of where one sat at the Peace Corps. The fifth floor was the executive floor, although not all Peace Corps executives had offices there, nor did many care. Quite a few division heads and regional directors were just as happy to be at a remove from Shriver and his incessant ideas, whims, demands, and sudden appearances. Many thanked the Lord that they were located on the seventh, eleventh, or twelfth floor, out of harm's way and where the view was better. But not Betty Harris.

> Sally Bowles used to kid me about this. I was put up on the eighth floor in a little cubbyhole. The token woman executive. Oh, very, very token at first. I refused to settle in there and accept this Siberia. I meant to get back to the fifth floor. I had that much sense. In three or four weeks after my arrival, I had maneuvered my way back. One of the top male officials on the fifth floor had gone on vacation. I just moved myself right into his office, just physically went in there and sat down and went to work. Did it cause a row? Certainly. But I made my point. I had come to do serious work. Quite simply, I wanted some power. Coming out of Texas politics, what else would I want? Certainly not some nicey-nicey lady's job. No. I wanted to make policy, or at the very least influence policy. You can't do that from a cubbyhole.

It didn't take long, says Harris, for the inevitable question of women's issues to attach themselves to her. An unmarried Volunteer had gotten pregnant. What to do? "Oh heavens!" laughs Harris. "A catastrophe!" An emergency meeting was called on a Saturday morning, with considerable Peace Corps brass present. Betty was the only woman invited. "This ludicrous conversation ensued," says Harris.

> It went along these lines: Well, obviously, if you send all of these young, healthy women overseas, and for the first time in their life they would be free, and, well, yes, equal—uh, in a sense—then

one or two of them, perhaps, out of a thousand, might be expected to succumb to the temptations of the flesh, and uh, might actually, uh, *sleep* with a male Volunteer in some isolated post. You know, out of loneliness and loss of hometown moral compass. And who knew? There was nothing on the Peace Corps application form to screen out a nymphomaniac. Then the thought began to occur to these grown men that possibly the pregnant Volunteer had got herself in the "family way" by means of intimate contact with a *national*. Oh, God! Well, the guys were just falling apart. A Peace Corps woman is pregnant and she's not married to anybody! And who's the father? And what happens now? Do we bring her home? Do we inform her parents? Do we throw her out of the Peace Corps? One fool present at this meeting actually suggested that we "can" women Volunteers altogether. No one ever suggested that our male Volunteers might be shacking up with female "nationals," getting *them* pregnant, or what the implications of *that* might be in the host country. Oh no, it's the women.

People ask me, how did I get involved in the women's movement? [Betty Harris was founder of *Ms.* magazine.] I tell them: at the Peace Corps. For the first time, I had come to realize fully the very discriminatory nature of men's attitudes toward women.

Betty Harris, along with Dorothy Jacobsen, Ruth Olson (Jacobsen's deputy in Personnel), and the Peace Corps doctor sent over by the Surgeon General's office, Leo Gehrig, M.D., arranged with the Florence Crittenden home for unwed mothers in Washington to take care of any pregnant Peace Corps Volunteers. If a Volunteer got pregnant overseas, wanted to have the child, and was interested in putting the child up for adoption, the Crittenden people could manage it. The Crittenden home had been doing this for some time, with great discretion, and some of the most prominent obstetricians in Washington worked with the Crittenden people on such matters regularly.

"The main thing," says Betty Harris, "was that we 'clean up' the girls' records. No Peace Corps Volunteer in such a situation was going to look 'bad'—not if I could help it. Those girls were not going to be censured. I knew instinctively that that was wrong. And I was determined that they could return to Peace Corps service, if they wished, and if they had otherwise acquitted themselves well in the host country. And out of the thousands of women we sent overseas in the early

1960s, there were only ten or twelve who came home for reason of out-of-wedlock pregnancy."

Shortly after this first confrontation on the subject of female fertility as a fact of nature, another even more preposterous question on the general issue surfaced. Betty Harris got her hands on a memo to Shriver—no copy to herself involved—from the medical division.

> This memo raised the question: What if a married Volunteer got pregnant by her own husband? Oh! Oh! What if one of our precious, upper-middle-class American flowers got pregnant in one of those dirty, backwater countries? Surely, the Peace Corps would bring the couple home. A nice American couple couldn't risk having a baby in a country where women squat to deliver a child.
>
> I went in screaming over this one. I screamed to everyone I could scream to, including Sarge, saying that the one thing that all women in all countries have in common was childbirth, and if we really want to insult these countries—to say, in effect, that your country's so dirty that this healthy, nutritional American woman cannot bear a child there—if you really want to insult them, fellas, this is the way to do it.

According to Harris, her arguments "started a great bureaucratic squabble. A lot of the men were calling me 'that idiot woman,' 'that meddler,' and worse. Me versus most of the males at Peace Corps headquarters. I was not beloved—let us put it that way. Even Joe English, who had come on board during the middle of this squabble as Chief of Psychiatry, was almost as bad as the rest of them. We fought like cats and dogs the first few weeks and months. We are friends now, but we were not friends then."

The squabble resulted in Harris's authoring some fiery memos that became known as the "MOM and POP" memos—"Memo on Marriage" and "Policy on Pregnancy."

The outcome was entirely Kennedyesque.

Senator John F. Kennedy first mentions the Peace Corps idea on the steps of the Student Union at the University of Michigan ECK STANGER OF THE *Ann Arbor News*

About-to-be President-Elect Kennedy with his family and friends awaiting Nixon's concession speech. From left to right: Bill Walton, Pierre Salinger, Ethel and Robert Kennedy, Angie Novello, and Bill Haddad. November 8, 1960 JACQUES LOWE PHOTO

General James M. Gavin in Belgium during World War II

Ernest F. Hollings in 1960

Warren Wiggins, Peace Corps Associate Director for Program Development and Operations, and President Kennedy depart the South Portico of the White House on August 9, 1962, to address 600 Peace Corps trainees on the South Lawn

Bill Josephson

Tom Mathews does his own version of the West African dance, the High Life, to the amusement of Mitzi Mallina

Jack Vaughn and Frank Mankiewicz

Bill Moyers, Jack Vaughn, and Franklin Williams react in typical Peace Corps style to a State Department official's speech

Padraic Kennedy

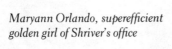

*Maryann Orlando, superefficient
golden girl of Shriver's office*

President Kennedy addresses Ghana I trainees the day before they leave on assignment

The first 50 Peace Corps Volunteers as they prepare to fly to Ghana aboard a chartered plane on which has been painted "Clipper Peace Corps"; August 31, 1961

Donovan McClure

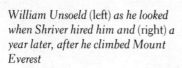

William Unsoeld (left) *as he looked
when Shriver hired him and* (right) *a
year later, after he climbed Mount
Everest*

Charles Houston in late 1963

Sally Bowles, capable daughter of the undersecretary of state

Jack Vaughn and Betty Harris

CHAPTER 4

"IN,
UP
& OUT"

B etty Harris had put Shriver on the spot by forcing the issue of whether married Volunteers could give birth while serving overseas. She had won many other concessions from him and her male colleagues concerning marriage, sexual mores, and fertility through her forceful MOM and POP memos and her intimidating willingness to shout down almost any man in the agency. But the issue of childbirth was the touchiest one yet, and Shriver was a man of his times, born in 1915 and in every respect a traditional family man. While his own wife, Eunice, was a strong-willed woman with formidable physical stamina (Peace Corps staff members had seen her jumping on a trampoline at the Shrivers' Maryland estate when she was six months pregnant), Shriver could not shake the notion, shared by even most of the younger men at the Peace Corps, that the United States of America and Switzerland were the only safe places to have babies.

Shriver had traveled the world during his first two years as Peace Corps Director; he had seen the conditions that existed in many developing nations; he was acutely aware of the health risks in these places. "On that first trip to Africa in 1961," says Franklin Williams,

we heard that a U.S. government official had just died of a tropical disease because he got no medical attention. And then we came upon this young American couple who had come over on their own to teach at a Nigerian boarding school. They were gaunt and covered with mosquito bites, and their baby was sickly and feverish. Shriver was appalled. Right then and there he vowed to assign at least one U.S. Public Health Service doctor to every Peace Corps program; he even cabled Washington and told them that this was going to be policy and to get moving on it. What's remarkable about that decision is that even the State Department had only a regional doctor who covered as many as five countries four or five times a year. But of course, the State Department people lived well, usually in a compound in the capital, whereas many of the Volunteers would be roughing it. There were philosophical contradictions in all of this, but Sarge was adamant. He said, "No

Peace Corps Volunteer must end up as neglected as that family we just saw, and no Volunteers are going to die because they didn't get medical attention."

Shriver's seemingly cautious stand on having one or more doctors for every Peace Corps program overseas encouraged the medical division to push Shriver, ever more aggressively, toward a policy saying that Peace Corps "girls" must return to the United States and the sanctity of their allegedly sterile American hospitals to have their babies, a policy that would also have the effect of forcing the couple to forfeit what remained of their time in the Peace Corps. Harris, as previously noted, thought that this policy was prissy and probably also terminally insulting to the host countries. Thus, it was the all-male medical division, backed by the powerful Chief of Psychiatry, Joseph English, M.D., against Betty Harris. This was so, or Harris felt it was so, because she was often the only woman attending senior staff meetings and always the only one who would do battle with the men. (Some of the other women in positions of authority who were let in on policy discussions, such as Nan McEvoy, Diana MacArthur, Sally Bowles, Patricia Sullivan, and Alice Gilbert, were at least as much valued for their family connections as for their intelligence or the soundness of their opinions. In any case, they rarely crossed their male colleagues.)

While Harris did not want to embarrass or annoy Shriver by continually harping on the childbirth issue, she was brimming over with conviction. She had become a "women's libber" at least years before it was even remotely fashionable. (Betty Friedan's *The Feminine Mystique* was published in 1963, creating a furor no less revolutionary than The Pill, and at about the same time.) Harris had been shaken by the depth of prejudice against women among the senior men at the Peace Corps, whom she had originally assessed as being an uncommonly enlightened breed. Further, she had been a woman scorned herself and was out for revenge. The medical division, tired of her opposition to their far more conservative views about life and love in the Third World, had collaborated on a long and detailed "blind" memo ("a Stone Age tract," says Harris) to Shriver cajoling, even bulldozing him into "bringing our married Peace Corps girls home if they became pregnant." The memo called Harris irresponsible and dangerous. Harris, ever watchful for end runs, intercepted a copy and became "utterly, positively livid." But not livid enough to keep her from lobbying Shriver one last time in a reasonable tone and with persuasive rhetoric:

Look, Sarge. The Peace Corps is probably the most progressive organization in America. It's what America claims to be all about: equality. In the Peace Corps, blacks have equality. Women have equality. Our female Volunteers are paid the same living allowances as the male Volunteers. They have the same responsibilities, the same physical hardships. We have said, in effect, that the rules are no different in the Peace Corps; the same goes for both sexes. So to suddenly say that a female Peace Corps Volunteer is too fragile, too fine, and too clean to have a baby in a Third World country, especially if she is game to do this, is to go back on our word—is to reverse policy. The exercise gets to be something of a sham. The women are insulted and the countries are insulted. And don't think they won't catch on. The couple ought to have a choice, at least. Stay or go. My bet is, 99 percent of them will choose to stay.

Betty Harris handed Shriver a memo—the last of her MOM and POP memos—which was much briefer than that of the medical division. Also, unlike the medical division, Harris provided copies to the entire staff. She was going for broke. "It's all here," she said, adding, "I rest my case."

Three days later, at a Friday staff meeting, Shriver said, "I'm going to Hyannis Port for the weekend. [That statement never failed to send orgasmic ripples through the room.] I have two memos here on the same subject, but with totally opposite viewpoints. The subject is pregnancy and childbirth. ("The men grimaced horribly," chuckles Harris.) I will take this memo from the medical division and I will take this memo from Betty Harris. And when I come back on Monday, I'll have an answer."

Betty Harris was as sure of defeat as Joe English and the medical division were sure of victory. Shriver entered the fifth-floor conference room the following Monday, waving the two memos and saying, "Now, about these issues of pregnancy and childbirth," indicating that this would be the first order of business. ("More squirming," says Harris.)

Shriver continued matter-of-factly, "I have talked to my wife, Eunice. I have talked to my sister-in-law, Ethel. And I have talked to General Maxwell Taylor. They all believe that married Peace Corps Volunteers should be able to have their babies overseas."

The assemblage was stunned. Harris murmured softly, "Well, hooray and hallelujah," but took care not to look too smug about her surprise victory. Those on the side of the medical division stared at

Shriver in disbelief. At that point, it was for them not so much a matter of having lost the battle but of how and why? What had really transpired in the mythical Kennedy compound at Hyannis Port? Primarily, what in the name of God did General Maxwell Taylor, the head of the Joint Chiefs of Staff, have to do with the issue of pregnancy in the Peace Corps? Harris thought she knew. "What Sarge was revealing in all innocent candor was that the Kennedy family felt fully empowered to influence Peace Corps policy on matters of family. The Kennedy family would proclaim and decree at this level. Of course. Who else? The family, that is, and whatever hotshot celebrity was visiting them for the weekend in Hyannis Port. In this case, it was General Maxwell Taylor. He was *there*, and to the Kennedys, his rank gave him the privilege of pronouncing on *anything*. And Lord knows, the Kennedy women do know a thing or two about childbearing."

◆　　◆　　◆

It was good sport at the Peace Corps to disparage and make fun of the State Department, to call it "the Brontosaurus." But to Bill Haddad, the State Department was the *enemy*, and many of its policies made him rage:

> The State Department actually told us not to send Catholics to Latin America, blacks to Africa, Jews to North Africa. Those people managed to combine so many lousy things in that one directive: coyness, obsessive caution, ignorance, and bigotry. That we weren't going to operate that way was a policy decision that Sarge made early.
>
> Except for some of the stuff about marriage and pregnancy, which dragged on too long, the decision-making process went "boom boom" at the Peace Corps. It was usually short and snappy. It often happened when you were just walkin' down the hall talkin' to Shriver. Training was uppermost on our minds in the early days. We were learnin' how to use the universities, and the universities were thrilled to have the business and were developing techniques for cultural immersion. But Sarge kept sayin' we hadda go further—find something unique that the Peace Corps could claim and put its stamp on. It hadda be tough but also, in some way, glamorous. Like a World War II movie without the horror. One night I told Sarge I'd been readin' some absolutely fascinatin' stuff on the British Voluntary Service Overseas program [VSO].

It was supposed to be the best of all volunteer programs overseas, although small. Their most effective people had been trained at what they called Outward Bound Schools. That concept and name were new to us then; it wasn't invented in America. I told Sarge this kind of training had been developed during World War II by British psychologists to try to figure out why some people survived life-threatening situations and others didn't. A majority of the Peace Corps staff had seen combat in World War II and we'd survived, and I think that's what bound us together. That connection clicked with Sarge. He said, "Fabulous! Find out more!"

I called the British embassy the next morning and said, "What's this Outward Bound Trust all about? Who's in charge? Where do I find 'em?" I was told that Sir Spencer Summers was chairman of the Trust and also a member of Parliament and that the program was run by Captain Frederick Fuller, who was then headmaster of the oldest Outward Bound School at Aberdovey, Wales, but that the schools were all over the world. I got this rather understated explanation: "These schools stress a devotion to an ideal of community and service. They expose their students to unexpected challenges. This kind of training is meant to generate self-confidence and erase unreasonable fears of the unknown." But what it really came down to was this: "A ship is torpedoed. It sinks. There are twelve guys in a lifeboat. Six survive and six die. What kept those six guys alive? Especially if they weren't necessarily physically stronger than the other six?"

British psychologists, Haddad discovered, had devised tests to spot survival qualities during World War II and had even learned, to some extent, how to instill these qualities. After the war, the British began to apply these lessons to challenges ranging from the behavior of juvenile delinquents to the training of future leaders of British industry.

"Holy shit, this is great," thought Haddad. He persuaded Summers and Fuller to come to Washington and tell him more. He kept Shriver filled in. "We were all getting very, very excited, and Sarge just said emphatically, 'Let's do it. Let's have a camp like that.' Now, mind you, this was pretty rugged stuff, so Sarge was really takin' a chance, tyin' it to the presidency in a way, 'cause it was sure to get a lot of publicity. More heroics, more of that New Frontier 'vigah,' which the press just ate up, like Bobby Kennedy's fifty-mile hike later in 1963. But if it worked, ahhhhhh."

Haddad chose Puerto Rico as the first place to look for a site because he knew its governor, Muñoz Marin, personally and knew that he had created something called "Operation Bootstrap," which was similar to FDR's Civilian Conservation Corps (CCC). Bootstrap consisted of progressive agrarian experiments around the island that helped bring people up out of poverty, taught them new skills, employed them in such a way as to contribute to the commonwealth's development. The Commonwealth of Puerto Rico had a tropical climate plus obvious cultural and linguistic similarities to Latin American countries where Volunteers would serve. It all fit.

> Muñoz first showed us a site in the rain forest near San Juan, but I said, no, no, this is too close to civilization. That night I was sittin' next to a guy at the hotel bar who was an agricultural worker, kind of like a forest ranger, who was part of one of Muñoz's experiments. I asked about his work. He told me about this place, Arecibo, on the other side of the island in the mountains. The place actually had a dam, and Outward Bound was high on rappeling down dams. So the next day I got a helicopter, and Summers and Fuller and I went up and flew over to Arecibo and saw a clearing and some buildings and a dam, and we landed and it was perfect. I went back to Muñoz and said, "Can we get this place?" and Muñoz said, "Sure," and I said, "What's the twist?" and he said, "I'll rent it to you," and I said, "How much?" and Muñoz said, "A buck," and I said, "You got a deal." So I went back to Shriver and said, "I've found this great place and Muñoz will give it to us," and Sarge said "Fabulous." Muñoz, Summers, and Fuller used to kid me—called it "Camp Haddad."

In fact, the site in Arecibo was originally called the Puerto Rican Field Training Center. Captain Frederick Fuller stayed on for six months to help set up the Peace Corps training program there. Governor Muñoz Marin's protocol officer, Rafael Sancho-Bonet, saw that the camp was equipped in what he then called a "beg, borrow, and steal" campaign, and later coordinated all Peace Corps activities in Puerto Rico before taking over as Rep in Chili. Shriver brought in the magnetic young Yale chaplain, William Sloane Coffin, as camp director. The camp combined language and cultural training with a physical regimen so rigorous that it caused considerable controversy at Peace Corps headquarters. Frank Mankiewicz, the first Rep in Peru and nobody's sissy, objected to its macho and risk aspects, as noted in the previous chapter, and he balked at taking part in some of the more draconian exercises, even as he acknowledged their efficaciousness on most of the trainees.

Soon, the original camp was expanded into two facilities respectively named Camp Radley and Camp Crozier. David Crozier and Lawrence Radley were the first two Volunteers to die; they perished in a plane crash in Colombia in late 1961. Victor Crichton, a college classmate and Peace Corps assistant of Bill Haddad's, conceived this commemoration. Haddad rushed the idea down the hall to Shriver, who rushed it into reality. Crichton had been one of the first jack-of-all-trades staff members at the first camp, "Camp Haddad." A graduate of Columbia and a successful campus politician, this handsome, high-strung, light-skinned Negro who was born in Grenada and raised in Harlem confounded the camp authorities with his rock-climbing and rappeling abilities. How had he gained these skills? ("As a power line construction crew chief on Okinawa just after World War II, in part, but mostly by exploring the last frontiers of Morningside Park in the city of New York.") Crichton loved the rigors of the Puerto Rican camp.

"Camp Haddad" is no more, but it lives on in memory, vividly, as very, *very* New Frontier.

♦   ♦   ♦

To have been a founding father (or mother) of the Peace Corps had about it the quality of a torrid love affair, one that has no shame—a foolish, all-consuming passion with exhausting quarrels and sweet reconciliations. Stir in some high purpose and self-sacrifice, the propinquity of America's first royal family, the idea of being first at what you were doing, and that giddy, glamorous, manic time seems almost touchable even twenty-five years later. It is easy to forget the flaws. But at least two of the Peace Corps' founding members do not forget. "It was real. We did not just imagine the thrill of it," says Mitzi Mallina, who was technically the first Peace Corps employee (by dint of having been handed the first bona fide government paycheck after several seven-day *pro bono* work weeks) and who was, from 1962 to 1966, assistant to Dr. Joseph Colmen, the director of research. "But it was also arrogant and neurotic. Institutionally, there was the assumption that the Peace Corps was the center of the universe, a superior entity. It was on its way to being enshrined. Otherwise," concludes

Mallina, "how else can one explain that preposterous postcard incident," which was the boomerang to match the boast.

Al Meisel, one of the first training officers, who, in tandem with Padraic Kennedy, had escorted some of the earliest Peace Corps groups to their countries of assignment and had seen with his own eyes the beginning of the experiment, addresses the same point:

The Peace Corps was a program utterly peculiar to the early 1960s. Innocent and idealistic, yet bratty and brash. It could not have been created at any other time. John F. Kennedy did not invent it; still, it was the echo of his inaugural address that we were responding to. Stylistically, however, it was 100 percent Shriver—kind of an eagle-scout-on-the-make style. I wasn't all that great a fan of Kennedy at the time, and I am less so now, but I never said so at the time. I, too, was caught up in the elation of having a young president who was saying, "Let's get this country moving again," and let's open the windows and let in the fresh ideas, and let's get youth into the act. Let's make things *happen*! And there we were, most of us about thirty, in a huddle with the President's brother-in-law, *making things happen*. It was very seductive. I think that the Peace Corps was probably even more exciting, creative, innovative, and daredevil than anything in the New Deal. But—there were two sides of that coin. One was Vietnam, which turned out sourly, disastrously, because we sought to impose ourselves from the first with troops and guns, euphemisms about "advisers" to the contrary. The idealistic side of the coin was the Peace Corps. We had the same kind of attitude about saving the world. We thought we had the responsibility to do so and the ability to do so. But over half the world bought the concept. The Peace Corps did useful work, to be sure, and it still does. But how *much* good? Well, in the very early 1960s, we at least did such a fantastic job of selling our noble intentions, our all-American know-how, and our kindheartedness—and of course the whole world had just fallen in love with Kennedy—that when one lone Peace Corps Volunteer penned a postcard to a friend in the United States that was critical of Nigeria, her "host country," all hell broke loose. I thought at the time, My God, what expectations have we raised? What have we wrought in our hubris? Poor Margery Michelmore. She was the international scapegoat. But then, in that exaggerated, self-congratulatory atmosphere, someone eventually had to be.

Margery Michelmore was twenty-three and a magna cum laude graduate of Smith College, and she was blessed with many other advantages: good looks, good manners, and a sense of humor. On the face of it, a most unlikely victim, villainess, or scapegoat. She was one of the first to apply for Peace Corps service and one of the first to be selected. She was completing her second phase of teacher training at University College at Ibadan, fifty miles north of the capital of Lagos. Harvard had designed the training program in cooperation with the college (Margery had already trained for eight weeks at Harvard). She had been rated an outstanding trainee. But one day, Margery chanced to pass along her impressions of her new environment to a friend in Cambridge, Massachusetts. She was in a hurry; she jotted: "Dear Bobbo: Don't be furious at getting a postcard. I promise a letter next time." She added that, in spite of extensive training, she and her Peace Corps cohorts "were not prepared for the squalor and absolutely primitive living conditions rampant both in the city and in the bush. We had no idea about what 'underdeveloped' meant. It really is a revelation and once we got over the initial horrified shock, a very rewarding experience."

Unfortunately, the good Margery got more explicit as she scribbled on. "Everyone except us lives in the street, cooks in the street, and even goes to the bathroom in the street." (The last phrase has always been thought to be a quaintly American contradiction in terms.) Margery concluded: "Please write. Marge." She added in a cramped postscript at the bottom of the card: "We are excessively cut off from the rest of the world."

The postcard containing the above message was said to have been found on the grounds of University College at Ibadan near Margery's dormitory, Queen Elizabeth Hall. The finder was said to be a Nigerian student at the college. No native of the city of New York today, upon finding a random postcard from, say, a native of Sweden, describing the filthy, frightening subway stations would be much bothered, but it was another matter entirely in 1961 in Nigeria among the educated elite of a Third World nation in its first year of independence.

In any case, the word was out in a flash. Shock waves reverberated around the world. The Nigerian newspapers were in a lather of outrage. Major American newspapers headlined the story. The networks were reporting it, all but licking their chops over such a juicy morsel. It was as if the Shroud of Turin had turned out to be a hoax cooked up in Andy Warhol's studio.

Warren Wiggins says that the atmosphere at Peace Corps headquarters during the first few weeks of operations overseas in the early fall of 1961 was something like a hurricane watch: "We worried that some untoward event was going to blow us out of the water. With that many young people overseas, something was bound to go wrong. We didn't know what it would be, how awful it would be, what the people at home would think of it. We certainly didn't know what people abroad would think of it, whatever it was. When the news about Margery started to break on Sunday afternoon [October 15, 1961], we realized we were faced with a crisis that wasn't going to go away. Clearly, an indiscretion had occurred but no great crime had been committed. We had been worried about much bigger stuff. On the other hand, this one looked like it was blowing." What information could be gleaned at the time indicated that, indeed, a Nigerian student had picked up a postcard on the campus in Ibadan, had traced it to Margery, and had duplicated and distributed it around the college, which had resulted in angry demonstrations. An AP stringer had immediately put it out on the wire. The attention the media was paying to the story gave credence to that version. When several of the Peace Corps staff gathered at headquarters on that October Sunday, they were grasping at straws. There was an early rumor that the American ambassador in Lagos, Joseph Palmer, was trying to force Margery out of Nigeria at once. (Not so. They soon learned that Palmer had merely arranged to get her out of raging Ibadan and into Lagos, so that she could be sheltered at the home of Palmer's deputy, Jerry Greene, and his wife.)

"But who *really* knew?" says Wiggins. "Margery's life could be in danger. The Peace Corps could be thrown out at any moment. It could be the domino theory—first, we're kicked out of Nigeria, then out of Ghana, and so on. Anything was possible."

Wiggins says that the first reliable word as to Margery's immediate fate came from Margery herself, who cabled Shriver that it would be best for the Peace Corps and best for her if she came back to the United States right away, that she was prepared to resign, that she was ready to travel at a moment's notice. "It was a clear, unequivocal communication," says Wiggins. "And it swept away the very worst of speculation and rumor at headquarters."

But it did not sweep away the melodrama. A James Bondian scenario, with Shriver as its author, was in the works.

Wiggins insists that Shriver was always calm and cool in a crisis. Always. And that he looked disparagingly on those who could not control themselves emotionally in the midst of tragedy or under intense pressure, and that his behavior during the Margery Michelmore postcard incident was no exception. But Timothy Adams, who had come to the Peace Corps from the *San Francisco Examiner,* and who was, at the time of the postcard incident, a new public information officer at the Peace Corps, picked up different vibrations: "There was panic in Shriver's heart. There really was. That postcard had created a cause célèbre. It was temporarily the talk of the universe. So, above all, Shriver wanted to stop the talk. To do so, he felt he had to outsmart the press—divert them—get their minds off Margery and the Peace Corps and on to something else." To buy time, Shriver devised the following itinerary for Margery: She would fly from Lagos, Nigeria, to London, to Bermuda, and then on to San Juan, Puerto Rico, where she would impart cultural sensitivity caveats to the Peace Corps trainees at the Peace Corps' Outward Bound camp. "To us in the Public Information Office," says Adams, "it seemed as if Shriver was going to excessive lengths to avoid having Margery arrive in the continental United States." (Tom Mathews, then deputy director of Public Information, was dispatched to Bermuda to pick up Margery at that point and to fly on with her to Puerto Rico. Her escort officer from Lagos was Dick Ware, a tall, handsome, courtly black man who had been an AID official in Nigeria and was about to join the Peace Corps staff. All bases covered.)

Up to that point, Adams was not much involved in the "preposterous postcard incident" except to let it be known that he thought that Shriver and others were overreacting to something that, yes, might blow up, but might just as easily blow over if you'd just leave it alone. "But that was not to be," says Adams.

> Two nights later, at about 2:00 A.M., I got a call. It was Warren Wiggins. He had just talked to Tom Mathews in Bermuda. Wiggins's message was brief: "Bermuda is socked in. Tom is trapped."
>
> Warren was beyond panic. He was simply following orders and relaying information. He said that Margery was now due to fly straight into Idlewild, the last thing that Shriver wanted to happen. And would I please get up there immediately so that I could "handle things."
>
> When I first got to Idlewild, there was this *army*—there is no other word for it—an *army* of press people with tape recorders and cameras and microphones. And I thought, Oh shit. Margery was

arriving on BOAC momentarily and there was this horde of reporters. I fell in with them and asked casually, "Who's coming in?" I really thought for a moment that it might be Grace Kelly, given the size of the crowd. And they said, "It's the Peace Corps girl." And so I knew I had my hands full. By dint of being a government official, I got past the customs officials and whisked Margery and Dick Ware into an enclosed area with this mob of reporters, noses pressed to the pane on the other side, peering in angrily. I then called Peace Corps headquarters and got right through to Sarge, who said edgily, "Tim, I don't want the press to talk to Margery."

Adams, glancing over his shoulder at the heavy-breathing, avaricious, frustrated mass of media pawing at the Customs Office window, said very slowly and deliberately: "Sarge, there is no way to avoid that." Silence on the other end. "Sarge, Margery Michelmore does not have two heads. She's a very intelligent girl. She's holding up. I have every confidence that she'll handle herself well." No response. "Sarge, Margery will now meet the press. Gotta run." Click.

"I'd been a reporter, but never a lion tamer, and now that is what I had to be. I went out, got up on a chair, and made an announcement to the effect that Miss Michelmore was very tired, had flown many thousands of miles, but was willing to answer a few brief questions. I told the TV and radio people that they'd get five minutes over here and the print people that they'd get five minutes over there, and that would be *it*.

"I thought there would be bitching and moaning. But nothing. They acquiesced. They had their five minutes each and that ended it. Just at this moment, Tom Mathews came rushing in from Bermuda, saying breezily, 'Hey, Tim, you handled that beautifully. Just right.' "

Moments later, Ruth Olson arrived. Olson had established herself as a crisis manager par excellence while working in the personnel offices of a number of agencies during World War II and thereafter: the War Production Board, the Federal Security Agency, the Foreign Economics Administration, the vastly expanded Navy, and finally as the head of personnel for the Navy's Bureau of Aeronautics. Shriver had heard about her during the first week of Peace Corps operations and had corralled her immediately. Betty Harris had gotten to know her through her work in the Peace Corps Personnel Office and suggested to Shriver that he send Olson in to help ameliorate the Michelmore melee. Harris, no stranger to the ways of the mostly male media (having herself been a journalist and a political operative), worried lest Margery be harassed beyond endurance.

After the two five-minute press conferences at Idlewild, the Michelmore entourage had grown to five: herself, Tim Adams, Ruth Olson, Margery's boyfriend (an NAACP lawyer from Boston who had sneaked in undetected), and briefly, Tom Mathews, who, satisfied that all was now going well, departed for Washington to give Shriver a report. "Tell Sarge this," said Adams. "Margery was great. She is going to look very good on the evening news—*and she will be on the evening news!* She was so great that a lot of the reporters ended up muttering, 'It must have been the goddamn Nigerians.' " (As it happens, they were partly right. But more of that later.)

Adams continued: "Tom, tell Sarge that we are now off to Puerto Rico, according to plan. But I cannot guarantee how long that will last. Margery really does not want to go. She's heard it's a Tarzan scene down there, and that is definitely not her style. She wants to make restitution to the Peace Corps, but not this way. Tell Sarge I'll stay in constant touch."

As Michelmore, Adams, and Olson boarded the plane for Puerto Rico, blissfully believing all press involvement was at an end, Adams recognized Carl Mydans, a renowned photojournalist, one of the giants of *Life* magazine. This could be no coincidence, and it wasn't. "Mydans had with him an attractive young female reporter, also from *Life*, whose name was, crazily enough, Marjorie. Marjorie Byers. *His* Margery, as Ruth and I started calling her. Well, I wasn't going to let him near *our* Margery. Obviously, he had tracked us relentlessly. But once we were in the air, he came back to talk to me, and he was such a gentleman that I finally relented and we were able to negotiate terms under which Mydans and Byers could get an interview with Margery after we arrived in Puerto Rico."

They were met at the airport in San Juan by Rafael Sancho-Bonet, then the Peace Corps' overall administrator in Puerto Rico (and soon to become Rep in Chile). He took them to meet William Sloane Coffin, the director of the camp. "Coffin was like the camp," says Adams. "Very macho." According to Adams, Coffin (who was previously chaplain at Yale and later a prominent antiwar spokesman, and who is now the senior rector at Riverside Church in New York) was unhappy that Margery Michelmore had been foisted on him. "He felt he was doing Shriver an enormous favor. Taking the heat. This girl was not his problem; she did not belong at that camp. He was not charmed by Shriver's idea of having her provide cultural sensitivity training. Well, God, nobody was. Coffin growled, 'I want it made clear that this girl is going to be treated just like everybody else here. Up before dawn, rappel down the dam, do drownproofing, conquer the obstacle course, etcetera.' "

Margery was saying to Adams and Olsen, in effect, "I will do this for a couple of days to accommodate the Peace Corps, but I view it as an unnecessarily punitive action, and there is a limit. If I am not permitted to leave very, very soon, I will leave on my own."

"She wasn't kidding," says Adams. "She was ladylike, but tough. And she just wasn't going to take any shit from Coffin, who now represented to her a certain bizarre thread of an institution called the Peace Corps. She thought she was being whipsawed. It was clear what had to be done. Ruth, Rafael, and I negotiated her out of there in about three days."

Of the many possibilities suggested to her by Ruth Olson and Tim Adams, Michelmore chose to work with Betty Harris and Sally Bowles in putting out the first issue of *The Peace Corps Volunteer*, an appropriate choice since she was, after all, the first returned Volunteer, albeit sixteen months premature in that regard. During the time she worked at Peace Corps headquarters, she was gratified to see her unique and painful experience, which many had feared could be ruinous, turn to good. And the Peace Corps had not been expelled. The Nigerian government was asking for more Volunteers in 1962—nearly three hundred of them—and there were only forty Volunteers in Nigeria at the time of the incident. Tim Adams had been insisting all along that the glare of publicity on Michelmore had in the end only served to show what first-rate people join the Peace Corps. Harris tended to agree, with a reservation: "The Peace Corps lucked out on this one. If Margery hadn't been good looking, gone to the right college, come from an impeccable New England family, or if she'd been a sex bomb or even one tiny little bit strange, we could have gone out of business."

Roger Landrum, now a Washington businessman and chairman of the Returned Peace Corps Volunteer Association, was in Nigeria at the time of the postcard excitement. For him and his fellow Volunteers (who were not in Margery's particular group but had rather been trained at Michigan State), the situation at the time was nothing less than "ominous." Landrum arrived in Lagos, the capital, just after the incident. He and a Peace Corps friend were taking a walk in Lagos when a member of the Nigerian Parliament came up and introduced himself and invited them to come to parliament.

The Peace Corps was being debated—whether or not to kick it out of the country because of the postcard. We said we would be fascinated to go. We went to the Peace Corps office to tell them this, and they forbade us to go. Said we'd be too visible. Parliament debated it pro and con for a couple of days, but nothing was resolved. It was time for my group to take a six-hundred-mile bus trip upcountry to our assignment at the brand new University of Nigeria. We knew that there had been demonstrations at University College in Ibadan because the postcard had gotten into the hands of the president of the student government, and those student governments were very politically active, very anticolonial, because Nigeria had just gotten its independence. They used the postcard as a way to show that the Peace Corps was an insult to their country.

But where we were going, we did not expect any problems because it was so far away and so new. But even there the students staged a large anti–Peace Corps demonstration; they marched, sang war chants, accused us of being spies, said the Peace Corps should go home. They even nailed hostile signs to our doors. I was scared to death. They were behaving in a very threatening way. But shortly after this, several of them knocked on my door, sat down, and said I was not to take this personally. They said, "This is a political statement about your government. You are welcome as an individual."

Landrum and his fellow Volunteer teachers were harassed in their classrooms for something over a week, but the postcard incident "became a joke pretty quickly, but I think only because Margery was immediately removed from the country."

Similarly, in Ghana, sensitivity to the Peace Corps' behavior was keen. A few months after the postcard incident, Prime Minister Kwame Nkrumah remarked to the Peace Corps Rep, George Carter (a fellow alumnus of Nkrumah's from Lincoln University in Pennsylvania and now an IBM executive), "If that had happened in Ghana, you wouldn't be here now."

Two nights before the blowup, the Peace Corps' official photographer of the time, Paul Conklin, was in Nigeria on assignment and had dinner with Margery and some of her fellow trainees at the Harvard-sponsored training program at University College at Ibadan. It had been a happy encounter. Thus, Conklin was stunned to hear that the charming Miss Michelmore from Massachusetts was now at the center of an apparently ugly scandal. He could scarcely believe the turmoil and the denunciations in the Nigerian press. "I tried to get in touch with Margery but she was on her way home by then." Conklin adds, "That incident cannot be exaggerated. It was like a hurricane that roared in from nowhere."

One of the strangest versions of the postcard incident came to light just four years, almost to the day, after the fact. Bob Gale, the Peace Corps director of recruiting, traveled to Ibadan, Nigeria, in October of 1965, to run two End-of-Service Conferences. Changing planes four times in the process (from Washington to New York, New York to London, London to Lagos, Lagos to Ibadan), Gale was nonetheless eager "to party," and in the early evening, upon arriving in Ibadan, ferreted out a Peace Corps staff member who was willing to go out drinking with him. The staff member, a young black man, took Gale to "a very local bar where I was the only white person present." The tall, apple-cheeked, dimpled, blue-eyed Gale drew stares, but he paid it no mind. Soon, into the bar came another imposingly large white man accompanied by a small Nigerian.

> The sight of this absolutely huge white person with this little African stopped everybody. There was complete silence as the two of them walked in through an archway onto the outdoor patio where I was sitting. Everyone stared at him—the huge white person—and suddenly he spotted me, stopped in his tracks, and exclaimed, "What are you doing here, Mr. Gale?" Who should it be but George Koehler, the cocaptain of the Carlton College football team when I was vice president there. It turned out that he was a Peace Corps Volunteer in Ghana. He was on leave and hitchhiking through Nigeria. He was picked up by a Nigerian who, when learning his rider was a Peace Corps Volunteer, immediately poured out a story to the effect that it was he who had discovered the famous postcard of October 1961, four years earlier. The Nigerian driver claimed he was then working at the post office in Ibadan and had been told by a group of left-wing students at the University to look for any postcards from Volunteers that might

discredit the Peace Corps. He was quite matter-of-factly claiming to be the culprit.

Obviously, there is no one who could be trusted to verify the truth of that story. But I see no reason why he would bring up the subject four years later and know so much about the controversy unless he had participated. Was he bragging? Did he want some kind of late recognition for having caused an international flap? Was he guilt-ridden?

I asked my friend, the Peace Corps staff member, what he made of it. He just shrugged and said, "We've heard stories and stories. I think that no one knows the whole truth. But one thing is certain. Peace Corps Volunteers in Nigeria never send postcards. They are haunted."

Murray Frank, director of the Western Region of Nigeria for the Peace Corps from 1961 to 1964 must have the last word because he alone was at the scene in Ibadan before, during, and after the incident. He reports that Margery recalled writing several postcards on Friday night, October 13, 1961, that she meant to mail them Saturday morning but could not absolutely swear that she had done so, so that from the first there was the suspicion that the offending card had been deliberately fished out of the post office in Ibadan. In any case, says Frank today,

at lunch on Saturday, copies of the card were at all the places at all the tables in all the dining rooms on the campus, and the Volunteers who previously mixed at meals with the Nigerian students were now isolated and segregated by them. The message on the card was printed on the front page of all, repeat all, Nigerian papers on Sunday and Monday. Leaders of the progressive Nigerian students led rallies demanding the removal of the Peace Corps. Articles appeared in the daily press for a week. Deputy Chief of Mission, Jerry Greene, came up from Lagos to Ibadan right away and he, Margery and I escaped the campus to eat at the Green Springs rest house. An AP stringer recognized Greene and deduced the rest with some investigation. He cabled the story to the States and it hit the U.S. papers. Margery went with Greene to Lagos and then left the country. It happened very fast.

The Volunteers and I had marathon meetings without Margery on Saturday afternoon and Sunday before she left. Some were angry with her; some defended her. Some thought 'there but for the grace of God go I' and some wanted to disassociate publicly from her. Some were against an apology of any kind and others wanted to go public with statements about what the Peace Corps stood for. In the end, we decided not to make any public statement which would extend the debate but that each one of us had to find a way to live with this situation simply by applying friendship and the principles of nonviolence. The isolation in the dining halls began to break down when the Volunteers, led by Aubrey Brown, announced to the Nigerian students that they were being unfair to him, that if he could not eat with them he would not eat at all. They invited him to sit down.

When the furor was almost ended, former president Eisenhower made a political speech in Madison Square Garden in which he suggested that the United States send Peace Corps Volunteers to the moon since it was also an undeveloped country and they could do less harm there. That brought the postcard back into the news briefly. I was asked at the time to speak at the U.S. Information Library in Ibadan. A very large crowd of young people and students showed up. They were not unfriendly. It was really over.

"Think of it!" says Warren Wiggins:

The greatest thing that could have happened to the Peace Corps in the beginning was a postcard from a Volunteer mentioning that people pee in the streets in Nigeria. It was like a vaccination. We all knew we were going to get sick, all of a sudden and by accident. But when? Where? From what? Well, it was Margery—a very, very minor bug in the system. But boy, did it take. *Everybody* was vaccinated. Never again would a major newspaper, under the worst of conditions, streamer anything negative about the Peace Corps. Since then, the Peace Corps has had rape, manslaughter, bigamy, disappearances, Volunteers going insane, meddling in local politics, being eaten by crocodiles, but never again did it get a bad play in national news. The vaccination took; we were immune.

The postcard incident had several times the force of a major policy decision.

Margery Michelmore left the Peace Corps in early 1962 to marry the lawyer from Boston. One can only hope that she has found anonymity, prosperity, and, yes, peace.

♦   ♦   ♦

No policy decision was ever made faster and with less debate than the one called "In, Up & Out." There was constant talk at the early Peace Corps of how to keep the organization fresh and vital, how to avoid falling into the trap of entrenched government bureaucracies, layered as they were with sluggish sinecures and "inhabited by corpses," as Haddad was fond of saying. Haddad was the most obsessed of all Peace Corps founding fathers about the dangers of calcification. Others worried, too, because the energy level of the Peace Corps was so high that it was intoxicating; it would be tragic to see it flag. But most believed that it would not flag; the honeymoon would last forever. So then, Haddad worried that people didn't worry enough. Wiggins would occasionally tell Haddad not to worry so much, that the Peace Corps wasn't anything like the foreign aid bureaucracy out of which he, Wiggins, had come. By and large, the Peace Corps didn't attract the same kind of people, wasn't structured the same, had a built-in burnout factor—people could work at that pace for just so long. And the Peace Corps had the Volunteers. Therefore, the Peace Corps would be forever young. "The Volunteers are it," agreed Haddad. "You know, we ought to make it a policy—not just a dumb rule, but an honest-to-God *policy* that in this outfit there are no lowercase volunteers, only uppercase ones."

Wiggins said, "Great. I'm for it. Write Sarge a memo. He'll love it." Haddad did, and capital V it was. The First Annual Report consecrated it.

Franklin Williams had an assistant, "an extremely clever, precocious, young man right out of Harvard," to whom he threw random but difficult challenges. Addressing Haddad's relentless quest for methods to fend off calcification, the young man wrote Williams (then special assistant to Shriver for almost everything) a memo that, in effect, stressed the point of Haddad's capital V. "If we were serious about keeping the Peace Corps young and dynamic," says Williams, "then he would suggest this: Deliberately, within eight years, move from an organization staffed by people who had never served as Volunteers to an organization staffed totally by former Volunteers. And the only way to do that was to set up a system whereby people either moved up after two years or they got out. The point was mobility— not hanging around to feather a long-term bureaucratic nest. Make room for that successful, returning Volunteer. It would be a gradual process. But move these people up, and eight years later, one of those guys at the bottom of the pyramid at the start would be the director. Or close to it." Williams says that he actually had this in mind when he got the memo—that a returned Volunteer should be director by the end of the decade. He was astonished to find that his assistant had so perfectly expressed his fantasy. (Twenty-five years later, there has never been a Peace Corps Volunteer to sit in the director's chair, nor even to hold the post of deputy director. Yet there are stunning success stories among the ranks of the early Volunteers, some of which are noted in Chapter 9.)

Williams took his young assistant's "brilliant exposition," rewrote it in his own idiom, and submitted it to Shriver under his own name. "Sarge wouldn't have even read it if it had been from the guy. He didn't know the guy. The guy had no access. However, he would read it if it was from me." Shriver was excited by the idea and asked Williams to send copies to all of the senior and upper-middle-level staff.

Says Wiggins, "The idea just whizzed through. I was all for it. I remember no opposition. It became policy."

"I totally supported it," says Jack Vaughn. "We couldn't become staid or career oriented. This was going to have to be a burst of glory."

"It was a disaster, in my view," says Charlie Houston. "It fostered panic and desperation. People started climbing and pushing and shoving and playing politics like mad. 'Grab it while you can' kind of thing. It got cutthroat. People were no longer putting the best interests of the Peace Corps first. They were all out for themselves. It robbed the place of a lot of its idealism and commitment."

"It never mattered to me," says Don McClure. "I was always planning to go back to the San Francisco Chronicle anyway." (He never did, however. The McClure family still lives in Washington.)

Twenty-four years later, in February 1985, Shriver voiced some doubts about the "In, Up & Out" policy. The occasion was a luncheon at the Federal City Club at the Embassy Row Hotel on Massachusetts Avenue in Washington, with Shriver and President Reagan's Peace Corps director, Loret Ruppe, as the featured speakers. They were describing the "old" Peace Corps and the "new." After Shriver had concluded his remarks and called for questions, one apparent "old-timer" asked, "Sarge, when you started the Peace Corps, one of your great concerns was that it might become a bureaucracy like everything else. Is the five-year flush still alive?"

Shriver looked surprised and amused:

Did you all hear that? Do you know what that is? The five-year flush is the name that was given to the policy originally called "In, Up & Out," adopted by the Peace Corps in the early 1960s, whereby nobody was allowed to serve in the Peace Corps for more than five years. That went against the grain of the civil service system. [It was and is very difficult to dismiss a civil servant, no matter how incompetent he or she might be.] The Civil Service Commission then consisted of three people, one who was for the five-year flush and another who was opposed. John Macy was the chairman. He wasn't sure what he should do. He said to me, "If you can get the president to tell me that it's all right with him to initiate the five-year flush, it's okay with me." So President Kennedy calls him up and says, "John, would you please support us on that." And John Macy did, and the policy was inaugurated. I think it's still the only agency in the government which has an automatic firing after five years. Fortunately, I left on the last day of my fifth year! But the policy is still in operation, if modified a little bit. The fundamental idea is still good but it's not the perfect solution. There are a lot of people who think it's a mistake. Because it's true that such a policy interferes with institutional memory. It's true that the Peace Corps continually has to break in new people. And it's true that the Peace Corps has to let people go just when they're getting good at their jobs."

Ruppe then smiled enigmatically: "It is a challenge to manage an agency that has 30 percent turnover every year."

CHAPTER 5

WITH SARGE:
ON LAND, ON SEA,
AND IN THE AIR

The Peace Corps had gotten lucky. Undersecretary of State, and former Ambassador to India, Chester Bowles was an old friend and former mentor of Harris Wofford, who was helping Shriver set up the Peace Corps. Bowles knew and had good rapport with Julius Nyerere, then prime minister and later president of Tanganyika, an East African country that was about to gain independence and change its name to Tanzania.* Bowles talked to Nyerere about the Peace Corps and found him receptive; he was interested in having a contingent of Peace Corps surveyors, geologists, and engineers for a road-building project in the early fall. Shriver immediately dispatched Lee St. Lawrence to Tanganyika's capital, Dar es Salaam, to "get it in writing" before Nyerere changed his mind. St. Lawrence had a rascally side and he could match Haddad in any profanity contest, but he was shrewd, learned, amusing, utterly unafraid, an almost legendary taker of risks. In addition, he was fluent in several languages and had led an "Indiana Jones" existence as a foreign aid official, serving in Belgrade, Yugoslavia; Vientiane, Laos (where he shared a house with the late Dr. Tom Dooley); and the Congo in its most turbulent period since it gained independence. There, he was twice beaten by mutinous Congolese soldiers and barely escaped being hanged. Although St. Lawrence enjoyed projecting a devil-may-care image, he was as tough a man as ever held a job on the New Frontier. A good man to send in "against" Julius Nyerere, a young and influential African leader known for his towering intellect, dynamism, and charisma.

Franklin Williams recalls St. Lawrence's triumphant return to Peace Corps/Washington. Shriver and the staff "turned phosphorescent" as St. Lawrence described "bushwacking the country from end to end in order to see the exact conditions under which Volunteers would live and work, all this glamorous stuff about trudging through

*President Nyerere relinquished his post on November 5, 1985, after twenty-four years as Tanzania's leader. In the twenty-five years since most of Africa gained independence from colonial rule, only two other African leaders handed over power willingly: Senegal's Leopold Senghor and Cameroon's Amadou Ahidjo.

the high grass, seeing giraffes and Masai warriors, talking politics with the prime minister, with words like "schistosomiasis" hanging out— that was a disease, we were told—and a few bars from the Tanganyikan national anthem in Swahili—that was the language. Jesus Christ," says Williams, still in wonderment, "we were impressed. Most of us idealists hadn't even heard of Tanganyika."

Harris Wofford says, "We were certainly relieved to get that invitation from Tanganyika. But Sarge had a problem. He was telling the president and the country that the Peace Corps would go only where it had been asked. And people were naturally asking, therefore, where it had been asked. So it was important to have a few more invitations fast. We particularly hoped for requests from India, the largest democracy in the world and leader of the neutral bloc; Nigeria, the most prosperous and populous nation in Africa; and Ghana, whose leader, Kwame Nkrumah, was a great force in the struggle for African independence. We were not supposed to fish for invitations, obviously, but we were certainly going to try to prime the pump of foreign interest." When Wofford learned that India's ambassador to the United States, B. K. Nehru, a cousin of Prime Minister Jawaharlal Nehru, had expressed interest in the Peace Corps, he quickly arranged a dinner meeting at his house in suburban Virginia to introduce the ambassador to Shriver. (Wofford had lived and worked in India in the early 1950s, and through Chester Bowles, he had met many of India's ruling elite.) As Ambassador B. K. Nehru was leaving Wofford's home, having listened impassively to Shriver's pitch about the Peace Corps, he suddenly queried, "Am I correct, Mr. Shriver, in thinking that you would not be averse to an invitation from our prime minister to visit India and talk about your program?" And soon, the formal invitation came by cable.

Once the visit to Jawaharlal Nehru was on Shriver's schedule, and known to be, other meetings with important Third World leaders were easily arranged. Shriver would be welcome in the sanctum sanctorums of Ghana, Nigeria, Pakistan, Burma, Thailand, Malaya, and the Philippines. When Shriver asked Wofford to accompany him on the trip, Wofford "jumped at the chance." It was then late April 1961, and the Bay of Pigs debacle had just occurred. A pall hung over the White House, where Wofford was spending half of his days as Kennedy's advisor on civil rights and the other half in helping Shriver set up the Peace Corps. Franklin Williams was also asked to accompany them. "I know that I was asked to go because I was black, and Sarge really wanted the appearance of an integrated U.S. team—and that sort of thing was very new then; and because I was supposed to find out what international organizations were doing in the Third World, since theoretically that was my Peace Corps role; and also because Kwame Nkrumah had been a classmate of mine at Lincoln University (a black institution southwest of Philadelphia). And Ghana was the first country we were going to."

When the Shriver entourage arrived in Accra, Ghana, in late April 1961, Shriver, who allegedly had never been sick a day in his adult life and who could not tolerate the indispositions of others, had laryngitis and could barely speak. But he gamely croaked to the greeting party at the airport: "Sorry, I've lost my voice. But that's all right. The Peace Corps' purpose in Ghana is to listen and to learn." (It occurred to Wofford that Shriver's laryngitis was providential. Ghana's president, Kwame Nkrumah, was then the leading spokesman for African nationalism and was also known as *Osagyefo*, meaning "Savior." Such an influential near-diety could only be effectively addressed by the respectful attitude of listening.) Wofford says that "Shriver and Nkrumah had a meeting of the minds on a point that Arnold Toynbee had made: There were radiations coming out of the heart of America, the heart of the West. Some of them were benign, some destructive, and some neutral. A developing nation like Ghana, according to Nkrumah, had to be sophisticated and choose the beam that was benign and resist the malevolent beam. Nkrumah believed that the CIA was such a negative beam. Ghana had to be careful, Nkrumah pointed out, in making these distinctions. Nkrumah told Shriver that he did not want American Peace Corps Volunteers "indoctrinating our young people. So don't come as social science teachers," he said, "and perhaps not even as English teachers. You should come to teach science and mathematics. We don't want you to *affect* them; we just want you to *teach* them. Agreed?"*

Naturally, Shriver agreed.

Nkrumah then said, "Fine. We will invite a small number of

*Nkrumah had also suggested in his meeting with Shriver that perhaps America might entertain the idea of welcoming volunteers from Ghana sometime in the near future. Shriver agreed instinctively to this understandably prideful idea of reciprocity. The idea of a "reverse Peace Corps" surfaced during the Kennedy and Johnson administrations at different times, and a pilot-project "reverse Peace Corps" was sponsored privately by Alfred W. Jones in 1965, featuring young volunteers from India (see chapter 8). But a reverse Peace Corps from Ghana never materialized.

Peace Corps teachers, and we could use some plumbers and electricians, too. Can you get them here by August?"

Fifty Peace Corps teachers—but no plumbers and no electricians—arrived in Ghana on September 1, 1961, singing their well-rehearsed song in Ghana's primary language, Twi.

"These were very delicate conversations that Sarge was having with these Third World leaders," says Franklin Williams.

The Bay of Pigs was just two weeks behind us and it was haunting us all along the way. Third World officials did not hesitate to bring it up. So this negotiating trip was no pushover situation. But Shriver had to succeed, and we had to make sure that he succeeded. And that presented the problem of how you related to him. You couldn't be his buddy. Wofford was his buddy, if anyone was. Wofford carried the classified papers. I had never seen classified papers before, and I couldn't quite take it seriously. Wofford took it very seriously. I used to imagine that he slept with the briefcase of classified papers lashed to his wrist. But I learned one thing very quickly: You leave Sarge alone. You leave him absolutely alone. When the loudspeaker at the airport announces that your plane is leaving, *now*, from Accra, Lagos, Peshawar, or wherever, and you see Sarge over there casually reading a newspaper, you do not run over and say, "Oh, Sarge, the plane is leaving." You do not do that. You just go ahead and get on the plane. You leave his ass alone. Otherwise, you will lose him. Sarge would not tolerate being shepherded.

Williams also learned that Shriver was "absolutely indefatigable," that he had no time "for personal things or socializing on a trip like this. He kept a Bible with him. He often consulted it. He got up at 5:00 A.M. to go to mass in any city, town, or village, in any country, where there was an available Catholic church that held early mass." Williams also learned that Shriver "would go far, far out of his way to avoid the appearance of being on a 'junket'—the idea of a government official taking his ease on an alleged 'fact-finding tour' at the taxpayer's expense"—that he would arrange to suffer, and to be seen suffering, the average traveler's discomfort. Williams adds,

Sarge was so adamant on this point that on the way home from the long, long trip he would not permit a one-day layover in Hong Kong, which was logical and which would have given us some rest. Oh, no. Instead, Sarge had us flying a day out of our way from the Philippines to Singapore, where we landed, changed planes, and took off again. Our one bit of leisure time on that whole grueling trip consisted of having a beer together at some little nothing place in the boondocks in the Philippines. Oh boy, we went, went, went. Twenty-six days in and out of eleven countries, if you count all of the detours and airports. Sarge never got tired. I found it irritating.

Ed Bayley, the Peace Corps' first director of public information, was the fourth member of what was breathlessly being called *the* trip. For many years the political reporter for the *Milwaukee Journal*, and more recently executive secretary to Governor Gaylord Nelson of Wisconsin, Bayley would handle the press in all eight countries: Ghana, Nigeria, India, Pakistan, Thailand, Malaya, Burma, and the Philippines. The plane trip to Africa was the last fun Bayley would have for twenty-six days, to be sure. He encountered Justice Thurgood Marshall on the plane; they commenced to drink martinis and play gin rummy through the night. But many times thereafter, Bayley was heard to ask in exasperation, "Why does Sarge insist upon running the Peace Corps as if it was the last stage of a presidential campaign?" In Ghana, Bayley raced from newspaper to newspaper to spread the good word of the Peace Corps. He got Shriver interviews with all of the leading editors and got him on Radio Ghana as well. In Nigeria, Bayley did the same, this time succeeding in getting Shriver on television. Nigeria had both oil and television, unique in a developing nation in 1961. Such a bonanza inspired Shriver to ask for more: "Ed, I hear that *Holiday on Ice* [a precursor to the Ice Capades] is playing here in Lagos, which is incredible, you know. Why don't you go over there and get the best looking blond in the cast, put her on television, and have her say how great the Peace Corps is?"

"That's a terrible idea, Sarge," said Bayley. "And I won't do it." According to Bayley, "Sarge sulked a little but he did not insist."

Nigeria had not only oil, television, *Holiday on Ice*, vast territory (357,000 square miles), and enormous population (82,643,000), it also had an ambitious and dynamic leadership, which had big plans for Nigerian education. As Harris Wofford records in his 1980 book, *Of Kennedys and Kings*, "There were places in Nigeria's elementary schools for only 14,000 out of the more than two million eligible children . . . The government could build the schools but for a while most of the teachers would have to come from overseas and speak

English, the language of instruction." Thus, negotiations between Shriver and His Excellency the Rt. Honorable Dr. Nnamdi Azikiwe, governor general and commander in chief; the Rt. Honorable Sir Abubakar Tafawa Balewa, prime minister; and the Honorable Sr. Ahmadu-Bello, Sarauna of Sokoto, premier of the Northern Region, were agreeable and pragmatic. As Wofford points out, Azikiwe ("Zik"), who had "called on Nigerians to 'go Gandhi' in their campaign for independence, was concerned that their British-style educational system was producing an educated elite alienated from the people. As the first Ibo [tribesman] to go to school in the United States, he had been impressed by Jefferson's ideas of education and by America's success, through land grant colleges and universities, in shaping a curriculum appropriate to a new land. He wanted Peace Corps teachers to help Nigeria achieve a similar democratic system of education." The Nigerian leaders were not inclined to lecture Shriver, as had been the case with Nkrumah in Ghana.

If there was no sign at the airport in New Delhi, India, reading "Welcome to the Land of Spiritual Superiority," there might as well have been, for that was the prevailing attitude that Shriver and his companions encountered. If for Wofford a return to India was a sentimental journey, the Indian visit was to present Shriver with a field of ideological land mines. If Kwame Nkrumah of Ghana had lectured Shriver, Jawaharlal Nehru of India would positively sermonize him. And Wofford's Indian friends from ten years past were constantly questioning him about the true intentions of the Kennedy administration. Wofford, in *Of Kennedys and Kings*, noted:

> From our first encounters in New Delhi, I found that Kennedy had stirred strong but mixed feelings. His youth, charm and call to service, his concern for the progress of Asia, Africa, and Latin America, and his recognition of the right of India to maintain their neutrality in the cold war were all appealing. Indians were glad the torch had passed to a new generation, but worried where and how Kennedy would carry it.

Many Indians thought that Kennedy's inaugural rhetoric had "a disturbing imperial ring," were alarmed by America's support of the invasion of Cuba (the Bay of Pigs was now a month in the past), and were put off by the rhymed message of the aging American poet, Robert

Frost, who with memorable difficulty intoned the following ending lines of original inaugural poetry:

We see how seriously the races swarm
In their attempts at sovereignty and form.
They are our wards and we think to some extent
For the time being and with their consent,
To teach them how Democracy is meant.

One Indian friend of Wofford's was sufficiently irritated by Frost's poem to ask Wofford whether the Peace Corps had been conceived in its condescending spirit. Thus, Shriver and Wofford, in their discussions with Indian officials in New Delhi and in their tours of sites in the Punjab, where it was hoped that the Peace Corps would work, always took the humble approach. They would say that by permitting the American Peace Corps to participate in India's development efforts, they would be giving the Volunteers a chance to find themselves. Shriver and Wofford did not speak with forked tongue; that is precisely what they hoped would happen to the Volunteers in India (should there ever be any). They were careful to emphasize the spiritual side of the Volunteer experience at every opportunity. They were encouraged greatly by Ashadevi Aryanayakam, a friend of Wofford's, who had presided over Gandhi's ashram, *Sevagram* ("Service Village"); Wofford had first met Ashadevi there in 1952, five years after Gandhi's assassination. As Wofford writes, she told him, "Yours was the first revolution. Do you think young Americans possess the spiritual values they must have to bring the spirit of that revolution to our country? . . . India must not boast of any spiritual superiority. There is a great valuelessness spreading around the world and in India, too." Ashadevi remarked on Gandhi's idea, dating back to the early 1940s, for a *Shanti Sena*, or an "army," so to speak, devoted to the principles and practices of peace seeking and peacekeeping in which "character or soul force" must take precedence over all other motives and behaviors. Gandhi personified this ideal, said Ashadevi, adding with a touch of irony, that "Gandhi was the first Peace Corps Volunteer." (Inspired and cheered by Ashadevi's words, Shriver and Wofford were better able to accept the doubting and the criticism that they were encountering elsewhere. Meanwhile, Chester Bowles, who had been ambassador to India from 1951 to 1953 was doing what he could from

Washington to see that his own Indian friends, including Prime Minister Nehru and his daughter Indira, would receive the Peace Corps group cordially.)

Everyone knew that the Peace Corps' future in India would be decided by only one person, Prime Minister Nehru. Wofford warned Shriver to expect a lecture from Nehru to the effect that India was the mother source of all inspiration, that Nehru would not at first evince much interest in the Peace Corps, but that in the end, Nehru would somewhat begrudgingly invite a handful of Volunteers—entirely as a favor to the United States. Wofford's guess came very close to the mark. Nehru received Shriver, Wofford writes, wearing his signature tunic adorned by a small red rose and "wearily, as was his fashion, slumped back in his chair, almost going to sleep during Shriver's description of the Peace Corps." Nehru's response was:

> For thousands of years outsiders have been coming to India, some of them as invaders, sweeping down the plains of the Punjab to the Ganges. Many of them stayed and were assimilated. Others went home, leaving India more or less the same as it was before they came. India has usually been hospitable to these strangers, having confidence that its culture would survive, and that it had much to teach newcomers.
>
> In matters of the spirit, I am sure young Americans would learn a good deal in this country and it could be an important experience for them. The government of the Punjab and the Minister for Community Development apparently want some of your Volunteers, and we will be happy to receive a few of them—perhaps twenty to twenty-five. But I hope you and they will not be too disappointed if the Punjab, when they leave, is more or less the same as it was before they came.

The Peace Corps group was aware that this was no ringing endorsement on the part of the Indian prime minister, and none was expected. Shriver had been given a door prize to take home, and that was all. And yet, that was a lot. If the idea of sending twenty-five Volunteers 10,000 miles away to be sprinkled over the Punjab (which means "the land of five rivers" in Hindi)—an area of 47,205 square miles in a nation of half a billion souls—has its farcical side, Nehru's permission to proceed, "however patronizing," writes Wofford, "was the green light that Shriver needed. From then on the Peace Corps had Nehru's imprimatur, which helped open the door in a number of other Third World countries." Shriver, a past master at upping the numbers, any and all numbers, ultimately convinced the Indian government to accept seventy-five Volunteers. By the end of Charlie Houston's tour as Peace Corps Rep in December 1964, there were approximately four hundred Volunteers at work in the Punjab and several other sites in India.

Hours after the meeting with Nehru—before Shriver, Wofford, Williams, and Bayley had left New Delhi—a cable came in from Wiggins in Washington that produced the euphoria that they craved to give in to but had held back, partly due to an unspoken, shared superstition that premature jubilation would jinx them and partly due to exhaustion. President Kennedy had done an abrupt about-face on the issue of Peace Corps independence. He had set it free from the identity-crushing clutches of the Agency for International Development. Vice President Lyndon Johnson had produced a miracle. The Peace Corps four in India could not imagine how it had happened, but they knew what it meant: subcabinet status for Shriver, who would report only tacitly to Secretary of State Dean Rusk. The rest of the trip continued at the same frantic pace, but the mood of the group shifted and lightened. Huge barriers had come down. And so they flew on to Pakistan, Burma, Thailand, Malaya, and the Philippines—the leaders of which all invited Peace Corps Volunteers, with the exception of Premier U Nu of Burma. "The atmosphere was different in Burma," recalls Ed Bayley. "There was something strange about it, despite a warm welcome and a marvelous government reception and dinner. We talked to U Nu and Burmese government officials for a long time at U Nu's residence, but U Nu often spoke obliquely; we could not tell what he was driving at." Franklin Williams says that U Nu spoke semiprivately with Shriver at one point at his residence, with Williams, Wofford, and Bayley sitting ten yards behind Shriver. "Suddenly, U Nu said to Sarge, 'Mr. Shriver, do you believe that there are young Americans who would volunteer to work in the jungles of north Burma with the same zeal for democracy as young Chinese Communists are doing for their cause?' Sarge crossed his fingers behind his chair so that we could see and replied, 'Yes, Mr. Premier, I do.' "

Still, no invitation. But Shriver says to this day, "I loved U Nu."

"We got our most enthusiastic response in Manila," says Bayley. The Philippines had been the target country about which Warren Wiggins had written in his "architectural" position paper, coauthored with William Josephson, "The Towering Task." That the Filipinos wanted large numbers of English teachers, as Wiggins had originally projected, provided, as Charlie Peters, chief of evaluation, put it, "a reassuring symmetry."

Shriver came back to Peace Corps/Washington after *the* trip "with a lot of important scalps on his belt," says Peters. "He had negotiated successfully with some of the most fabled and powerful Third World leaders during a period when the Third World was not anti-American *per se*, but which was certainly suspicious about any kind of neocolonial approaches and which was by and large burning up with independence fever. Sarge had no previous training or experience in international diplomacy nor any experience in the federal bureaucracy, and yet, while he was accomplishing the former he was also pulling off the latter, forcing the issue of bureaucratic independence for the Peace Corps at a remove of ten thousand miles. Having accomplished all of this in less than thirty days, he came back home *more* than the brother-in-law of the president." A lot of bright, young, ambitious people came to the Peace Corps in the early 1960s with the mistaken notion that they would become very important simply by doing so, believing that if they were holding hands with Shriver, in effect, they were all but whispering their brilliant advice directly into JFK's ear. But as Charlie Peters notes, "No one had that kind of access to Shriver, especially in the early days, and Shriver didn't have that kind of access to or support from Kennedy's White House."

No help from the White House? How could that be? Is revenge too extreme a notion? Is "paying a political price" a mite too melodramatic? After twenty-four years, Shriver has no inclination to label the situation; he merely tells the story:

> After I got back from that first overseas trip in the spring of 1961, I started preparing a strategy for getting the legislation through in September, when it was scheduled to come up for debate. Naturally, I assumed that I was supposed to work within the administration, but nobody seemed to be particularly interested in getting the legislation through. Not the Bureau of the Budget, not Larry O'Brien, who was in charge of congressional affairs at the White House. I couldn't figure out why that was, since the Peace Corps was now real and functioning successfully. One weekend early that summer my wife and I flew up to Cape Cod on the president's plane. I was telling her how perplexed I was, really, that I was

having so much difficulty in getting the cooperation I had expected. She said she'd speak to Jack about it. She went back and talked to him. He asked, "How's Sarge? What's he doing?" and she said something to the effect of, "Well, he's having trouble with the Peace Corps legislation. He's puzzled because he's not getting any cooperation." And it was she, my wife, who came back and told me that Jack had said to her, "Well, Sarge and Lyndon Johnson wanted to have a separate Peace Corps, separate from AID, and so I think they ought to take charge of getting it through Congress. I've got plenty of other legislation I'm struggling with." Kennedy went on to say to his sister that if the Peace Corps had remained within the overall foreign assistance bureaucracy, he, Kennedy, could ask a particular senator or congressman for one vote for everything and "would not have to fuss with separate legislation."

"Well, that's all I needed," said Shriver, who had been living in Washington for about four months and who had never dealt with Congress before.

> When it was checked off to me that way, I just said, "I'm putting this piece of legislation *through!*"
> In wanting to have the Peace Corps separate, to have it have a separate identity, a separate contracting system, a separate life overseas, I then found myself saddled, you might say, with *all* of the responsibility, because I had made that request. So I said, Okay, if it's my baby, I will never ask anyone for help again. And I never did. I never asked anybody ever after that—nobody, nobody—for help. Nothing. Nobody. I just took the bull by the horns and said, Okay, it's the Peace Corps against everybody else. If it had to be done entirely by ourselves, I was damned well sure it was going to be done successfully.

Enter Bill D. Moyers, age twenty-six. Moyers had gotten his political education at the feet of the master, Lyndon Baines Johnson, for whom he had worked on and off since he was a nineteen-year-old college student in Texas. He had seen this larger-than-life boss reach all but the highest of heights in American politics: Senate majority leader and vice president. Moyers had been by Johnson's side through many political campaigns and legislative battles. Few, if any, young men of his age have been more knowledgeable about the workings and the mentality of Congress. And he landed in Shriver's lap at just the right time. Even before the Executive Order of March 1, 1961, had been signed, James Rowe, an influential Washington lawyer and beloved local personality, who was also an intimate of Lyndon Johnson's and a former aide to President Franklin Delano Roosevelt, called Shriver: "Sarge," he said, "I think I have good news for you. I don't really understand how this has come about, but did you ever hear of a fellow named Bill Moyers?"

Shriver replied, "No, I haven't."

Rowe went on: "Well, Bill Moyers is about twenty-five years old. He works for Lyndon; he is one of the top people in the vice president's office. But he wants to work for the Peace Corps. I can tell you, I've been in Washington for thirty-five years and I think Bill Moyers is the smartest person that Lyndon Johnson has ever had work for him. Secondly, I think he's one of the most gifted young legislative persons I've ever seen. I have no idea why in the world he wants to work in the Peace Corps. Frankly, I think it's sort of crazy for him to want to do that. But he definitely does. He wants to meet you. I would recommend that you talk to him."

Moyers became the Peace Corps' first associate director for Public Affairs at twenty-six, its second deputy director (after fellow Texan Paul Geren) at twenty-eight.* In the late summer and first three weeks of fall 1961, Shriver and Moyers stalked the halls of the House of Representatives and the Senate from sunup to sundown selling the peace corps idea.

Peter Grothe, foreign relations advisor and speech writer for Senator Hubert Humphrey in 1960 (and now a professor at the Monterey Institute of International Studies), says that Humphrey who had introduced similar legislation in May of 1960 on the eve of the U-2

---

*To become deputy director of the Peace Corps at the age of twenty-eight meant that Moyers would be the youngest presidential appointee in history. During his confirmation hearings before the Senate in early February of 1963, Moyers was suddenly challenged by Republican Senator Frank Lausche of Ohio. Lausche dyspeptically cited Moyers's youth and lack of administrative experience, declaring that Moyers was "still wet behind the ears." This remark brought Senator Russell Long, Democrat from Louisiana, to his feet, saying that Lausche had just insulted the sovereign state of Louisiana, its people and himself, and that was because, Long explained, he, Long, had first been elected to the Senate when he was only twenty-nine. A third senator then asked, "Exactly how old are you, Mr. Moyers?" Moyers replied, "Twenty-eight," and then, in a fully audible aside, added, "and a half." Laughter rippled through the Senate chamber. Moyers was installed in the executive suite of the Peace Corps within the week.

incident and West Virginia primary (which Grothe had drafted and in which the phrase "peace corps" first appeared), now got behind Shriver 100 percent since the idea seemed at last to have a chance of becoming a program. Humphrey told Shriver, who had been criss-crossing the country making speeches, "Sarge, forget about talking to women's clubs in Detroit. They don't get your bill passed. We in Congress do. Don't sit down to another meal between now and the time your Peace Corps bill comes up for a vote unless there is a senator or a congressman sitting by your elbow. Remember that there are one hundred of us prima donnas in the Senate who stand around and debate about how the government ought to run, and we envy you guys because you are doing it. So make each senator feel like you care about his views. Massage our egos." According to Grothe, Humphrey then ticked off each member of the Senate Foreign Relations Com-mittee and told Shriver how to approach each man. "Bill Fulbright (D-Arkansas), no problem. Frank Lausche (R-Ohio) is very conserva-tive and an ornery son of a bitch. I'll buy you a steak dinner if you get his vote. John Sparkman (D-Alabama), no problem. (Sparkman had been Adlai Stevenson's vice presidential running mate in 1952.) Now, Albert Gore (D-Tennessee). Albert's a very fine senator, very distinguished, hard-working. But Albert's a loner; Albert's a maverick. So he'll need a little loving. I want all of you at the Peace Corps to love Albert. Go to his office. Sit down dutifully. Take notes on what he's saying. As soon as you get back to your office, call him and thank him for the points he made—A, B, and C—about how to get Peace Corps legislation through. I don't care if his darling daughter does work at the Peace Corps. Albert's very independent and this is what you'll have to do to make sure of his vote."

Grothe concludes: "Shriver and Moyers carried on the greatest romance act with the Congress since Romeo and Juliet, and they literally saw over 400 House members and senators. And with Hum-phrey managing the bill in the Senate, the bill passed overwhelm-ingly."

Shriver and Moyers operated as Batman and Robin, and sometimes the roles were reversed. Shriver trusted Moyers's knowledge of the Senate implicitly. But once, Shriver's instincts bested Moyers's inti-mate knowledge of Congress. "We were walking down the Senate corridors and I notice a sign on a door: 'Mr. Goldwater,'" says Shriver. "I stopped and said, 'I think I'll just go in and ask him whether or not he would vote for the Peace Corps.' Moyers said, 'Oh, you're never going to get Goldwater.' I said, 'Well, I'm sure that we're not going to get him if we never even ask him.' So we rapped on the door and went in, and fortuitously he was there and willing to talk to us. We talked for an hour, after which he said, 'That sounds like a great idea. I'll vote for it.' "

The Peace Corps was signed into law on September 22, 1961.

◆　　　◆　　　◆

Twenty-five years later, early Peace Corps staff members remember, with the clarity of yesterday, not only the high voltage of the Shriver persona, but certain of the Shriver "tricks," as well. Or were they devices?

One such device was known as the "pencil signal." Betty Harris describes it:

> At senior staff meetings, Sarge kept a bunch of finely sharpened pencils in front of him on the conference room table, along with a legal pad, because he was a great jotter-downer of ideas. If you made a suggestion and Sarge jotted it down, you had scored. But if Sarge was beginning to get bored with what was being said, he would pick up a pencil and start twiddling it between his fingers. The pace of the twiddling would increase according to how bored or annoyed Sarge was. If you were talking and he was twiddling, you were beginning to feel ill.
>
> But if he got bored to the point of exasperation, he would snap the pencil in half. With one hand. Snap! If the poor idiot who was boring him kept on blathering after the first pencil got broken, Sarge would pick up another, twiddle very fast—and snap. That usually did it. If the offender was a new staff member, he had little chance to become an old staff member.

Al Meisel, one of the first two training officers at the Peace Corps, was hired and survived because, like his cohort Pat Kennedy, he was a fast-talking, acerbically precise and witty fellow. Like Pat Kennedy, he shared certain traits with Shriver: impatience and the ability to spot a phony or a bore. He was always amazed when a phony or a bore slipped through the thorough and somewhat devastating interviewing process at the Peace Corps. He could not understand how anyone who entered the portals of Peace Corps headquarters could not sense the electricity that could spell danger as soon as the elevator doors opened, or how, having met Shriver, the job-seeker could not appreciate the necessity to perform crisply, briskly, and with utmost dispatch.

"But phonies and bores and incompetents did slip through occasionally," says Meisel, "partly because Sarge was just a bit too credential-happy." Meisel recalls an occasion when a well-dressed, well-recommended—and inordinately-pleased-with-himself—sociologist who had survived his first round of Peace Corps staff interviews (but who had yet to meet the Final Pronouncer, Shriver) attended his first senior staff meeting. He had come to explain his theories about culture shock, a subject of great interest to the early Peace Corps staff. The sociologist, who looked uncannily like the actor who played the dotty commandant of the movie series, *Police Academy*, seated himself next to Meisel who was going over some correspondence about a training program for Thailand. Looking over Meisel's shoulder, the newcomer commented, "Oh, how very interesting your work must be. My specialty is West Africa, but I'm curious. Is Thigh-land a large country? Is it densely populated?" Meisel, not looking up from his papers or missing a beat, replied, "There are forty-six million Thais in Thailand which adds up to ninety-two million thighs."

The eminent sociologist was, says Meisel, "a droning, pontificating bore whose expertise went no further than having interviewed several fundamentalist Protestant missionaries in Africa." The sociologist windily strove to gain Shriver's approbation by dropping deliberately "show-off" social science phrases such as 'cognitive dissonance,' punctuating every other fog-shrouded point with a coy, condescending "and parenthetically, for your purposes . . ."

On this occasion, Shriver achieved a record on the "pencil signal" scoreboard. "Sarge broke three of them in two minutes," says Meisel. "One, crack . . . two, crack . . . three, crack. On the third crack, the guy got the picture. He might speak no more. It was all over. I mean, it was just *all over*. The guy was dead."

Meisel recalls the aftermath of such situations: "The offender would hang around for a while, hoping for a second chance. He would cringe around the walls for a time, and then disappear.

"You see," says Meisel, "if you muffed it at a senior staff meeting, you became an instant walking cadaver. It was really quite a cruel reality."

In the early days of the Peace Corps, says Meisel, "when Shriver was in fact the brother-in-law of the Sun King, I used to think of Saul in the Bible. The Lord turned his face away from Saul, and Saul went around the rest of his life saying, 'What did I *do*? What did I *do*?' He never knew quite what he did."

Another quick route to a windowless office at the Bureau of Mines was to deny Shriver one of his pet public relations gambits. "His mind churned out thousands of these ideas a week, it seemed," says Meisel, "and he would pop them on anyone at anytime. You might get a call at midnight or at 7:00 A.M. He might collar you in the men's room. He didn't appreciate a negative reaction; he didn't *understand* a negative reaction. He was crazy about these ideas, and many of these ideas were, in fact, crazy. He might hit you with three or four of them at one time. When he did, you had to think fast. You had to argue him out of the most undoable ones, but you had to pick one that had some remote possibility of succeeding, and usually that was his favorite one, thank God.

"At a staff meeting in the summer of 1961, Sarge looked around the room with a glint in his eye, which always meant he was about to pop one of his wild ideas. You could read your colleagues' minds: 'Here it comes, but where's it going to land?' "

On this occasion Shriver asked, "Who's the training officer for Nigeria I at UCLA?"

"No way out of it," says Meisel. "I said that I was."

Shriver then said, as he always did, "You know what would be a great idea, Al?"

Shriver had read in the sports pages that morning that a Nigerian middleweight boxer named Dick Tiger was going to fight in Los Angeles the following week. "Since this guy, Dick Tiger, is fighting in Los Angeles just when our first group for Nigeria is training there, why don't we get the trainees to wear Dick Tiger T-shirts and go out to the fight and cheer him on?"

Meisel says, "I just thought, Oh holy God. This can't be real. Wait until the director of Nigeria I program out at UCLA hears me laying this one on. He'll think I've gone nuts. And everyone around the conference table was already rolling their eyes back into their heads in disbelief and sympathy, so glad it wasn't them."

Meisel got up his courage and called the training director for Nigeria I at UCLA. "I said, 'Look, you'll never believe this but Sarge Shriver wants . . .' "

The training director at UCLA didn't believe it, couldn't believe it, wouldn't believe it. "He was almost screaming," says Meisel. "He thought it was the silliest thing he'd ever heard. There was no money for this, he said, and no time for this, he insisted. No way to do it. Can't do it. Won't do it."

Meisel, although full of pain and embarrassment, replied icily, "Look. Sargent Shriver is the director of the Peace Corps. He *wants* this. And he wants press coverage. You can't say you won't do it; you can't even say you will maybe *try* to do it. You have to *do* it."

Poor guy, thought Meisel. He wasn't hired to do public relations acrobatics. He was hired to train Peace Corps Volunteers how to teach English to Nigerian youths. He'll need some help. He's probably having a nervous breakdown right now.

Meisel convinced Shriver to fly him out to Los Angeles to help pull off the stunt. The press were alerted "and actually seemed quite charmed with the idea," says Meisel. Fifty Dick Tiger T-shirts were produced in small, medium, large, and extralarge. The Peace Corps trainees, according to Meisel, "were warming to the idea, getting into the good-old-Sarge-Shriver spirit. I was amazed. The training director at UCLA was much more amazed. And by God, we got those kids on two buses, they went to the fight, had prime seats, the press covered it, they cheered on Dick Tiger of Nigeria, and whadaya know, Dick Tiger won! And everybody got the point."

"I was right," says Meisel, "in thinking that it was a crazy idea in the first place. Sarge was right in seeing its potential, its value to the Peace Corps image, *if* it worked."

"It was almost impossible to deny Shriver his fancies unless you knew how to handle him, which I didn't," says Meisel, "or if your job put you in constant contact with him, which thank God mine didn't. I traveled all the time. And after the Dick Tiger episode, which succeeded against all odds, I stayed out of Shriver's sight when I was infrequently at headquarters. Sometimes I actually hid from him, so sure was I that he would ultimately cause me to make a fool of myself. But Ed Bayley and Tom Mathews were always being hassled." Ed Bayley, being closer in age to Shriver than most of the staff (Shriver was born in 1915, Bayley in 1918), could say a peer's *no* to Shriver and could also invoke his journalist's ethics in such a way as to make Shriver back off from some of his more far-fetched publicity schemes. Mathews's strength was that he could kid Shriver out of his wildest notions; he had a comedian's timing and could divert Shriver's attention. Shriver would go away happy, believing that he had convinced Mathews to commit whatever wild whim he had conceived on the spur of the moment. Mathews counted on Shriver's forgetting what he had just proposed and Shriver usually did. But Tim Adams remembers an occasion when Bayley got trapped.

"Shriver called Bayley saying that he wanted an editorial in the *New York Times*. Now, the *Times* had been consistently good to the Peace Corps from the first, almost too good to be true," says Adams. (In 1961 alone, the *Times* published 209 items about the Peace Corps.) But Shriver wanted more. Bayley demurred, saying that it simply wasn't ethical to lean on people who wrote editorials, that it could easily be taken as greedy and undignified, especially by the *Times*, the "newspaper of record," which had already sent many bouquets to the struggling Peace Corps. In addition, reasoned Bayley, the Peace Corps' place in the Third World was far from being cemented; the handful of programs were brand new. Wasn't it a bit early to toot the horn so loudly? Shriver ignored all of these caveats, commanding Bayley to "call John Oakes! Bayley was very sheepish and embarrassed about calling John Oakes," says Adams, "and he would not have done it except that Sarge kept calling him every ten minutes to see if he had done it. Bayley told Oakes that he was calling at the request of Sargent Shriver and Mr. Shriver wanted an editorial the following day. Oakes said, 'I'm terribly sorry, Mr. Bayley. It's too late for tomorrow, but we can do it the next day. Would that be all right?' "

Bayley, dumbfounded yet relieved, called Shriver and told him that his wished-for editorial in the *New York Times* would appear miraculously the day after tomorrow. Bayley expected some sign of gratitude. Shriver merely chirped, "See? That wasn't so hard, was it?" (Bayley retired in June 1985 as founding dean of the Graduate School of Journalism at the University of California at Berkeley.)

There was an interlude beginning in late 1962 that became known as the "Year of the Buzz Bomb." It did not last very long, for reasons that will soon be apparent, but it is vividly remembered. The "buzz bomb" was not fundamentally revolutionary; it was merely an intercom system that connected Shriver instantly with staff members he most frequently needed to reach. The system worked in only one direction: Shriver to staff; not in reverse. To have a "buzz bomb" on one's desk conferred status, of course, but many were asking, "What price status?"

Donovan McClure, in his position as a key public information officer during the first two years of Peace Corps operations and as a frequent traveling companion of Shriver, had a "buzz bomb." He describes it as making a sound that was "sickening."

In a meeting that Shriver was aware of but did not attend, "the 'buzz bomb' would inevitably go off," says McClure. "And it didn't ring—it *went off*. Those who weren't too secure would lose muscular control upon hearing it, start twitching violently in some cases. Even those who were quite secure were pretty badly jolted for a moment. It wasn't a fingernails-on-the-blackboard noise, but it had the same effect. The secretaries were just terrified of the thing. They wouldn't pick it up; they were too paralyzed by the sound of it. They knew it was Shriver in person, that he wanted something impossible. They knew that they couldn't help him; they knew he didn't want to banter with them, and they didn't want to banter with him, either. They kind of liked to worship him at a distance, but they wanted no part of the 'buzz bomb' scene. So, when it went off, they'd jump up and come screaming after us.

"They would try anything to find us. They'd come pounding on the men's room door, pleading for us to come out quick, that the goddam *thing* was going off."

By various accounts, the *thing*, the "buzz bomb," made a sound that resembled one of the following: "WhooAhhhank," "Waaannnknh-ugh," and "the sound of a really terrifying death gurgle combined with a scream from the attic."

Nan Tucker McEvoy had a "buzz bomb" in her office in her capacity as head of the "Talent Search." (She had originally been deputy director of the Africa Regional Office.) The "buzz bomb" so little became her persona that it was almost ludicrous; people constantly remarked on the incongruity of the "buzz bomb's" ugly, vulgar sound emanating from the desk of the agency's resident patrician.

Because Nan McEvoy was charged with finding people for overseas staff positions, Shriver called her with stunning regularity. "I heard that horrible sound several times a day for over a year. It was always a hideous prelude to an impossible request. I learned to cope with it by counting to five very slowly every time it went off so that I wouldn't sound addled when I answered. I'd just say breezily, 'Oh, hi, Sarge. What's up?' And he'd say, 'Nan! Listen! We've gotta have a Portuguese-speaking basketball coach for Brazil.' "

Was the "buzz bomb" a sick joke? Did it reveal a not totally repressible devilish streak in His Bubbliness (a Shriver nickname that made the rounds for a time)? Nan McEvoy and Don McClure think not.

"Why would a delightful guy like Shriver want to be represented by the most revolting sound on earth?" asks McClure. "Besides, Shriver did not go in for practical jokes."

However, Bill Moyers did, no doubt as a result of having spent most of his adult life to date practicing Texas and Washington politics, a combination so fraught with intrigue, pressure, quixotic behavior, and high-wire stunts that one could easily get addicted both to danger and absurdity. Moyers had a frisky way about him but you had to have a mad gleam in your own eye to notice it. Those who noticed that "young Bill Moyers," as he had gotten tagged by not just a few members of Congress, enjoyed sophisticated mischief were "even younger Dick Nelson," as he had gotten tagged by the Peace Corps staff, and Blair Butterworth, who at twenty-three had been classmates at Princeton. Nelson was Moyers's assistant. "Bill had to have someone around who was younger than he was." But no one knew where Nelson's office was and Nelson had fun keeping it that way. Butterworth's father was ambassador to Canada at the time but Butterworth blithely says, "As I recall, I was a file clerk." (He now runs a political consultancy firm in Seattle.)

"One Sunday in the fall of 1961," says Nelson, obviously warming up to some kind of revelation, "Moyers came over to Blair's and my little house at Two Pomander Walk in Georgetown. Judith (Moyers's wife) and the kids were visiting relatives in Texas. We decided that Bill was too much the Baptist and we ought to teach him how to drink. After a couple of drinks, I did my imitation of JFK and Blair did his of Bobby Kennedy. Bill thought this was uproariously funny. He said, 'Dick, why don't you call Warren Wiggins and pretend you're the president?' I said that Warren would smell a rat and just hang up, so what would be the fun? Then I voiced a sudden horrible thought: 'But what if he *believed* me?' Moyers replied, 'Then we'll *really* have some fun.'"

Butterworth remembers Nelson dialing Wiggins at his suburban Virginia home and in the purest possible Kennedy tonalities saying, "Uh, this is the president. Is Sahge theah by any chahnce?" According to Butterworth, Wiggins's wife, Edna, who had answered the phone, "went berserk, as who wouldn't? And shouted, hand over the mouthpiece, 'Warren, get out of the shower! It's the president!' With which Nelson says, 'Mistah Wiggins, I am looking for Sahge. Do you know wheah he is?' Warren crisply says, like the good trooper he is, 'No, sir. But I'll find him, sir.' Hangs up. We'll never know exactly what happened next," says Butterworth. "But Warren must have called the White House because those White House operators were famous for being able to find anyone, anywhere in the world. He finally gets connected to Sarge. He says, 'Sarge, this is Warren. The president's looking for you.' And Sarge says, 'Warren, someone is pulling your leg. The president is right next to me. I am in his car.' We heard about that part later because Warren did tell a few people he had been hoodwinked, and of course, Shriver was *there*. But at the time, Moyers, Nelson and I are just collapsing, thinking how hilarious it all is. When suddenly Nelson says, 'Hey, the Secret Service can't trace that call, can they? What about the FBI?' Then we got panicked. We pulled down the shades. We shook. Were they coming after us? Moyers suddenly got up and just flew out of the house. He races down to Peace Corps headquarters, signs himself in, back-dates the time two hours so it looks as if he was at the Peace Corps at the time of the call. And when Sarge calls a senior staff meeting the next day and complains that somebody has been imitating the president on the telephone—and that it must be somebody on the staff—Moyers immediately speaks up and volunteers to get the FBI to find out who did it!"

Nelson told the comely Carol Welch, one of Moyers's two secretaries, the story, swearing her to confidentiality. Welch promised to let Nelson know if there were any further repercussions. "There weren't," says Nelson, "but for weeks, Blair and I thought we saw Secret Service agents everywhere. Moyers made it worse by saying things like, 'Hey, who's that on the corner? Why is he looking at you so suspiciously? Wasn't he sitting next to us in the restaurant?' " Nelson and Butterworth did not do their Jack-and-Bobby routine again—at least, socially—for almost a quarter of a century. (In 1963, Nelson went into the Marine Corps. He is now an investment banker in New York. Butterworth became a Peace Corps Volunteer in Ghana II and is now head of a political consulting firm, FDR Services, Inc. in Seattle.)

♦   ♦   ♦

March 1, 1962, was rolling around and everybody at Peace Corps/ Washington knew what *that* meant. Happy birthday, dear Peace Corps. A year had been survived. There were over one thousand Volunteers in fifteen countries, with another twenty-nine hundred in training for seven more countries.

A few days before the first anniversary, McClure gathered the male San Francisco contingent for lunch to decide how to celebrate. The male San Franciscans, McClure, Tom Mathews, Tim Adams, Jim

Walls, and George Kittell, agreed that they would get some wine and cheese and try to have what they called "our famous San Francisco French bread" flown in from one of their favorite San Francisco restaurants, La Trianon. McClure recounts:

I gave the owner of La Trianon, Jean LaBriatt, a call and told him we were planning a little surprise party for Sarge Shriver to acknowledge the Peace Corps' first birthday and that we'd love some of his fantastic French bread. Could he have it flown in? Would he let me know when it would arrive? I'd go out and get it. He was very enthused, very flattered, and promised to do so.

The morning of the anniversary, we were thinking about ordering the wine and cheese and having everything ready in the fifth-floor boardroom. Later that evening, we'd call Sarge in and toast him.

All of a sudden, at about 11:00 A.M. in rolls all of this heavy equipment—hand trucks with ten ducklings, vegetables, dessert, you name it. And of course, the San Francisco French bread. Right off the elevators onto the fifth floor. My God, we were so flabbergasted. What had happened was this: Jean LaBriatt had decided that for his old friends, for the Peace Corps, for Sargent Shriver, it had to be nothing but the best. He had brought a beautiful menu, and he himself arrived cradling some special kind of lettuce in his arms. He had brought staff, tablecloth, flatware, everything. He had arranged for some ovens to be brought in to cook the dinner.

He had arranged for the West Coast PR man for American Airlines, Tom Barber, to get involved. He brought Art Hoppe, the *San Francisco Chronicle* columnist, with him. He was going to put on, by God, a sit-down dinner for twenty. Jean paid for it all. He absolutely insisted. He was so honored to be asked to participate. He said it was the high point of his life.

There were Tom Mathews and me, standing there at the elevators, watching this stuff roll out. It was a terror-stricken moment for us. We were so totally embarrassed we didn't know what to think, what to say. And we sure as hell didn't know what we were going to do, because here's the Spartan image of the Peace Corps, people are out rotting in the jungles, and here we are with *canard à l'orange* and cherries jubilee being flown in from California. Tom and I went out and had several drinks.

The next day, Deputy Director Paul Geren was showing some nuns around headquarters. The nuns wanted very much to see Shriver's office, or at least, get as near to it as possible. Geren explained that he was not allowed to take groups into the director's office, but he could show them the conference room where Mr. Shriver and his staff made all of their "important decisions."

Geren opened the door, stepped aside, and gestured for the nuns to enter ahead of him. Immediately, cries of shock and disbelief were being emitted by the good sisters. Geren peered in and himself issued a gasp of genuine horror. There lay the remains of what appeared to have been a regular Roman orgy. Empty wine bottles and duck carcasses.

Geren hustled the nuns back out in to the hall, gasping, searching his mind for an explanation: "Mr. Shriver is away—someone has used his conference room for a private party. Shocking! I'm so very sorry. This is terrible, terrible. Now, let's go up and have a look at the Selection office." After some sleuthing as to the perpetrators, Geren called Mathews and confronted him. Mathews and the "San Francisco Mafia" would *pay*, he promised with blissful bitterness. Shriver would have to be told. Mathews shot back gleefully, in a deliberate parody of Shriver, "T'rrfic! Do it! *Tell* Sarge. We had to *drag* him away!"

◆   ◆   ◆

There soon came to be two things that the senior staff of the Peace Corps dreaded most: One was not being asked to accompany Shriver on an important overseas trip; the other was being asked.

To travel with Shriver had certain fantasy-laden, Hemingwayesque possibilities: snowy peaks, lush valleys, the heat of the desert, the hope of a glorious dawn over a campsite by a jungle waterfall, the thrill of paddling furiously through a rush of white water on an uncharted river, the certain knowledge that one would behave bravely and efficiently when the lion charged, unlike the doomed, weak-willed Francis Macomber.

However, tales of Shriver's all-work-and-no-play-or-even-sleep schedules had been going around since his invitation-hunting trip in May and June of 1961, and there were some on the Peace Corps staff who found these tales not just a little bit unsettling. Men ten and fifteen years younger than Shriver (who was forty-six in 1962) wondered whether the status-drenched invitation to travel with him was worth the bone-aching rigors and life-risking escapades that were apparently involved. Not to mention the element of fear. It wasn't fear *alone* that caused people to recoil from joining Shriver on a Third World jaunt; it was the double terror of imagining Shriver witnessing your weakness, watching in disgust as you helplessly indulged in craven behavior.

"I certainly didn't want to go on one of those wild trips," says Donovan McClure, who was as tall, strapping, and athletic as Shriver. "I hated flying. I still do. I mean, I really *hate* it. I am a white-knuckler. It's obvious. I can't fake it. And I'd been hearing all of those stories about how Sarge loves to fly, is crazy about it, nothing ever bothers him. He can take a *nap*, it was said, in a little Piper Cub when the plane is being flung all over the skies with horrible updrafts and downdrafts. I figured I could take the crazy workload, but I could never take the flying; and when you're traveling with Sarge, flying is the crux of it. With Sarge, you're in the air most of the time. I had good rapport with Sarge, and I wasn't about to destroy it by making a fool of myself on an airplane."

But McClure had no choice.

In mid-October 1962, President Kennedy stunned the nation and the world with his ultimatum to the Russians to remove their missiles from Cuba, or else. On the morning of the third day of the Cuban missile crisis, McClure's phone rang at 7:30 A.M. It was Shriver's ever-alert, ever-coping secretary, Maryann Orlando, saying that McClure should hustle over to the Department of Health and get certain in-oculations because he was leaving that night for East Africa with Mr. Shriver. "In my shock and panic at this message—and Maryann could really zap it to you in a crisis—I formed the brief but totally insane notion that with the Russian missiles pointed at us, Shriver, always resourceful, was aiming to set up a government-in-exile.

"I was watching the news when Maryann called. It was tense. God knows, it was tense. All of a sudden, those 1950s doomsday novels like *On the Beach* and *Seven Days in May* didn't seem so far out.

"But of course, I got my shots and packed my bags and flew up to New York that evening to meet Sarge, and as it turned out, Joe Colmen (director of research) and Joe Kauffman (director of training) were going along, too, thank God. They were thinking what I was thinking: Why East Africa *today*? It's easy to get paranoid during an international crisis if you live in Washington."

As the group left New York that night, neither McClure, Colmen, or Kauffman knew exactly where they would be landing in East Africa, or why, "and nobody asked Sarge that question," says McClure, "because you just didn't ask Sarge a question that you knew would sound so *dumb.*"

Over the Atlantic, with Shriver safely asleep—under the seats— McClure, Colmen, and Kauffman chatted sotto voce about the possible destination and mission ahead.* "Sarge was talking with Ethiopia at Idlewild," said Kauffman. "He's very concerned that Wofford is out there coping with nearly 300 teachers, which, if you can believe this, automatically doubles the number of secondary school teachers in Ethiopia. So you can bet Sarge wants to check this situation out, but we'll be going to other countries, because Sarge never goes to just one. But that's all I know."

◆　◆　◆

That was Donovan McClure's first trip out of the United States, as it was Colmen's and Kauffman's. And they were, indeed, headed for Addis Ababa, Ethiopia, with additional trips to Somalia, Tanganyika (now Tanzania), and Tunisia. As their plane flew on through the night, the three chatted about the weirdness of it all—this strange trip, the abrupt summoning of them to it that very morning as Kennedy was staring down Khrushchev over Russian missiles in Cuba. As they discussed the weirdness, their boss, the brother-in-law of the man who was staring down Khrushchev, slithered out of his sleeping space underneath the set of seats just behind them, looking, as always, fresh as a daisy, saying he had had a "t'rrfic nap," and wondering whether

*Shriver actually did sleep under the seats of airplanes. When later interviewed by a reporter from the New Yorker magazine, who asked why it was, as legend had it, that he could always appear so fresh after such grueling flights, Shriver explained calmly that such flights were not grueling to him, at all, that he found them restful, that he got more sleep than usual on these flights. Why? Because he had discovered a way to curl up under the seats and sleep for many hours, undisturbed. The New Yorker summarily printed a story that made Shriver seem eccentric and possibly given to prevarication. How could a grown man of six feet or over stretch out and sleep under the seats of a crowded airliner? When Shriver read the story, he was offended, and on his next trip to New York arranged to have a drink with the author, at which time he explained in detail how one did it: how to slide under, where to position one's head, how to point one's feet, what obstacles one should be aware of, and gave comparison figures as to which airlines had the better under-the-seat sleeping space. (TWA, apparently, had more under-the-seat space than Pan Am.) The New Yorker writer was convinced, and wrote a retracting story praising Shriver's inventiveness.

he could see all of the Peace Corps Volunteers in Ethiopia in four days, plus have some time with Wofford, plus see the emperor, Haile Selassie, in the same amount of time. "Sarge opened two bulging briefcases and went right to work," says McClure.

He asked me to come sit with him and help him comment on a massive pile of memos and reports that he had with him. But I never got a chance; Shriver was grabbing at those papers as if they were rolling off the presses, adding in the margins—or right on top of the copy—notes such as "Who he?" and "Why not?" and "Let's do it!" and "T'rffic!" (Sarge was aware that we had shortened that word to fit the way that he and the Kennedys pronounced it.) Then he'd say, "Howdaya think old so-and-so will like *that?*"

Sarge was convinced he could see all 275 Volunteers in Ethiopia, which of course was impossible, but he gave it a good try. He was racing around in a jeep from sunup to sunset, shattering the poise of countless Volunteers by suddenly appearing in their classrooms or at the doors of their houses, hand extended: "Hi! I'm Sarge Shriver. Greatameecha. How many students do you have? How many hours do you teach? Whereya from? Oh! I know that town. I know the mayor. I campaigned in Wisconsin for three weeks. President Kennedy is behind you all the way. Say, what's that on the blackboard?"

For Shriver, McClure, Colmen, and Kauffman, breakfast in Ethiopia would be a boiled egg in a government rest house. Lunch was a bottle of warm beer with Volunteers between classes. "Dinner was the one real meal, and frankly, I would have preferred another boiled egg or a warm beer," says McClure. "The local specialty in Ethiopia is something called a *wat*. It can be chicken *wat*, lamb *wat*, or beef *wat*. The *wat* is what makes it what it is—it's a highly seasoned stew of fantastic strength. I reacted to it more severely than most, since I have an unadventurous meat-and-potatoes stomach, anyway."

The group from Peace Corps/Washington had their first encounter with *wat*, in this case with chicken, on their second evening in Ethiopia. A relative of Emperor Haile Selassie's feted the Shriver entourage in Harar, 230 miles from Addis Ababa, in addition to the six Volunteers stationed there. "We were all seated around a banquet table," says McClure, when two large pots of *wat* were carried in. Bright, shiny ladles were provided. The princess was beaming, but I detected a look of keen interest that bordered on the sinister in the faces of the Volunteers as they watched Shriver ladle out a heaping bowl of the stuff. I poured mine over sparingly. Beside each bowl was a plate of bread made of local grain, rolled thin, like a pancake. It looked like one of Stan Musial's old sweat socks. Our glasses were filled with the local beverage, called *tej*, an orange-colored fluid. There was nothing for it but to begin, so I took a *tiny* spoonful of the *wat* and just burst into flames. Oh God, I thought, I'm going to *die*. I grabbed my glass of *tej* and took an enormous gulp hoping to douse the fire. I gagged. I was horrified. Could this be A. B. Dick correction fluid? Then I chomped on the sweat sock in desperation, and it stayed in my mouth like Plasticine. I was frantic. I looked at Sarge, who was at the head of the table, for a clue as to how to cope. Tears were pouring down his cheeks, so I knew he had dug deep into the *wat*. His glass of *tej* was almost empty and a huge hole had been chewed out of the side of the sweat sock.

But he was smiling. "That's real *stew*," he said, and the princess beamed more widely, and Sarge just went ahead with this culinary ordeal until he had finished everything. I finished half, explaining nervously that I was on a diet, under doctor's orders, and so forth.

After the meal was over, I looked around and noticed that the six Peace Corps Volunteers had hardly touched their food and were staring at Shriver with unabashed admiration.

On the fourth and last day of the visit to Ethiopia, Emperor Haile Selassie summoned Shriver to the Imperial Palace in Addis Ababa. Shriver had expected an invitation to the palace; all of the cables and other correspondence had indicated such a meeting would take place. But Shriver was not prepared for its being a highly formal occasion due to the informal nature of the Peace Corps, which had been repeatedly stressed by Shriver in every public statement; the Peace Corps would not dress or behave as U.S. embassy officials did. But no doubt the Emperor, in contemplating a proper greeting for the brother-in-law of the president of the United States, felt that protocol on such an occasion should be at its most precise.

"Sarge was usually wearing wash pants and sports shirts because he was spending most of his time in a jeep, bouncing around dusty roads to see Volunteers," says McClure. "And when he looked into that big bag of his, he mumbled. 'There's no tux, and I only have brown shoes. Hmmmm.' U.S. Ambassador Arthur Richards was then called. He offered to lend Sarge the necessary formal attire; the owner was an aide at the U.S. embassy who was said to be about the same size as Sarge. The outfit arrived, Shriver put it on, and—oh, God— he looked like Buster Keaton. The striped pants were too short. If worn normally, the cuffs missed the shoe tops by six inches. If he tugged the pants down to meet his shoes, the trousers left a wide expanse beneath the vest. But Sarge is a problem solver by nature. We were somewhat panicky, but Sarge then figured out that by pulling the trousers down to meet the shoe tops and walking slightly hunched over, it looked as if the vest and the trousers met in the middle."

Thusly attired and contorted, Sargent Shriver was ushered into the office of the Imperial Palace of Ethiopia's emperor, Haile Selassie, while his Peace Corps companions waited outside.

During their wait in a majestic hallway outside the office, Mc-Clure, Colmen, Kauffman, and Pritchard (Ross Pritchard had just flown in from Washington) were informed—by an obsequious junior U.S. embassy official who was the Peace Corps group's escort officer— that word had leaked out that the meeting between Mr. Shriver and the emperor was going extremely well and that their boss, Mr. Shriver, was making a fine impression on the emperor. The emperor was much impressed, said the escort officer, with Mr. Shriver's deferential manner. It was so sensitive of Mr. Shriver, he said, to bother himself to bow to the "Lion of Judah," as Selassie was also known. Such behavior indicated America's enormous respect for the venerable Ethiopian leader, and it also incidentally minimized the inevitable comparison of Shriver's tallness in comparison to Selassie's shortness. All of this bode well, said the escort officer, for the Peace Corps' fate in Ethiopia.

The Peace Corps group kept straight faces throughout this sincere, groveling recitation, nodding soberly and appreciatively. Soon Shriver, still hunched over, emerged from his meeting with the emperor and, with more cheery bravado than he probably felt after two hours of diplomatic ritual in spinal agony, announced that the Peace Corps group would now be given a tour of the palace.

"As we reached an outer corridor of the palace, a sort of colonnade bordering on a garden," says McClure, "we almost collided with a full-grown lion, attached to a small tree by a long rope, who was actually prowling the area pretty much at will. We all stopped in our tracks. Oh, God. What now?"

"This is Tojo," said an Ethiopian palace guard. "He is the emperor's favorite."

"Is it all right if I pat him?" asked Shriver.

"Uh, if you wish," said the guide.

Colmen turned to Kauffman and whispered, "What is the line of succession at the Peace Corps, anyway?"

Joe Colmen, a behavioral psychologist from New York, ran the Peace Corps Research Division. He was one of Shriver's foils who could, like Mankiewicz and Gelman, make Shriver laugh his great whooping laugh and cause him to make light of things in tense situations. Colmen was an obsessive punster and an instigator of mass guffawing at senior staff meetings. Like Mel Brooks, whom Colmen physically resembles, Colmen likes to see the group dynamic reach the brink of craziness. Like Brooks, Colmen likes to provoke "dangerous laughing." But as Colmen was now finding, face to face with Tojo, it was one thing to crack up Sarge in a staff meeting in the relative security of a Peace Corps/Washington conference room and quite another to find something amusing to say when on Instant Safari with Sarge. Colmen was thinking, as were McClure and Kauffman. "Ahhh, Francis Macomber wasn't such a sissy."

Colmen backed off to see exactly where Tojo's rope was attached, if at all. "God. This huge beast was tied to a tree that was only three inches in diameter, just outside the palace corridor, and the rope was yards long. I didn't like it.

"But Sarge, who has no fear, has patted the lion to no ill effect. The lion just stared at him benignly. Pretty pleased with himself, Sarge now says to the rest of us, 'Now *you* pat the lion.' And he says to the palace guide, 'My colleagues will now pat Tojo.' "

"Uh, if you wish," says the guide.

"I kept going to the back of the line, and would have preferred to go to the back of the lion," says Colmen.

"Then Ross Pritchard goes up and pats it, then McClure, then Kauffman. By that time, the lion is really getting *annoyed*. It's my turn. And how do I know? Maybe Tojo doesn't like behavioral psychologists. But you don't welch around Sarge. So I slowly reached out and put my trembling hand on Tojo's head, smiling very sweetly, and the minute I did, the lion let out the most enormous MGM roar."

Colmen jumped back as if on springs. Shriver roared even louder than the lion. Colmen, who had not been actually attacked, consoled himself with the thought, "Gee, just like staff meetings. I can even get a laugh out here."

When you traveled with Shriver, says Colmen, "you were always working yourself to the nub, or something dangerous and crazy was happening to you. It was true what Frank Williams had said: Sarge never stops. He doesn't need sleep, or if he does, he can sleep when the rest of us can't. He can sleep standing up; he can sleep in a jeep that is careening around; he can sleep on the floors of airplanes in turbulence; and he gets up at the crack of dawn, or before, and bounds off to Mass. He bounds back, and we go to work. It was all true; we had seen it all."

McClure says that Shriver "didn't carry money; he didn't worry about money. I think that he didn't know what it was, exactly. We'd breeze out of all of these flea-bitten hotels in Africa, right by the reception desk, and Sarge never paused to ask for a bill. He figured they'd bill the Peace Corps, I guess. He wasn't trying to get away with something; it just didn't occur to him to pause. The proprietors of these hotels didn't seem to mind; they were so honored that President Kennedy's brother-in-law had stopped their way. Did they render bills? I don't know. They probably didn't know how to. I later learned that the Kennedys never carry money, just as royalty does not carry money."

"But Shriver didn't behave like royalty," says Colmen. "He behaved like a Great White Hunter on safari with a bunch of dudes who were not quite up to it, which we often weren't."

"I once said to Sarge, in some African hotel, when we were all exhausted and hot, 'Sarge, why don't we just stop for a while, relax, have a drink or something?' Sarge said, in the jolliest way, 'Now, come on, Joe. You're younger than I am. Why cantcha take it? It's not so bad. You know, I work as a dollar-a-year man.' "

Colmen replied, "Yes, Sarge, and you are worth every penny of it."

◆   ◆   ◆

Wheels were up for Somalia, courtesy of the Somalia Air Force, which was said to consist of three careworn DC-3s, courtesy of the U.S. government. "We put our bags alongside of this awful-looking, beat-up DC-3 at the airport at Addis Ababa," says Colmen. "But once we got on board, we could see that there was no place to stow the bags. No shelves, racks, closets, cubbyholes, no overhead compartments. It was bare bones. No carpeting, no curtains. Our seats were being screwed into floor bolts, facing the tail of the plane. The seats were torn, caved in, grimy. The interior was filthy—hadn't been cleaned in years, if ever. There was this huge, burly, scruffy Somalian pilot who was just heaving our bags into the plane willy-nilly. It was clear that there would be no flight attendants, no food, no drink, no nothing. Just pure hell, going into nowhere."

Shriver walked around the plane, making upbeat comments about the durability of the DC-3, the "gooney bird" of World War II, recounting tales of how a DC-3 had once been known to "land itself" after a pilot had bailed out.

"Well, *nonsense*," says McClure. "The two Joes and Ross and I could see how bad it was going to be, even as our intrepid leader was acting as if he were doing an ad for the latest Oldsmobile for TV: 'See this, notice that; oh, so many magnificent features.' "

The Peace Corps five strapped themselves in. "The straps were frayed," says Colmen. "The buckles were weak and rusty. What a farce. What a horrible farce."

"Wheels were up, all right," says McClure, "but that's all. I mean, we did take off, and we heard the wheels clamp up into place, but what no one had ever told us was, when you take off from Addis Ababa, Ethiopia, you are at a very high altitude to begin with, and you take off over a cliff, and when you're over the cliff, the plane just goddam *drops*. You gain altitude in the takeoff, sure, but then you *drop*. It was really quite horrible, and I have never known anything worse."

When the drop occurred, just over the cliff, McClure was so undone that he was moved to curse Shriver, out loud, for his big suitcase; the suitcase out of which he never took anything; the suitcase that did not reveal a tuxedo, but only brown shoes; the suitcase that was so heavy, two men had to lug it out at every stop. McClure had come to hate and resent that suitcase, and now, he *knew* that that suitcase was dragging the pathetic Somalia Air Force DC-3 down. Death was moments away.

"When we dropped," says McClure, "the luggage was just flying all around the damn plane. I was in a terminal state of white knuckles. I was well beyond trying to conceal from Sarge my absolute terror. The two Joes and Ross were doing somewhat better, but not much."

"I don't think that we are gaining proper altitude," said Colmen in a soft voice.

"It's hard to tell, isn't it?" said Pritchard quietly.

"Sarge, we're in *trouble*," hissed McClure, through clenched teeth.

"Well!" whooped Shriver. "The only way to find out is to go talk to the pilot. Right?"

Colmen recalls that "somehow Sarge got to the cockpit, which was behind us, without falling down. It seemed as if he was gone for a half an hour, but maybe it was just a minute or two. When he returned to his seat on this roller coaster, he said nothing, opened his briefcase, and started reading memos and reports. We all started yelling at him: 'Sarge, *what the hell is going on here, anyway?*' "

Shriver looked up from his reading only to remark, "Oh. Well, I couldn't find out too much. The pilot is asleep and the copilot is reading."

"We all laughed hysterically," says McClure, "because we were, in fact, hysterical. But the plane almost immediately stabilized."

As it did, the burly Somalian pilot emerged from the cockpit carrying a plastic tray of paper cups filled with a liquid concoction that McClure says "resembled failed *tej*, a sort of orange glue. To be polite and to take our minds off the whole horrible experience, we accepted it. It was awful, but we gagged it down, thanking him profusely." Thinking that he had done the Peace Corps group a great kindness, the pilot returned three more times for refills. "We never refused," says McClure. "We'd just throw it back, gag, and hope that our apparent gratitude would inspire him to keep the heap in the air. When he came out the fourth time with more of the stuff, just delighted with himself, Sarge said out of the corner of his mouth, 'Is there any way we can lock that door?' "

The plane landed at dawn "at some absolutely godforsaken place in northern Somalia," says Colmen. "We had to refuel for the next hop to the capital, Mogadiscio, to the south. We'd had no sleep, no food, no water, no coffee in hours—only that hellish orange glop. But we were glad to be on land with Sarge for a while instead of up in the air with Sarge, especially in the kind of air we'd been in, which was also hellish. Sarge, of course, looked as if he was ready for a screen test, and the rest of us looked like shell-shocked combat troops. As we got off the plane, we looked around, and I don't suppose that any of us had ever seen any place more bleak or depressing. The end of the world. 'Moonscape' is too cheerful a word for it. We were in a dusty nowhere, surrounded by miles of desert. We had taxied up to two seemingly deserted ramshackle buildings. But at least we could get out and walk around."

Shriver addressed the pilot upon disembarking: "It must be tough, flying in this bad weather, all of this wind."

"Ah, no," the big, burly pilot replied with equanimity. "It's just these big old airplanes."

The Somalian Air Force pilot then said to Shriver: "Sir, your country gave us all of the planes that we ever had. Your country gave us three of *those*" (meaning the wretched DC-3 on which they had just flown).

"And that's the last one we've got."

"We were ushered into the other ramshackle building next to the so-called air terminal," says McClure. "It was called a 'rest cottage.' It had nothing but a table and some chairs; it was totally down at the heels. Everything about it was worn out, falling down, decaying, dirty. Yeah, the end of the world. But at this point, even Shriver was beat. I see the sign. I reach down into my bag and I pull out that fifth of scotch—Ballantyne's Scotch—that I had reserved for an emergency. Even Sarge, who hardly ever drank, looked pleased to see it. We would like a cheeseburger, a shower, clean sheets. But no hope of same for days and weeks to come.

"When I pulled out the bottle of scotch, I said wearily to Sarge, 'Sarge, will I be named deputy director?' "

"*Yes!*" replied Shriver without a moment's hesitation.

The scheduling of the trip to Somalia was dictated as much by the alleged ineptitude of the Peace Corps Rep there as it was for Shriver to visit Volunteers. A preliminary report from a Peace Corps official who had recently done the rounds of the Peace Corps in East Africa had indicated that the Rep in Somalia was doing a poor job of administering the program and that the Somalia I Volunteers were miserable, as Gelman had earlier reported them to be in training at NYU.

Ross Pritchard, who had joined up with Shriver and company in Ethiopia, had been tapped as the replacement for the Rep in Somalia, should Shriver find truth in the dire rumors. Pritchard, who had been happy in his job as planning officer at Peace Corps/Washington, was none too happy about the report that had described Somalia as he had just seen it: "desolate, dusty, bleak, truly underdeveloped."

"Poor Ross Pritchard," says McClure. "Sarge had hauled him out of Washington via a cable from Addis Ababa to get there fast. He would have to take over in Somalia. Somalia was going wrong. The fact is, we had heard dire reports about the Peace Corps project in Somalia when we were in Addis. The Peace Corps staff in Ethiopia would say to us, 'Geez, have you been to Somalia yet? It's a disaster. You gotta pull that guy out.' " Ross Pritchard had arrived in Ethiopia the day before the Peace Corps/Washington group departed for Somalia. "Imagine how Pritchard felt," says McClure. "He had been suddenly yanked out of Washington, had been flying for eighteen plus hours, and had landed in such a strange place as Ethiopia only to find that his pals had been patting lions and eating fire, and then, the next day, he is transported on a terrifying flight to a country that God forgot, and he may have to *stay* there."

David Gelman had been surprised that so few Somalia I trainees dropped out before going overseas, and he was even more surprised that so few had dropped out once they actually got there. The Somalia I trainees had now become Somalia I Volunteers. There were forty-five of them who were teaching mathematics, science, biology, English, and carpentry. They had been in the country three months by the time Gelman arrived to do a follow-up evaluation of this program in the field, which coincided with Shriver's trip. By the time Shriver's entourage arrived in Mogadiscio, Gelman had personally met and talked with every Volunteer in Somalia I. That was Gelman's style in any case—to focus intensely and patiently on the individual Volunteer. He did not have much taste for discussions with ministries of health and ministries of education. He was not interested in bureaucratic discussions about program structure. The Somalia I Volunteers were rumored to be in a state of misery bordering on the mutinous, and the administration of the program was said to be bad, bordering on disastrous. "There wasn't much to discuss," says Gelman. "I just needed to get the Volunteers' story."

"I didn't remember these Volunteers very well," says Gelman.

I had spent only three days with them at NYU eight months before and had done other evaluations in between. This was a teaching project. I found that many of them liked their jobs well enough; that wasn't the problem. But they hated Somalia, and it wasn't difficult to see why. Somalia is a very hard country. The Somalis are very tough people. The conditions there were probably the dreariest I experienced anywhere in Africa, but that wasn't the real problem, either. We had already learned that the Volunteers who served in tough places—where there was a lot of physical hardship—came to like it *because* it was hard. It ultimately made them proud. The marine mentality. But they hadn't been there long enough to form this mentality.

No, the problem was, as rumored, the Rep. The irony is, this man looked and acted in so many ways like the ideal Peace Corps Rep. He was big, attractive; he had an easy drawl. He was an outdoorsman; he had been a sheep rancher in California. He rode horses the way he drove jeeps—at full tilt. He had tremendous physical courage. He had even been a congressman. He was smart. He had a sense of humor. He was a sweet, lovable guy. So how could he be a disaster as a Peace Corps Rep? *How?*

Well, here's how. This man hated the Volunteers. He had absolutely no patience with them. He thought they were just a bunch of culture-shocked, spoiled crybabies. This man could not tolerate the fact that the Volunteers were having trouble adjusting, were griping and complaining about this or that. He could not *tolerate* this. He wanted very badly to make a success of his job as Rep in Somalia. He believed in the peace corps idea. But he could not be bothered with the Volunteers' problems; their problems sickened him, and by the time I arrived, he had, in effect, withdrawn from them. He wanted no relationship with them, and he had none. A Peace Corps Rep who has no rapport with, or even any basic liking for, his Volunteers is, by definition, a disaster.

I was torn. This man just fascinated me. He reveled in tearing up the countryside on a motor scooter, and this was rough country. I rode with him many times on the back of that machine, and it terrified me, but I admired his exhilaration and skill. The first time I ever rode with him, he told me to fall if he should fall, and how to do it. He was inexhaustible, and it was up and down on those rutted hills and zooming through towns, villages, tiny outposts. He would take me to see Peace Corps Volunteers, but he didn't want to see them himself. It made him too angry. I could tell he thought that I would come to see what he saw: a bunch of neurotic, infantile whiners. But that is not what I found. I found forty-five genuinely frustrated, underadministered people—in the most desolate areas of a rugged, *really* underdeveloped country— who needed a leader who cared something about them. And this man simply did not. Here was a potential hero who tore through the country on jeeps and motor scooters, who took all kinds of John Wayne risks, but who would not pause to hear them out. And that's all they needed: to be heard out.

Gelman tried to coax the Somalia Rep into accepting the frailties of persons not of his generation or of his "rugged individual" stripe. Gelman would say, "You've got to roll with it. This project is in its early stages—things will change, things will get better, the Volunteers will adjust; they have adjusted all over the world; it's not so bad, you know. Give them a chance. Just try to get on their wavelength."

But the first Peace Corps Rep in Somalia could not and would not and did not give the Volunteers a chance. He felt totally alienated from them, and vice versa.

When this Rep got the word that some of his Volunteers, posted in some desolate area in some nonadministered project in northern Somalia, were in a state of frantic discontent, he would send a deputy up to see them. One such deputy was a puritanical Protestant minister who had somehow conned his way into the Peace Corps by convincing the Selection Division that he was totally able to distinguish missionary work ("convert the heathens to Christianity") from the far more pragmatic, nonreligious goals of the Peace Corps. But this minister went up to a Volunteer site in northern Somalia, and, says Gelman, "he did no good whatsoever; he only made things worse. He was sanctimonious and terribly Victorian and was almost as intolerant of the Volunteers as was his boss."

Gelman, in his travels around Somalia, had to agree that the Peace Corps Rep in Somalia had a point: The Volunteers were ranting and raving to an extent that was extremely annoying, sometimes boring, and always enervating. But Gelman, who was endlessly fascinated by the individual Volunteer experience, came back from his travels around Somalia with the conviction that the Somalia I Volunteers were miserable because they knew that their Rep had no confidence in them and held them in so much contempt that he would not even deign to meet with them.

"This was not the way that the Peace Corps was supposed to be, and I knew it," says Gelman. "In my evaluation report to Charlie Peters, which of course Sarge would then read, I tried to be sympathetic in my treatment of that Peace Corps Rep in Somalia. I liked him; I appreciated his personal valor, and I did not want to do him in. But the fact is, he was all wrong for that project, or possibly any other.

"In any case, the Somalia Rep and his Volunteers were a colossal mismatch. It wasn't working; it was never going to work the way it was. It could only get worse. And so, I reluctantly recommended in my evaluation report that he be replaced, and ultimately, he was, as was the sanctimonious minister. I was told that the Somalia Rep returned home brokenhearted.

"He was my first victim. All Peace Corps evaluators have victims. It makes you feel just lousy."

But upon the arrival of Shriver and his entourage, it seemed for a while that the Somalia Rep would stay on the job in spite of Gelman's negative conclusion. Like Gelman, Shriver's first impression of the Somalia Rep was favorable. Shriver also found the man likeable and was impressed by his colorful background. Shriver, too, warmed to the man's intelligence and sense of humor. And certainly not the least of Shriver's interest in the Rep was his swashbuckling way with a motor scooter or a jeep.

With the Rep at the wheel, the Peace Corps group was whisked off to visit the infamously unhappy Somalia I Volunteers. "It was a mad, mad ride. The Rep had picked up on the fact that Sarge was the sort of fellow who, like himself, enjoyed taking some risks and going for broke, and he was showing off for Sarge," says Gelman. "While the rest of us were being jolted out of our senses in this old jeep, Sarge just nodded off at one point. Well, he didn't even *nod*. He just sat there bolt upright, closed his eyes, and actually went to sleep for ten minutes and awoke as refreshed and cheery as if he'd had eight hours of perfect sleep in the most comfortable bed on earth. None of us could get over it. I had heard that President Kennedy could also nap at will, but could he nap in a jeep careening over the ragged terrain of Somalia?"

Gelman recalls that Shriver had several tough conversations with the Somalia I Volunteers. "I had painted a very rosy picture of Sarge to the Volunteers. They were very eager to meet him. And I had thought that his bubbly, upbeat presence would boost their sagging morale. You could see their eyes light up when they met Sarge. They were so goddamn grateful to meet any authority figure, especially the big boss from Washington, when they hadn't even been visited by their Rep but once. But unfortunately, they were so demoralized from having no other therapeutic outlet except for me in three months, that they kind of let Sarge have it. And of course it all centered around their dislike of the Rep, who on this occasion, as well as on others, stayed in his jeep, avoiding contact with his charges."

McClure says, "The Volunteers were saying to Sarge, 'Oh God, this guy is so bad, so bad. He doesn't give a damn; he pays no attention; he has no respect for us. We never see him. And we have problems here, but he won't respond. This country is tough enough, and we need support, feedback. But there isn't any. So what are we supposed to do when the guy who is running the program isn't running it? When he hates our guts?' All that pent-up frustration and rage being directed at Sarge, the eternal optimist.

"But Sarge responded. He was concerned. 'Is it really so horrible?

You know, you people haven't been here very long. Everyone needs time to adjust. You're doing useful, important jobs. You are t'rrfic. How bad is this guy, anyway? *How* is he so bad? Be *precise*. What has he done that is really so terrible? What did you expect? What, exactly, do you want him to do for you? Did you come over here expecting to be pampered? This guy isn't evil, you know. He wants the program to work. He is a dedicated individual. He has lived a challenging life. He has been successful. He is no fool. He has the credentials. Be patient. Give it a chance. You have a great opportunity here. Make the most of it.'

"It was unfortunate that Sarge gave the most depressed Volunteers in the Peace Corps a locker-room pep talk. In trying to cheer them up and put the best light on things, which is Sarge's forte, he came across as glib, facile, even cavalier in his treatment of them, which just plunged them into a deeper well of despair."

But help was soon to be on its way. Once back at Washington headquarters, Shriver added up the negatives about Somalia I: the brief pre-Gelman report that told of trouble and discontent, the gossip about the Somalia Rep Shriver had heard in Ethiopia, the actual visit to Somalia with the unhappy Volunteers, and, finally, Gelman's much longer report, which delved deep into the problems there. Shriver made the decision to pull out the swashbuckling, jeep-driving, rough-riding, motor-scooting, sheep-ranching, Volunteer-hating ex-congressman. He was replaced by another Californian, Salvatore Tedesco, who had been Deputy Rep in Ghana, the Peace Corps' first program, whose early omens had been as bright as Somalia's had been gloomy. Tedesco was tough, voluble, and approachable—the right man at the right time to take on and to turn around the program in Somalia.

Shriver did an odd thing just before leaving Somalia. "He strode through the lobby of our hotel as we were leaving," says Gelman, "and startled everyone by throwing his arms in the air and shouting the African freedom call, '*Uhuru! Uhuru!*' I cringed. I was sure the Somalis would think he was making fun of their aspirations or that the brother-in-law of the president of the United States was nuts. Obviously, I don't have Shriver's uncanny instincts for public relations. Everyone thought it was *fine*. Great. There was even a sprinkling of applause. Smiles all around. This important man from Washington, D.C., had made them the ultimate compliment."

◆　　　◆　　　◆

The Tanganyika visit was vastly different from the one to Somalia. To begin with, the capital city, Dar es Salaam, was far more modern and western than Mogadiscio. That observation prompted Colmen to reply, "Look. Let's not get all carried away. Mogadiscio is *not* a hard act to follow."

In addition, the Peace Corps Rep in Tanganyika, Bob Hellawell, was a dapper, efficient young man who bristled with intelligence and energy. Shriver had personally recruited him from the Cleveland law firm of Jones, Day, Cockley and Revis to be associate general counsel in April 1961. At thirty-two, Hellawell was one of the youngest partners of a major law firm in the United States. Shriver considered him quite a "find." Before any Volunteers had finished their training, Shriver was discussing with Hellawell the absolute necessity of getting first-rate people to run the programs overseas. The Peace Corps would be *happening* overseas, said Shriver, not in Washington. Shriver mused that it would be no simple matter to lure fifty to one hundred highly intelligent, creative, and successful people out of burgeoning careers and lucrative positions to "pioneer" with a program in the developing nations, a program that had yet to be signed into law by Congress. But, Shriver added, this would have to be done in the next few weeks.

Hellawell replied, "Would you consider me?"

Shriver later remarked, "I was amazed—amazed that an honors graduate of Williams College, an editor of the *Law Review* at Columbia Law School (where he graduated eighth in a class of two hundred), a man clearly well on his way to the top of his profession, and a man who, just a few weeks before, had packed up his family and moved to Washington, would now ask to go to Africa for the Peace Corps. This," said Shriver, "was the spirit that got the Peace Corps going."

While many of the Peace Corps programs were primarily teaching projects, Tanganyika I was to be composed of thirty surveyors, geologists, and engineers. They were the first Peace Corps trainees to graduate, in this case from Texas Western University in El Paso, and the first group to be put through the "macho" paces at the Peace Corps' Outward Bound camp in Puerto Rico. Tanganyika was also one of the first Third World nations to have requested Peace Corps Volunteers. Tanganyika I was the first program not to be negotiated by Shriver personally and the first to be run single-handedly during most of its initial two years; Hellawell was on his own.* (The British-supervised

*There was another "first" attached to Tanganyika I: the first picture of a Peace Corps Volunteer at work overseas that the staff at Peace Corps headquarters had ever seen,

system of government was still functioning in Tanganyika on the eve of independence, and government officials there did not see why a large Peace Corps in-country staff would be needed; there seemed to be resentment of such an intrusion, even though the officials welcomed the idea of young American Volunteers with certain necessary technical skills. Compliance by Shriver on this score seemed the better part of wisdom, since Tanganyika's very early invitation lent credibility to the Peace Corps' ambitious, and announced, intentions. Shriver was grateful that he had such a proven "winner" in Bob Hellawell to send on this challenging mission.)

Shriver, McClure, Colmen, Kauffman, and Pritchard arrived in Tanganyika in early June of 1962 to find Hellawell, if slightly harassed and overworked, nonetheless confidently in control of his Volunteers and their various projects. The Volunteers were fully "employed" in work that was of tangible use to the host country and that could be judged as being useful to them in the future in their chosen professions. Roads and bridges were being built by the Volunteers, culverts were being installed, and the first of thousands of miles of surveys had begun. There were problems, though, such as the projects smacking too much of straight technical assistance—as was associated with AID—as opposed to the "people to people" involvement that was the central point of the Peace Corps. But that would change. Meanwhile, Shriver and company were delighted to find order and lack of Volunteer hostility and demoralization.

There were the usual grueling jeep trips to see Volunteers who were stationed in several sites around this country of some 300,000 square miles. Some of the terrain was sparse, but less so than Somalia. There was the relief of the Livingstone Mountains in the distance as the group drove through the famous Serengeti game preserve. The afternoon movie travelog of youth was made manifest; sightings were made—close up and far off—of giraffes, zebras, elephants, lions, antelopes, leopards, gorillas, ostriches.

"Sarge was going berserk," says Colmen, "and he was at the wheel, with Hellawell navigating. He was fascinated by anything that moved. So were we all—but, you see, not *that* fascinated—partly because we

---

which was reprinted on the cover of early publicity and recruiting brochures. The Volunteer was Eugene Schreiber, a tall, scholarly looking young surveyor with his transit. For a while, that picture typified the Peace Corps in the public's mind, and to the Peace Corps staff, that Volunteer was all Volunteers.

had had no time to find cameras and buy film for this trip, and he had, and partly because Sarge was the kind of person for whom every day was like Christmas morning. Sarge kept slamming on the brakes, jumping out, and photographing anything and everything. This was Sarge at his most Sarge: 'Wow, look at that! T'rffic! Gotta get it! Only be a minute.' And then he'd get up much too close to the creature or creatures he wanted to capture on film, and then he'd race back to the jeep and we'd roar off again. More slamming of brakes. More running around and snapping pictures. He was ecstatic. But we were getting tired of it. At one point, Sarge saw a very ordinary piglike animal over in some bushes. Not interesting. Slam. Leap. Snap, snap, snap."

"What is that thing, anyway?" asked Joe Kauffman with infinite weariness.

"I think it's a wild boar," replied Colmen listlessly.

"I think it's a crashing bore," said Kauffman.

Along the way, Hellawell had been shouting directions and tour-guide information. "He couldn't exactly be John Nesbitt of the 'Passing Parade'; the whole excursion was too jolting," says McClure.

Hellawell "ordered" Shriver to stop in a clearing surrounded by some shade trees, "convincing him by bellowing over the roar of the jeep's engine," says McClure, "that this was the nicest, coolest place anywhere around; that we could stop for some cool, cool water out of a flask and a snack."

Shriver was persuaded. The group piled out, gratefully gulped water, munched on mysterious sandwiches and questionable fruit, stretched their legs. "Fortunately," says Colmen, "there was nothing moving. No pigs, no zebras, nothing."

Suddenly, Shriver, who was looking about with binoculars, spotted some movement among the trees. "Who's that, do you suppose?"

"What do you *mean*, Sarge," asked Hellawell, not without a touch of exasperation.

"I see this guy walking through the trees. He's t'rffic! Take a look," said Shriver excitedly, handing Hellawell his binoculars. Hellawell saw what Shriver saw and became instantly furious. Hellawell saw a tall, strong, stately, and stunning Masai warrior stalking the territory, bedecked in an elegant robe, dripping with exotic jewelry, and carrying a spear that he seemed to be using as a walking stick.

"I see the guy, Sarge," said Hellawell. "And Sarge, that's all you should do, too. Just *see* him. Don't go near him. I can tell by his markings that he's a Masai warrior, Sarge, and the Masai are unpredictable. You don't mess with them."

McClure recalls feeling initial relief that Hellawell had been so stern in his warning. But that feeling shifted suddenly to one of total horror as Shriver broke loose from the group and headed straight into the clump of shade trees toward the Masai warrior as if late on his paper route.

The group watched helplessly as Shriver, who himself was attired much in the mode of a country-club golfer, strode directly up to the Masai warrior and thrust out his hand. "Sarge was always animated, and a seasoned political campaigner, and I suppose he was saying what he always said: 'Hi! I'm Sarge Shriver from Washington, D.C. Nicetaseeya.' The Masai couldn't have understood one word, but he suddenly broke into a big, friendly grin, and he and Sarge were just pumping each other's arms up and down, both of them just beaming," says McClure.

"Hellawell just cannot believe this. Then, Sarge marches this magnificent-looking ebony warrior over to meet us. And what do you know, Sarge is making formal introductions, and we are all shaking hands. We were all but clicking our heels and bowing, body language that everybody understands—we hope. Sarge hoots to Kauffman, 'Hey, Joe. We'll line up together and you take the picture.' "

The picture now hangs, much enlarged, in McClure's den in suburban Virginia. It shows an apprehensive McClure off to the left, eyeing the warrior warily, and Shriver front and center with his arm around his new Masai buddy (McClure says it looks as if Shriver is a presidential candidate who has just announced his choice of a vice presidential running mate whom he supports 1000 percent), and Colmen off to the right, smiling the forced smile of Dutch courage. The Masai himself is somber, dignified—as if he were suddenly aware of his new responsibilities.

The Masai then departed, with a few appreciative nods, and disappeared into the brush.

What remains foremost in the minds of the Peace Corps group is not so much their quirky encounter with the Masai warrior, but the vastness of Tanganyika, its striking variety of topography, the scope of seemingly endless sparse plains set off by the sudden emergence of snowcapped mountains in the distance. "The isolation of the thirty Volunteer geologists and engineers in Tanganyika overwhelmed me," says McClure. "I am a person who gets severe withdrawal symptoms—

chills and tremors—if I have to go two days without at least one informative daily newspaper. Our trip to East Africa was too action-packed, too stimulating, and too physically and culturally taxing—and often, too terrifying—to induce news tremors, but I kept thinking, everywhere we went, How do the Volunteers cope in such news vacuums? Nothing to chew on, no one to talk to. I was projecting my feelings silently, of course. I didn't want to express such a potentially demoralizing thought. I imagined, as we visited the Volunteers, that they must be suffering some version of my own pangs. I imagined wrong. No one seemed to be. They were having a personal, spiritual, life-changing experience that we had hardly dared hope for and one that we were then unable to grasp—except to acknowledge that it was real."

Since Shriver had been the driver on most of the Peace Corps/Washington forays to visit Volunteers in Tanganyika (and his companions the often alarmed passengers and/or victims of Shriver's exuberant way with a jeep accelerator), there was much talk about the roads in this quixotic and fascinating land. Any definitive volume on the Peace Corps experience in Tanganyika from 1961 to 1963 might well be titled *Roads* or *Lack of Roads* or *Weird Roads* or *Road Talk* or *All About Roads*—or even *Road-a-Mania*. (Shriver had once driven his Peace Corps pals into a murky river at full tilt because that's where the road went and abruptly stopped. But the jeep didn't. With the jeep mired in the mud, the group had to climb out and push the vehicle up on to dry land. "No big deal, when you travel with Sarge," says McClure, "except on this occasion we were being treated as stupid medical students by Joe Colmen, who, while he had a Ph.D. in psychology, did not have a medical degree. But he had been instructed by the Public Health Department in Washington to warn us of certain strange African diseases, mostly found in rivers. So Joe Colmen, who *did*, anyway, have the title of doctor, is yelling at us as we push the jeep out: 'You've heard of schistosomiasis—snail disease? Well, now you've got it. Count on it. You always wanted to die in Tanganyika? No problem.' ")

Shriver, who knew that his "karma" would not allow him to die in East Africa in a minor jeep mishap, yelled back. "C'mon Joe, shut up about snails and *push*."

As it happened, that night after the Peace Corps/Washington group arrived at sundown at a rest house where three Peace Corps engineers were quartered, an illness occurred.

"There was moaning and groaning coming from McClure, who

had the bedroll next to mine, in the middle of the night," says Colmen. "McClure was bleating, 'Joe—help!' I asked him what was wrong, and he said 'stomach cramps,' and I thought, Oh yes, the first stage of schistosomiasis. We are all doomed. But I didn't convey this thought to poor McClure. I told him I had just the thing for him. I fished around in my medical bag, and I *did* have a medical bag from the U.S. Public Health Service, which even contained quinine for malaria. But there was no electricity in this rest house, and I couldn't find the flashlight. I pulled out a bottle that felt like good old Pepto-Bismol, and I found a spoon, and I figured in my exhaustion and confusion that that would have to be that. Because there is no cure for schistosomiasis, anyway. I spooned it into Don's mouth—several spoonfuls. He dropped right off to sleep and seemed to be all right. So I went back to sleep."

The next morning, the entire group—the three Peace Corps engineers and the Peace Corps/Washington Four (Pritchard had since gratefully returned to 806 Connecticut Avenue, N.W., Washington, D.C.)—awoke to a glorious sunrise, fresh air, and blissful quiet. McClure was alive and even well. "Boy, oh boy, Joe," exulted McClure. "I feel great. What did you give me?"

Colmen looked around and found a bottle of high-strength cough medicine—heavily laced with codeine—and one sticky spoon on the floor.

"Snail oil," replied Dr. Colmen. "An antidote. Guaranteed to stave off schistosomiasis, which you obviously had."

"How can I ever thank you, Joe?" asked McClure. "Excuse me. *Doctor* Colmen."

"By never letting Robert Sargent Shriver, Jr., drive any damn vehicle anywhere, ever again, with you or me in it. Especially in Tanganyika."

"It's a *deal*," said McClure.

In an evaluation report a few months later, David Gelman commented upon the obsession with roads in Tanganyika, an obsession shared by Tanganyikans and visitors alike. Almost all of the Peace Corps Volunteers in Tanganyika were involved in building roads or in doing some kind of work that was related to road building.

Gelman wrote in an early 1963 evaluation report:

You don't begin to appreciate the significance of roads until you go to . . . Tanganyika, where the tarmac ends eighty miles out from the capital (Dar es Salaam), at Morogoro, and the rest is bush track or now-you-see-it-now-you-don't gravel surface meandering all over the countryside. People talk about roads in Tanganyika as Americans talk about baseball, integration, or good restaurants. You talk of roads in pubs, the hotels, the village store. You get up in the morning, stretch, look out the window, and wonder where the roads are going.

Usually, they're pretty bad. Under British rule, the Public Works Commissioner presided over a near anarchy. Headquarters had little idea of what its Regional Engineers were up to. Reconnaissance surveys were submitted to the Colonial Development Fund which forked over money—in limited amounts—virtually for the asking, and construction would then proceed. The resulting roads . . . were a sight to behold, if you could find them. Many of them seem to be trying to shake you off as you drive along. They wind endlessly. If an obstacle appears, no matter how slight, they build around it. When they should build around it, they build over it. A couple of roads run up grades so steep, nothing less than a cable car could traverse them . . . [One of the main objectives] was the construction and improvement of feeder roads to enable the small farmer to bring his produce to the main market centers.

Such had been the roads over which Shriver had driven.

The Peace Corps/Washington group noticed, as Gelman later reported in his 1963 evaluation, that the thirty Peace Corps surveyors, engineers, and geologists did not live lives of great deprivation by contrast to Tanganyikan technicians, who were few. The five Peace Corps geologists, in particular, who were engaged in mapping some ten thousand miles of the country, lived well. Their drill included six months of fieldwork and then a return to their headquarters to complete their maps and reports.

"During their field phase," wrote Gelman, "they lived rather like white hunters, operating out of a tent in the bush . . . [with a] driver, a guard, two [Tanganyikan] survey assistants doing low-level work, and a cook.

"The engineers and surveyors often lived under similar circumstances. They were doing reconnaissance and detailed surveys in every region of Tanganyika, plus a miscellany of actual construction jobs or construction supervision. All of them were based in comfortable housing, but roughly half lived in tents or rest houses in the bush from Monday through Friday and [then] returned to their homes on the weekend."

Shriver was enormously pleased by Peace Corps accomplishments and lifestyles in Tanganyika. The Volunteers indicated to Shriver what they later spelled out in more detail to David Gelman: They had been given more responsibility and experience in Tanganyika in a few months, than they could have gotten in the United States in ten years. (For that matter, Tanganyika was able to train only two engineers in one year.)

The day before departure from Tanganyika for Tunisia, the last scheduled "Peace Corps country" on this whirlwind trip, there transpired a nice moment on the top of a hill. McClure describes it:

> We roared up one of those incredibly steep hills in our jeep to a little house where just one Volunteer lived. He had no warning that we were coming. But we had heard about him, his isolation, his ability to go without speaking to another human being for two months at a time and his not minding it. [Gelman later wrote: "He was very closed-mouthed by nature."] He was a geologist, a young kid who was doing research on his own. How he survived, how he got food, we couldn't imagine. But he was there, and Sarge just had to see him. We had with us the usual sparse provisions—some pathetic snacks, a few Cokes, and water in flasks. This guy was totally surprised and absolutely delighted to see us. He told us that we ought to have a picnic, and he suggested a hill where we'd have a marvelous view of the plains and the mountains, and he offered us "a few slightly stale cheese sandwiches."
>
> As we sat there on that hillside eating our humble victuals, this Volunteer commented casually, "You know, your trip up here is amazing to me, but another amazing thing happened to me just a few days ago. Chester Bowles came through this area, and he heard that I was up here alone, doing geological surveys, and he made the effort to come up here and talk to me. He brought me these cheese sandwiches."

◆   ◆   ◆

Lee St. Lawrence, who had negotiated the Peace Corps program in Tanganyika and who was about to become the Peace Corps' regional director for the Far East, was then sent to negotiate the first Peace Corps program in Tunisia in late June of 1961. This program was to become the most complicated Peace Corps endeavor in Africa, and possibly the world. The first sixty-five Volunteers arrived on August

14, 1962, and were met by the acting Rep in Tunisia, Reuben Simmons. The group included heavy-equipment mechanics, architects, town planners, building-construction supervisors, and physical education teachers. They had been instructed in two languages—French, during their training program at the University of Indiana, and a smattering of Arabic after their arrival in Tunisia. The heavy-equipment mechanics had also taken training at the Caterpillar Company plant in Peoria, Illinois—the first time a Peace Corps training contract had ever been signed with a private business firm.

The astonishing diversity of skills, levels of education, social status, ethnic background, and age in this group guaranteed that it would present management problems galore. (And two more groups would be added to the contingent within a year: twenty agricultural workers assigned under the technical supervision of the United Nation's Food and Agricultural Organization and twenty-five nurses.)*

When the first sixty-five Volunteers arrived, Simmons was on his own, the lone administrator, with only Ralph Morris, M.D., the Peace Corps doctor, to complete the in-country staff. George Klein, who joined Simmons as associate Rep in mid-October 1962, arrived in Tunis only to be informed of three totally jarring and unacceptable facts: One, the Cuban missile crisis had begun; two, Simmons would have to leave Tunis at once and go out in the field to help with some serious settling-in problems among the Volunteers; and three, Sargent Shriver and his Washington entourage would be arriving in two weeks for a three-day look-see of Tunisia I, which was in anything but marvelous shape. Klein was charged with preparations for Shriver's visit.

Just a few weeks before Klein had arrived, the new American ambassador to Tunisia, Francis Russell, had flown into Tunis to take up his post at the U.S. embassy. He understood Klein's predicament,

---

*George Klein believed that Tunisia I contained an individual who must surely be the most original, unusual, quaint, and unlikely Volunteer in all the Peace Corps: "He was about seventy years old, he had been a farmer in Minnesota all of his life, and Tunisia was his first trip out of Minnesota. He spoke English with a heavy Norwegian accent—when he spoke. He had not been able to master a word of French or a word of Arabic. No one could understand his English. I only got one sentence clear: 'Need a space heater; room cold!' But he was a fantastic Volunteer. He worked in the port of Tunis teaching Tunisian workers how to repair heavy machinery of all kinds. He was an expert. His 'students' worshiped him for what he could do. And they learned. I had heard that he had barely made it through the selection process, yet here he was, one of our great success stories."

and Klein describes him as "a wonderful, wonderful, elegant, kindly, and intelligent man, and I was grateful that I would have his assistance in planning for Shriver's visit. But unfortunately, he had gotten the notion that I would be an authority on Shriver, which I was not in the least, having only met him briefly once. He was very keen that everything be perfect for Shriver."

Ambassador Russell asked Klein whether Shriver would like to stay at the embassy residence.

"Oh no, no," said Klein. "I'm sure he wouldn't. Shriver has made it a great point, you know, not to have the Peace Corps identified with embassy life in the host country. I understand that Shriver is very strict about the Peace Corps image. I have reason to believe that he might feel embarrassed or compromised if he stayed at your residence. I hear that he always meets with the American ambassador, and will accept an invitation to lunch or dinner at the ambassador's residence, but is dead set against being seen to live the life of an ambassador. You know, the Peace Corps is supposed to be very Spartan."

Klein says that it was difficult to say these things—that he dreaded offending the kind and courtly Russell—but that, at the same time, he was convinced that Shriver wanted to keep things simple, unostentatious.

"Well, then," asked Russell, "what do you suggest?"

Klein suggested that he might be hitting it about right to book Shriver and his companions into a good, but not elegant, hotel—that he find comfortable, but not fancy, accommodations for them. Russell reluctantly agreed, saying that one must do what seemed best, under the circumstances. "But," says Klein, "I could tell he didn't like it."

Klein made reservations at a better-than-average hotel. At the last minute, Ambassador Russell became anxious. "No," he said firmly, "It won't do. I cannot let this happen. I cannot take the responsibility for having a man of Sargent Shriver's high rank stay in a simple room at a hotel that is not also of high rank. It's just not suitable. His brother-in-law is the president of the United States. Therefore, he is an important emissary. How can we say that we have not done our best for him?"

Ultimately, Klein was convinced to book a suite for Shriver at a better hotel. He figured that if Shriver objected roundly, he, Klein, could aptly apologize and quickly make other arrangements. Klein was between a rock and a hard place; he could not offend the kindly, Brahmin ambassador, but neither could he present himself to his own boss, Shriver, as an insensitive, "worst case" Ugly American who hadn't grasped the basic Peace Corps message.

"I met Shriver, McClure, Colmen, and Kauffman at the airport on the last day of October 1962," says Klein. "I took them to the hotel where I had finally booked a suite for Shriver and a room for each of the others. They went their way. I took Shriver up to his suite. I didn't know in those days that you must check things out beforehand for big shots. I have since learned. But I hadn't surveyed Shriver's suite in advance."

Shriver walked into his suite, looked around, and said to Klein, "What *is* this?"

Klein felt frozen in terror for a split second. He then said, very evenly, "This is your sitting room. Ambassador Francis Russell explicitly instructed me to book a suite for you in the best possible hotel in Tunis. This is it.

"Shriver accepted this explanation. I set down his enormous suitcase and departed."

The next day, Shriver set off to visit Volunteer sites in the lead vehicle of a minimotorcade, a perfectly ordinary American station wagon, accompanied by Reuben Simmons—who had returned to Tunis to greet Shriver and take him through the paces—and Ambassador Russell. Two sedans carrying the Shriver entourage, George Klein, and an AP stringer, followed. As they moved out into the countryside, Simmons later told Klein that Shriver seemed somewhat uncomfortable at the idea of the motorcade arrangement, and once, glancing back, he noticed that a fourth car had joined the procession. He wanted to know who was in it, and why. It turned out to be a car full of USIA officials. Shriver bristled. "Get that car out of here! Send it back!" he shouted. The procession stopped, and the USIA men were persuaded to drop out.

The first stop was in a town called Sfax, where the group would visit Volunteer architects and town planners. Klein was carrying envelopes with the Volunteers' monthly stipends, which he left locked in his car. When the group returned from their visit with the Volunteers, they found the car had been broken into and the money stolen. Klein was not keen to have Shriver know this, and he didn't tell him. While Klein went running off to find a policeman, the station wagon with Shriver, Simmons, and the ambassador whizzed off for Monastir, the next stop.

"Suddenly," says Klein, "a big, hulking Tunisian cop appeared, dragging a teenage boy by the ear. He and a pal had done the deed, and the cop had seen them do it and had chased them on foot. The money was returned, but I had to go to the police station briefly, which meant almost an hour's delay in following Shriver to Monastir."

There was a girls' school in Monastir where some of the Volunteers were teaching physical education. Just as Klein pulled up, Shriver was walking out of the school with a good-looking, self-confident, young black female Volunteer whom Klein had not met for the simple reason he hadn't had time yet. He thought, "Well, thank God I've got her stipend with me, and I'll have to give it to her, but then Sarge will wonder why we deliver money in this fashion, and he will also discover I have not met this girl."

But there was nothing for it but to confront the situation. Klein went up to the girl, shook her hand, and said "Hi. I'm George Klein. I just arrived two weeks ago and I've been looking forward to meeting you."

Klein says the young woman was cordial and friendly, thanked him for her stipend, and said her name was Glynn Barr. "I was utterly aware that Shriver was taking in this scene with great interest. He gets it. A Peace Corps staff guy hasn't met one of his Volunteers.

"With a little twinkle, Shriver says, 'Oh yes, Glynn, I want you to meet George Klein, the associate Rep here. You see, Glynn, the reason that I travel from Washington to go on these field trips is to introduce my overseas staff to their Volunteers." He said it only half-jokingly; there was an edge to it.

"The following day, on the way back to Tunis, Shriver spotted a lone farmer in a field behind his plow. The motorcade came to a screeching halt, with Shriver leaping out of the first car. I wondered what was so fascinating. Don McClure explained that *everything* fascinated Shriver. So, we all scrambled up this muddy bank and out into the field. The old farmer looked terrified as he sees this band of Americans heading straight for him. He stood there, frozen, behind his ancient, rudimentary hornlike plow. Shriver indicated in sign language that he wished for the farmer to pull his plow. The farmer did so, eyeing Shriver with the utmost suspicion. God knows what he thought we had come for. 'Aha!' says Shriver, just delighted with himself. 'It has a steel tip, just as I thought.' "

On their last day in Tunisia, Ambassador Russell feted the Shriver party at an elegant luncheon at his residence. Later in the afternoon, the group drove out to Hammamet, a beautiful place on the Mediterranean where the government kept a villa for western musicians and writers to take up residence to do their work—an arrangement not unlike Yadow, the writer's colony near Saratoga Springs, New York. A formal tea was being held in Shriver's honor, hosted by high-level Tunisian government officials, cultural leaders, and bank presidents. "We were behind schedule, and I, as the advance man, so to speak, was already feeling embarrassed," says Klein. "But then, Shriver's car pulled over to the side of the road and stopped. Reuben Simmons declared that Shriver was feeling awful, seemed to be developing something akin to flu, was in agony, and they would have to return to Tunis. Oh, boy. So it was my unhappy duty to finish the drive to Hammamet, walk into that gorgeous villa, and tell two dozen of the top people in Tunisia that Mr. Shriver wouldn't be coming. You know, kill the messenger."

Dr. Ralph Morris attended Shriver in Tunis, and the next day Sarge was on his feet. It was time to go home. George Klein and Reuben Simmons took Shriver and his staff to the airport. It was early in November 1962, and the talk turned to football. McClure said, with a gleam in his eye, that he looked forward to three weeks of newspapers his wife, Maggie, had been saving for him. Shriver was uncustomarily quiet.

"But at the airport," says Klein, "there was trouble. Some Volunteers had showed up—some just to see Shriver, but a few had come to complain. Poor Reuben. Poor Sarge. One infamously articulate but malcontent Volunteer from Florida was there, leading the complaining session. He would not be stopped. He was letting both Reuben and Sarge have it. His plumbing didn't work, he was too isolated, he had grown up in Miami and couldn't take the boondocks of Tunisia, the language training had been poor, there was no lock on his door, why did he have to live in semisqualor, and on and on. Shriver was taken aback. Reuben said something about there being two ways to slice an apple, meaning there were two sides to every issue, and it depended upon your attitude.

"Shriver wasn't feeling well and he was fed up. He snapped at Reuben, 'I don't know what apple you are talking about.'

"The last thing I heard before they boarded the plane," says Klein, "was this exchange between Shriver and Colmen: 'I shouldn't have snapped at Reuben. He's got too much on his hands. But he'll have to get tough with that Volunteer. He's much too intense.' Colmen replied, 'No, Sarge. His problem is that he's *not* an in-tents guy.'"

Bill Haddad arriving in Arecibo, Puerto Rico, 1961

Barbara Wiggins (mother of Warren Wiggins) at age 65, rappelling at the training camp in Arecibo

Tim Adams, a Public Information Officer, deals with the press at New York's Idlewild Airport before the arrival of Volunteer Margery Michelmore

Margery Michelmore   PHOTO BY CARI MYDANS, LIFE MAGAZINE)

George Carter

Shriver and entourage arrive in Rangoon, Burma, in May 1961, on the fifth stop of a seven-nation trip to open the Third World's doors to the Peace Corps. Edwin Bayley is at far left, Harris Wofford is over Shriver's right shoulder, and Franklin Williams is to Shriver's left. Others are U Soe Tin, on Shriver's right, and Terry Sanders, Chargé d' Affaires of the American Embassy, far right   USIS PHOTO

Wofford, Shriver, and Bayley visit the Shwedagone Pagoda
USIS PHOTO

Peace Corps Volunteers bound for Nigeria on December 27,
1961, gather around a Christmas tree in the Pan Am terminal
at Idlewild Airport to serenade Director Shriver
PAN AMERICAN WORLD AIRWAYS PHOTO

Shriver meets Prime Minister Jawaharlal Nehru, May 2, 1961   USIS PHOTO

Young Bill Moyers, deputy director of the Peace Corps at "28½," the youngest presidential appointee in history

The pencil signal

Al Meisel

Shriver, in his borrowed trousers, meeting with Emperor Haile Selassie

Peace Corps Volunteer Glynn Barr, Ross Pritchard (over her shoulder), George Klein, Ambassador Francis Russell, Joe Kauffman, and Shriver in Monastir, Tunisia

Donovan McClure, Peace Corps Public Information Officer (left), looks uneasy, and Joe Colmen, Director of Research (right), smiles wanly, as Shriver surprises them with a no-nonsense Masai warrior in the Tanganyika bush

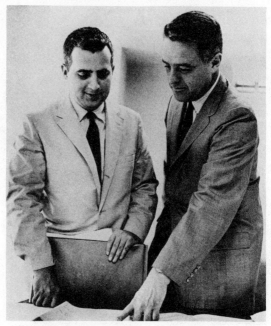

Charlie Peters, just named Chief of Evaluation, and Shriver plan the first around-the-world fact-finding trip

Dick Elwell, evaluator

Nancy Gore

Bob Gale

Douglas Kiker

CHAPTER 6

CHARLIE PETERS:
THE BURR
UNDER THE SADDLE

"You are an inch away from being fired."

This message was conveyed to Charlie Peters, the chief of evaluation, during the late summer of 1962, by his immediate boss, Bill Haddad, the associate director of the Office of Planning, Evaluation and Research.

Peters loved the Peace Corps and relished his job. He had put together the first self-evaluation unit in the federal government, and he was unabashedly proud of it. It had been Bill Haddad's idea to form such a unit. As an investigative reporter, Haddad hankered to go out and get the story, to dig for the truth even if, in this case, it was one's own truth—the truth about the Peace Corps. Haddad had told Shriver: "Let's get our own guys to go out there and find out what's goin' on, and if there's something wrong, we'll be the first to know and can correct it before the press gets onto it and starts screamin'."

It was also Haddad's idea to hire talented reporters to do the evaluations. He believed that academics, let alone bureaucrats, would get so mired in programmatical detail and plodding recitation that the people who would need to read the evaluations, and perhaps act swiftly on their recommendations, would simply start tossing them into the wastebasket. After all, there would be several hundred of these reports; one on virtually every Peace Corps project, just in the first three years; therefore, these reports must, above all, be readable, even entertaining—occasionally riveting and dramatic. "We want people to look forward to getting these reports, not dread them. We want them to be read eagerly and thoroughly because the true story of the Peace Corps will be in these reports," Shriver had told Peters when he first put him in charge of Evaluation. Shriver and Haddad then both recommended David Gelman to Peters; Gelman, they said, had precisely the qualities Peters should be looking for: He was a thorough and experienced reporter from a major city newspaper, a gifted writer, a man of wit and originality. Gelman became Peters's first full-time, on-staff evaluator.

Shriver, never blind to the glitter of celebrity, also urged Peters to hire popular and respected authors as consultant evaluators. It would be difficult to ignore the observations and recommendations of such vaunted scribes as Richard Rovere, Calvin Trillin, James Michener, Fletcher Knebel, and Mark Harris. Shriver intended that the Peace Corps be seen as a magnet to talent, as a source of fascination to people of immense storytelling ability, to political analysts, to historians, to wits, to men of letters. These men would, in turn, become advocates, fans, constituents, supporters. "Get the opinion makers on your side!" exhorted Shriver. And Peters did.

"But there was danger as well as beauty in telling the true story of the Peace Corps in these evaluation reports," says Peters. "These reports, whether written by me, my staff evaluators, or by well-known authors of the time, *did* focus on the reality of the Peace Corps, *did* present it, *did* define it—and of that, I am vain. But of course not everybody wanted to know the truth, or would accept it. So, in my first few months as chief of evaluation, it was always my word against the word of those who were conceiving and executing the Peace Corps' programs overseas"—namely, Warren Wiggins, associate director for program development and operations (PDO), his immediate deputies, and the regional directors (of Latin America, Africa, the Near East/ South Asia, and the Far East). The Wiggins coalition was a formidable one, and this was true not only at Peace Corps headquarters. The Peace Corps' overseas Reps, too, fell within the Wiggins coalition, a bureaucratic Goliath to Charlie Peters's David.

A year earlier, in the spring of 1961, well before Peters had been handed the hot but delectable potato of the Evaluation Division, he had found himself agreeing completely with Wiggins in an agencywide controversy over the eventual shape of the Peace Corps. There were options as to how the Peace Corps' programs would be administered. One option, popular and likely at the very beginning, was to contract out the majority of Peace Corps programs to the United Nations, the universities, and private agencies. This "establishment" view of field operations was for a brief time the prevailing one, because the agency had not yet got a sense of itself, of what it could do entirely on its own.

Peters was dismayed at that approach. "Here we had this new, miraculous agency," he says, "We had got hold of an idea that was golden—that had people banging on the doors to get in—and yet there was talk of turning the whole thing over to entrenched institutional bodies who hadn't had a new idea in years. Why would we do this? We had just fought our way clear of the clutches of AID, so why would we now say, okay, let's go the Boy Scout route? Furthermore, although I hadn't been in Washington very long, I could see that these outside organizational controls would rip us off. We'd just be a holding company. We'd draw up guidelines, hope for the best, and write big checks to private consultancies who had no real feeling for the movement. I could actually feel in my bones that Volunteer spirit out there just drying up. Warren Wiggins did too, thank God, because he had so much influence around the place."

Wiggins held many of the same views as Peters, and for some of the same reasons, but he saw them more graphically. Before Peters had been given his mandate to bluntly criticize Wiggins's programs overseas, Wiggins had already built an empire at the Peace Corps. He had gained control, as he had told Franklin Williams he would at the very beginning, of all of the money for overseas programming and all of the money for overseas travel. Wiggins saw that if multiple outside contractual arrangements were to be the case, his job would be dull and his power nil. Wiggins says, "I came from the bureaucracy and I knew how to staff up. I knew how to get my people in place and functioning, and all of my key people were from ICA and they also knew how to staff up and get moving. We were all experienced in mounting government programs overseas; we knew how to organize and roll ahead. We knew what expertise to draw on, what levers to press. We had our signals straight, whereas many others did not. The head of the Experiment for International Living, Gordon Boyce, wonderful man that he is, did not. Let's just say that if Boyce, whom Sarge had brought down from Vermont to be the first director of private organizations, had been able to staff up as fast and as completely as I was, the Peace Corps might have been very different. But Gordon did not think in bureaucratic terms.

"When Shriver left on his first overseas trip in May of 1961," says Peters, "Warren Wiggins and Bill Josephson immediately started a campaign to kill the option of U.N., university, and private agency control over programming. They gave very persuasive arguments against this option. I didn't need any convincing; I agreed with their view totally. They had little trouble lining up the majority of the staff on their side; Wiggins and Josephson were the acknowledged experts on the federal bureaucracy at the Peace Corps. And of course, Wiggins had a very vested personal, political interest in keeping control of the overseas programming. Franklin Williams was the main opponent, and a formidable one. But Warren was absolutely right, and I told him so. This was the right thing to do and the right time to do it, with Sarge out of the country." And in fact, the word was out that Shriver wasn't keen about this option, anyway—was losing interest in it—and probably hoped it would be shot down by consensus. The word was also out that Shriver had been recently made aware that the U.N. was not popular with Congress. Thus, Shriver certainly wouldn't want to be shackled to the U.N. when asking for appropriations from Congress.

Peters chuckles ruefully about his having been in such total agreement with Wiggins at this crucial time in the Peace Corps' development. While Peters instinctively grasped the perilous aspects of outside control, he also knew full well how awesomely powerful Wiggins would become as a result of retaining all control over programming. "And it all came to pass," says Peters. "Warren gained tremendous power, breathtaking power, during Sarge's first overseas trip in April and May of 1961. A virtuoso performance. He had taken the agency, yanked it around, shaped it. To his eternal credit. When Sarge returned, triumphant, having sold a world the Peace Corps, the agency was *formed*."

Peters and Wiggins began their Peace Corps adventure as friends. At the beginning, the Peace Corps was awash in idealism, hope, excitement, camaraderie. The Peace Corps staff at Washington headquarters, the Volunteers, the overseas staff were united in mutual admiration and congratulation. The energy-and-euphoria level was dangerously high; family men abandoned family for the greater glory of saving the world. Workaday mortals stalked the halls of the Maiatico Building, at 806 Connecticut Avenue, N.W., imbued with the notion that something akin to the Second Coming was at hand. Wives of Peace Corps officials frowned deeply and waxed cynical as their young husbands (their average age was thirty-three) embraced their new love object.

Charlie Peters would be excoriated by Peace Corps wives as the devil himself. He was the one who sent the thirty-three-year-old husbands off to India, Sierra Leone, Togo, Venezuela, Borneo, and Afghanistan for weeks on end. The wives stayed behind in a new city as lonely young "peace brides" and mothers with squalling babies, only to have their husbands return babbling about their exotic cultural immersions and the need to meet Charlie Peters's deadline for the big evaluation report that had to hit Shriver's desk in a week. These reports were labeled "Authorized Eyes Only." (Later the reports were verbally designated "Eyes Only"; and sometimes folks just said "Eyes.") "Big deal, big deal," the wives would mutter.

Dick Nelson, the twenty-three-year-old assistant to twenty-six-year-old Bill Moyers and recent Princeton graduate, always found the "sacred secrecy" syndrome amusing: "You'd think this place was the War Room of the Pentagon combined with the Vatican. Here I am, just a kid out of college in hardly an exalted position, but I was investigated by the FBI and the Civil Service as if I were very likely a double agent—just in order to walk through the front door. But I never saw anything you could call 'sensitive' or 'top secret.' The most exotic thing I ever saw was the burn bag. The burn bag was brought around regularly so that we could dump the carbons—there were no Xerox machines in those days—of our supposedly important papers into it, and then the burn bag was taken to God knows where and incinerated."

Nonetheless, some of the evaluation reports did contain sensitive material and "in-house" intrigue, and the "eyes" who saw them were very few; regular circulation was limited to only a handful of the top brass—those who had either the power or the responsibility to act on their recommendations.

At times, Peters and his evaluators, with their mandate to tell the truth no matter how painful, were required to recommend drastic restructuring of individual Peace Corps projects in which the Volunteers overseas were working, perhaps to eliminate them and to create new projects. Sometimes it was clear that a Rep should be transferred, demoted, or fired, and the same might be true of troublesome deputies and associates. Occasionally, an evaluator would happen upon a program so well conceived, structured, and administered, a staff so compatible and a group of Volunteers so well trained and highly motivated—all enjoying full and satisfying employment, all finding excellent rapport with the host country officials and its citizens—that the evaluator would be moved to write a report that amounted to a "rave review." But usually something needed fixing: too few nurses at one provincial hospital, too many community development workers not keeping busy enough in an urban slum, an inappropriately assigned Volunteer experiencing too much isolation, an unhealthy cliquish grouping of Peace Corps English teachers at an elitist urban university, Volunteers who were living in squalor they could not tolerate, Volunteers too bunched-up in a village too small to utilize their individual or combined talents, Volunteers merely living much too well for the "Peace Corps image."

Peters and Wiggins, both men of integrity and great intelligence, were offering, more often than not, opposing views of Peace Corps field operations. Who was right? Who was wrong? And why? Perhaps an evaluator, with his analytic mandate, was too rigorously critical, too carried away with his power to criticize any small imperfection in an operation that was characterized by its inevitable but charming imperfection. Perhaps Wiggins, with his powerful coalition, was too defensively subjective, having been charged with the conception and administration of the programs that Peters and his evaluators were now so free to criticize.

Thus, the relationship between the Wiggins coalition and Peters and his evaluators, which was built up over the months and years of Shriver's reign, became an acrimonious one. The adversary relationship was built in.

"It was hairy, and everyone who knew anything about what was going on in the agency knew it was hairy," says Peters. There were screaming matches behind closed doors, behind half-open doors, and even in the halls. Haddad had set the style, feeling at all times free to yell and to employ florid language. Others followed suit. Peters was not confronted by Wiggins himself in the beginning; Peters did not at first have Shriver's full trust or a large enough power base to take on PDO at the top.

In spite of his problems with the powerful Wiggins coalition, Peters was gaining impressive respect among disparate but influential pockets of the senior staff and the semisenior staff. Peters would say a blunt, fearless, unequivocal no to Shriver when others were saying yes or sure or why not? He would go against the whole staff in a meeting with Shriver without getting pugnacious, confrontational, or rude.

"Frank Mankiewicz, Joe Colmen, and Dave Gelman used the technique of joking and joshing and punning Sarge out of a wild idea or impossible project," says Don McClure. "Tom Mathews and I used the same technique. Sarge liked to have a staff meeting break up on a note of hilarity, anyway. But Charlie was the one to say 'No, Sarge, it just won't work.' He marshaled his facts like the lawyer and politician that he was, spoke in a soft southern accent, and was very lucid. Charlie never pandered."

Still, Peters daily confronted the spectre of getting his walking papers. The fellows in PDO never ceased to want his head, never ceased to hope and plot for his removal as chief of evaluation. If the PDO coalition could not get rid of the Division of Evaluation—because they knew that Bill Haddad had utterly convinced Shriver of the need for such a division—then at least they knew that, by the most clever and relentless of machinations, a more benign, more malleable, and less self-starting character than Peters could be found to do the same job.

"It got to the point," says Peters, "where I knew that even though it was clear that some of the PDO people respected me and even kind of liked me on a social level, they wanted me out, and the sooner the better. I was feeling harassed and scared of their hostility to the point that I'd avoid them, those PDO people, when I saw them coming down the hall. I'd duck into the men's room or slip into someone else's office. I didn't want to think about them, and I didn't want them to think about me."

The peak of the adversary relationship between Peters and PDO came soon after Peters had finished writing evaluation reports on several early Peace Corps programs. "I had committed myself to finding a view of the reality of the Peace Corps. In early March of 1962, I left on a very long trip; I visited the very first Peace Corps programs in Ghana, Nigeria, West Pakistan, East Pakistan, Thailand, and Malaya. I had already been to the Philippines and Saint Lucia. I felt that I was able to say to Sarge, in effect, Here is the truth about the Peace Corps. Here's what works, here's what doesn't, and here's why. Much of what I saw overseas was amazing and inspiring, and I said so, but I wrote a pretty devastating report on the first Peace Corps programs in East and West Pakistan, which I did find appalling, and I recommended in this report that the person or persons who were responsible for conceiving it and organizing it ought to be fired for lunatic stupidity. Only fifteen out of sixty-one Volunteers had real jobs. Within a month of my delivering it to Sarge, the people who were responsible for mounting and administering this program were fired. Sarge had acted on my recommendation. And one man who got the ax was in a rather senior position in the Wiggins coalition. So now the PDO people *really* hated me, were out to get me. Sarge had taken my word over theirs. They were livid."

Peters says that the reason a program could go bad, stay bad, and not reach the attention of Shriver was that there was a conspiracy of silence. Peace Corps Reps wrote monthly reports, but the reports from Pakistan reported nothing amiss. Host country officials did not write to Shriver and complain. Their feelings were that they didn't want to offend President Kennedy. Without the benefit of an evaluator on the spot, seeing things as they really were, it all looked rosy. "This happened time and again," says Peters. "Sarge was deceived. I was deceived. Even people in PDO at headquarters were deceived at times.

The host country governments—the whole free world—was in love with John F. Kennedy, and nobody wanted to displease him. If I had not gone out when I did, on that long trip in 1962, I wouldn't have known. The PDO man who was ultimately fired for the mess in Pakistan knew what was going on, but he wasn't telling anybody. Talk about gilding lilies—when you got down to where lilies were being gilded, you found out that there were no lilies."

It was in the late summer of 1962 that Peters got the grim message from Haddad: "You are an inch away from being fired." The PDO people were converging on Shriver and finagling for Peters's ouster. Haddad was arguing Peters's case, but the opposition was formidable.

"I sat down at my desk and drew up a long, two-columned, ten-page memo to Sarge," says Peters. "I knew that I was in mortal peril and thought that the Division of Evaluation was in mortal peril, as well. So I laid it all out. I wrote on one side of the page what PDO was telling Sarge, and on the other, what I was telling Sarge about these first Peace Corps programs. Needless to say, these two accounts were mostly in opposition. I ended this memo by saying, in effect, 'I realize that there is disagreement as to what the truth about the Peace Corps is. But only you can decide what is right. I believe that you should go out almost immediately and have a look at our field operations. Observe closely; talk to the Volunteers, who are themselves the truth, and then come back to this memo and compare what the Division of Evaluation says to what PDO says, and decide which is right.' "

In October 1962, on the cusp of the Cuban missile crisis, Shriver took off from New York's Idlewild Airport with Donovan McClure, Joe Colmen, and Joe Kauffman in tow and with Ethiopia, Somalia, Tanganyika, and Tunisia on the schedule. Peters's "last ditch" memo was in Shriver's briefcase on this trip.

Peters had reminded Shriver of David Gelman's training evaluation on Somalia I at NYU, which had pointed out negative attitudes, unpleasant episodes, low morale. It was Peters's theory, borne out time and again, that if a training program did not go well, if the about-to-be Volunteers did not form a team feeling—and worse, developed a certain prejudice toward the country to which they were headed for two years, as had been the case with the Somalia I group—the program could not possibly begin well and might not find its footing till near the end, if at all, even with brilliant administration—and the latter element was said to be woefully lacking in Somalia.

Peters had used the example of Somalia I in his memo to Shriver to point out the disparities between what PDO was saying about its programs and what he, Peters, was saying about them. It was now for Shriver to see for himself, with special attention to the situation in Somalia. Luckily for Peters, David Gelman was already in Somalia doing an extensive evaluation and would be concluding his analysis just as Shriver and his entourage arrived. Shriver, Peters knew, was already well acquainted with Gelman, liked and respected him. And Gelman had gained the reputation at the agency of seeing and speaking the truth and as someone who had a therapist's gift for drawing out the Volunteers. And now Peters's destiny would be decided seven thousand miles away, on another continent, with David Gelman as his best and only witness to the truth as Peters perceived it. Gelman was now seeing at first hand what Peters suspected about Somalia, and had heard rumored. If Gelman was concluding that the Somalia program was a mess, or even worse than Peters had suggested to Shriver in his ten-page memo, then Peters was exonerated and due for true baptism. But if Gelman saw a much rosier side to the situation than Peters had portrayed, that would surely reduce Peters to less than an inch from being fired. Maybe an eighth of an inch. Maybe less. Peters could not pick up the telephone and dial the Peace Corps Rep's office in Mogadiscio, Somalia, not only because it was technologically impossible to do so, but also because, even if it were possible, most likely Gelman would not be there—and even if he was, he would not be able to talk freely. In any case, Peters knew that Gelman could not and would not pull back from any position he had taken, would not lie to Shriver to save Peters's job, would not play games. Better not think of it, any of it, Peters concluded. Gelman was now God, in effect; he had the power to determine Peters's fate.

As noted in Chapter 5, the Somalia program was indeed a sorry one, and a good bit more so than Peters had even suggested in his "last ditch" memo to Shriver. Gelman had interviewed each and every Somalia Volunteer—had told Shriver unwaveringly and relentlessly of their misery—and Shriver had gone out into the field and seen and heard it for himself, as well. Unbeknownst to Gelman, Shriver sent a cable out of Mogadiscio to Washington, D.C., saying this: "Tell Peters his reports are right."

Peters's previous anxiety stemmed from many roots. He did not much fancy the practice of law, and he did not want to return to it—not at the Peace Corps, not anywhere. He did not want to return to the West Virginia State Legislature, where the issues at hand were local and parochial compared to the global ground he was now dealing with. In addition to having a law degree (from the University of Virginia), Peters had a masters degree in English (from Columbia). He was at home with the written word; he enjoyed writing and editing and was adept at both. As a lawyer, he had been trained to dissect. "But of course," says Peters, "everybody likes to dissect, whether they are any good at it or not. The trouble is, nobody wants to be dissected. So, on the one hand, I had it made—I was doing exactly what I wanted to be doing with my life, on top of which I was serving a cause that I truly believed in and thought was critically important. Living in Washington during the Kennedy years was a giddy experience. Working for guys like Shriver and Haddad was exciting beyond belief. Having all those tremendously talented journalists and authors working for *me* was glorious. And yet, I lived in terror for many months. I lived in terror of losing it all, all of the time. Because I was the whistle-blower, albeit an *appointed* whistle-blower, I became the hated guy, the guy who said what was wrong—who was *hired* to say what was wrong. So if I was not hated personally—and I believe I was not—I was certainly roundly hated for my role. And I became so established in my role, so quickly, that I really was the guy you loved to hate."

The evaluators liked each other enormously; they saw each other socially, and their wives became close friends. "Their favorite sport was to complain about me," says Peters, not without a measure of pride.

They even complained in front of Beth. But that was okay. Beth complained, too. The rhythm of an evaluator's life could give anyone cause for complaint. My first year was a killer. June 1961: two trips to Puerto Rico, three to four days each. July 1961: a ten-day trip to Berkeley, California, and El Paso, Texas. August 1961: Notre Dame in South Bend, Indiana, and Ames, Iowa, to Iowa State University—all training programs. End of August: to Penn State for Philippines I training and to Harvard for Nigeria I training. Back to Washington to be present for the White House send-off receptions of the first groups going to Ghana and Tanganyika. September 1961: out to Colorado State. On the plane coming back, I ran into an old friend from Charleston who asked, 'How's Beth?' My answer gave him quite a start: "Threatened." October 1961: it was Michigan State in East Lansing and then to the

University of Michigan for Thailand. Back to Washington. Then in November 1961, I was off to Saint Lucia for my first overseas evaluation of a Peace Corps program. December 1961: out to the Philippines for my second overseas evaluation. January 1962: back to the University of Michigan for the Thailand training program graduation. Took a month's leave to sit in on the West Virginia legislature. Then in March 1962, I began my long trip from Washington to Ghana to Nigeria to West Pakistan to East Pakistan to Thailand to Malaya. I did an evaluation on each trip and was gone for seven weeks.

The extent to which Charlie Peters found himself in opposition to various elements of the extended Peace Corps "family" is succinctly summed up in remarks made twenty-three years later by Thomas Quimby, the first Peace Corps Rep in Liberia, the first Peace Corps Rep in Kenya, and later the Peace Corps' regional director for Africa at Peace Corps headquarters.

Tom Quimby is a man of the "old school"—tall, courtly, precisely spoken, orderly of mind and manner, obviously well bred and well educated. If he were introduced to you as an ambassador, as a deputy chief of mission, or as a headmaster of an elite New England boarding school, you would think to yourself, Oh, but of course. Quimby was aware that Kennedy-style political gamesmanship and sometimes violent in-house power struggles went on at Peace Corps headquarters, but he did not indulge; it was not his style; his metabolism and belief systems rejected shouting and going for the jugular. Still, he was, by definition, a member of the Wiggins coalition.

"Charlie Peters could never understand why I was so vehement about some aspects of his operation," says Quimby. "He couldn't understand why I was so critical of his methods and his observations, or why I took issue with him so often. He chafed at the fact that I had written a thirty-page rebuttal to Sarge defending myself against certain negative statements made in his division's first evaluation report of my program in Liberia. He couldn't understand why I thought that many of his evaluations of other projects were unfair, because he believed, above all else, that he and his evaluators were fair. Awfully tough sometimes, he would admit, but *fair*, he would always insist."

A division of evaluation, Quimby says, "was, I feel, in retrospect, a very good thing to have. It's good to have a burr under the saddle. And Charlie Peters was certainly a burr.

"But one of the things that bothered me was the emphasis on getting good writers to go out in the field and write highly readable reports, rather than getting good developmental people to go out and analyze the development problems. I thought that too much attention was being paid to getting down on paper the fine phrase that would titillate Sarge. I realize that's how you develop a constituency, without and within, and for many of those fashionable writers who got exposed to the Peace Corps in the field, it was no doubt a good education for them. But I did then and I do now question the emphasis on readability over serious, deep analyses of development problems in these countries."

Peters would remind the PDO people, the regional directors, or the overseas Reps, that he had not hired "a bunch of innocents or a bunch of troublemakers." His evaluators were, he would constantly insist, "damn bright people—the best I can get—and they are as keen to see the Peace Corps succeed as anyone." But PDO versus Evaluation was a fight that had no end—and could have no end.

Peters took immense pride in producing a written history of the Peace Corps. A record. The true story. He liked to think that future researchers and writers would read these evaluations with admiration, if they were ever made available to the public (as they now are, in expurgated form, through the Freedom of Information Act). Peters can admit that not every evaluation report contained unassailable truths; it was altogether possible that an evaluator might have misunderstood or misread apparent programmatical problems, might have misinterpreted a situation in the field, or could have been manipulated by the Rep. Still, he was stubbornly and utterly convinced that his reports contained as true a picture as was possible.

Peters's first three evaluators were David Gelman of the *New York Post*, Philip Cook of the *New York Herald Tribune*, and Timothy Adams of the *San Francisco Examiner* (who would later serve as Rep in Thailand). Peters then hired Richard Elwell, who was living in Los Angeles and working for the Ramo-Woolridge Corporation after having worked at the *San Francisco News*. Elwell had worked with Haddad on a California congressional campaign in the early 1950s. He came to the Peace Corps at Haddad's bidding; he made a sudden announcement to his wife that this was going to happen, and in five days he had packed up the family, sold his house, and driven east with his three young sons, while his wife, Patty, flew east with their two-month-old son. Elwell had not been told what his job would be, and he had no place to stay when he arrived in Washington, but he, too, wanted *in* and had simply yanked up his roots and got on with it. A man of no frills, an Iowa native who eschewed elitism and luxury, Elwell (and his sons) had camped out in sleeping bags along the way. "We spent New Years Eve, December 31, 1961, sleeping on the ground by the Salton Sea near the Arizona border."

When Elwell arrived at Peace Corps headquarters, he was first interviewed by Dick Graham, "a selfless self-made millionaire, I was told, who had left the corporate life to serve the Peace Corps. People told you things like that immediately and all of the time at the Peace Corps." Graham, says Elwell, "sat on a chair in the middle of a cluttered room and I sat on a box. He asked me where I was living. I said, 'Well, that's a good question. Nowhere exactly.' " Graham said, "Oh, well, then, just move in with us." Elwell couldn't get over his magnanimity, but adds, "That's how it was in those days at the Peace Corps." Elwell was then interviewed by Charlie Peters, who quizzed him about his job goals at the Peace Corps. "I suddenly realized that I didn't have a job. I was only being *interviewed* for a job. But I trusted Haddad. I knew I'd be okay."

Peter hired Elwell at Haddad's urging, but had no trouble in deciding to do so, as Elwell was obviously a competent writer/editor and had an originality (which would today be described as Garrison Keilloresque) that Peters saw would pay off well in the psychodynamics of the Evaluation Division. "Politically, I was very naive, and Charlie found that intriguing, given the power struggles he was engaged in. Charlie would often say things like, 'You certainly do have a peculiar view of the world.' But he wouldn't fill me in."

When it came time for an evaluation of the Peace Corps program in British Honduras (now Belize), Peters never considered anyone for the job except Elwell. "It's a funny little enclave," says Elwell, "which probably wouldn't have gotten a Peace Corps program if Willy Warner hadn't been on the staff. Willy was an expert on Latin America and he had an eye for all things quirky." Warner had become fascinated by British Honduras, sometimes called the Mosquito Coast, a country the size of New Hampshire which borders on Mexico, Guatemala, and the Caribbean Sea of which Aldous Huxley once said, "If the world has any ends [the British Honduras] would certainly be one of them." There were only twenty-six Volunteers in this land of 140,000 people who were descended from English pirates, African mahogany cutters, Spanish-speaking mestizos from Yucatán, German-speaking

Mennonites, Mayan Indians, and seagoing Caribs. And the Volunteers there "certainly weren't high achievers or worriers. They were in fact people who'd been assigned to other Latin American countries but who couldn't learn Spanish," says Elwell, laughing.

These were mostly nice but forgettable country kids. But the two most memorable Volunteers I ever met, I met there. Two grown women, both of them retired schoolteachers. One was a black grandmother from California in her fifties. The other was seventy and white. They shared a little cabin in a little town called Silk Grass. (Other places in British Honduras were as quaintly named: Guinea Grass, Orange Walk, Hummingbird Highway, Monkey River Town.) There was a problem in the cabin because the black lady liked listening to hymns and preaching on the local station and was being formally courted by the local postmaster who would come and sit in the parlor. The white lady enjoyed getting stoned and listening to opera on an old Victrola. As luck would have it, I arrived in Silk Grass on Opera Night. The white lady had also invited a Dr. Connally, the Peace Corps doctor who doubled as a mechanic for Peace Corps vehicles, and one of her students and her mother. She was a punctilious hostess, saying, "We have to start at 7:00 P.M. on the dot because the opera lasts two hours and the electricity goes off at 9:00 P.M." The temperature was 98 degrees Fahrenheit and 98 degrees humidity, and we are all crammed into this little room. Dr. Connally turns to me and says, *sotto voce,* "What do we do if the electricity *doesn't* go off at 9:00 P.M.?"

The next day, Elwell accompanied the doctor on his rounds. Stopping at another Volunteer's cabin, they heard on a shortwave radio about the Cuban missile crisis. "Oh God," moaned Elwell, in an attempt to apply some gallows humor to a sudden attack of panic. "The rest of my life in Silk Grass listening to *Götterdämmerung.*"

In mid-1963, Peters hired Kevin Francis Xavier Delany, a tall, slim, handsome young man from CBS News who had become a boy wonder of publishing in the mid-1950s. He had a front-page byline at the *New York Telegram* when he was only twenty-six—a feat in those days—and his future as a "hotshot" seemed assured. He came to the Peace Corps on his own; he wanted *in,* as others had, but did not have specific Kennedy/Shriver/Haddad "pull" or important contacts in other influential corners of the Peace Corps.

When Delany got off the elevator on the eleventh floor of the Maiatico Building in May of 1963, a young woman whom he had known in New York in the mid-1950s spotted him. "F. X.!" she called out. "How great to see you. Are you coming to work here?"

"Well, I hope so," said Delany. "But it seems that I have to see so many people. I mean, two or three, okay. But why seven or eight?"

Delany's old friend from New York replied, "Kevin, this place is different from any other place. Remember, I worked for a fashion magazine for eight years; I grew up in a Republican suburb; my husband taught at a military academy. I was hardly the perfect Peace Corps candidate, and *everyone* wants *in* here. So you might ask how I did it. I did it because I wore my heart on my sleeve."

Delany looked annoyed. "I can't wear my heart on my sleeve. I'm not the type. But thanks for the tip."

By early afternoon, Delany returned to his old pal's office. "I am screwing up, I think. Things are not going so well in these interviews. They are giving me the fishy eye."

"Wear your heart on your sleeve," keened his old pal from New York.

Whatever Delany did next will never be known, but it got him the job. He became an evaluator within weeks and went on to be deputy director for the Peace Corps' Asian Operation and, ultimately, Rep in Thailand. Delany soon recruited Dick Richter, a former colleague at CBS News. Richter, like Delany and other evaluators, eventually succumbed to the Peace Corps adventure in the field and became a Rep in Kenya.

Peters also hired as evaluators Paul Vanderwood from the *Nashville Tennessean*, Herb Wegner from AID, and Thorburn "Trip" Reid from the American Bar Association Special Committee on World Peace Through Law. Shortly after the assassination of President Kennedy in November 1963, the first trickle of returning Volunteers found their way to Washington headquarters. They were looked upon as rare specimens. They were gawked at, worshipfully questioned. They were celebrities within a near-magical fellowship and much in demand. "I got my hands on two of the best," says Peters. "Mick McGuire from Pakistan I and Maureen Carroll from Philippines I."

McGuire, a native of Washington, D.C., had been one of the fifteen out of sixty-one Volunteers in the Pakistan program, which Peters had so unmercifully denounced, who had had a job by dint of his own efforts. He was sophisticated, smart and half the womenfolk at the Peace Corps were in love with him. (He later married the Belle of Ghana I, Georgianna Shine.) When Peters was interviewing Maureen Carroll with the thought of hiring her as the first female evaluator in his all-male den, he suddenly found himself so bowled over by her "maturity, wisdom, and humor" that he actually conceived of making her his deputy somewhere down the line. It was a revolutionary thought for the times, but most of all, it was revolutionary for Charlie Peters, who, along with Bill Haddad, had been targeted by Betty Harris—the keeper of the feminist flame, such as it was in the early 1960s—as a particularly egregious male chauvinist. ("Pig" was added in the early 1970s.) "Yet here I was," says Peters, "seriously thinking about making this twenty-three-year-old girl, uh, woman, my second-in-command. And this woman had never had a job before, other than having been a Peace Corps teacher for eighteen months. It was not out of any concern for feminism or to placate Betty Harris, who was always asking me, sarcastically, 'Will there ever be a female evaluator, Charlie? Will there?' I did it for myself. Maureen had tact, whereas I did not. She had stamina and courage, which the job demanded. She was interested in administrative work, whereas the other evaluators were not. She was not power-happy or bitchy, so she'd come across as no threat to the guys. Our secretaries, who were very bright girls, would not resent her for being so young to have such a big job, because in those days, returning Peace Corps Volunteers were looked upon as heroes and heroines.

"So, Okay, I'm a male chauvinist. But I was a pioneer in the bureaucracy. I gave high responsibility to a twenty-three-year-old female, and *nobody* else was doing that in 1963."

◆   ◆   ◆

"Charlie thinks we're the RAF and this is the Battle of Britain," said Phil Cook in early 1963. Indeed, there was an embattled quality to the Division of Evaluation at times. Frantic departures and arrivals to and from places nobody had ever heard of were the order of business. At first, the evaluators, including Peters, had to feign knowledge and even expertise about places called Togo, Cameroon, Somalia, Sabah, and Sarawak. And they had to produce what amounted to a Ph.D. thesis every six weeks. But journalists are "quick studies" and an inventive, curious lot, and they will, often as not, "Bugs Bunny" their way through peril and apparent impenetrability. They had to adapt themselves quickly to hitherto unknown countries, cultures, political systems, languages—and most important, they had to be able to grasp how American Peace Corps Volunteers were bouncing off all of these elements, including abject poverty, most of them during their last gasps of adolescence and within a period of profound social, economic, and philosophical change in countries that had never before experienced self-rule. And this, before the peace corps *idea* had been fully integrated into their intellectual processes.

One of the least troublesome and most amusing aspects of all of this complicated but fascinating newness was inventing a vocabulary to describe exactly what was going on. Peters admitted that he did not know, and he encouraged the evaluators to pound out on their new electric IBM typewriters (which none had ever seen or used before) what they had seen and sensed overseas, to exchange first drafts, to edit one another, and therefore to learn—to learn a common language, a viable Peace Corps Evaluation Division language, one that would persuade Shriver and the more specifically knowledgeable and ever-ready-to-pounce PDO crew that they rightly represented the "division of record." They howled with laughter as they struggled, and even "Napoleon Bonaparte Peters" was seduced out of his workaholic isolation to howl along with them. David Gelman, the first evaluator (and soon to replace Bob Gale as director of Special Projects), was everyone's most feared but favorite editor. "Who is infrastructure? What is she?" he wrote in the margin of one colleague's report. When the tone of a report went wrong—suddenly too pompous or too soupy— Gelman would simply write "GAK!" in the margin adjacent to the most offensive passage. But Gelman reached his height as an arbiter of the language of overseas development in one of the first evaluation reports on Nigeria. Gelman's fellow evaluator had written, "Peace Corps Volunteers are filling badly needed gaps in Nigeria's secondary schools." Gelman scribbled in the margin, "If these gaps are so badly needed, why are we filling them?"

◆　　◆　　◆

Peters had sailed into the Peace Corps in late March 1961 on a sea of misconceptions—his own and those of the people who counted at Peace Corps headquarters. Kenny O'Donnell had called Shriver saying that he was sending over Charles Peters of Charleston, West Virginia— a lawyer, a state legislator, and a member of a prominent family in Kanawha County—who had organized the president's successful primary campaign there. He was ready to give up an exceptionally promising political and legal career to be part of the Peace Corps; that is what he wanted to do most, said O'Donnell. O'Donnell could vouch for Peters, as could Larry O'Brien, Ted Sorensen, and Bobby Kennedy, all of whom had been impressed with Peters's performance on the campaign. By the time Shriver passed the word to Moyers, Peters had become a miracle worker and a genius. Moyers told his assistant, Nancy Gore, the Peace Corps' resident Scarlett O'Hara and female political sage (as the daughter of Tennessee's Senator Albert Gore), to go out to the elevators and greet "the man who carried West Virginia for Jack." Gore, expecting someone on the order of John Wayne, glanced at the short, vaguely roly-poly man with the racoonlike eyes and eyebrows whose cigarette was dripping ashes on his tie, and dismissed the possibility that he was Peters the Powerhouse of recent legend. But Peters asked Gore for directions to Moyers's office, and she realized that this was the man they were waiting for. Peters was immediately offered a job as a consultant in the general counsel's office, which Peters describes as "a position of almost pathetic obscurity when you consider the structure of a bureaucracy. I thought I was a patronage case pure and simple—you know, the poor idiot who had worked hard in some essential capacity. I figured Sarge had been *ordered* to take me. But what the hell, I thought. I had landed where I wanted to land. I had my foot in the door."

Kenny O'Donnell had advised Peters to get to know Bill Haddad because Haddad had "a lot of energy and is politically sophisticated," which implied, Peters thought, that O'Donnell believed Peters was going to need all the help he could get, which further fed Peters's feeling of being a patronage case on shaky ground. Haddad, however, was predisposed to be impressed. He had been in Shriver's office when the White House called, and if Bobby Kennedy, Haddad's boss on the 1960 campaign, was prepared to endorse Peters, Peters must be tops. Haddad further conjured up the notion that Peters must somehow have some very special "pull" at the White House if so many of the Kennedy insiders were willing to endorse him.

"I really liked Haddad," says Peters. "He was enormously tough and creative and self-confident, and of course I was not going to be fool enough to let such a guy know I felt even remotely insecure. Certain death. Haddad was at that time dreaming up a training operation in Arecibo, Puerto Rico. It sounded to me as if it would be a public relations dream come true if it worked, and if it didn't—oh, brother." Haddad wanted it launched officially as quickly as possible;

Governor Muñoz Marin had given Haddad his word that it would be done. But now, somebody had to negotiate the agreement with the attorney general of Puerto Rico. Haddad mentioned that the Latin world was not known for its efficiency; it was the land of *mañana*. So someone with legal skills and political know-how should be sent to bring off the deal. A two-hundred-watt light bulb lit up in Peters's head. Such a mission would have been the natural province of Bill Kelly, the Peace Corps' director of contracts. "But I knew," says Peters, "that Bill Kelly, however competent, had a healthy regard for making his 5:00 P.M. carpool and not working on weekends. People in carpools did not make policy." Haddad knew that since coming to the Peace Corps, Peters worked late, worked on weekends, and was always looking for more work. He was dangling some tantalizing bait in front of Peters. Peters was biting.

"So, feeling like Robert Morse in *How to Succeed in Business without Really Trying,* I said to Haddad, 'Would you mind if I went down to San Juan and did this thing?' "

"Go ahead, Charlie," said Haddad with a devilish smile.

"In those days," says Peters, "my zeal was going well past what I knew I was doing. And two days later, there I was, down in San Juan, Puerto Rico, in the reception room of the office of the attorney general of Puerto Rico, without any firm grasp as to what happened next. Fortunately, the A.G. was on a long lunch hour. I furiously started going through his law books, which were right there in the bookcases, trying to pretend to the A.G.'s secretary that I was just passing the time. Five minutes before the A.G. came back from lunch, I found the right book that gave the jurisdiction for contracts involving the creation of American institutions not on home turf.

"I was able to go into his office and say, 'Mr. Attorney General, Section 3282 of the U.S. Code, annotated, points out that . . .'

"He was utterly snowed. An agreement was signed immediately.

"To deal with the Latin world—the Latin mentality—and to get a decision in one day was just something beyond belief to everyone at Peace Corps headquarters. I had returned with what Warren Wiggins used to call 'the program in your pocket.' "

Shriver and Haddad thus agreed that he was the right man for the difficult, vitally important job of chief of evaluation. He held this job from April 1962 until April 1969, entering and exiting on the same day, April 27.

The process of evaluation had by then entered Peters's bloodstream, come to personify him. In such a case, what do you do for an encore? In Peters's case, he did what came naturally, though by no means easily. At great financial and professional risk, he started his own magazine, *The Washington Monthly*, which examines and exposes corruption, wrongheadedness, mismanagement, stupidity, waste, and catch-22 ironies in all bureaucracies, be they of the public or private sector. *The Washington Monthly* . . . well, it *evaluates*. It is a burr under the saddle.

Charlie Peters's mother is proud of her son. But she worries a lot. She recently said to Charlie's wife, Beth: "I think Charlie is making too many powerful enemies. Why does he insist upon ruffling so many feathers?" Beth replied that she, too, had often worried and had often asked Charlie the same question, to which Charlie had replied, "Well, *somebody* has to."

But Peters acknowledges the dangers of telling the truth. Reflecting on his perilous months in 1962 at the Peace Corps, when he was too often "an inch away from being fired": "The more I understand about the federal bureaucracy, the more I understand about bureaucratic momentum, the more I think that it's a miracle that I *wasn't* fired. Because the rejection of the truth from the body of the bureaucracy is so great that it triumphs over any medical immune system that has ever been invented."

CHAPTER 7

MATING
SEASON

Robert Lee Gale, a native of Saint Cloud, Minnesota, reported to work at Peace Corps headquarters in Washington in March 1963, which was late by "founding father" standards. Yet his arrival was perfectly timed for him to perform a service that was absolutely crucial to the Peace Corps' continued success and possibly to its survival—a service that he alone among humans could have performed. Gale had no idea of this natural matching of man and job that was soon to evolve, nor had Shriver or Haddad when they first interviewed Gale.

Gale had been vice president for development at Carlton College in Northfield, Minnesota, when Cupid's arrow struck him, besotting him with passion for the Peace Corps. At Carlton (of which he was a 1948 graduate), Gale had made a name for himself in college administration circles for raising over twelve million dollars for an endowment to increase faculty salaries and student aid and to launch an era of building. He was also known in these circles for the unique metabolism that made it possible for him to work twelve hours a day consistently, with six hours off for play, four hours of sleep, tennis at 7:00 A.M. (weather permitting), and off to work again. His friends and colleagues agreed that there was no one quite like Bob Gale; he was an original. Six foot two, eyes of blue, a great big, jolly, pink-cheeked Santa Claus of a man with a creamy disposition, a cast-iron liver, and the wicked serve you could not return at 7:00 A.M., even though he had been partying till 3:00 A.M. and you had nodded off in the middle of Jack Paar's first joke.

Gale initially knew no one at the Peace Corps, but he arranged through Senator Hubert Humphrey of his home state of Minnesota (who had sponsored legislation for an all-male, lowercase "peace corps" in the spring of 1960, during which season he himself was a candidate for president) to be introduced to Bill Haddad. Haddad found Gale so versatile (Gale had also been editor in chief of the Maco Publishing Company in New York and had been involved in the production of the famous pictorial essay, *The Family of Man*) that he persuaded Shriver to create a division for him within Haddad's bailiwick of Planning, Evaluation and Research. Haddad wanted to call that division "Special Projects" in order to leave it free to be absolutely anything, a combination ombudsman and gadfly, a close cousin of the Division of Evaluation both logistically and philosophically. Only Haddad could get away with such an impulsive bureaucratic whim, and only Haddad could persuade Shriver that to let such a talent as Bob Gale slip away bordered on being a criminal act. Shriver alone could wave the magic wand that would produce a new division that did not fit on the organization chart. Gale was understandably ecstatic about all of this until the day of reckoning, in which he had seven interviews and then was kept waiting for three unsettling hours before he could see Shriver. Meanwhile, he had become paranoid about his interview with John Alexander in PDO, whom he was convinced had disliked him. (Alexander had in fact given him his most glowing report.) He had been made triply nervous because Haddad kept running into Shriver's anteroom where Gale was cooling his heels, plopping portions of the first draft of the Peace Corps' "Congressional Presentation FY [Fiscal Year] 1964" into his lap, exhorting Gale to, "Read this. Cut it. Fix it. Anything you do will make it better. I'll be back in half an hour." After Haddad's third such manic visitation, Gale begged, "Bill, I've read the first sentence a dozen times and I can't absorb it. I'm too goddam nervous. Tell you what. If Sarge hires me, I'll stay here for two days and nights and read everything and fix it all up for you. But for chrissake, not now. Okay?"

Maryann Orlando, sensing Gale's anguish, suggested that Gale go out for a cup of coffee. "Coffee. Ha!" recalls Gale. "What I wanted was a double martini." But he went out for the coffee and Shriver was ready to see him immediately upon his return. His nervousness and paranoia evaporated instantly. The Shriver charm was turned up to full blast. "You'd think I'd remember every word we spoke, but I remember nothing except that I was totally overwhelmed by the guy and he hired me. I went out of there on cloud nine. I went straight to a phone and called Barbara."

"I was thrilled at first when Bob called me," says Barbara Gale. "I was just as turned on by the Peace Corps idea as he was. We had worked our tails off for Hubert [Humphrey]. We didn't much like the way that the Kennedy people had just mowed him down in the West Virginia primary. But we decided that only Kennedy could beat Nixon. And he showed some idealism in proposing the Peace Corps, so we switched over. When Bob called me to tell me that Shriver had hired him and given him his own division, I'm afraid my next question was, 'What's the salary?' I was sure it would be more than you could get in academia. Bob said, 'Oh, God. I forgot to ask.' I said, 'You forgot to *ask*? You mean you're going to be bringing three little children and a pregnant wife and several huge debts to Washington, D.C., and you don't know what your salary is? Suddenly, I was very alarmed."

As it turned out, the impractical Gale made fifteen thousand dollars as chief of special projects. By 1965, when he left, as acting associate director of the Office of Public Affairs and director of recruiting, he made twenty-five thousand dollars. The latter was a hefty sum for a young man in government in those days. In fact, Gale started out making as much as a staff assistant at the White House and ended up making as much as a senior special assistant to the president. (Since then, upper echelon White House salaries have more than tripled.)

To placate his worried wife, Gale told her they were going out on the town to celebrate. Haddad suggested the Jockey Club in the Fairfax Hotel (now called the Ritz Carlton). "You never know who you'll see there: Marlon Brando, Aristotle Onassis, Lee Radziwill. Albert Gore has an apartment there."

"We walked in," says Gale, "and there was Minoru Yamasaki [the esteemed architect who had designed five of the new buildings at Carlton College, for which Gale had raised the funds]. *Time* magazine was just finishing a cover story about his having been picked to design the World Trade Center. They were celebrating, too, and asked us to join them. We were all so jubilant that Jacques Vivien, the maître d', didn't present any of us with a check. In fact, it got to the point where he was sitting down and drinking champagne with us." Soon, the Gales were installed in a house at 3749 Jocelyn Street in the District of Columbia, where during the next three years there would be more parties than Jocelyn Street or any six of its neighboring streets put together had known in all of time. At work, Gale was installed in a rabbit warren of four oddly shaped offices on the eleventh floor "with an absolutely sensational view—maybe the best in Washington—of Lafayette Park, the White House, the Executive Office Building, the Washington Monument, the Tidal Basin, the Jefferson Memorial, and the landing pattern at National Airport. Why was I up there when Shriver, Moyers, and Haddad were down on the fifth? By all rules of corporate and bureaucratic life, it should have been the other way around. But I never got around to asking. Twenty-three years later someone explained that when Shriver was trying to get his Peace Corps task force moved out of the Mayflower Hotel and into a building identified with government in midtown, the fifth floor of ICA headquarters was offered. So he took it, and there he stayed. My spectacular view didn't really count; the fifth floor was the floor of maximum prestige."

Gale began Peace Corps life as editor of the "Congressional Presentation FY 1964," as he suspected would be the case. Haddad had decided that Gale, with his editorial experience and his mellow, jocular personality, could rescue this important document from prolonged interoffice squabbling, as had recently been the case.

Nonetheless, storm clouds gathered and over just such a petty issue as Haddad had hoped to avoid. When Gale and his Special Projects staff were close to finishing the final draft, Howard Greenberg, director of the Office of Management, stopped him in the hall. "By the way, Bob, I assume that you're putting the budget figures I sent you right up front in the presentation, ahead of everything else. I mean, you are, aren't you? Because that's what Congress wants to see. They don't want to read a lot of little stories about how great the Peace Corps is."

Gale felt his composure beginning to crack for the first time since his arrival. "Why no, Howard, quite the opposite. The introduction comes first, naturally. Then the country reports. Then the maps and graphs. The budget figures come last. After all, we say we're asking Congress to appropriate thirty million dollars in the first paragraph. The country reports reflect how we spent the money we got last fiscal year. They justify it. Haddad is very keen that this thing be as good a piece of journalism as we can make it. Shriver wants it to be readable. He wants to capture the imagination of Congress. So far, Congress really likes the Peace Corps. Sarge wants them to *love* it. So that's the approach I've taken. This is what I was hired to do."

Greenberg bristled. "The budget, you say, is *last?* Well, that's crazy and that's wrong and I won't stand for it." Gale lowered his voice almost to a whisper: "Haddad wants it this way. And it has been my experience that Haddad asks for what he knows Sarge wants. So you'd better see Haddad."

Greenberg then pulled a time-honored bureaucratic trick on Gale, suggesting that Haddad, Gale, and Shriver meet in Greenberg's office at about 4:00 P.M. The ploy: Lodge a complaint against the greenest member of the staff and then propose a conciliatory gathering on your own turf with the principal adversary and the highest power present. Gale caught on within seconds, although he was just the innocent newcomer that Greenberg imagined him to be. But he thought, "I can see it now. I walk into Bill Haddad's office and say, 'Hey, Bill. I just ran into Howard Greenberg and he's mad that the budget's going to be at the end of the presentation and he wants it changed and he says he won't let it out of the building as it now stands. Wants a meeting with you and me and Sarge late this afternoon in his office. Asked me to set it up with you.' " Gale shudders at the thought of Haddad's reaction had he actually blurted out the situation. "He would have gone completely bananas, probably fired me on the spot, maybe killed Howard."

A meeting did occur that evening. Score one for Greenberg. But it took place on the eleventh floor. Score one for Haddad and Gale. Both Haddad and Gale attended. Score another for Greenberg. But the meeting was held at 10:00 P.M., four hours past Greenberg's usual departure time. (Haddad swore he could not get there a minute earlier; he was meeting with Shriver!) *Many* points for Haddad and Gale. Bill Moyers, the twenty-nine-year-old deputy director of the Peace Corps and Washington wunderkind, showed up expressly at the request of Haddad, partially to intimidate and partially to mediate. No such luck. The meeting actually took place in the Division of Evaluation, down the hall from the Division of Special Projects. Bob Gale arrived carrying the by-now eighty-page congressional presentation, and the double doors to the Division of Evaluation were closed. Gale's assistant was in the front office of Special Projects that muggy spring evening when all hell broke loose, as Gale had thought it might. Haddad and Greenberg were suddenly in a ferocious shouting and swearing contest. Gale had asked his assistant to prepare to stay until midnight, if necessary, "in case I need someone to drive me or anyone else to the hospital." His assistant explained that she drove a 1961 "Unsafe at Any Speed" Ralph Nader Corvair and could not take too many of the wounded.

The eleventh floor elevator doors opened and the assistant of "Young Bill Moyers," known as "Even Younger Dick Nelson," stepped off. Nelson was twenty-two years old. ("Bill had to have someone younger than himself working for him," says Nelson, now forty-four.)

"How's it going?" Nelson inquired. Gale's assistant replied, "Very noisily. Even your boss and my boss have begun to shout, and as you know, they are known for never shouting. Could you break in on it?" Nelson agreed to break in on the thunderous meeting down the hall on the pretense that either Cope or Suzanne Moyers, the very young children of his boss, was running a fever and Dad was needed at home immediately. Nelson went down the hall, threw open the doors, and everyone froze. Not a sound except the buzzing of a half-dozen flies that had flown in the huge opened windows. It was hot in the cavernous room, the temperature being in the eighties, as it could easily be in late April in Washington. The "gladiators" were soaked with perspiration and looked drained. Each stood in a different part of the room, as if to avoid potentially disastrous bodily contact with one another. Gale was pale and still clutching the congressional presentation. Haddad and Greenberg were purple from their vocal exertions. Moyers was poised warily by the door, his eyes darting anxiously back and forth among the other three as if to anticipate who would do or say any unsettling thing next. Nobody moved.

Nelson was about to make his preplanned announcement about Bill Moyers's sick child when Moyers suddenly shattered the hot, still air with a long banshee shriek, dashed across the room, and flung himself out of the eleventh-floor window.

Haddad, Gale, and Nelson were aware that Moyers had not committed suicide; they knew that there was a walled parapet around the eleventh floor of the Maiatico Building. "Young Bill Moyers" had simply vaulted out onto the narrow but safe terrace. But Greenberg was horrified: "Oh no, Bill, noooooo! Dear God, Bill, NO!" howled Greenberg in unbearable distress. Running to the window from which Moyers had just jumped, Greenberg got another shock: Young Bill Moyers was standing on his own two feet, outside the eleventh-floor window, peering in with a fiendish glee: "Come on in, the water's fine."

The budget came last.

A week later, "Congressional Presentation FY 1964" was finished. The next day, members of Special Projects and Evaluation proofread the final version of the document furiously, Gale had it printed on an emergency basis, and at midnight, Victor Crichton, an associate of Haddad's on loan to Gale, set off on his Vespa to deliver it to Shriver in Rockville, Maryland.

◆　　◆　　◆

In late April of 1963, Bob Gale received a late-night phone call from Haddad. "I can't make the senior staff meeting tomorrow. Got to go out of town. You go in my place. It's time you saw the group in action. Take notes, but don't speak unless spoken to. Don't get trapped. If

Sarge asks you a question, don't try to fake it. Just say, 'I don't know, Sarge, but I will find out right away.' "

Shriver began the meeting with the remark: "We're almost at the point where the requests for Volunteers will outnumber our supply. We didn't expect this to happen so quickly, since we started out on opening day with over twenty thousand banging on our doors and we didn't even have a single request from overseas. We've had excellent press and a steady stream of people applying since then, but by this time next year I predict we'll be in fifty countries and the ones we're in already are asking for as many as triple the number they now have. So we've got to be much more aggressive about the way we recruit. Much more imaginative. I'm open to any and all suggestions."

Gale was vaguely aware that recruiting, up until that time, had consisted of getting an adequate supply of Peace Corps applications to every post office in the country, to the deans of students at most universities, and to trade associations. Staff members from Washington, on an individual basis, were sent out to talk to interested students. The more Gale had heard, the more surprised he had become: Sometimes the staff member dispatched to a major university campus was a middle-level staffer who did not have sufficient dynamism or information with which to fire up likely recruits. But more to the point, the Peace Corps staff member was physically inaccessible, even invisible. His presence on campus had often not been announced at all, let alone with any fanfare. He was given an anonymous office and a telephone. It would take a very motivated student and a very turned-on dean of students to put the student together with the Peace Corps recruiter. "But this is ridiculous," Gale was thinking. "The students I'd seen at Carlton were wild about the Peace Corps. So were the faculty and administration. That's where a great many of the twenty thousand original applications had come from—the relatively small liberal arts colleges like Carlton. I had to conclude that those first twenty-thousand-plus applications, so to speak, had made the Peace Corps cocky. The Peace Corps thought that would go on forever. But nothing does, and furthermore, I gathered at that meeting that nobody really ever dreamed that the Peace Corps would become so fantastically popular in the Third World in so short a time. The Peace Corps was now dealing with a success the size of which it hadn't quite bargained for. Not even Sarge, obviously, thought it would get so big so fast, and Sarge thinks very, very big."

Senior staff members began throwing out ideas that Gale found "naive, ill-informed, even disastrous." He was irresistibly moved to break his vow of silence. "Look," he broke in suddenly, "you can't communicate effectively that way on a big university campus, or for that matter, not very well on even a small one."

Time stopped. Nobody moved. All heads turned toward the new guy, Haddad's stand-in. "Oh, God," thought Gale immediately, panic clutching at his chest. "What have I gone and done? Queered myself permanently, that's what. Half of these people don't know me and don't care what I think." But no. The looks he saw on the faces of the senior staff, and especially the look on Shriver's face, expressed only rabid interest and thankful deliverance.

Shriver leaned forward and asked urgently, "Well, then, what would *you* do, Bob?" And by way of explanation, Shriver added, "Bob Gale here is the only one among us who has had very recent first-hand experience in an academic bureaucracy and the only one who has had constant contact with college students lately."

"Off the top of my head," said Gale, "never having given it any thought before, I said, 'Well, I'd send in some kind of a team, not just one person. I'd send in senior staff. I'd send in famous names. I'd made a big thing of it. I'd get the college administrators and the faculty fully on my side, get them involved. I'd alert the campus newspaper and the campus radio station. I'd try to co-opt office space in the Student Union—that's where a lot of the action is at a big university. [Gale was beginning to feel foolish; he was stating the obvious, wasn't he? But he couldn't stop now.] I'd send out . . .' "

Shriver stopped Gale abruptly, startling him badly by pounding the table. Then came the famous Shriver hoot: "T'rffic!" he yelled jubilantly. "Go try it next week. Hey, what about in the next couple of days? I mean, why not? In case some of you didn't know, Bob Gale here wrote and published the congressional presentation in only four weeks."

"Next week? Next couple of days?" Gale realized he now was about to sound like a cop-out, a weak sister, after coming on so strong. But he was alarmed by Shriver's sudden electrification. "Sarge, honestly, it would take a bit more time than . . ."

"Where would you like to try it?" asked Shriver, now wildly excited.

"Well," said Gale, beginning to perspire, knowing he had opened Pandora's box, "I guess I'd pick the University of Wisconsin." (Gale says he mentioned Wisconsin because he knew most of the top administrators and knew that it was a "swinging" school. The highest compliment that Gale could pay a person, a place, or an entity was to call it swinging, which meant, to him, progressive, lively, politically aware. He said that the University of Wisconsin was a Peace Corps "natural." He did not add "pushover," but he prayed "pushover.")

Shriver then turned to Douglas Kiker, then the director of public information (following Ed Bayley and Tom Mathews in that job), and said, "Doug, you go with Bob." Kiker looked startled but blinked only once before nodding a nod that Gale suspected was the utmost in hypocritical enthusiasm.

Kiker, now and for many years a reporter for NBC-TV News, had come to the Peace Corps from the *Atlanta Constitution* and had preceded Gale by a few weeks at the Peace Corps. They had been introduced once, saw each other infrequently—Kiker's office being on the seventh floor, Gale's being on the eleventh. It says something for Shriver's instincts that, without knowing Gale or Kiker well himself, he had instantly put the two together to launch the first big, daring Peace Corps recruiting drive. Perhaps Shriver noticed that both men had similar metabolisms: Both Gale and Kiker were "night owls," enthusiastic party people, enthusiastic heterosexuals, joke tellers, risk takers, "idea men." Gale knew academia; Kiker knew the media. Birds of a feather with complementary abilities.

"And so there we were, Kiker and me," says Gale. "Hardly acquainted; but now we were supposed to go out to the University of Wisconsin together and actually *do* this thing.

"I went back to my office, pulled out my little black book and frantically started calling my friends at the University of Wisconsin: the president, the dean of students, the development people. They put Doug and me in touch with department heads on the faculty. We were given names at the campus newspaper and radio station and other important contacts in the community. Everyone out there was very excited. This was a first for all of us. They were saying euphoric things like, 'This university is the Peace Corps' university.' I mean, these were old pals of mine, but they were going ape on the phone."

But Gale knew that there were going to be problems in spite of the enthusiasm and the rosy promises over the telephone. The University of Wisconsin at Madison was and is a huge place. In 1963, its undergraduate student body numbered 17,452; its graduate students numbered nearly 7,000. There were then 1,650 members of the faculty. The Wisconsin campus in 1963 covered nine hundred acres on the shores of Lake Mendota. Gale realized that to do the kind of public relations job that needed to be done there, he and Kiker would be stretched to the limit of even their remarkable endurance levels. After a week, they would be worn out. "This thing," says Gale, "was going to be like a presidential campaign, I could tell already, only it was going to be more grueling because there were just the two of us. Come to think of it, that's no doubt why the idea attracted Sarge so much. People who've been in a winning presidential campaign never lose the taste of it. It gets their blood pumping." Thus, Gale decided to put together another team, a follow-up team, as he called it, who would come in, carry on, and "mop up." Gale and Kiker would drive to the airport Sunday evening to meet the follow-up team, take them to a motel for a briefing, hand them their speaking and interview schedules for the week, give them a map of the campus and a list of names they must memorize that very night. He and Kiker would then fly home to Washington.

"You had to have your advance team, as in a political campaign," says Gale, "and then you had to have your second wave, who came in and took full advantage of what the advance team had lined up. That was the beginning of the team concept as I envisioned it just before leaving for Wisconsin." Gale lined up a follow-up team for Wisconsin that was guaranteed to knock 'em dead: John D. Rockefeller IV, Padraic Kennedy (no relation to the president; his arrival at the Peace Corps is described in Chapter 3), and Camilla Sorensen (then in divorce proceedings with Ted Sorensen, JFK's counsel and speech writer).* "Jay, Pat, and Camilla. Three gorgeous human specimens with turn-on names. Perfect!" says Gale gleefully. "If the students hadn't picked up on *that* one, I'd have been very surprised. Those kids at Wisconsin were *swinging* kids." (It was all over Washington headquarters two days after the follow-up team arrived on the Wisconsin campus that the *Daily Cardinal*, the school newspaper, had carried the headline: "Kennedy, Sorensen and Rockefeller Arrive Today"—"today" meaning the Monday after Gale and Kiker had left. Actually, while the paper had indeed noted the arrival of the "famous threesome" on the front page, and where to find them, the purported headline came instead in the form of a big sign placed in front of the Student Union with an arrow below it to indicate "right inside.")†

*Shortly thereafter, Camilla married Louis Hanson, an aide to Governor Gaylord Nelson. She is now a Regent of the University of Wisconsin.
†A surprise follow-up recruiter was Ellen Kennedy, Padraic's wife, who had been a

When Gale and Kiker first arrived at the university the third week in April 1963, Kiker took over his natural beat, the campus newspaper, the *Daily Cardinal*, and WIBA Radio, a station that was an NBC affiliate and was owned by the local Madison newspaper, the *Capital Times*. WIBA featured a disc jockey who was enormously popular with the university students: Papa Hambone by pseudonym, George Vukelich (pronounced voo-*kell*-ick) by name. Papa Hambone (who also taught creative writing at the university) came on the air at 7:00 P.M. every night of the week. He mixed show tunes with folk music and jazz, framed it all in a talk-show, call-in format, and fashioned a style that Gale calls "a white man deliberately 'talking black' but in a non-insulting way" and that Papa Hambone himself calls "mellow/laid-back/hip."

Kiker had heard about George Vukelich, a.k.a. Papa Hambone, through Bob Gale's contacts in the University of Wisconsin administration before leaving Washington. Kiker was told, "You get Papa Hambone, you've got the whole university." Obviously, therefore, he was the first campus media man Kiker sought out. And Papa Hambone did put not only Kiker on the air frequently, but Gale, as well—and the following week, Kennedy, Sorensen, and Rockefeller. Kiker had begun with uncharacteristic caution and shyness, asking Papa Hambone if the Peace Corps might be given a bit of time one or two nights on his program. (This kind of recruiting was new; no one knew how the campuses would take it.) Papa Hambone said cooly, "I'm on every night of the week. You've got one hour every night. Just bring on your people."

Papa Hambone was a rarity. As Gale was to find in subsequent encounters with administration officials at other major universities, many were strangely out of touch with what was churning within the student body, or they misread the clues. But Papa Hambone had his ear to the ground, and he heard the subterranean rumblings for what they were. "I liked the peace corps idea," says Vukelich. "I liked the Peace Corps people I met. I liked the way they did things. They were daring and refreshing. They stirred things up. It was fun to work with

---

graduate student in French three years earlier at the University of Wisconsin. She "worked" the senior and graduate French classes. The Wisconsin French majors were bowled over by the sight and the sound of a young, curly headed blond woman by the name of Mrs. Kennedy describing Peace Corps programs in French-speaking Africa— in fluent French.

them. The whole thing was unique, yet inevitable. Here at Wisconsin, we had these idealistic students who were really looking for something, and then along came the peace corps idea and the Peace Corps people at the same time, and there was cross-pollination. I was astonished at how little the great monolithic federal bureaucracy was allowed to get in the way of this new creation. Maybe it was the almost evangelical fire in Kennedy's inaugural speech that did it. Clearly, a great story was there to be told, and when Doug Kiker and Bob Gale and all of the others came out to Wisconsin, I just opened it up and let them tell it."

Gale was thinking that Kiker was having all the fun, dealing with Papa Hambone and the *Daily Cardinal* while he, Gale, had to do battle with the bureaucracy. Even though many of the top officials at Wisconsin were old friends—especially the vice president for public affairs, Bob Taylor—Gale found just what he feared he might:

I had to start from scratch. I had hoped that we could just go right into the classrooms with our message and that we could schedule the follow-up team to do the same. Despite all the good will at Wisconsin, there is, in the end, really only one way to deal with an academic community. You start with the president, then go to the deans, then to the department chairmen, then to the individual professors to line up the speakers for certain classes. Speaking in classrooms was something new, but then, everything we were doing was new, and nobody was saying no to any of it. Except, apparently, for one guy. My old friend, Bob Taylor, who was close to the president, Fred Harrington, told me at the beginning that Porter Butts, the guy who ran the Student Union, never let any outside group use it. He never made any exceptions. Don't bother calling or going to see him, said Taylor, because there's just no use. But I went to see him anyway because, one, I was determined that we set up the Peace Corps recruiting booth in the Student Union no matter what. On a big university campus, that's the only place to be. And two, I had a sneaking suspicion that Porter Butts might be, just *might* be, related to a student I'd known at Carlton who'd been the first one on that campus to join the Peace Corps. She was one of my favorites and I recalled that she came from a college town. I called on Butts and the first thing I said was, "Are you by any chance Priscilla Butts's father?" He was amazed. "How did you know my daughter, Priscilla?" I explained that she'd joined the Peace Corps way before I had. Well! I had been a vice president of his daughter's alma mater and now I was a Peace Corps official. From then on, Butts just tore the whole place apart for us, gave us the whole schmeer. Found students to make signs for us. Everything.

By midweek, Gale got his hands on what was allegedly a highly guarded mailing list of all graduate students at Wisconsin—they numbered nearly seven thousand—which included law and medical students. He realized they might be less motivated than undergraduates to become Peace Corps Volunteers due to the fact of their having invested so much time and money on their professional educations. "But seven thousand skilled young professionals at a great university that loved the Peace Corps and were within shouting distance—it was just too much to pass up." Gale called Washington headquarters to see if they could get a special mailing out by Friday morning so that the students would have it on Monday, just as the follow-up team rolled into town. He, Gale, could dictate a press release over the telephone and then send headquarters a printout of the mailing list on labels by special delivery *and* . . . The answer was an adamant no. Washington, in the person of Howard Greenberg, said it couldn't be done that fast, not possibly. Gale was told that it was a crazy idea, out of the question. A dozen reasons were given. All of them sounded realistic, Gale had to admit, but he was too fired up to give up quite so easily.

"All right," Gale told Kiker, "we'll show 'em. We'll do it ourselves."

Kiker was appalled. "Just what in the hell makes you think we can do that?"

"You go write a release that reminds them that Kennedy, Sorensen, and Rockefeller will be on campus as of Monday and will be able to discuss options with them. Make it sound like Peace Corps service is another year or two of graduate school, but *free*. All expenses paid. Stipend at the end of service. A nest egg before entering their chosen professions." Gale was becoming incandescent with delight at his scheme. "Then go see Bob Taylor. I'll bet he can get someone in the president's office to run off the releases for you. They'll probably even type it for you on a mimeograph sheet. I'll see about getting a printout on mailing labels of all the names and addresses and then I'll try to find a store that has seven thousand number ten envelopes in stock. Of course, there goes the May rent and the grocery money, but what the heck?

We'll need extra hands. I'll ask Porter Butts if he can round up a few students, and then off we go."

"But what do we do about a return address, Bob?" asked Kiker. "I mean, that is *key*, man. We can maybe stuff, lick, and apply mailing labels to seven thousand envelopes if we don't eat or sleep for the next three days—any of us—but we couldn't write 'Peace Corps, Washington, D.C.' seven thousand times by hand even if we had nothing else to do. Anyway, it would look damned unprofessional. But there's got to be a return address or those kids won't even open the thing. Here's this anonymous envelope that looks like third class mail, so who cares?" Kiker sensed that he had begun to dampen Gale's ardor for the scheme. But no. Suddenly, Gale sparkled all over. "I've got it! I'll con one of those movable type stamps from somewhere and we'll frank 'em ourselves—saying 'Peace Corps, Washington, D.C.'— or have the kids take turns doing it. It's gonna be wild, but I swear, we can do it."

"Are you sure that's legal?" asked Kiker with a slight, nervous laugh.

"Oh sure. Why not?" replied a now unstoppable Gale.

By early Thursday evening, Gale and Kiker had actually acquired all of the necessary materials. Eight students corralled by Porter Butts showed up in the Student Union and they, Gale, and Kiker formed two assembly lines, stuffing, licking, applying mailing labels, franking the envelopes, and tying them into bundles. By about 3:00 A.M. the job was three-quarters done, but no one had the energy or will to go on any longer, not even Gale. Thanking the students profusely, and realizing that it was a miracle of sorts that had kept them going for so many hours at boring, repetitive tasks for no pay and no glory, Gale and Kiker gave them their business cards and wrote their home addresses and phone numbers on the back, urging them to call or write them for job references when the time came. "Honestly, we mean it," said a weary Kiker. "Call on us. We can never thank you enough for all of your help."

As it later turned out, five out of the eight joined the Peace Corps after graduation, but at the time, they looked perplexed, even stunned. Finally, one of the girls said, "Oh, but we expected to see you again tomorrow. The job isn't finished. We always intended to finish it. That is, if you can use us."

"Doug and I got all choked up over that," says Gale. "All we could do was mumble our thanks and nod."

One week had passed. It was time to go home. Gale and Kiker had not slept more than four hours a night.

As they were driving to the airport in a rented car on Sunday evening, they tuned in Papa Hambone one last time on the car radio. Papa Hambone was just closing his program. "He said, very slowly— and I'll never forget it," says Gale, "Ah likes the Peace Corps [pause] because it swings [pause] just a little [pause] *all over the world.*"

Doug and I just screamed and yelled and punched each other and laughed and cried and almost ran off the G.D. road."

♦　　♦　　♦

At the first senior staff meeting attended by Kiker and Gale after their trip to Wisconsin, they were greeted by applause. "That was something new," says Gale. "I certainly wouldn't call it a hero's welcome, but then, any kind of compliment was hard to come by from that competitive bunch. Howard Greenberg was the first to speak, which was unusual, even unheard of. And God knows, he and I had had our differences. But he said 'Bob Gale and Doug Kiker here, went out two weeks ago to the University of Wisconsin. They broke more rules and regulations than anyone in the United States government, as far as I know. Though I won't go so far as to say they've broken the law, they did come close a couple of times. [The staff chuckled appreciatively, thinking that Greenberg was joking.*] But we aren't going to fuss about trifles. These guys and their follow-up team, Pat Kennedy, Jay Rockefeller, and Camilla Sorensen, brought back 485 completed applications—that is, to be precise, 485 nine-page questionnaires *and* 485 Peace Corps tests. Four hundred and eighty-five students at the University of Wisconsin took the time to do all of that with final exams approaching. The most we ever got before from a recruiting trip was forty or fifty." (Gale was getting anxious; it wasn't like Howard Greenberg to gush. Was he being sarcastic? Had he been rehearsed? No. Couldn't be. Nothing was ever rehearsed at the Peace Corps. But what was this preamble all about?)

Greenberg continued, seeming now to strive for great dramatic

*Since a few of the envelopes sent to the Wisconsin graduate students were inevitably misaddressed, they landed back at Peace Corps headquarters in Washington. Howard Greenberg lit upon them and saw what Gale had done. Greenberg liked to tell Gale later that he could have gotten five years in prison for every illegally franked envelope. Given seven thousand envelopes, that comes out to thirty-five thousand years in prison, Greenberg would say. "I let Howard have his little joke," says Gale.

effect: "I'd say we had a revolution on our hands!" Gale could not believe his ears. This must be a setup for a letdown. He waited for the censorious other shoe to drop.

"Exactly!" whooped Shriver, rising a few inches out of his chair. "And that means that Bob Gale is no longer chief of Special Projects, but is now director of Recruiting. Effective as of this minute."

Dollar signs lit up on many foreheads. Many hands clapped. Maps of hitherto undreamed of territory flashed up on the big screen of colleagues' imaginings. Fantasies of loftier titles and larger staffs were suddenly aswirl. Quite simply, more Volunteers meant more of everything else. The "numbers virus" had been hatched in the Peace Corps laboratory. The effect was epidemic. Most of the staff scrambled out of their chairs at the conference-room table and rushed for the door as if a presidential press conference had been in session and the commander in chief had issued a statement that amounted to breaking news.

Only two people were not happy about Gale's sudden, melodramatic elevation: Gale and Haddad. They stayed behind to talk to Shriver, each for his own reasons. Haddad objected violently to Shriver's having moved Gale out of his, Haddad's, bailiwick. "Goddammit, Sarge, you're always stealin' my best people," hollered Haddad, real tears brimming in his eyes. "You say you want Planning, Evaluation and Research to be the most creative arm of the agency, and then you go and take away my most creative guy. Recruiting is just a lot of bullshit. You can find other people to do that. Bob Gale can run Recruiting out of his hip pocket from Special Projects. Special Projects—we *created* it for Bob. Recruiting . . . Recruiting? Recruiting is, is, is, oh God, I dunno . . . Recruiting is *nothing!*"

"For once you're wrong, Bill," said Shriver quietly and with a trace of irritation. "Recruiting is not nothing. Recruiting is crucial. At least, it is, with Bob Gale running it. Clearly, he's got the Midas touch. The trouble with Recruiting is that it never has been approached creatively before. We've been thinking like the army and the navy. But this is new, what Bob has done. And it works. And Bob Gale is director of recruiting for life, as far as I am concerned. And Bill, that's that."

Haddad stormed out of the room in a fury.

Gale felt wary and trapped.

Shriver, seemingly unperturbed by Haddad's ire, chirped merrily, "Where to next, Bob?"

"What do you *mean*, Sarge? The school year's over, in effect. It's the end of April. The students spend May studying for, and taking, final exams. It's a pretty tense and panicky time on campuses in May. I don't think we should impose ourselves. It would just irritate people and it wouldn't be productive. It could, in fact, be counterproductive. We hit Wisconsin at a perfect time, but there won't be another perfect time until next fall. During the summer, we can concentrate on people like nurses and electricians, engineers and plumbers and master carpenters, people who have specific skills and who work all year, who are available . . ."

"Oh, *no*." said Shriver. "Summer recruiting, okay. But we could recruit on some campuses the first two weeks of May. Maybe hundreds of them wouldn't actually fill out questionnaires as they did in Wisconsin, but you could get them *interested*. They'd apply during the summer. What's the nearest equivalent to a school like Wisconsin— big, liberal-leaning, yeasty, a place where you've got contacts?"

"Michigan," said Gale, somewhat weakly. He knew there was now no turning back.

"*Great!* You know, that's where it all started. That's where the president made his first pitch for the Peace Corps during the campaign. You can't go wrong. Just get the same group to go with you. Advance and follow-up."

Gale already felt sorry for Rockefeller, if it is possible for an impecunious married man with three young children and a pregnant wife to feel sorry for a bachelor millionaire. He knew that Jay Rockefeller would just be returning from an inspection tour in the Philippines and would therefore be totally exhausted when it was time to go off to recruit again at the University of Michigan. He called Rockefeller and told him what Shriver wanted. Rockefeller agreed. "He, Pat Kennedy, and Camilla Sorensen, were fired up and ready to do it all again."

However, when the reality came to pass, it did not much amuse Rockefeller. He arrived in Ann Arbor, Michigan, one day after he had arrived in Washington from the Philippines. And he was, in fact, exhausted.

Gale, however, had impulsively locked Rockefeller into a "situation" the day before he arrived. Gale had met an attractive, charming young woman named Lennie Radley, a student at the University of Michigan. She had made it a point to seek out the Peace Corps people on campus to see if she could help out. Immediately upon hearing her name, Gale realized who she must be: the sister of Lawrence Radley, one of the first two Volunteers to die. (Radley and David Crozier perished in an airplane crash in Colombia in 1962. The Peace Corps' two training camps in Puerto Rico were named in their memory, Camp Radley and Camp Crozier.) "Lennie was a senior at Michigan and chairman of the Student Committee and she was ready to turn herself and her friends and colleagues over to the Peace Corps recruiting effort completely," says Gale. "But even though, in every way, she was prime as prime could be for Peace Corps service, she was under orders from her family not to join the Peace Corps. Understandably. But she did work her head off for us on campus, and it was no small thing. When she heard Jay Rockefeller was coming in on the follow-up team—she'd heard that he was not only six foot six and handsome, but nice and intelligent, as well—she said to me wistfully, 'I'd love to meet him. Just be introduced to him.' "

Gale was seized by an uncontrollable urge to right the wrong done to the Radley family by cruel fate in taking their son as one of the first Peace Corps casualties, and by a desire to thank Lennie Radley for all of her help to the Peace Corps' advance team at a key university that Shriver was going to be watching with a beady eye. And Lennie was so likeable, so intelligent, so deserving. "Lennie," said Gale, with the certitude of a person who has just mastered Advanced Astrology, "you have a date with him."

Any possibility of such an arrangement would have come a cropper quickly had Gale not decided to stay over one more day and work with the follow-up team, and having done so, been rooming with Jay Rockefeller for one night at the Student Union (where Kennedy had, on October 14, 1960, suggested some semblance of a peace corps).

"I told Jay, pretty much the minute he arrived at Michigan, that I'd arranged for him to go out with this wonderful, pretty, bright girl that evening," says Gale.

Rockefeller balked. "Well, look, Bob, I'm not. I am going to bed. I have traveled fifty thousand miles in the past five weeks. And now I am going to bed."

"You *can't*," wailed Gale.

"But I *am*," insisted Rockefeller.

Gale says that he was feeling so desperate that he grabbed Rockefeller "and kind of shook him. And I guess fearing for my sanity, he relented and said, very quietly, 'Okay. But I'll do it only if you take out her roommate and go with us.' "

"I can't," I said. "I am a married man." (Gale couldn't believe how prissy he sounded.)

"I don't care," said bachelor Rockefeller.

"She may not have a roommate," said Gale, feeling very foolish.

"But she certainly has a *friend*, if she's as great as you say she is," countered Rockefeller.

Lennie Radley had a roommate, and the four of them went out to dinner at a typical campus eatery, Gale trying not to marvel at the unlikelihood of the whole situation. "We had a wonderful time," says Gale. "Both Lennie and her roommate wound up as Peace Corps Volunteers the following fall. Lennie's parents relented."

The two-week Michigan recruiting effort reaped 170 question-naires, more than Gale had thought possible given the timing: early May 1963, with panic over final exams setting in, but as many as Shriver had unrealistically hoped for, even knowing the odds. (And, just as Shriver had predicted, another 300 came in from Michigan the following summer.)

"We made a strike on the Mayo Clinic in Rochester, Minnesota, that summer," says Gale, chuckling. "I had my doubts about that one. Who was going to leave the vaunted Mayo Clinic to join the still pretty new and kind of radical Peace Corps? But a few nurses did. It proved to me that no matter where we went in that era, we'd always find a few fans. Except maybe fundamentalist institutions like Bob Jones University, whose students, faculty, and administration bom-barded Shriver with letters about our being Communists and sinful mixers of the races."

For Peace Corps staff members and some of the first returning Volunteers, the most famous recruiting trip was the "Big One" to California in early October 1963, the one that gave rise to the term *blitz recruiting*. Gale assembled five advance teams and five follow-up teams. Each team spent a week in southern California and then a week in northern California, visiting every major campus in both areas. For instance, one advance team consisting of Nan McEvoy, then deputy director of the Africa Regional Office, and Frank Erwin, then deputy director of Selection, were assigned first to Los Angeles State University (where there was only modest interest in the Peace Corps) and next to San Francisco State University (where there was consid-erable interest). Bob Gale, Linda Lyle (his secretary), and Doug Kiker took on the University of Southern California (USC) in the south and then the University of California at Berkeley in the north. Gale had friends at both schools who could be of help, but Berkeley, Gale knew, was going to be an all-out Peace Corps school in any case. Of USC he wasn't too sure; he had heard more than once that its undergraduate student body was, well, politically indifferent and intellectually lazy.

"Since I was now director of Recruiting, I had to go where I knew I'd do well. I didn't necessarily have to do better than anyone else. No. That's not true. I *did* have to outdo everyone else. And at Berkeley, I did. At Berkeley, Doug, Linda, and I got nearly two hundred questionnaires in one week—and the advance team is not really required to get *any* applications—and then the follow-up team came in and mopped up about seven hundred more. Sarge came out and spoke at most of the schools where we were recruiting, and at Berkeley and San Francisco State he got absolutely tumultuous welcomes."

The spectacular numbers gleaned at Berkeley—plus the response to Shriver personally—made everyone forget that Gale's effort at USC had been a flop. "Even though a friend of mine, Tom Mickell, who was vice president for public relations and development at USC, did everything he could for us—got us a booth in the plaza in front of the library, which was the best possible spot, and helped us schedule in our speakers, gave us contacts and entries—it just didn't matter. The last day we recruited there—a warm, sunny October Saturday— only seven kids, in a student body of several thousand, passed by our booth on the way to the library. And none of them gave us more than a glance. Those who had stopped during the week apparently thought we were an early-day version of Club Med. I've heard that the scene has changed enormously since."

The working day for the advance teams began at about 8:00 A.M. and ended between 11:00 P.M. and midnight. Both in Los Angeles and in San Francisco, the word would get passed from team to team in the early evening where everyone was going to congregate that night. "And we'd congregate until about 3:00 A.M. in various restaurants and bars. Everybody wanted to compare notes, and nobody felt like passing up a night out in these two cities, which offered such great nightlife. Washington was *important*, but Washington had no nightlife."

The advance teams tended to be more rambunctious than the follow-up teams, partially—indeed, if not wholly—because "advancing" was Gale's "beat," and as the Prince of Partying, he tended to pick people whose skills, attitudes, and metabolisms were similar to his own.

In Los Angeles, by night, it was Dino's for dinner. ("A table for *twenty-five*, Mr. Gale?" an incredulous maître d' would inquire. "At 1:30 in the morning?") Once it was a strip joint, the Body Shop, just off Sunset Boulevard in Hollywood, with a smaller, game group that would not be shocked and tell tales to the higher-ups at Peace Corps headquarters.*

In San Francisco, nighttime leisure hours were spent at such famous places as the Top of the Mark. ("We took most of the tables. We called ahead to say, 'We are in Mr. Shriver's party.' Sarge was still in Washington," chortles Gale.) Just as many fun-filled wee small hours were spent in North Beach, a Bohemian, ethnically various section of the most beautiful city in America. Interteam and intrateam romances bloomed as the moon rose over the Golden Gate Bridge and the second or third stinger was consumed.

Jim Walls, a former reporter for the *San Francisco Chronicle* and subsequently a writer for the Division of Public Information, often played "tour director" for the Peace Corps horde, since he knew his way around. One evening he appeared in one of his favorite old North Beach haunts, Enrico's, with a tall, striking brunette named Yvonne. Yvonne (whom Walls called "Y" and who bore a slight resemblance to Vivien Leigh) was a top model in San Francisco and an "old and dear friend" of Walls. According to Walls, who enjoyed being outrageous, Yvonne had a terrible hangover. "Y," coaxed Walls, "Tell 'em about your hangover." Y said, slowly and evenly, with no expression on her splendidly chiseled porcelain face, "My hangover is so large that you could make *awnings* out of it." The Peace Corps gang thought that they had never met anyone so divinely decadent. Walls, who bears a close physical resemblance to John Cheever and whose wit approaches that of Peter DeVries, had upstaged all others for the time being. However, his preeminence was short lived. At 3:00 A.M., even when the most dedicated of Peace Corps advance team revelers were beginning to wearily disperse and head for their hotels, a finale of surprising vigor took place. Sally Bowles stood on a North Beach

---

Because the Peace Corps group at the Body Shop didn't look like anyone else on the premises, or like Californians in general, some of the other patrons got curious. "They were also curious because we were laughing and joking among ourselves and not gaping every second at the proceedings on stage," says Gale. "They started asking us who we were. I kept whispering 'For God's sake, don't tell them we're from the Peace Corps.' Here we were, the Holy Ones, in a strip joint. I told the gang just to say that we worked for a government agency, and then to clam up and look mysterious. By the time we left, everyone thought we were from the CIA, which was fine with us."

street corner and began belting out, quite to the astonishment of her colleagues, "He's Got the Whole World In His Hands," slamming her right fist into her left palm to keep the beat. The last man on the advance team and the last man from Peace Corps headquarters whom anyone could have imagined joining in—namely, Warren Wiggins—did so, and with as much heart, soul, and resonance as Sally. Pretty soon, they were joined by some others—Peace Corps colleagues and strangers—but since nobody really knew the words or could stay on key for more than a couple of bars, the chorus soon petered out. Only three hours until the alarm clock went off.

As it turned out, certain people back at Washington headquarters had heard that more was off-key about the first "blitz" advance-team recruiting trip than just the late-night street-corner spiritual.

Right after Gale and Kiker returned to Washington, once again triumphant with another record number of Peace Corps applications in their valises (there were over sixteen hundred by the end of two weeks), Gale was called by Deputy Director Bill Moyers for a private meeting in his office. This had never happened before and Gale was apprehensive; it wasn't like Moyers to have hushed tête-à-têtes. As soon as he had walked into Moyers's fifth-floor executive suite offices, Gale knew there was trouble. Moyers was uncustomarily edgy, and for one so young, was wearing the frown of a disapproving father. "He started reeling off what he'd heard of our after-hours antics on the California advance trip. That, as head of Recruiting and leader of the advance team, it was my responsibility to behave myself and to see that others did, as well. That it was dangerous to cavort into the night in cities where the press was very alert and sophisticated. That our antics could bring shame to the Peace Corps. That we had no right to 'play' on a business trip at government expense. Oh, boy—was he being the Baptist. Obviously, he had been thoroughly informed as to all of our doings, had exaggerated them in his mind, or his informer had ex-aggerated them. As *he* saw it—I could just tell—our escapades had been *lurid*.

"I broke right in. I said, 'Look, Bill, these people were working fourteen to sixteen hours a day out there, seven days a week, two weeks in a row. They have to stay in kind of seedy places. Their per diem doesn't cover their expenses. Sixteen dollars a day doesn't cover a fifth of what it costs. But they did a fantastic job. They brought in more applications than ever before in the history of the Peace Corps. *By far*. And that's what Sarge wants. What they do after hours is certainly not my business, and I don't think what I do after hours, here or there, is your business. And if you ever bring the subject up again, I'll quit.' I walked toward the door, mumbling something about why didn't he just find someone else to run Recruiting. He ran up to me, as if he wanted to continue discussing this thing, but I was so mad that I didn't let him speak. I just repeated what I'd been saying, only in stronger terms. I said, 'Don't get me wrong, Bill. I'm not kidding and I'm not bluffing. I am absolutely totally prepared to quit on the spot if you ever bring up the after-hours subject again.' And he never did."*

The next team recruiting effort, in Pittsburgh in November 1963, was modest compared to the California trip. In fact, most recruiting efforts—with the exception of a blitz of New York in December 1963— were forever after modest compared to the California trip. Gale was just as happy that they were. It had been complicated and exhausting to organize the California trip. It had been complicated and exhausting to carry out. It had been expensive—perhaps too expensive to justify even the stunningly successful results—and it had been risky. Even Gale had to admit it. The Peace Corps presence had been large, busy, and visible. Approximately one hundred Peace Corps staff members had been swarming over the famous turf for the better part of a month at different times. The candle had indeed burned at both ends. Further, while Moyers had thereafter refrained from hectoring Gale about the Peace Corps recruiters' not altogether discreet or tidy social antics, word had gotten around at headquarters that *the* trip to get assigned to was the *next* California blitz. Fun in the sun three thousand miles from home. And all in the cause of world peace. The gap between instant florid legend and actual fact was as vast as the distance between the Potomac River and San Francisco Bay. But the legend persisted. The trick was: Have excellent excuses for turning down trips to the

---

*Gale was so mad at Moyers on this occasion that he forgot to defend himself with the best defense he had. The entire San Francisco Peace Corps group had been feted by one of San Francisco's most elegant social leaders, Mrs. George Cameron, in her pink Loire Valley chateau in the ultra-affluent exurb of Burlingame. Her niece, Nan McEvoy, had regaled her with tales of the group's hard work and sacrifice. Mrs. Cameron, a Coco Chanel look-alike who lived surrounded by lush gardens, paintings by Monet and Cezanne, and rugs by Aubusson, had a social conscience and a butler to boot. He smiled a tiny smile of discreet amusement as he served the bedraggled recruiters gin and tonics on a silver tray. In the spirit of the early Peace Corps, it was another first.

boondocks, and ingratiate yourself with Bob Gale, the Czar of Recruiting.

Gale was aware that he was being "lobbied" for the best trips. Slavishly sycophantic behavior is not hard to decode, and Gale realized that his sudden, dazzling popularity following the California trip was not due solely to his mastery of the workings of the American college campus or the record number of Peace Corps recruits he had been able to lure. Gale had acquired, in a word, power. With a snap of his finger or a flick of his pencil, he could dispatch you to San Francisco in October or Syracuse in January. It was bound to happen, anyway, that the most glamorous people at the agency got the most glamorous trips, since the most glamorous colleges tended to be politically yeasty and pro-Peace Corps—and were, in turn, very responsive to attractive, articulate people from the New Frontier. "This reality became quickly obvious," says Gale, wincing, "and resentments were built up—against me personally, against the whole idea of recruiting generally. But what could I do? I had to save my 'stars' for the *real* Peace Corps schools, as we used to call them, like Wisconsin, Michigan, Berkeley, Harvard. Particularly some place like Harvard. I mean, you couldn't send someone who wasn't pretty sensational up there. At Harvard, there were all of those superbright young men, mostly liberal Democrats and very much turned on by the peace corps idea, but who had fabulous career opportunities out there just waiting to be taken the day after graduation. Now, the more affluent ones—okay; they could afford to take a chance. But the less affluent ones, the ones whose parents had sacrificed and struggled to send them to Harvard, they were harder to get. Their parents were saying, 'What? We spend our life savings to give you a Harvard education and you want to throw it away on some malaria-infested backwater of the world? Nothing doing.' These guys were hard to get even when they were highly motivated for Peace Corps service. You therefore had to send someone absolutely persuasive and compelling to talk to such people. Because high motivation is very important. You don't want to lose these really motivated guys."

There were other problems in the quirky realm of Peace Corps team recruiting. Recruiting was hard work. Just plain hard work. A lot of it was tedious and repetitive, some of it even simple-minded, a bit of it excruciatingly boring. Thus, even in the most attractive of environments, there was the danger of burnout. To avoid burnout or crippling ennui, one had to amuse oneself. It was difficult to amuse oneself if one did not have compatible fellow recruiters, comfortable accommodations, and extra spending money. Uncle Sam was not paying for your gin and tonics at the Top of the Mark. Your government per diem did not cover dinner at Dino's. If you ended up with incompatible, frightened, or just downright inept teammates, the whole effort could become, at best, a waste of time and, at worst, a profound embarrassment, which might mean little or no cooperation from the college administrators in question the next time the Peace Corps came a-courting.

No matter how controversial, complicated, or combative the process of team recruiting became at any given time—from the selection of teams to go out to the campuses to the actual conduct of business in the field—Shriver was vigorously in support of it. Whenever anyone complained about Gale's methods, right in front of him at staff meetings or behind his back, Shriver simply stated the gospel: Without Volunteers, and really good ones, the Peace Corps is nothing. Without team recruiting, we cannot get enough Volunteers, or enough good ones. The Peace Corps is growing too fast. We have to keep up. Bob Gale's method is not only the best method, it's the only method.

Gale was proud of the fact that Shriver, on his own, wrote and issued an agencywide memo saying that everyone on the Peace Corps staff "*had* to give me three or four weeks a year in recruiting time. Sarge was aware that I was being pressured and lobbied about recruiting assignments, that some people balked at going at all, and others balked at going to unglamorous locations. Sarge stated that if somebody did not wish to go when or where I wanted to send them, they could not come to see *me* about it. They would have to go to Maryann Orlando first and explain their problems, and then to Sarge himself and give him an explanation. Needless to say," says Gale, laughing the laugh of sweet revenge, "that policy cut down considerably on people bugging out."

Following the infamous California trip, a moderate team recruiting assault was planned for the city of Pittsburgh in late November of 1963. Gale thought that Pittsburgh was not Peace Corps fodder. He did not believe that the University of Pittsburgh, Carnegie Tech (now Carnegie-Mellon), and Duquesne University—the city's largest and best-known institutions of higher learning—would offer up many Peace Corps Volunteers. However, Gale had friends in high places at the University of Pittsburgh and Carnegie Tech who were keen to have the Peace Corps come.

Although Gale did not expect a high yield of Peace Corps recruits in Pittsburgh, he knew at least that he would get the maximum number *possible* out of Carnegie Tech and the University of Pittsburgh. His friends at both places would want to put on a good show for the Peace Corps and they would go to superhuman lengths to get Shriver in person. At Carnegie Tech, there would be H. Russell Bintzer, vice president for public relations and development, and Tom Lindsay, director of development. At the University of Pittsburgh, there would be Ed Litchfield, the chancellor, and Ed Cale, vice president for fundraising.

At Duquesne University, there would be nobody. What?! Bob Gale did not have a pal at Duquesne? (He did not, but Peace Corps recruiters came to know the dean of students there, Geza Grosschmitt, a slight man with thick glasses and a toothy smile that he liked to display in a theatrically sinister way while talking in the manner of Peter Sellers playing Dr. Strangelove. If Shriver would come to speak at Duquesne, Grosschmitt said, with a deliberately mad gleam in his eye, he could be sure of a grand turnout. "I vill stand behind ze children with my vhip, and they vill go into ze auditorium!"

The Pittsburgh blitz was the first not to be led by Bob Gale. But Shriver had promised to show up if the advance team was able, after all, to produce a Gale-like phantasmagoria—grand welcomes, full auditoriums, a press conference, radio and television coverage. Shriver was not being a prima donna in this regard; he was in demand as a speaker all over the country; his Reps pleaded for his presence overseas; host country governments were eager to honor him. It was a matter of going where he could do the most good. And as it turned out, Pittsburgh surprised everyone (and the Gale-less recruiters astonished themselves) by turning on fully to the Peace Corps, including having the mayor proclaim it "Peace Corps Week in Pittsburgh."

Even though Shriver had opted to compress three speeches, a press conference, and a radio and television interview into something less than a day and a half—sending the three advance teams, the three colleges, and KDKA into a scheduling frenzy—his sweep through Pittsburgh was flawless.

Jubilant over his wholly positive reception in Pittsburgh, Shriver left on a morning plane Friday, November 22, 1963. Although he rarely had time for luncheon dates, he made one that day with his wife, Eunice—then pregnant with the Shrivers' fourth child, Mark—at the Hotel Lafayette two blocks from the Peace Corps.

It was there that he heard of the assassination of the president.

An ambitious and complicated semiblitz on New York City, which Gale had been orchestrating for weeks and which was to commence during the last week of November, was abruptly canceled. Peace Corps headquarters was paralyzed. People sat at their desks with their heads in their hands and wept inconsolably for days. Some could not stay in the building for long. It was not unusual to see someone pounding the wall in bitter, angry grief. People whispered to one another that they could still hear the drums.

Shriver was composed but expressionless. No one could look him in the eye. Everyone knew all too well that it was he who had organized the funeral, had walked just behind the President's widow and his two brothers, Robert and Edward, in the funeral procession. Everyone had seen on television his pregnant wife, Eunice, kneel down in the Capitol Rotunda at her brother's coffin. Only one thing was known: Nothing and no one would ever be the same again.

But when the Kennedy family learned from Shriver that the Peace Corps had come to a standstill, that an important recruiting trip to New York had been canceled, they reacted quickly. As Gale remembers it: "They said, no, go ahead. The president would have wanted it. The Peace Corps meant a lot to him. It is important to go on with the work." This was a signal that the Kennedy toughness, the Kennedy courage, and the Kennedy magic were still at work. It was a sign that the Peace Corps was still special, still had a purpose—was, in fact, a living legacy.

"That message from the Kennedys got people back on their feet," says Gale.

In a couple of hours it was humming again. People were again running around like crazy, laughing, arguing, trying to outdo each other. Whew! But it was really something to put back together what had been completely and utterly dismantled. We had to reschedule everything for the first and second weeks in December, telescoping a lot of it. We had to get to those schools before the kids left for Christmas vacation.

I flew up there before anyone else on Friday, November 29; got myself a suite at the Warwick Hotel out of which I ran an advance-advance operation. I went right to my old printing broker, Allied Graphic Arts, with whom I had worked when I was editor in chief of the Maco Magazine Publishing Company. Allied was the biggest in the world. A guy named Salie Weiker was my contact there. Salie is one of the toughest guys in the world. I asked him if there was any way to get posters done in a hurry—like, overnight. Salie said, "You get the material to me by 5:00 P.M. today. We'll get five thousand posters to you by 8:00 A.M. tomorrow. In color."

I found out later that Salie had called someone he did twelve million dollars worth of business with and said, "You will *do* this." And he never charged me for it. The next morning, Saturday, November 30, at 8:00 A.M.—no kidding—five thousand three-color-process posters arrived at my suite, announcing the Peace Corps' presence the following week at such-and-such locations—colleges where we were recruiting, where you could take the Peace Corps test, et cetera. The next day, Sunday, December 1, six advance teams of from three to five people flew in from Washington. Over half of them had previously lived in New York. Some were natives, and boy, the sense of swooping down on the old home town, the biggest city in the world, was just phenomenal. Very competitive. Manic. I mean, people were working off their grief. The attitude was: My team'll lick your team. These people— I had them running all over the city with those posters. And a lot of them were senior staff. But everybody put up posters. Everybody mimeographed. Everybody collated. Everybody phoned professors to schedule classroom visits.

Ironically, one of the people on my team was Jack Vaughn. Now, Jack was already senior staff. As regional director for Latin America, he outranked me. But he never complained. Little did I guess—and Jack didn't either—that he was just about to be appointed ambassador to Panama.

The Peace Corps recruiting trip to New York encompassed Manhattan (Columbia, Barnard, NYU, Hunter, CCNY, Manhattanville), Brooklyn (Brooklyn College), Queens (Queens College), and the Bronx (Fordham). Approximately eighty Peace Corps staff members in all came to town to do the advance and follow-up work.

"Somehow, Craig Ward [a Peace Corps public relations officer] found a huge recreational vehicle to rent," says Gale, "and he drove it right into the middle of the Quadrangle. The administration at Columbia had never allowed anyone to do anything like that in its history. And probably any other time, they'd have called in the police and had us run out and maybe even had us arrested. But the country was still in mourning. The Peace Corps was associated with Kennedy— totally. So they left us alone. We just ran the students in the front door, answered their questions, gave them an application, told them when and where to take the Peace Corps test, and out they went at the back of the van."

Gale requested the largest auditorium at Columbia for Shriver's speech. The dean said, "Oh, no. You don't want that. You would be humiliated. Columbia students never come to hear *anybody* speak, especially someone like Sargent Shriver, who nobody has ever heard of."

Gale was appalled. "I have spent the last nine months of my life on American campuses all over the country," he said. "Before that, I was vice president of one. And I have yet to see a student body that would not turn out for Sargent Shriver and the Peace Corps."

The dean would not be budged. "Columbia is different," he said impassively. "These students are blasé. Nothing impresses them. They are not joiners. I'll wager you could not even fill our smallest auditorium."

Gale, barely able to resist knocking the dean to the floor, replied between clenched teeth, "Where, I wonder, were these blasé, sophisticated Columbia students during the president's funeral just two weeks ago? I'll tell you where they were. They were glued to their television sets just like every other American citizen. They were watching it, transfixed, just like everybody else. And since they were, they saw Sargent Shriver marching right behind Jacqueline Kennedy in the funeral procession. And that is not easy to forget. And they were told repeatedly that it was Sargent Shriver, director of the Peace Corps, and that Sargent Shriver had, in fact, arranged the funeral. So do not tell me that these kids do not know who Sargent Shriver is. The whole *world* knows who Sargent Shriver is!"

The dean reddened: "I am telling you what I know, and what I have seen for years. Students at Columbia pride themselves on being totally unimpressed with celebrities of any sort. Oh, maybe they'd turn out for a counterculture figure like Allen Ginsberg or Timothy Leary, but certainly not for an all-American type like Shriver. Forget it, Bob. And believe me, I am doing you a favor. In the end, you will thank me. It's the smaller auditorium or nothing."

Gale was on the verge of telling the dean that hundreds of hot-eyed, eager Columbia students had already passed through the Peace

Corps van in the Quadrangle and were actually applying for service, but stopped short of doing so, since the administration at Columbia had so far not called out the police, nor had they even requested that the Peace Corps van be removed. Gale knew that Craig Ward's brazen notion of driving it right onto the grounds had shocked just about everybody, including the students, but the act had also gathered unto itself a kind of Robin Hood panache that drew admiration. And anyway, what harm could come of it? Since the Peace Corps was being indulged as to its mischief, Gale decided, why push our luck any further? He concluded his argument for the bigger auditorium with a sigh and a shrug. He was about to walk away when the dean said, "Okay, okay. You can have the big one, but it's your neck."

As it turned out, just a few minutes before Shriver appeared on stage, Gale, Jack Vaughn, and Craig Ward were huddling at the entrance to the auditorium trying to figure out not only how to deal with the standees, who were now packed like sardines into the rear section of the hall, but also how to broadcast Shriver's speech to the overflow crowd outside, which was made up of about fifty plainly disappointed and irritated students. Could they somehow get amplifying equipment to set outside at the last minute?

At this point, the dean appeared, looking more than a bit sheepish and shaking his head: "I would never, never have believed this possible when we had that, er, conversation the other day. Please accept my apologies. This is absolutely *incredible*."

There was no time to savor the sight of the Dean eating crow, nor to solve the problem of getting sound equipment. Shriver, having peeked out and seen the packed auditorium, decided to go on stage immediately instead of waiting for a signal from Gale. His instincts were exactly right; the second he appeared the students, who had been seated, were on their feet, applauding vigorously. A less blasé reception could hardly be imagined. (After the speech, with no urging, Shriver "worked the crowd" outside the auditorium. He knew exactly how and when to do these things, and Gale found himself thinking, not for the first or last time, "presidential.")

"This was great," says Gale. "Not even I expected anything this good. But it never failed—the better it got, the harder it was to pry Sarge away. And it always seemed that I was with him when one of these real 'turn-ons' occurred, coupled with the fact that it also always seemed to be *me* who had to get Sarge to the airport. It was just as important to get Sarge on the right plane as it was to let him interact with the students. But he hated to be coaxed and tugged at. He would just ignore you or glare at you. But if he missed a plane, he could be unmerciful. You couldn't win. So there I was, tugging at him, tapping him on the shoulder, saying, 'Hey, Sarge, we gotta go. *Now*. Hey, Sarge, we're gonna miss the plane, no kidding. Hey, Sarge, please.' "

As it happened, Gale had enlisted the aid of a young man named Mike Sher for this complicated New York trip. Sher was a well-to-do New Yorker who found the Peace Corps fascinating and was willing to work without salary. But he was not particularly interested in going overseas. It was the Kennedy glamour, the politics, the stateside drama that attracted him. "Which was fine with me," says Gale.

I needed all the help I could get. And luckily, Mike had a crisis mentality, because we were always in crisis. Mike was willing to do anything. *Anything*. On this particular trip, I told him that his main responsibility was to hold the plane for Shriver. Mike had a lot of imagination and New York chutzpah. If anyone could hold the plane for Sarge, Mike could. Still, there was of course a limit as to how *long* you could hold a plane.

I finally dragged Sarge away from the crowd at Columbia. We were practically socking each other by the time I got him into the car. I looked at my watch and my stomach turned over. We had only twenty-five minutes to get to La Guardia. It wasn't rush hour so I couldn't blame missing the plane on that. It was a clear day, so there would be no reason the plane would be delayed. I had to count on some freak thing. I could not see how Mike could manage this one. Well! We got to La Guardia, raced to the gate of Eastern—and in those days, you walked out on the tarmac to the plane—and by God, the plane was still there. Sarge and I were running toward it and I suddenly saw *why* the plane was still there. Mike Sher was lying down in front of it. Lying down on the tarmac for R. Sargent Shriver.

The kids were there for Shriver. The kids were always there for Shriver.

♦   ♦   ♦

The blitz instantly became a thing of the past the moment that Mike Sher picked himself up from the tarmac at La Guardia airport in December 1963.

Team recruiting, as Gale had conceived it and as Shriver had invigorated it, went on as before. If anything, the New York trip had convinced many holdouts—many doubters—of the usefulness of the "Gale Method." And since it utilized eighty staff members, a great many more people at headquarters now understood how it was done and had acquired the skills that would make them effective recruiters. This had been a goal of Gale's and of Shriver's. Another goal of theirs had been achieved in the first nine months of team recruiting: The Peace Corps was now a part of campus life. Peace Corps recruiters would be invited back every year, and would be welcomed, often with the same deference and cooperation shown in 1963. Administration officials and faculty members on campus were now attuned to the "Gale Method" and would be more likely to fall in step with Peace Corps recruiters the minute they arrived, and in some cases, act unofficially as surrogate recruiters. Finally, the first nine months of intensive, spectacular, blitz recruiting had allowed the Peace Corps to discover the "real Peace Corps schools," ones where the well would never run dry. The five most potent at that time were the University of California at Berkeley, the University of Wisconsin, the University of Michigan, Carlton, and Swarthmore. "But percentagewise, Carlton was first," says alumnus Gale, beaming.

Ah, Berkeley. Gale and his new deputy in Recruiting, Frank Erwin, personally "hit Berkeley three and sometimes four times a year for the next two years" before they both left the Peace Corps for other government jobs (Gale to be deputy to Franklin D. Roosevelt, Jr., at the Equal Employment Opportunity Commission, and Erwin to be special assistant to Secretary of Labor Willard Wirtz).

"Even with just the two of us working that huge campus," says Gale, "we always came home with a fantastic number of applications. Almost every student we talked to personally about Peace Corps service ended up as a Volunteer."

Berkeley, of course, was also the center of maximum student unrest and protest against the Vietnam War in the mid-1960s to late 1960s. "Without realizing it, I glimpsed the shape of things to come in spring 1964," says Gale.

The students at Berkeley always knew when the Peace Corps was visiting. We made sure they knew, of course, but it was such a great Peace Corps school that word traveled very fast. The first day I was there on my third visit, a guy who used to be a student at Carlton, and had actually done some baby-sitting for us when I worked there, looked me up. Skip Richeimer. He was by this time getting his Ph.D. at Berkeley. He had seen my name in the campus newspaper. Skip also belonged to a radical student group called the Free Speech Movement, whose leader was none other than Mario Savio, who would later become one of the most famous campus radicals in the country. Skip asked if I'd come and talk to the group. Or rather, *listen* to them. They did not think the Berkeley administration was listening. Skip knew that Barbara and I were liberal Democrats, had worked for Hubert Humphrey in 1960, and were now associated with the Peace Corps, and he figured I'd therefore be sympathetic. Well, I didn't see any harm in that. I was willing. I went and listened.

Those people were a bit more hostile toward the administration at Berkeley and the administration in Washington than I thought they'd be. They hoped I'd kind of intercede for them, I guess. They asked me to speak to a very influential, very high-placed female administrator at Berkeley. I had to speak to her anyway, so I mentioned that I'd met with the group and that I thought the problems they perceived as to the social issues and as to their right to speak out were legitimate. I mentioned the group's concerns about nuclear power, the quality of the environment, the possibility of growing involvement in Vietnam. She replied rather icily: "I have my spies, and I know what is going on. And I am asking you to keep out of it."

Gale suddenly thought the whole situation "was potentially more volatile and more ominous than I ever would have suspected." I told her that I'd stay out of it because, one, I was really just a guest; two, because Berkeley was the premier school for Peace Corps Volunteers; and three, because I'd be busy recruiting full time anyway. She looked relieved."

The last thing Gale heard from Skip Richeimer was his voice over a P.A. system that broadcast regularly on campus: "Be sure to visit the Peace Corps booth in front of Sproul Hall this week." Gale still marvels that this about-to-be revolutionary group took it upon itself to benevolently promote the Peace Corps just six months before the group uncorked its revolution. "I've never been sure," says Gale, "whether the Peace Corps' very existence and purpose kept the lid on the uprising for six months, when it might have blown earlier, or whether the very existence of the Peace Corps signaled 'go' in the first place."*

*It was in front of Sproul Hall, the administration building at Berkeley, that in

Ah, Sproul Hall. Gale and Erwin have so many memories of that place. One trip stands out because they almost quit over it. Gale recounts: "It was one of those trips that Frank Erwin and I took to Berkeley not too long after we'd discovered that it was an absolute gold mine for the Peace Corps. We were out there, the two of us, for six days. Standing on the steps of Sproul Hall. The sun never went behind a cloud. We stood on those goddamn steps of Sproul Hall for twelve hours a day talking to students. No relief. As Frank said, our ankles were up to our knees. As a result, we came back to Washington very worn out but with very expensive looking tans on our faces and hands. Now, Sarge knew that we had been at Berkeley, but I guess that he had forgotten. Or he'd just been traveling himself and was distracted. Anyway, he saw us in the hall the first morning we got back to Washington. He stopped in his tracks and just bellowed at us: "Good grief! What are you guys thinking of, anyway? Here it is, the most important recruiting season the Peace Corps has ever had, and you two go off on vacation."

Gale and Erwin looked daggers at Shriver. They turned on their heels and stalked off to their offices, away from Shriver. Their body English was clear: "We quit!" (Not only had no one at Peace Corps headquarters taken so much as a day's vacation since the Peace Corps began, but of all people, Gale and Erwin believed themselves to be the two hardest-working individuals at the agency. They traveled more than the evaluators. They traveled more than Shriver. Their sixteen-dollar-a-day allowance from the government covered only a fraction of their expenses on their numerous recruiting trips. Their hours were longer, their days off—such as an occasional Sunday—were fewer, and their work was more tedious and more physically demanding than anybody else's. Like Peters in the Division of Evaluation, Gale presided over controversial turf. Both Evaluation and Recruiting were the constant targets of sniping and jeering by other individuals and factions. Both operations existed and thrived because Shriver personally stood behind them, personally sanctioned them and encouraged them, gave them high priority. Otherwise, as both Peters and Gale have since put it, "Life would have been impossible.")

September 1964, "Jack Weinberg, 24, a lapsed graduate student in math, set up a card table with leaflets . . . to protest the university's rule . . . which forbade recruiting for political causes . . . and was arrested . . . The Free Speech Movement . . . was born" (Life, vol. 7, no. 13, December 1984).

As Gale and Erwin noisily started to clean out their desks in the seventh-floor Recruiting Office—to the horror of their onlooking colleagues and minions—the phone rang in Gale's office. "It's Mr. Shriver's office," said Linda Lyle, Gale's secretary, tremulously, connecting the call with the wild leave-taking behaviors in the Recruiting Office.

Gale was thinking: "Kennedys never apologize. We've all heard that a million times. So what could this be?" He picked up the phone and, thinking that he had nothing to lose, snarled, "Yeah?"

"Bob, this is Maryann. Mr. Shriver believes that he's made a mistake. He has just remembered that you and Frank were recruiting out at Berkeley. He realizes that of course you have not been on vacation. He's sorry. He apologizes. Honestly."

At that point, Shriver came on the phone: "Hey, Bob. I wondered if you and Frank could join me for dinner tonight. See you in the lobby at 9:30?"

"Okay, Sarge," said Gale. "Nine-thirty. In the lobby."

Could it be that Gale had caved in so easily? Erwin was incredulous. "Yes and no," Gale laughs today. "Three things struck me all at once. One, a Kennedy, so-called, had apologized. A bit indirectly, but still, an apology had been offered. Two, I had calmed down just enough to remember that I still had a wife—and one who had since had a miscarriage—three little kids, and debts up to my ears. Just as I had been when I came to Washington. I couldn't afford to quit. So much for bravado gestures. And three, I started thinking about another truism that applied to the Kennedys: They never carry money. Any of them. Sarge included. Their companions, no matter who they were or where they might be, always ended up forking over.

"I was down from boil to simmer. But I was still sore enough to consider playing a little trick on Sarge." Gale told Erwin: "Tell you what. We'll lock up our wallets in our desks when we go out. That way, we can't bail him out even if the situation gets so embarrassing we'd be tempted to."

"This is crazy, you know," said Erwin. But when the time came, Erwin locked up his wallet, chuckling wickedly.

Shriver took them, as they knew he would, to the Black Steer, a steak-and-hamburger, checkered-tablecloth eatery a block and a half from the Peace Corps on 17th Street. The conversation was entirely amiable, with Shriver making a point of saying how successful the recruiting efforts had been, how impressed Congress was with the numbers (ah, the numbers; always the numbers). Everything Shriver said during dinner clearly was meant to be directly or indirectly complimentary to his two guests. It was obvious that he was trying to make up for impulsively lambasting them earlier in the day. Gale and Erwin were cynical enough—and by that time, clearheaded enough—to know that Shriver really could not afford to alienate his two prime recruiters; on the other hand, it was so uncharacteristic of any Kennedy to let you know that *he* needed *you* (especially more than once in a day) that Gale was beginning to feel a bit guilty about what he was about to do to Shriver, but not guilty enough to go back to the office and get his wallet.

The waitress brought the check. "Typically, Sarge reached around at his pockets and declared that he seemed to have no money, which was no doubt true," says Gale, "because he never did. Frank and I, in turn, reached around in our pockets and mumbled some version or the other of, 'Gee, I don't seem to have any money, either.' Sarge looked nonplussed; this had never happened before. The waitress began to fidget. She was a little embarrassed for us.

"Suddenly, I said, 'Ah. I'll bet you'd take Mr. Shriver's signature, wouldn't you?'

" 'Oh!' she gushed. 'Of *course* we would.'

"And so, Sarge had to sign the bill. *That* time."

◆   ◆   ◆

The worst thing about being director of Recruiting, for Gale, was the incessant carping by a few extreme purists on the staff who could not tolerate the combination of passion and pragmatism that guided the Peace Corps. They wanted a more monastic entity. They did not last long, however; but as they departed, they tended to focus all of their disapproval on the Division of Recruiting. In their view: (1) Recruiting was impure; Peace Corps Volunteers should be like pilgrims and/or missionaries—*called* to serve in the manner of priests and monks; it was wrong, wrong, wrong to go out and importune; (2) Recruiting trips were orgies in disguise at government expense; (3) Recruiting trips were outrageous publicity gambits designed to launch the political careers of certain Peace Corps senior staffers; (4) Recruiting was a Madison Avenue stunt, a numbers game. The fact was that the people who made the most cutting remarks about Gale's approach to recruiting had never recruited.

Gale always declined to reply to these charges and/or insinuations, partly because they were stuffy and exaggerated and partly because, since he had Shriver's full support, he had no need to reply. Occasionally, when pushed a bit too far on the subject of chasing numbers for numbers sake, Gale would snap, "I am merely responding to unreasonable expectations."

Which was true. Shriver was the original numbers addict. But he, too, was responding to unreasonable expectations—of Congress, of the Kennedy family, of the press—and numbers reassured him. In time, he came to like percentages better than numbers. Percentages were somehow less crass. Gale and Erwin were ready for Shriver's percentage phase.

"Fairly often, in staff meetings," says Gale, "Sarge would suddenly turn to me and ask, 'What's our percentage at Harvard?' And I'd say, '6.4 percent,' which meant the percentage of the student population that had applied to the Peace Corps in a given year. Now, I knew approximately what they all were. I just *knew*, after a while, by the type of institution, a very close approximation of what they were.

"But to make it sound utterly convincing, on about the third question of this kind that Sarge would ask, I'd say, for instance, '5.7 percent.' And Frank Erwin would be cued to say, 'No, no, Bob. It's 5.6 percent.' I'd then say, 'Oh, yes. Dammit, Frank. You're right. It's 5.6 percent, Sarge.' "

◆　　　◆　　　◆

Franklin Williams's controversial memo espousing the policy of "In, Up & Out" had set junior-senior, senior, and senior-senior staff members to thinking seriously about their futures sooner than most would have otherwise done. While no one thought of making a career out of the Peace Corps—it was not the sort of place where you dug in forever, in any case—it was a bit unnerving knowing that you *had* to clear out in no later than five years. Many staffers spent inordinate amounts of time figuring out how they could get around the rule, now being called the "Five Year Flush," and some succeeded, ultimately, in tacking two or three years on to their designated tenure (the more senior they were, the more easily this was accomplished).

However, by early 1965, Gale had no thought of staying longer than three years, having arrived in March 1963. Nothing could ever replace the Peace Corps in his heart, and no experience he could ever have would be so rich. Still, there were Shriver's edicts: "Recruiting is the key to the Peace Corps," and "Bob Gale's formula works better than any other," and "Oh, by the way, Bob, no matter what other titles you might ever get here, you're never getting Director of Recruiting out of your complete title."

Bob Gale did not want to be Director of Recruiting for Life. Indeed, he knew that by the end of three years in this job, he would be a squeezed lemon, a much-too-familiar face to college administrators, a potential Johnny-One-Note. He knew that he could not sustain the enthusiasm, the energy, or the spirit to have it be otherwise. Furthermore, the pressure of "responding to unreasonable expectations" ever since the Wisconsin trip, combined with what he termed "mindless criticism," had taken its toll on the normally jolly Gale disposition. He felt he would soon rival John Alexander and Bill Haddad for exorbitant displays of temperament. Gale had had his flashy time—very flashy—and he knew it. During the 1963–64 academic year, his recruiting techniques had bought in thirty-six thousand applications. During the 1964–65 season, his formula attracted forty-six thousand. "We were better organized the second year," he says. "But what were we going to do for an encore? At what point were Sarge's expectations going to level off? How long were history and the national mentality going to stay on our side? I really wanted to quit while I was winning. To have gone stale at the Peace Corps would have been a sad thing. I was catching on to the terrifying importance of timing and image in Washington. I was becoming a creature of the city."

Gale had stopped worrying about quitting his Peace Corps job with a wife, three children, and debts on his hands. Because the Peace Corps was a speeded-up agency and the Division of Recruiting was an even more speeded-up operation within it, Gale and Erwin had come to know, and be known by, scores of influential people in half the time it usually takes in Washington. The Peace Corps became known as a "talent bank," and its excellent press coverage gave it a sheen that piqued curiosity. Thus, by early 1965, Gale and Erwin were getting job offers that they could seriously consider.

It was a nice feeling, the best kind. But it was not a specific job offer that sent Gale scurrying for the door. It was basically a case of fright.

While the forsythia blazed forth in Washington and the temperatures climbed to seventy degrees in March 1965, it was frigid and snowing hard in Bloomington, Indiana. Bob Gale was completing his advance work at the University of Indiana, and Shriver was winding up his speech to an overflow crowd of about two thousand students. "It was a Shriver classic," recalls Gale, already beginning to shift uneasily in his chair in the remembering.

He was doing his Pied Piper number. He had given this stem-winder of a speech, quoting from Thomas Aquinas and Thomas Jefferson and the Greek philosophers and the Bible and JFK's inaugural speech, and the kids were going wild. As usual, the kids were chasing along behind him as he left the auditorium, asking for his autograph, wanting to shake his hand. Mobs of them. Shriver enjoying every second. In this wild snowstorm. And, as usual, I am pleading, "Sarge, we're gonna miss the plane. We gotta *go*. The car's right over there." The kids are all but clawing him. So I commence pulling at him, as usual, and he starts sort of socking me, as usual, and we are having this pulling and hitting contest.

I finally get him into the car, and he is *so* happy because everything is going *so* well, the kids are shouting and running alongside the car, and I am inching along, trying not to run over them, not knowing exactly where I'm headed in this blizzard. We get out on the main road, and now Sarge wants me to *step* on it, *step* on it, and my nerves are so frazzled I miss the turnoff. We can't get up on to the cloverleaf. And I don't know how to double back and get onto it. Because I have never been there before. And Sarge is having a fit. "Go up the *other* way," he shouts.

"That's the opposite exit ramp, Sarge. We *can't*."

"Sure you can, sure you can. Just blink your lights and honk your horn. Keep blinking and honking."

So there I am in a blinding snowstorm, driving up an exit ramp the wrong way at sixty miles an hour, and the president's brother-in-law is just as excited as hell, cheering me on, laughing and yelling and having a wonderful time. Lights blinking. Horn honking. Total madness. Then, an insane, suicidal U-turn, and we're off! Made the plane by a split second. To Sarge, making the plane was simply the happy ending to a series of delightful episodes. To me, it was simply The End.

"Shortly thereafter," breathes Gale luxuriously, "I left."

Then he laughs and laughs and laughs. The joke, he clearly thinks, is not on him.

CHAPTER 8

SHRIVER'S REPS: MEN OF THEIR TIMES

"The Peace Corps Representative occupies the pivotal position in the Peace Corps administration," wrote Shriver in 1962. "From the day we decided that the Peace Corps would manage its own programs overseas, I knew that this would be so. The 'Rep,' as we have come to call him, would be crucial to the success or failure of the Peace Corps effort."

At the very beginning, Shriver charged Bill Haddad with coordinating the operation called Talent Search; it was another of Haddad's many ad hoc, hip-pocket jobs that some of his colleagues secretly referred to as the "hero hunt." In the fall of 1961, the job fell to Glenn Ferguson, who came to the Peace Corps with an M.B.A. from Cornell and a law degree from the University of Pittsburgh, where he had also been assistant dean and assistant professor of the Graduate School of Public and International Affairs. Most recently he had been an official of the management-consultant firm McKinsey & Company. Shriver thought the experienced, sophisticated Ferguson would be a valid replacement for Haddad, who was now setting up the new Division of Evaluation. Ferguson was, but he almost immediately succumbed to 'Rep fever,' and Shriver delightedly dispatched him to run Thailand I on November 3, 1961. Talent Search was then successively run by the dashing Franklin Williams, the suave Willy Warner, the towering scion Jay Rockefeller IV, his aristocratic roommate Bill Wister, and the winsome bluestocking Nan Tucker McEvoy. By putting so many of his "stars" in the Talent Search job, Shriver was serving notice that his standards for overseas Reps were exceedingly high. (The initial screening process eliminated all but about one in thirty applicants; those who survived were then subjected to the famous "interview mill" at Peace Corps headquarters.)

It was taken for granted that the first Reps would be men between the ages of thirty-five and fifty-five; no women were ever then seriously considered for the top overseas jobs, although a handful became associate Reps in the first three years. It was also taken for granted that the first Reps would have "star quality." And indeed, the "hero hunt" did produce some genuine heroes. While the early Peace Corps was obsessively antimilitary and antibureaucratic in all of its attitudes (and some outsiders thought comically so), there was this irony: For men between thirty-five and fifty-five at that time, military service was a "given." It was the one experience that all of them had in common, and it was generally the experience that had shaped them more than any other. Most of the first Peace Corps Reps had served in World War II or the Korean War, or—as in the case of Don McClure, who was too young for the wars—had performed some form of military service for two years. The first Reps came out of a generation that had worn a uniform. Most had seen combat and some had been decorated.*

Frank Mankiewicz, the first Rep in Peru, had enlisted as a private in the army after one year at Haverford College and before his eighteenth birthday. He was first sent to language school to learn Spanish and ended up with a mortar company in the Sixty-ninth Infantry Division, which went into combat across France, Belgium, and Germany. "I wound up," says Mankiewicz, "in the battalion which met the Russians at the Elbe. I personally didn't meet any Russians. My jeep had a flat tire that day." Mankiewicz's deputy Rep in Peru, Bill Mangin, joined the navy V-12 program after one year at Syracuse University. He was later commissioned an ensign and assigned to amphibious forces, was sent to the Pacific, and participated in the invasion of the Marshall Islands. Darwin Bell, Mankiewicz's third in command in Peru, the calmest and most good-natured of men, had a particularly harrowing wartime experience. After two years at Utah State, he enlisted in the army as a private in 1942 and, like Mankiewicz, was sent to language school and wound up in a mortar company in France. But Bell and his whole division were captured by Germans in the Battle of the Bulge and were taken to Stalag 9-B in Bad Orb. Bell escaped from the prison camp twice and was recaptured twice. The third time he escaped, the Germans found him again but, thinking he was dead, left him in a field, where he was picked up by nuns and taken to an infirmary. A German doctor told him he had to have his appendix out and that he would be back the next day to operate. "But the next day," said Bell, "American tanks came rolling into town and the war was over for me." Bell spent the next nine months in hospitals in Europe and the United States recovering from severe malnutrition

*All Peace Corps Reps had college degrees and 86 percent of them had advanced degrees, the latter usually having been acquired after military service.

and a damaged coccyx. (In Peru, nineteen years later, as Bell and Mankiewicz compared wartime experiences, they suddenly realized that after Bell's division had been captured, Mankiewicz's division had taken its place.)

Charles Houston, M.D., the first full-time Rep in India, in addition to his rigorous and daring mountaineering escapades, had served in World War II as a naval officer and flight surgeon attached to high-altitude training units. Houston's deputy Rep, Brent Ashabranner, spent four years in the navy, first with the Seabees and then with amphibious forces in the South Pacific.

Andres (Andy) Hernandez, the first Rep in the Dominican Republic (and later Rep in Guatemala) enlisted in the army in 1942 and won three battle stars for combat duty in the Battle of the Bulge, in the Ruhr, and at Aachen and Cologne.

Eugene Baird, the first deputy Rep in Ecuador, was a gunner's mate on the aircraft carrier *Yorktown* and then on the destroyer *Stormes*; he participated in the invasions of Kwajalein, Tarawa, the Truk Islands, Palau, Saipan, and Guam. David Boubion, the first Rep in Panama, served aboard a destroyer in the campaigns at Iwo Jima and Okinawa at the age of eighteen. David Stauffer, the first Rep in British Honduras (now Belize) was a member of the army air force reserve and a sophomore at Amherst when he was called to active duty in 1941. He first flew B-24s for the Eighth Air Force out of England while his twin brother was also flying B-24s in Italy. He later shifted to B-17s and flew twenty-two combat missions in Europe and won the Distinguished Flying Cross.

Ross Pritchard, the first full-time Rep in Turkey, joined the navy right after Pearl Harbor, when he was all of seventeen years old. This adolescent male from Paterson, New Jersey, was assigned as a tail gunner and radio operator in a patrol bombing squadron and was cited for bravery under fire while serving in the South Atlantic and North Africa. William Saltonstall, who at the age of fifty-four resigned as headmaster of Phillips Academy, Exeter, to be the Peace Corps' second Rep in Nigeria, served as an officer aboard the USS *Bunker Hill* during World War II.

Thomas Quimby, who directed the first Peace Corps program in Liberia, graduated from high school in Grand Rapids, Michigan, in the class of 1936, along with a pretty young lady named Betty Bloomer, whom he briefly dated and who later married another Grand Rapids native named Gerald Ford. Four years later, Quimby graduated from

Harvard in the class of 1940 with a handsome young man named John Fitzgerald Kennedy. Quimby joined the U.S. Navy in June 1941. His fleet oiler was sunk in January 1942, one of the first U.S. ships hit in the Pacific after Pearl Harbor. How did he survive this calamity? "Swam," says Quimby. (He was ultimately rescued by a U.S. destroyer.) Almost exactly twenty years later, he was instrumental in rescuing a Peace Corps Volunteer and a Catholic priest after their fishing boat capsized in the Atlantic Ocean off the West African coast. Also taking part in that rescue operation was Walter Carrington, the first Rep in Sierra Leone (which borders on Liberia). Carrington, although a graduate of Harvard and Harvard Law School (class of 1955) and a member of the National Board of Directors of the NAACP, was given the title of clerk-typist in the United States Army from 1956 to 1958, "although I spent most of my time serving as defense counsel at courts-martial."

Haddad says: "The Peace Corps always reminded me of a World War II movie without the horror. That spirit filtered down to the Peace Corps. There was always that self-effacing humor, the kind of humor that develops in times of hardship or danger. And we were arrogant in a funny kind of way. We were guys of the forties who thought there was nothing we, or America, couldn't do."

DONOVAN McCLURE

Don McClure had traveled with Shriver countless thousands of miles all over the United States as speech writer, briefer, press handler, and crisis manager from September 1961 to September 1962. On a moment's notice, he had packed his bags and accompanied Shriver to Ethiopia, Somalia, Tanganyika, and Tunisia in October 1962—a trip so exhilarating yet so exhausting and dangerous that he found himself saying to his wife upon his return, "That trip was one of the most profound experiences of my life. But I never want to do *anything* like that ever again."

Still, he had had the lion's share of New Frontier fun. Traveling across the United States and through Africa with Shriver, McClure had met governors of states in America, heads of state in Africa. He had played touch football at Timberlawn (Shriver's estate in Rockville, Maryland) with the Kennedys. In effect, McClure was living on the edge of the golden circle that was universally imagined to surround the magic core of Camelot. What more could a young journalist of his political persuasion want? He was leading millions of people's fantasy lives. But a year intensively in the company of Shriver during the pulsating formative stage of the Peace Corps' development had left McClure feeling stretched thin. Anyway, his promised one-year-off-only had already passed. He'd left his heart in San Francisco. It was time to go back.

McClure called his former boss, Abe Mellincoff at the *San Francisco Chronicle*, to say that he would soon be heading west. He then went to see Shriver, hoping that his parting words of appreciation would be adequate to the "unprecedented, fantastic opportunity" that Shriver had given him.

Shriver was having none of it. "Hey, come on, Don. Don't be ridiculous. You're not leaving the Peace Corps. You're going overseas. You're going to be a Rep."

McClure was somewhat stunned, since the subject of Rep-ship had never come up before. He reminded Shriver that he had had no real experience as an administrator, and further, had no facility for foreign languages. None whatsoever. Hopeless.

"That's okay. We'll send you to an English-speaking country. How about Gabon?"

"Sarge, they speak French in Gabon," said McClure patiently, knowing that Shriver knew it.

"Well, then," said Shriver, "How about Sierra Leone?"

McClure pretended to be interested. "You didn't exhibit poor sportsmanship in front of Sarge, no matter what. But I wasn't worried. I could afford to play the game. I knew that Maggie would shoot it right down, anyway. And if a Peace Corps wife balked at going overseas, Shriver would relent."

But that evening, McClure got one of the biggest shocks of his life. "Maggie was all for it. She actually wanted to go. We had never discussed this possibility, just as I had never before discussed it with Sarge. The deal had always been, we were going back to San Francisco. But Maggie was now saying that the children, being only three and five, could adjust. They wouldn't be leaving longtime friends or schools. And *she* could adjust. I'd been traveling with Sarge for the better part of the year and hadn't been home much. She figured she and the kids would see more of me in Sierra Leone, with Sarge five thousand miles away. And mainly, she said, we might not ever have a chance to do something like this again. We'd never have the nerve.

"So there went my last line of defense. I couldn't exactly tell Sarge that Maggie refused to go when in fact Maggie was dying to go." But what of Abe Mellincoff at the *San Francisco Chronicle*, who had already given McClure a year's leave of absence and was expecting him back momentarily? "Abe was so sure I'd always go back—and so was I—that he gave me another two years leave. He was convinced that additional exposure to government and international affairs during the Kennedy administration would make me that much more valuable to the *Chronicle* in the long run." So, with Shriver insisting, his wife encouraging, and his former boss acquiescing, McClure was on his way, in March 1963, to the continent that he had so recently sworn he would never step foot on again.

Where is Sierra Leone? What is it?

If you took a large world map, scissored out the continent of Africa, and then picked the cutout up, explains McClure, "your left thumb would likely rest on and cover up Sierra Leone. It's that small, hot, humid, very wet yet also very dry, thumb-shaped country on the west coast of Africa." (Sierra Leone is on the west coast of the African continent, the portion that juts out into the Atlantic Ocean. If that "jut" were to be compared to a head and a chin, Sierra Leone might be a tiny dimple in that chin. Guinea is to its north and east, Liberia to its south.)

Sierra Leone was the first British colony. It had achieved independence in April 1961, and it had become the one hundredth member of the United Nations. Sierra Leone was one of the first half-dozen Third World nations to receive Peace Corps Volunteers. While English was the language of instruction in Sierra Leone, and while all signs and menus in the capital city, Freetown, and environs were printed in English, *Krio* was the lingua franca, and 220 hours of it was taught to the Volunteers in university training programs in the United States. (Other tribal dialects were spoken in Sierra Leone: *Mende* in the south, *Temne* in the north.)

"In language, the Volunteers were way ahead of the staff. But thank God," says McClure, "the sixty Peace Corps teachers who arrived in September 1963 had been trained at Cornell, had learned to love the little green lizards that would be scampering across their bedroom ceilings. They had learned host-country customs, traditions, economy, politics, religions, and dialects. Volunteers who had been garbling phrases of 'The Star Spangled Banner' all their lives could render all three verses of the Sierra Leone national anthem perfectly."

Unfortunately for McClure, Walter Carrington, the Rep in Sierra

Leone for the first year, was transferred to the Peace Corps hierarchy in Tunisia before McClure had a chance to get briefed by him. Indeed, some of what the McClures came face to face with during their first few days in Freetown had sent them reeling. As McClure explains, the worst of it was this: "In Freetown, open sewers ran along either side of the main streets. They were three feet deep and immediately adjacent to the narrow roads. An unknowing or miscalculating passenger, hopping out of a vehicle, all too often slid into the muck, screaming in rage and disgust—arms and hands flailing wildly in the air. And it was not at all unusual for me to encounter, on my way to and from work, at least one taxicab or lorry (the British word for truck—better still, decrepit truck) lying on its side in the ooze, like a wounded buffalo. In early autumn, during the rainy season, these sewers would fill to overflowing and disappear from sight altogether, giving the streets the illusion of being broader than they actually were. And so, again, this caused the uninitiated or distracted person to attempt to wade across what appeared to be mere puddles, only to drop chest-deep into a swirling sewer."

Freetown, however, was not altogether uncivilized. In fact, in some ways it was a bit too civilized to suit the McClures, who had fantasized something more on the order of a genteel-seedy Graham Greene novel. (Coincidentally, McClure had been reading Greene's *The Heart of the Matter*, which is based on Greene's experiences in Sierra Leone as functionary of the British government, just as Shriver popped the Sierra Leone question.) "Supermarkets were springing up," says McClure. "You could buy aerosol shaving lather, stainless steel blades, bourbon, frozen meat, and Polaroid film. Soon after we arrived, a Lebanese restaurant opened up, offering hot dogs and hamburgers. There were two air-conditioned, wide-screen cinemas with ten-year-old Tab Hunter movies. Jukeboxes blared Ray Charles, Burl Ives, Elvis Presley, and the Limeliters. Local television showed "The Flintstones" and "The Beverly Hillbillies," which appalled me, in my Graham Greene romanticism, but delighted my children. Our other major culture-shock experiences were campy Arabic films, inevitably featuring bosomy two-hundred-pound heroines, and—oh, yes—the daily sight of topless salesgirls in the open-air markets. Quite unnerving. The thought occurred to me that the topless ladies were responsible for so many taxicabs and lorries running off the road. But that's an American thought. Sierra Leone had been topless for centuries with no fuss. And the lorries were in lousy shape."

But what Americans fear and fret about above all else when contemplating life in a Third World nation is that ultimate cultural factor: food. "Can we eat it?" "Will it kill us?" "If we can't handle the local food, what can we find to eat instead?" "Might we actually starve?"

McClure had reason to fear the food in Africa. In spite of his six-foot-two height and his athletic frame, McClure could tolerate only bland fare; he had the digestive system of a hummingbird. He had been forced to eat the highly spiced chicken *wat*, the signature dish of Ethiopia, six months before on his trip with Shriver through East Africa, and he had thought at the time that he might actually die from it. And he had been unable to ingest or digest the local fare of most other African countries. He had lost eighteen pounds in eighteen days. The thought occurred to him when he said good-bye to Shriver on his way to Sierra Leone that he might just end up looking like Mahatma Gandhi while "asking not" in Africa. Thus, he was profoundly relieved to find that there was at least some American-style food available in Freetown, and that the principal dish of Sierra Leone, Jolloff rice and ground-nut stew, was edible. *Fufu* and *bonga*, also local fare, never reached his lips, let alone his stomach. He was warned by other American officials in the country to steer clear of it altogether. Even one Sierra Leone native, whose own tastes ran to things British, intoned, "*Don't.*" McClure never found out what *fufu* and *bonga* actually were. He preferred to think of them as incantations rather than as something to eat.

"Ironically," says McClure, "Freetown looks like San Francisco with the money removed. It's built on a series of dramatic hills overlooking a beautiful bay. It's the only city in Africa with that kind of topography, and the harbor is the third largest in the world. For all of its basic potential to be cosmopolitan, it had, in 1963, only one first-class hotel, the Paramount. The Paramount stands on one of those magnificent hills overlooking the bay. But none of the rooms have a view of the bay. They overlook the parking lot. It was explained to me that you can always see the bay, but how often can you get to see a really first-class parking lot?"

Such skewed priorities and catch-22 thinking were rampant in African nations as they achieved independence in the early 1960s. Sometimes the rush to freedom brought on a compulsion to modernize, and modernize inappropriately, as in the case of the Paramount Hotel. Other opportunities inherent in throwing off the colonial yoke were not just mangled, they were missed. People long used to the values of a dominant outside culture may be slow, and even stubborn, about accepting new and more flexible ideas and systems. For many Peace Corps Reps in the early 1960s, when freedom (*uhuru*) was a-flower in Africa, these problems were constant and often bedeviling.

McClure eased himself slowly into these ironies and paradoxes with the help of Mike McCone, his twenty-eight-year-old deputy, who had also been deputy to McClure's predecessor, Walter Carrington. McCone, a Philadelphian with a degree from Yale, had spent summer vacations as a choker setter on highload logging operations for the Weyerhaeuser Timber Company in Oregon. He had also been a naval officer on board a destroyer, serving as a communications officer. He had left his job in San Francisco as a stevedore superintendent to join the first Peace Corps program in Sierra Leone. (McCone had the kind of background, on paper, that made Shriver all shivery—the kind of chic-tough credentials that found him hitting the "buzz bomb" button and barking, "Find this guy! Find McCone!")

McClure describes McCone as "a tall, lanky guy with sandy hair, pale blue eyes, high-pitched laughter, a far-out sense of humor, an enormous capacity for work, and a fierce loyalty to the Peace Corps." McCone dragged out a raft of papers, McClure recalls of their first meeting—reports, accounting sheets, ledgers, and purchase-order forms. He began to explain to McClure the intricacies of overseas administration procedures.

"It was a bleak moment," says McClure twenty-two years later. "My mind boggles at the most simple figures, and here I was confronted with debits and credits and allotment symbols and obligated and deobligated funds.

"Mike paused, noting my distress. 'You got all that, didn't you, dad?' He smiled what I very soon came to recognize as the McCone leg-pull smile."

McCone then told McClure not to worry about it. "I'll handle it, and when I'm not here to handle it, we've got a Sierra Leonean over at the embassy, named Sawyer-Williams, who can give Washington whatever figures they want."

McClure replied that, while he was grateful for McCone's careful explanation of bureaucratic financial procedures, he found them somewhat confusing. But he vowed to make an attempt to "learn something more about these matters."

"Oh, Christ no!" growled McCone. "Out here, you're Shriver. Did you ever see Shriver pouring over ledgers and trying to find out how the hell many footlockers there are in the Volunteers' houses? This is staff work, and I'm your staff. You stay fresh to mess with the big issues, like Sarge-baby does."

McClure thought: "Godammit, McCone, we just might get along."

"Now, about those big issues," said McCone. "Let me give you my view of the state of our projects as of this moment."

The Peace Corps Volunteers were working in three major fields. There were forty-six secondary schoolteachers spread around the country. There were twenty rural-development workers and ten medical Volunteers—two doctors and eight nurses who were assigned to a government hospital upcountry. In September 1963, there would be another sixty schoolteachers arriving, at which point the Sierra Leone contingent of Peace Corps Volunteers would rise to 156.

Each group had exquisite problems, of course.

For the forty-six teachers already at work, the main gripe was the transfer. The strong Volunteer, said McCone, would stick with a frustrating situation until he licked it, but a weak one—"and we have a few"—would rather switch than fight. Several teachers were at that moment clamoring for a change, said McCone, either to another house or another school. McClure would have to meet those involved and decide for himself.

The most troublesome aspect of the Volunteer teacher's life was that it was quite often segregated. On school compounds, McClure was told, there was senior-staff housing and junior-staff housing, and the two encompassed a world of difference in size, furniture, upkeep, and the amenities. Volunteers were invariably assigned to senior-staff housing, while the African teachers were relegated to the poorer junior accommodations. This arrangement, said McCone, set the Volunteers' teeth on edge. By their lights, it was the opposite of what was supposed to be going on. But their pleadings with their headmasters and with the minister of education were to no avail. Perhaps McClure ought to intervene in due course, McCone suggested.

The rural development (RD) Volunteers were hindered by two factors: the "rain that won't stop" in the early fall—thirteen feet of it—and snakes.

In the worst of the rainy season, "the jeeps won't start, which doesn't matter all that much," said McCone, "because the roads are impassable, anyway." And you can't build roads and bridges while being pummeled by opaque sheets of water. During this period, the RD Volunteers became demoralized and stir-crazy, said McCone. It was clear to McClure that there was no solution except to encourage the RD Volunteers to write home for Monopoly sets and more paperbacks.

As for the snakes, McClure was far more sympathetic. He had three phobias: air travel, accounting, and snakes. His Peace Corps duty had brought him into close contact with all three. Even if there was nothing he could do about the snakes, he could be *understanding* when the RD Volunteers complained. (McClure never forgot the Rep in Somalia who had hated his Volunteers for complaining and called them crybabies. And he had been fired.)

McClure had a special feeling in his heart for the RD Volunteers, who were all males. He himself could never have been an RD Volunteer; RD Volunteers lived and worked in "the bush." McClure had an aversion to the countryside, remembering visits to his grandparents' farm in rural West Virginia as a child. Insects, outhouses, and snakes. He knew as a boy it wasn't supposed to be a masculine trait to recoil from such entities, and he knew as a man that it was positively stigmatizing to exhibit loathing and terror in this regard. But the snakes were the worst of it. Still, he also knew that there were others like himself out there—otherwise strong men who feared reptiles. On his first trip out to see the "RD boys," clomping through the tall grass with them, McClure learned that one of their number, Tony Longi— who wore a black eye patch and a beard and was "built like the middle guard of the Green Bay Packers"—shared his trepidation. McClure told him confidentially that he had read somewhere that a snake is as frightened as you are, and if he knows you're coming, he'll get out of the way. Longi looked grateful. "When I go through this tall grass in my work, alone, I stomp and sing and make all kinds of noise," said Longi. "I don't want to sneak up on anything. You know?"

The Peace Corps medical team in Sierra Leone had had a communications problem so total, in the beginning, that it was almost funny. In training, the Volunteers had been told that they would work in public health. "Unfortunately," says McClure, "this message did not filter through to the Ministry of Health in Sierra Leone, which assigned them to clinical medicine at Magburaka Government Hospital (which was at the geographic center of the country). The hospital's superintendent, a Dr. Harding, was told nothing at all. One day the medical team just arrived." The buck was passed and passed. Blame was placed and replaced, from the Ministry of Health to the former Peace Corps Rep in Sierra Leone to the American embassy to the AID office to Peace Corps headquarters in Washington to the White House and back again. The fact was, of course, the Peace Corps medical team was very welcome indeed. Extra trained hands are welcome in any hospital in the world, especially in a provincial hospital in Africa. And even though the Peace Corps nurses were initially appalled—as American nurses invariably are—at hospital standards so removed from the sanitized and sterile conditions they were accustomed to in the States, "they took this in stride, confident in their own technical skills, and gradually reconciled their initial shock by marvelous improvisations," says McClure.

◆　　　◆　　　◆

On Mike McCone's advice, McClure's first act as Peace Corps Rep in Sierra Leone was to introduce himself to George Davies, the Peace Corps' contact at the Ministry of Education.

From McClure's journal and notes and story outlines of that time comes this account:

George flicked a cigar ash on the floor by his chair and repeated my question. "How is the Peace Corps doing in Sierra Leone? Let me put it this way. The people who two years ago were saying 'When *you* invited the Peace Corps to Sierra Leone' are now saying, 'When *we* invited the Peace Corps to Sierra Leone.' "

George laughed uproariously, displaying a gold tooth. He struck another match to his cigar that had gone out in the vigor of his laughter. George Davies was about fifty—a lean, soft-spoken Sierra Leonean who had lived several years in England, had been educated there, and still went there every couple of years for what he actually called Home Leave. His accent was so British I could barely understand him. I could see he was having the same difficulty with my West Virginia English.

Mike had briefed me earlier on George Davies. When the Sierra Leone government requested Peace Corps teachers in the summer of 1961, the Ministry of Education's professional staff was wildly pessimistic. Their concern was not that the Peace Corpsmen would have difficulty living here, which had been the concern back in Washington. It was the American education of the Volunteers that was suspect. To be fair, there was room for reasonable doubt. Lord knows, Americans can't spell. Such simple words as tyre, programme, colour, and gaol are invariably misspelled. And would they understand the importance of sticking to the syllabus and pointing every effort toward the exams? Could they adapt to the British system, with its African deviations? Were they qualified to teach? Several at the Ministry thought not.

Still, the country's secondary schools were hopelessly under-staffed and new ones could open only if teachers were available. A developing country must gamble. Skeptics at the Ministry crossed their fingers and breathed a compassionate sigh for George Davies. As the Principal Education Officer for secondary schools, George was the fall guy on whom this dubious new program had fallen.

George responded in the only way a professional could—with a buoyant optimism. He behaved as though he had been tossed the Ministry's juiciest plum. George, with his law degree from Cambridge, his education classically British, was rapturous over the magnificent things they were doing in education at West Dakota State. He quietly but thoroughly conned doubting headmasters with his outrageous prediction that in another year, all schools in Sierra Leone would be clamoring for these energetic Americans and they had best get a foot in the door now while the first few were still available.

That was two years ago. As George Davies sat in my office now, puffing on a yellow English cigar, we were making plans for the arrival of 60 new Volunteer teachers. Headmasters had asked for 110. It was the seller's market George had so facetiously predicted. This was not to say that all skeptics were now believers, for it was still early, but the atmosphere around the Ministry was decidedly warmer, and George Davies was no longer the man in the Edsel. *

---

*Forty-one of the forty-six secondary schools in Sierra Leone were established by Christian missionaries, and while they received most of their financial support from the Sierra Leone government, the headmasters were primarily Catholic priests and Protestant ministers of various denominations. McClure found it fascinating to see that the church groups had carved out areas of influence on the map of Sierra Leone in a pattern similar to the French, British, and Belgian colonizers on the map of Africa. In the north, Catholic mission schools were administered by the Dutch brothers. In the south, it was the Irish fathers. Various Protestant mission schools were located north and south, but rarely in the same community with their Catholic competitors.

McClure learned to time his visits to the Protestant schools in the morning and early afternoon, "hitting the Catholic schools in the late afternoon or evening, since the Catholic fathers invariably greeted me after a long, dusty jeep ride with a cold bottle of Heineken. The best I could ever do at the Protestant schools was Coca-Cola."

Since the communications breakdown between the Peace Corps and the Ministry of Health, resulting in the surprise arrival of the ten medical Volunteers at Magburaka Hospital (where they were assigned to work for which they had not been trained), McClure vowed to stay in closer touch with the ministries concerned with Peace Corps projects than was normally the custom. He would certainly not want to let George Davies out of his sight for very long. Here was a host-country official who literally spoke the King's English and had a European mentality, political and bureaucratic skills, and a sense of humor. A rare find. And rarer still, Davies understood completely the nature and the purpose of the Peace Corps. He wished it well, wanted it to succeed. And he was keen to be involved, but not so keen as to be meddlesome. McClure was grateful. Many other Reps were not so lucky in their host-country contacts; indeed, enough Sierra Leonean officials did not fully comprehend the Peace Corps' stance and mission. It was very, very important to have a friend at the Ministry of Education, McClure mused, especially when, with the arrival of 60 more Volunteer teachers within days, the number of Peace Corps teachers would climb to 106.

McClure, McCone, and Davies worked on the Volunteer assignment sheets together. Davies asked how long the in-country orientation program should be. McCone and McClure agreed that three days would suffice. "In the early days of the Peace Corps," says McClure, "host-country orientation programs often lasted several weeks, much to the irritation of Volunteers weary from stateside training and eager to get on with the job. An abbreviated orientation now served mostly a protocol function—an opportunity for the Volunteers to meet the minister of education and the American ambassador and to get their pictures taken for the newspapers."

McClure was envisioning working around the clock to prepare for the new Volunteers' imminent arrival, when Davies announced casually, "I'll get the invitations and programs printed up for the orientation. Just send over a list of who you want invited from the embassy."

Too good to be true, McClure said to himself. "Well, thanks, George. That will be a big help."

Then Davies did himself one better. Pausing at the door, he turned to McClure: "Mike tells me you like to play poker."

"It's a way of life," McClure replied, the light in his eye unmistakable.

"Good. Be my guest tomorrow night at the Reform Club. We play every Friday. Bring money.""*

♦   ♦   ♦

Friday night poker games at the Reform Club in Freetown quickly became a staple of McClure's life there. And he found, to his delight, that his poker colleagues were none other than canny, clever Sierra Leonean officials from the various ministries—interior, justice, agriculture, health, education—men like George Davies; men he would be dealing with, in any case, in his job as Peace Corps Rep. When push came to shove, as it was bound to occasionally between Peace Corps staff and Volunteers and the authority figures of Sierra Leone, much could be smoothed out and solved in the smoke-filled poker parlor (or parlour) of the Reform Club. Or over lunch. And, sometimes, over tennis. The arrangement worked out so well that McClure added another evening of poker at his own house every Tuesday. This practice continued until his departure in early 1965.

"These men were bright and amusing," says McClure, "people you'd love to have dinner with anywhere in the world. They had a realistic sense of their own country. They knew what progress was rationally possible and what was not possible. There was nothing subservient about them, but they didn't have the ego-trip syndrome, either. For instance, they did not take the attitude—as did Ghana, in their view—that they were 'a power to be reckoned with.' They thought Nkrumah's stance in Ghana was offensively arrogant."

But McClure had promised himself, McCone, and the Volunteer teachers that he would do battle with the most stubborn government officials and with the headmasters of the secondary schools of Sierra Leone on the question of the segregated housing. George Davies steered

*After McClure concluded his tour in Sierra Leone and returned to Washington, he arranged for George Davies to visit the United States and participate in training programs for future teaching projects in Sierra Leone. McClure, remembering the great disappointment that Davies had earlier expressed in not having met "your Sargent Shriver" on a brief visit to Sierra Leone in 1962, during Walter Carrington's tour as Rep, arranged a time for Davies to meet Shriver at Peace Corps headquarters. Given Shriver's packed schedule, this had not been easy to do, but McClure had been able to convince Shriver of Davies's pivotal role vis-à-vis the Peace Corps in Sierra Leone (and it did not hurt that Davies had a law degree from Cambridge). McClure couldn't wait to tell Davies the good news, imagining how thrilled Davies would be. "Oooooo. Yesssss," intoned Davies. "I would like to meet your Sargent Shriver. But first, can I meet your Jay Rockefeller?"

McClure to a particular gentleman at the Ministry of Education who was said to be Keeper of the System.

"We make housing assignments on the basis of qualifications," said the official intransigently. He seemed puzzled that McClure, a white American male from a southern state, would object to segregated housing. He seemed annoyed that McClure, a representative of the oh-so-sensitive-to-local-customs Peace Corps would confront The System.

"But our young people simply don't like living in the best quarters available. We didn't come over here to do that," countered McClure. "Our Peace Corps teachers don't want to be separated from the Sierra Leonean teachers and living better than they do. It upsets them. They don't want special, preferential treatment. Can you understand that?" McClure was feeling slightly desperate, since he was very much afraid that the official absolutely did not and could not understand.

"I hear what you say. But that is not the way it works here. Let me repeat your own question: Can you understand that? The status of the superior teacher must be maintained. If he or she happens to be a Peace Corps teacher, so be it. We will end up with no standards and no system if your people go mucking about, mixing up the established procedures. We like to give our guests the best we have. You could call on the poorest family in any village and, what little they have, the best would be yours. Is that so difficult?"

"I think you know that's not what I'm talking about."

The official smiled. "I do know. But you must realize that in Sierra Leone our teachers are paid very poorly. Aspiring to that senior-staff housing is a major incentive. Not to earn it would destroy that incentive. There will always be senior teachers here, with junior teachers coming up. We have to preserve the system. Your people are very adaptable. I am sure they can adapt to good housing."

Elitism, McClure concluded early in his tour as Rep in Sierra Leone, is the great crippler in Africa, independence or no. It isn't the lack of industry, an interstate highway network, or twenty-eight flavors that harms this society, thought McClure. The British-oriented class distinctions were dying hard. Attitudes about education among the young were as rigid and self-hindering as they were among their elders, and often more so. Some of the adults, as illustrated in the conversation between McClure and the Keeper of the System, had at least a mordant sense of humor about the situation, and often, the Peace Corps Volunteers—with their unaffected enthusiasm for "creative" teaching, learning, and thinking—elicited that kind of exasperated, sardonic response. To the young, however, merely having landed in a secondary school—which in turn gave them a chance for a white-collar job in the civil service—was such a bonanza that they would permit no deviation from the rote-learning routine that was aimed unwaveringly at The Exam. To pass The Exam meant you were now separated and distinct from your illiterate neighbor in the village. This distinction summoned up an almost immediate arrogance and lofty disdain among the exam-passers. The Peace Corps teachers, with their egalitarian instincts, watched this inexorable process with sadness and frustration. More than one Volunteer who had tried to depart from the straight-and-narrow path of the syllabus, to make the student reason for himself rather than learn by rote, had been interrupted by his class with angry cries of "That isn't on the syllabus" or "We won't have that on the exam." A few students were so upset they walked out.

The would-be exam-passers, who were otherwise enormously fond and admiring of their friendly, energetic Peace Corps teachers, were further nonplussed by other unorthodox behaviors. Watching them cheerfully pitching in to help dig wells on the school compounds, the students would sidle up and ask in sincere astonishment, "Please, *why* did you get an education if you are still going to do dirty jobs like this?"

On both sides, it was always a case of, "Will wonders never cease?" McClure had occasion not only to shake his head—more in sorrow than in anger—at the antidevelopmental attitudes that he encountered in postcolonial West Africa, but also to marvel at the ingenuity, the pluck, and the swashbuckling nerve and courage of the Sierra Leonean.

At no time was McClure more bowled over—both literally and figuratively—by the native dash and energy than while driving his Peace Corps jeep through the countryside to visit Volunteers in out-lying areas. By August 1963, there were forty-six secondary schools in Sierra Leone, one-third of which were located in the two largest cities, Freetown and Bo (the latter being located up-country). All of the others were scattered from the Liberian border at the Mono River to the south, back over the thumb-shaped hump of Sierra Leone, up to the northern and eastern borders shared with Guinea. If the roads went several miles out of Freetown, they were called highways, even if they consisted only of one and a half lanes with deep gutters and/or soft shoulders. In 1963, there were only 162 miles of paved road in Sierra Leone. The rest of the roads, as in neighboring Liberia, were made of laterite, a substance that dissolved into impassable molasses in the rainy season and was transformed into a washboard texture—its ruts choked with red dust—in the dry. Driving on the left side of the road—and shifting gears on the left—was not so much a challenge to a thirty-seven-year-old American as was the death-defying trick of avoiding collisions with the lorries.

Lorries, or trucks, are the chief mode of transportation of people and goods in Sierra Leone. They are key to the life of the country. McClure explains:

> Really, they are a law unto themselves. When they stop to pick up passengers, goats, or firewood, it is generally on a curve. And it is always in the center of the "highway." To find a lorry in such a spot, let alone to confront one head-on as it pounds down the centerline of the highway toward you on tires bound by gunny sacks, is traumatic. You slam on your brakes and you hope for the best. There is no going *around* a lorry, a fact which every lorry driver absolutely counts on. Now, this is maddening and danger- ous, but you gain a powerful respect for the lorry driver's ingenuity and perseverance.
>
> I had always been told that what Sierra Leone needed most was experienced auto mechanics and that few were available. Yet, I saw lorries running that would have stymied the entire engineering division at Chrysler. I once peered over the shoulder of a lorry driver (he was stalled in the middle of the road, naturally, so all I could do was wait) as he "fixed" his vehicle. He raised the hood (bonnet, they call it, according to British custom) and we both looked inside at the remains. The only thing recognizable was the engine, and it was wired, taped, and soldered. The driver pushed aside a coffee can functioning as the air cleaner, pulled loose a fistful of wires, pushed and shoved and hammered at the engine, replaced the wires and the coffee can, closed the hood, climbed back inside, and roared off.

Observing such miraculous feats of "can do" on the part of the Sierra Leonean lorry drivers, out in the middle of nowhere with no technical training and no tools at their disposal, helped McClure put his own vehicle in perspective. He had at first complained long and loud about "that heap" or "that sorry excuse," even though McCone kept re- minding him that he was driving the "pride of the fleet." He was also motivated to stop complaining when he realized that lorry drivers were not the "hard hats" or the Ralph Kramdens of their society, but were in fact solidly middle class. They had steady jobs and led stable lives. Their children went to the best schools. You did not "write off" a lorry driver in Freetown, Bo, or Magburaka any more than you would "write off" the chief loan officer of your local bank in the United States. The Volunteers were discovering the same. Lorry drivers were significant citizens. Lorries were a central, important fact of life in Sierra Leone. Indeed, despite the antiquated look and condition of many of their vehicles, they constituted a monopoly in the country. Volunteers who did not have access to jeeps traveled about by lorry, and they would chide their jeep-riding colleagues about the rich cultural experience they were missing. And they were right to do so. At least half of the charm of the lorries were the gaily painted signs across the front that read "Trust in God," "Doris Day," "Me Worry?," "Slow but Sure," "Let Them Say," "Pray for Me," "Zorro the Great." McClure's favorite was "Except God."

However, "slow but sure" was the way McClure characterized his own acceptance of the topography of Sierra Leone. It was simply too unappealing visually for a man who had been living in two of the most attractive cities in America, San Francisco and Washington, D.C. McClure's lack of lust for the land itself he ascribes to his "swing through East Africa with Sarge the year before. There, I found a constant excitement, whether it was the occasional burst of zebra through the elephant grass of Tanganyika or the breathtaking mountain scenery of Ethiopia. Or maybe it was Shriver who provided the excitement. West Africa is flat and has few wild animals. What it does have is lush plant growth provoked by 150 inches of rain each year, dry winds and dust during those months when it isn't raining, and little else in the way of shifting scenery. But Sierra Leone was, in other ways, the perfect Peace Corps country—hospitable, mellow, delightfully uncomplicated. No huge bureaucracy such as in the U.S.A. or India." So McClure kept his negative observations to himself. "I found myself telling the people at the American embassy, who never got out of Freetown and who would ask me what it was like out there in the bush, 'It's just *beautiful.*' "*

*Graham Greene, who lived in Freetown for two years during World War II, wrote of that environment in his 1948 novel, The Heart of the Matter: "In the evening the port became beautiful for perhaps five minutes. The laterite roads that were so ugly and

The monotony of the landscape did not bother the Volunteers. They had other things to grouse about. Such as the *teefs*. "There are no syndicates and nobody robs banks," says McClure, but what Sierra does have aplenty is petty crime perpetrated by petty thieves, called teefs (a mispronunciation of "thief"). They are especially active during the rainy season because the heavy downpours drown out the sound of bare feet on a tin roof. They are positively aswarm during the Peace Corps Volunteer arrival season, according to McClure. Two weeks after new Volunteers arrive in a country, their air freight, with their personal belongings, follows them. This is a cue for the teefs to move into action. Most housing has "teef bars"—iron pipes placed in windows like a jail cell—to prevent physical entry. But Sierra Leone's teefs were too resourceful to be so easily stymied.

Some Volunteers would awake in the middle of the night to see a long pole extending into their sleeping quarters through the teef bars and then withdrawing, carrying with it their clothes, cameras, watches, shoes. One Volunteer, a sound sleeper, awoke to find not only had his clothing been stolen, but also his mosquito netting and bedding.

In Bo, Sierra Leone's second largest city, Volunteers Gus Allen and Paul Chantrey had attracted a teef man of staggering persistence. For three consecutive nights they heard him picking at the front door lock. Each morning they found that he had taken one additional tiny screw from the lock. The night came, as it was bound to, when only one screw remained. They were ready. Gus, sleeping with a baseball bat, heard a noise at about midnight. He crawled over to Paul's bed, whispering, "Paul. Paul! I hear him. He's here. Get up!"

Paul, still half asleep but getting the message, lurched to a sitting position, eyes blinking helplessly in the pitch dark, and plunged through his mosquito netting, landing on top of Gus, whom he quickly locked in a stranglehold. Unearthly choked gasps of "Paul, it's me, Gus. Lay off!" were to no avail. Finally, Gus unloaded three desperate punches that even through the tangled mosquito netting had their effect, break-

---

clay-heavy by day (in the rainy season) became a delicate flower-like pink. It was the hour of content. Men who had left the port forever would sometimes remember on a grey wet London evening the bloom and glow that faded as soon as it was seen: they would wonder why they had hated the coast, and for a space of a drink they would long to return."

ing the stranglehold and allowing Gus to scramble to his feet and get the lights on. The teef man was nowhere around, but Paul had a swollen lip and a bruised cheekbone and Gus was rubbing a sore neck and pondering new strategy.

McClure, who had studied journalism in college and subsequently had become a newspaperman (on the *Akron Beacon Journal* and then on the *San Francisco Chronicle*), was addicted to newsprint, news stories, politics, and sports. He never ceased to give thanks to whatever inspiration, or incidence of good luck, had put the Paris editions of the *New York Times* and the *New York Herald Tribune* on the news-stands of Freetown, Sierra Leone. He knew that other Peace Corps Reps were not so fortunate, that they had to get through the worst phases of culture shock without an American newspaper. The dread thought that he simply could not have survived such a circumstance occurred to him often, and he would shudder in gratitude.

The local papers left just about everything to be desired. Sierra Leone's one daily newspaper, the *Freetown Daily Mail*, which was owned by a press syndicate in London and staffed by Africans, had a schizoid, discombobulated quality; it could not decide upon a consistent identity or viewpoint, nor could it decide whose interests it should most rationally serve. The *Daily Mail* favored local intrigue and blood and gore on the front page. McClure describes the *Daily Mail* as containing

a rousing mixture of typographical errors, malapropisms, massacred idioms, patent-medicine advertising, "Wow! Wow!" headlines, and delighted disaster. The *Daily Mail* was justly famous in the diplomatic community and among expatriates for its exuberant handling of crime stories, particularly those involving rape, incest, and ax murders, when the gore was abundant. It strove to titillate its readers with every succulent detail, clinically describing those portions of the victim's anatomy bared, stabbed, chopped, sliced, severed, maimed, or bruised. In noncrime stories, *Daily Mail* reporters were less diligent. There was, for instance, a front-page photograph of the Prime Minister of Sierra Leone and three other dignitaries at the Lungi Airport. Classic diplomatic greeting scene. The caption read: "Here we see the Prime Minister speaking to the Governor-General, the British High Commissioner and an unidentified man wearing spectacles." The unidentified man wearing spectacles was the American ambassador.

The *Daily Mail* was neither to the political left nor to the political right and bore the Peace Corps neither ill nor well. "Generally," says McClure, "the *Daily Mail* treated the Peace Corps fairly enough, when they treated us at all, since circulation in Africa is based on steamier stuff than good works and human understanding."

However, in addition to the *Daily Mail*, there were several small weeklies in Sierra Leone, including one virulent leftist sheet, *We Yone*, which McClure describes as "bitterly anti-American." Its so-called editorial office was a tiny cubicle, which also housed a shoeshine stand, in a building next door to the American embassy. The paper was mimeographed on a machine that still bore the handclasp emblem of AID (Agency for International Development), who had donated it.

In a special box on the front page of *We Yone* one day in the fall of 1963, this title appeared, "shrieking," says McClure "in bold thirty-six-point type": "AMAZING REVELATIONS! HOW DID A WHITE SOUTH AFRICAN RACIALIST FIND HIS WAY INTO THE U.S. PEACE CORPS? SEE OUR ISSUE NEXT WEEK!"

How indeed, McClure wondered. He and Mike McCone invited *We Yone*'s editor to go over their Peace Corps Volunteers "mug books" and pick out "that dastardly South African." He went through the material with great care but could not find what he was looking for. "As he left our office," says McClure, "he said he still planned to carry out his big exposé the following Saturday." Based on what, McClure could not imagine.

Meanwhile, McClure launched an investigation on his own. He learned that the offending South African in question was one Mr. John Graydon, who had recently published an article in the *Johannesburg Times*, which in and of itself made him suspect in the mind of the editor of *We Yone*. Mr. Graydon was in fact a South African, was employed by the Ministry of Education in Sierra Leone, taught school in Freetown, and had entered the country a year earlier on a British passport. (The Peace Corps had a Volunteer in Freetown named John Gray who had never been to South Africa.)

Two days before *We Yone* had scheduled its "exposé," McClure called on *We Yone*'s editor in his miniscule office next to the shoeshine stand and confronted him with the facts. Simultaneously, Lamont Draper, the USIS chief, got in touch with Siaka Stevens, a Sierra Leonean political leader (now the president of Sierra Leone), and filled him in on the situation.

On Saturday, as threatened, *We Yone* printed its "exposé" but, according to McClure, went on "to make journalistic history of sorts by printing a front-page retraction of the exposé, which it had already laundered, taking out any reference to the Peace Corps."

Before McClure could turn his mind to winding up his job in Sierra Leone and returning to Washington—only to pack up for the final trek back to San Francisco—Shriver pounced. Shriver had caught McClure unawares many times before, but McClure thought those days were over. As much as he liked and admired Shriver, and that was an understatement, he had concluded as he turned thirty-eight that he was too old to be job-city-and-continent hopping, changing plans on the spur of the moment, and most important, postponing his chosen career in journalism any longer. Shriver had a charismatic and controlling personality; if he wanted you to stick around, it was almost impossible to escape his grasp. One had to be on guard. But Shriver knew instinctively just when one wasn't.

He cabled McClure in late 1964 and offered him the position of associate director of the Office of Public Affairs. McClure was stupefied. On the organization chart, the five associate directorships were just a notch below Shriver. While in reality they did not have equal power, each associate directorship had considerable territory and prestige.

Shriver's offer to McClure to become associate director for Public Affairs was something he had never imagined happening, and he was therefore having a difficult time coming to terms with it. He had to deal with two warring ideas. On the positive side, it was an enormously flattering offer; being named an associate director meant near-autonomy over one's own territory (in this case, the increasingly important functions of Public Information and Recruiting) and a place very near the top of the pecking order in the most glamorous agency in the nation's capital. For a fellow who had come to town with no administrative credentials or pretensions and who had merely meant to test the waters for a year, to take a crash course, as it were, in the workings and the language of the federal government, this sudden potential elevation was heady stuff indeed. Abe Mellincoff at the *San Francisco Chronicle* would certainly not stand in his way, would in fact be likely to give an enthusiastic thumbs-up signal as McClure made himself yet once again more valuable to his former employer. But there was the negative side: What if LBJ succeeded in gobbling up Shriver for the poverty program full time just days or weeks after McClure returned to Washington? McClure was solidly identified as a man who could think and write in the Shriver idiom, a man who knew and effectively employed the Shriver brand of public relations. McClure could not imagine that any successor to Shriver would be a man who could tolerate such a "Shriveresque" person as himself as an associate director. Shriver cast too long a shadow.

Yet the title of Associate Director for Public Affairs at the Peace Corps had first belonged to Bill Moyers, who was, by late 1964, being referred to by some journalists as "Deputy President" in Lyndon Johnson's White House. The associate directorship would never have more luster than it did just at that moment.

"Take it!" said Maggie McClure, knowing in her heart that they might never see their beloved San Francisco again except as tourists going down mem'ry lane.

There was a poignant farewell party for the McClures in March 1965, attended by the Volunteers and the host-country officials with whom McClure had spent so many pleasant hours solving Peace Corps problems during evenings around a poker table. The McClures' farewell party did not go unremarked; a reporter and photographer from the *Freetown Daily Mail* covered the event. As McClure and his family were about to board their plane the following day, at Lungi Airport, he was handed that day's edition of the *Daily Mail*. There on the front page was the friendly farewell tableau of the day before. Above it in arrestingly bold type was this headline: "McCLURE LEAVES FOR GOOD."

FRANK MANKIEWICZ

Not all of the early staff members of that younger-than-springtime era were comfortable with Shriver's every-man-for-himself, jump high, jump higher, if-you-can't-stand-the-heat-get-out-of-the-kitchen style of leadership and the intense, sometimes vicious, competition that it spawned—aided and abetted by the quirky policy of "In, Up & Out." Indeed, some were destroyed by it. But many thrived and grew beyond their wildest dreams because of it; and Mankiewicz positively luxuriated in it. He was a man after the Kennedy clan's own heart.

Time—which was always in short supply at the hire-and-work-at-a-gallop pace of the early Peace Corps—was also on Mankiewicz's side. Purely by chance, Mankiewicz had time to handpick his own Volunteers. He had time to travel twice to Peru in advance of his official posting to meet and negotiate with Peruvian officials, to carve out jobs for the Volunteers; time to rent living quarters for his family and to set up a Peace Corps office in Lima; time, even, to hire and install a Peruvian secretary, Nina Portaro. He had time to get to know Sargent Shriver and Jack Vaughn, the key men in his life at that time. He had time to polish up his somewhat rusty Spanish and, because of the military takeover in Peru on the eve of his departure, he had time to acclimate himself to the ways of Washington, a factor in shaping the "political Mankiewicz" of the later presidential campaigns of Robert Kennedy in 1968, George McGovern in 1972 (whose vice presidential running mate was none other than Sargent Shriver), and Gary Hart, briefly, in 1984. (Mankiewicz himself ran unsuccessfully for Congress in 1974, from a few yards over the district line in Maryland, just beyond Westmoreland Circle, on the partially tongue-in-cheek promise to put some "fun" into Maryland politics.)

And he was not the son of Herman "Citizen Kane" Mankiewicz and the nephew of Joseph "All About Eve" Mankiewicz for nothing. He thoroughly relished the exercise of casting his own production, Peru I. To his credit, he did not fashion an elite Ivy League youth brigade for Peru (what his late sister, Josie, would have called "Croysters"—boys who went to New England prep schools such as Groton and St. Paul's and then on to Harvard and Yale and said "Oh, Croyste" for "Oh, Christ"). However, Mankiewicz could have easily done that, since the majority of applicants during the first three years of the Peace Corps were from the cream of American colleges, in their early twenties, upper middle class, and in the higher percentile scholastically. He knew better than anyone what a public relations bonanza could be reaped in having a member of a famous film family leading a bunch of blond, beautiful, and brilliant Kennedy clones through the world's mountains and jungles, and how irresistible that would be to a media already marked by its obsession with all things Kennedyesque. But Mankiewicz refrained and instead went about exporting that true hallmark of America, variety. He wanted people of all ages and backgrounds. He thought it was important to demonstrate to the Peruvians (or to any Third World nation) that the Peace Corps was not just a passing fad for which "gringos" were so famous, but a commitment at every level of our society to the idea of service and the possibility of growth. And in full Mankiewiczian style, he proclaimed that a good mix would be "more fun, anyway." (Betty Harris escorted the second group of Peace Corps Volunteers to Peru. The group included Barbara and Chester Wiggins—sixty-two and sixty-five, respectively—who were the parents of Warren Wiggins, the powerful associate director for Program Development and Operations. Barbara Wiggins was scheduled to teach nursery school. Chester Wiggins, who had been a plant maintenance manager for United Airlines in San Francisco, had come to be a construction supervisor in a slum-relocation project in Arequipa. Both Harris and Mankiewicz were beaming broadly over this extraordinary juxtaposition that could happen only in America, and they hoped that it was not going to be lost on the host-country government or its citizens.)

With that precious extra time that luck and a political upheaval in Peru allotted to him, Mankiewicz was also able to put together an overseas staff that was close to perfect. Never known for his promptness, managerial skills, or attention to detail, Mankiewicz was wise enough to seek out people who would balance his charismatic, creative, "big screen" view of things with solid, patient administrative work and intimate knowledge of the country. He asked for advice and took it. Warren Wiggins and Jack Vaughn had worked with a native of Logan, Utah, named Darwin Bell in La Paz, Bolivia, some years earlier, when all three were employed by the foreign aid program, then called ICA. Bell was a management *genius*, Wiggins and Vaughn declared. He had an M.A. in industrial relations from the University of Chicago and had worked for automotive, insurance, and engineering companies both in the United States and overseas. Mankiewicz gratefully hired Bell as his associate director for Management in the Lima office. "And it was all true," says Mankiewicz. "Darwin Bell was that good. In fact, he was so good that the Latin America Regional Office kept borrowing him from me."

Bell and deputy Rep William Mangin were setting up the Lima office and preparing for what was to become the second most dense concentration of Peace Corps Volunteers in the world (after Addis Ababa, Ethiopia, which in the space of a few hours had found its secondary-school teacher force had doubled with the influx of nearly three hundred Peace Corps Volunteers on July 18, 1962) when the *golpe*, or military takeover, occurred and diplomatic relations were temporarily broken off. With the first Volunteers and Mankiewicz waiting impatiently in the United States and the Peruvian operation at a standstill, Bell was sent to Ecuador to help set up the Peace Corps office in Quito. He was next dispatched to Honduras in October 1962, just three weeks after Mankiewicz and the Volunteers had arrived and were digging into their jobs. Mankiewicz was annoyed. Mankiewicz was furious when, in November, Washington yanked Bell away yet again to set up shop in Jamaica, and thereafter Mankiewicz was merely wearily resigned when Wiggins and Vaughn sent Bell to Costa Rica in January 1963, to Panama the following April, and then on to Venezuela for some administrative first aid. Bell's reputation as a roving administrative troubleshooter got around quickly among new Reps in Latin and Central America and the Caribbean who had had no administrative know-how but were otherwise glamorous and interesting Shriver "finds" of the time. "Get me Dar Bell," they were braying in unison. If Bell was unavailable—and Mankiewicz was increasingly unwilling to release him as his own program in Peru ballooned—the cry would increase in anguish: "Well, then, get me a Dar Bell *type*, for chrissake!"

Peace Corps/Peru was slated to grow in geometric progression during Mankiewicz's stewardship. Volunteers would be located all over that large country of almost 500,000 square miles, whose dramatic terrain started in many coastal areas at well below sea level and rapidly rose to Andean peaks rivaling those of the daunting Himalayas. (Peru's highest mountain, Huascarán, is 22,205 feet; the world's highest, Mount Everest, is 29,028 feet). Volunteers in remote locations could be three days' difficult travel from Lima, often including shin-splitting treks by foot up cracked riverbeds and awkward journeys on horseback or mule-back. Thus, Mankiewicz posted associate directors to such strategic points in the country as Arequipa—Peru's second city, an oasis far to the south of Lima in the Atacama Desert—and Cuzco, the ancient capital of the Inca that lies high in the Andes. At Shriver's suggestion, Mankiewicz chose Emery Biro—an admired former colleague of Shriver's from the Catholic Interracial Council in Chicago—for the Arequipa office, and at Franklin Williams's suggestion he hired Dan Sharp—an urbane 1959 graduate of Harvard Law School and a former deputy attorney general of California—for Cuzco.

William (Willy) Warner, the most urbane of all Peace Corpsmen before or since, who was on leave from the foreign service with an expertise in Latin America and was serving as executive secretary (for he, too, knew how government worked), had met not long ago a young woman named Nancy McNulty at USIA's Bi-National Center in Lima. According to Warner, she was comely, exceedingly bright, and fluent in Spanish, having received her M.A. in Spanish Literature in 1951 from Boston University. He had since lost track of her but urged Mankiewicz to track her down. As it happened Mankiewicz ran into her a few days later at the Peace Corps' training camps in Puerto Rico, by which time she had begun to work on her Ph.D. in linguistics at New York University and was surveying Spanish language facilities at the camps for English Language Services, Inc., under contract to the Peace Corps. Mankiewicz was dazzled and hired her on the spot, soon thereafter giving her the title of associate director, thus making her one of the highest ranking Peace Corps staff women overseas. She arrived in Lima shortly after Mankiewicz in September 1962.

Key to the success that Peace Corps/Peru became during Mankiewicz's stewardship (although the program would expand to a barely manageable 427 by September 1964 and to 500 by the end of 1964) was the vanquishing knowledge of Mankiewicz's deputy Rep, William Mangin. Mangin, with a Ph.D. in anthropology from Yale, was in 1961 a professor of anthropology at Syracuse University (as he is today). Peru was almost a second home to him; he had done innumerable scholarly studies there over the years, ranging from gathering data on the drinking habits of Quechuan speakers in the high Andes in 1951 to scrutinizing the decision-making process in the Peruvian government in 1961. Needless to say, he, too, was fluent in Spanish.

Bill Mangin arrived in Lima on July 3, 1962. Darwin Bell arrived the next day. Bell said later, "There was the Peace Corps office in Lima—in the Lincoln Building on Washington Street. And I show up for work on July fourth. How patriotic can you get?" By the end of September 1962, all staff members and Volunteers were in place; and, diplomatic relations having been restored between the United States and Peru, morale was high. But even such happiness as that could not save Mankiewicz from two memorable bouts of culture shock, an affliction to which he had always thought he would be immune. First, there was the weather in Lima, for which he was not prepared after just two brief visits. "In Lima, the sun shines only three months of the year. It never rains. I mean, never. It isn't like Los Angeles where people say, oh, the climate is marvelous, it never rains. What does that mean? That means only about two or three weeks a year when it rains like hell. But when I got to Lima, it had not rained for sixty years. And I hear that it has not rained since. Oh, it drizzles a lot, but the water never really hits the ground. It hangs in the air, like fog. Probably the worst climate of any capital city in the world.

You know, it's crazy. They could have put the capital anywhere they wanted, and almost anywhere else would have been better." (Mankiewicz perhaps forgets that the same charge has been leveled at Washington, D.C., by foreigners for two centuries.)

Then there was the matter of the "dog boxes." Mankiewicz, in his two exploratory trips to Peru, had heard vague reference to the need for "dog boxes" when the Volunteers arrived. Thinking that the Peruvian officials had somehow made the odd assumption that the Volunteers would arrive with their own pets and would want dog *houses* (was it the Lassie legend?, he wondered), Mankiewicz refrained from getting further tangled in the discussion, since it could surely lead only to maniacal linguistic confusion. But when he arrived in Lima to settle in, he found that he had to deal with the formerly ephemeral "dog boxes" right away, that it was no laughing matter. It seemed that health authorities in Lima, realizing that the squeaky-clean new American Peace Corps Volunteers would be going into squalid, impoverished urban areas and isolated mountain villages where health standards and medical facilities were nil (even though many of the Volunteers would be trained as health workers just for that reason), felt that they would not be prepared for the omnipresent hazard of rabid dogs. The Volunteers, as foreigners and strangers, were more likely to be prey to this scourge than natives, went the theory. "The deal was," says Mankiewicz, grimacing half in revulsion, half in "Saturday Night Live" satirical glee, "there were rabid dogs all over the place, and people had died from having been bitten by them. The Peruvian government and the U.S. Public Health Service instituted a grim practice: If a Peace Corps Volunteer got bitten by a dog that had no tag and the Volunteer was in doubt as to the dog's identity—or if the dog exhibited unnerving behaviors such as extreme irascibility—the Volunteer was instructed to kill the dog and mail its head back to Lima. Nothing focuses the mind more than to have to say, 'Okay, son, here are your water purification tablets, here is your footlocker of Thornton Wilder and other American classics, and oh, by the way, here also is your box for mailing in the head of any rabid dog that happens to bite you.' "

But Lima had its charms. In 1963, it was an elegant, European city where the mixture of Spanish and Incan cultures combined to cast a spell over visitors. Shops with beautiful and often inexpensive silver jewelry were all around the spacious plazas. The palaces and villas of the rich, which surrounded elegant formal inner courtyards, came with many servants. The rich of Lima slept on the purest of linen sheets and privileged haciendas often contained a private chapel and their own priest. The gardens of Lima were always green, despite the lack of rainfall, and vineyards dotted the countryside to the south, where grapes were squeezed by hand as they had been in the seventeenth century. There were plentiful and excellent restaurants; and the hotels ranged from comfortable to grand. And much of what Lima had to offer in 1963 was affordable to the middle-class North American pocketbook.

But that was not the Lima that the Volunteers usually saw. Surrounding Lima were the squatter settlements. Such settlements were called *ranchitos* in Venezuela and *favelas* in Brazil, but in Colombia, Ecuador, and Peru they were called *barriadas*. "People came down from the mountains in the middle of the night, put up houses, and just moved in," says Mankiewicz. "They'd come in, dig four holes, stick four posts in, string straw mats from one post to the other, and then put a big straw mat on the top, or a piece of tin. But usually straw, because it never rains in Lima. And so, there is a lot of dust. It may sound hopeless but it wasn't necessarily and it didn't have to be. These people had goals. They wanted jobs, schools, medical attention. Many of the *barriadas* had a leader who had some idea of how to organize and who understood the necessity of getting credit, and the Peace Corps could work with these people. But at the beginning, these people were powerless. Utterly powerless." Many Volunteers lived and worked in the *barriadas* in straw huts without plumbing or electricity. Very few asked for transfer out of the *barriadas* because they could not endure the living conditions or because their hearts were breaking over the poverty and powerlessness of the people. On the contrary, most of the Volunteers living in straw houses rarely complained or got despondent. Herb Wegner, an evaluator who visited the Peace Corps program in Peru in early 1963, reported that *barriada*-bound Volunteers in and around various cities considered themselves comfortable and felt their living quarters were "adequate"—this in spite of the fact that "breakfast is cooked on Primus stoves on packing boxes in one corner and is served on a cement mortarboard placed on top of a washtub set between two cots."

Most of the Volunteers thrived on the experience; they had never been so needed or appreciated as they were in the *barriadas*. It wasn't a case of their providing more and better services with more consistency and compassion than had been done in the past—educational, medical, nutritional, financial, entrepreneurial, political—it was rather a case of the Volunteers providing the very first services of any kind that these people had ever known. The people of the *barriadas* were tabula rasa, and the Peace Corps Volunteers had the chalk. Mankiewicz was seized by the possibilities inherent in such a situation and his vision of progress and change sent him into raptures. They were calling it "community development" at Peace Corps headquarters: a way of getting into and galvanizing a community by means of organizing sports teams, crafts cooperatives, school lunch programs, dental hygiene demonstrations, adult literacy courses, small libraries, and credit unions. Soon enough, Mankiewicz was calling it revolution. Mankiewicz's passion for the technique and potential of community development took hold about midway in his tenure as Rep and continued to obsess him throughout his tour as director of the Regional Office of Latin America, which ran from 1964 to 1966. Mankiewicz said then, said later, and says now: "Community development offends a bureaucrat's sense of order because it is basically revolutionary. I mean, the purpose of community development is to overthrow the existing order—social, political, economic—whatever it is." Needless to say, Mankiewicz's community development rhetoric made a few "bureaucrats" nervous back at Peace Corps headquarters, and it continued to make them nervous when he returned to Washington to direct all Latin America programs. No one was terrified, however, because Mankiewicz was no arm-flinging firebrand, and when he uttered inflammatory words such as "overthrow" and "revolution," it was generally assumed that he meant peaceful, if radical, social change at the bottom of the socioeconomic order in Latin America—that he merely meant that he hoped that the Peace Corps would be able to show the powerless how to get just a little bit of power at first and then, later, more. According to Mankiewicz, the Volunteers would truly be "agents of change" in the *barriadas*, the *favelas*, and the *ranchitos* of Latin America. After all, who else but the Peace Corps Volunteers were living and working on a daily basis with these people? And whom did these people trust? "Certainly not their own governments," says Mankiewicz. Those who were not leery of Mankiewicz's rhetoric were highly skeptical of the efficacy of community development on a large scale; they thought it too unstructured a business, too haphazard, too likely to end with underemployed Volunteers and underimpressed host-country officials.

But criticism of, and opposition to, community development and

Mankiewicz as its "philosopher king" (as Kevin Lowther and C. Payne Lucas somewhat facetiously put it in their 1978 book, *Keeping Kennedy's Promise*), would not gather momentum until the mid-1960s. Meanwhile, from 1962 to 1964, Mankiewicz was an unequivocally popular fellow, someone to marvel at, Shriver's most charismatic Rep.

Enter Herb Wegner, an evaluator from Washington. Wegner descended on Peace Corps/Peru on February 19, 1963, and stayed until March 8, 1963. Mankiewicz had yet to be seized by revolutionary theory. The Volunteers had been at work, mostly in community development projects, for only five months. Before Wegner left for Peru, his boss, Charlie Peters, warned him with a helpless smile, a shrug, and upturned palms not to be too beguiled by Mankiewicz (although Mankiewicz was a champion beguiler, Peters conceded) or the "propaganda" emanating from the "operational people" at headquarters, particularly from the knowledgeable Dick Ottinger, whose administrative responsibility was the west coast of Latin America, where Peru was then the prize program. Peters also worried that Wegner, a tall, blond, ever-affable former AID official who was the only former government man then working as an evaluator (the rest were all journalists), would not want to be too critical of a U.S. government program. AID (formerly ICA) had no more been a self-correcting agency than any other arm of the government. "Look," said Peters, "Frank is one of Sarge's favorites, and one can see why. But you can't let yourself be intimidated by that. Be ruthlessly objective. Tell the truth. I'll back you up, no matter what," promised Peters.

Wegner ultimately produced a ninety-page evaluation report that amounted not only to an exhaustive review of Peace Corps/Peru under Mankiewicz but one that no one could find serious fault with, not the "operational people" and not the Evaluation Division. There was an uncommon stillness at 806 Connecticut Avenue for a while.

Wegner visited all of the major project sites: Lima, Arequipa, Cuzco, Vicos, Chimbote, and Puno. Of the total 200 Volunteers in Peru in February and March of 1963, Wegner was able to talk to 125 and question in depth over 50. The projects at that time were housing, health/nutrition, expansion of credit unions, savings-and-loan involvement, arts and crafts, and university teaching spread out over forty individual communities. "The question in Peru," Wegner wrote, "is not so much of going from bad to good—but from good to better . . . The two basic ingredients which combine to bring about this healthy situation: intelligent and flexible PCVs and an energetic, well-rounded staff to administer them . . . The failure of the Peruvian governmental agencies to provide that assistance which was promised has caused great gaps in our programming. It could have spelled disaster for the Peru program had we not had the high caliber of Volunteers plus the versatile staff . . . Job switches have had to come fast. Some PCVs have angled into their own new positions, and others have been maneuvered there by the staff."

Voicing a worry that was to preoccupy the Evaluation Division—and for that matter some of the "operational people"—throughout the 1960s, Wegner noted that "the increasing size of the Peru program causes me real concern. The staff has its hands full handling the present groups of PCVs. [Half of the staff's time was spent in travel.] It should not be expected to administer more and more." But, of course, it did. Advice to level off the numbers of Volunteers unless there was a proportionate increase in staff was rarely taken until a program got almost scandalously out of control. The "numbers game," as it was called, was real at the Peace Corps. Hubris reigned. Even if a particular Rep knew he was asking for trouble by requesting double or triple the existing number of Volunteers, he would request. To do so—and better, to get them—was to demonstrate the influence of the Rep with the host government, the popularity of the Volunteers with "the people," and the clout of the Rep's regional staff at headquarters.

Still, Wegner had enormous admiration for that early staff of Peace Corps/Peru, without exception. While he did not hold back in citing program and placement deficiencies, and while he recommended the dismissal of one very well educated and ambitious Volunteer, he was basically heartened by the program overall and even entertained by certain of its aspects: "The Peace Corps office in Lima occupies a three-bedroom apartment [that] usually displays a somewhat frantic but friendly atmosphere. It is obviously the communications center between the administration and the Volunteers, as well as between the Volunteers themselves . . . Itinerant Volunteers use the office as a place to live. It was virtually impossible in the office to talk to anyone with any degree of privacy. Two or three conversations would be going on simultaneously in one room. On two occasions I resorted to the use of the men's room as a conference chamber."

"There was no back door to sneak out of if you wanted to talk privately or avoid a troublesome encounter," recalls deputy Rep Bill Mangin. "You were trapped. One day the rector of a provincial university arrived. He liked to complain to the Peace Corps staff because his own ministry of education wouldn't listen to him. I hid in a narrow closet, and when he came in the office, everyone was giggling or guffawing. It made him extremely uncomfortable and he promptly fled. We moved ultimately and got an office with several back exits."

Wegner made only two strong recommendations that were negatively weighted: one, control the urge of Peace Corps/Peru to nearly triple the number of Volunteers unless Peace Corps/Washington is willing to increase the size of the staff from seven (counting the Peace Corps' public health doctor, John Starr) to at least twelve; and two, dismiss a Volunteer named Boris. Boris was twenty-six and considered himself, says Wegner, "to be educated above the level of the other PCVs. An economist, he described his interest as 'working with small industries in the city of Arequipa.' In his role, he would like to wear a shirt and tie and have an apartment close to the area of his operation."

Boris had been writing to Washington, citing his own superior abilities, the blindness to these abilities on the part of the entire staff in Peru, and their insistence in giving help only to the bottom of the social structure (incorrect on all counts). At first, Boris had been held in esteem by other Volunteers, who were impressed with his advanced degrees in economics, his apparent knowledge of industry, and his sophisticated plans. Although Wegner found that Boris's influence over other Volunteers was waning (partly due to his conceit and partly because he was a chronic complainer), Wegner was "concerned that in the normal course of events, some policy from the Lima office, or perhaps from Washington, may cause a momentary flash of discontent among the Volunteers. At this time, it is consistent with Boris's image of himself that he would try to take a position of leadership in organizing the Volunteers in rebellion against the 'administration.' This was the pattern of [his most recent accusatory] letter to Washington in December 1962 [only three months after the Peace Corps effort in Peru had begun]." Wegner believed that Boris was "capable of presenting us with another Venezuela." Wegner added that it was his feeling, "and I relayed it to Mankiewicz, Biro and Mangin that consideration should be given to sending Boris back to the United States as having failed to make an adjustment to his Peace Corps role in Peru, for basically, he is a professional malcontent and a negative influence on those with whom he associates."

"We should have thrown him out," Mangin now says. "But we wanted to go the two years without actually throwing anyone out. We liked to think we could solve such problems on the spot. In any case,

Boris soon got wind of the fact that he was in trouble and he quieted down. Soon thereafter, Frank and I perfected the technique of the 'forced resignation.' " (The reference to "another Venezuela" in this evaluation report is ironic. Just prior to Wegner's signing on with the Peace Corps, there had indeed been a Volunteer rebellion in Venezuela during its first weeks of operation. Shriver had paid attention to it because the Volunteers of Venezuela I had been articulate and well organized. Shriver had replaced the unpopular Rep in Venezuela with Milton Carr, a distinguished former newspaperman and first Rep in Ecuador. But before he could make this switch, which was acceptable to the Volunteers in Venezuela, Shriver sent Mankiewicz in on an emergency basis to quell the rebellion, reassure the Volunteers, and actually run the program until Carr arrived in June 1963, after serving nine months as Rep in Ecuador. Deputy Director Eugene Baird then replaced Carr in Ecuador and Mankiewicz returned to his post in Peru. Wegner noted in his evaluation that Mankiewicz was not in Lima at the time of his inspection, but he does not say where Mankiewicz was because he did not know. The fact of the Volunteer revolt in Venezuela was reasonably well known around Peace Corps headquarters; but the fact of Mankiewicz's having to save the day until Carr could be transferred from Ecuador was not. As a consequence, the press never found out about the "mutiny.")

Wegner's evaluation of the first program in Peru was perhaps the only evaluation report, ever, that made *favorable* comments that were later challenged by the in-country staff. Quite the opposite was usually the case. Wegner wrote that "Ken Harding, roving PCVL ["L" standing for "Leader"], is filling a job which [approaches] a staff function. The job wouldn't work unless it was filled with a person of good judgment, acute perception and sharp political acumen. Ken has these qualities and has remained acceptable to the Volunteers in spite of his obvious function of reporting to the Peace Corps Representative."

"Not at all!" insists Mangin. "It was tough for Ken, who was a nice guy. Frank and I made a big error. We never should have given Ken this kind of job. He realized it after eight months or so and asked to be relieved." (To single out certain Volunteers as leaders—PCVLs— was controversial in both theory and in practice. While the naming of a PCVL was one way of rewarding a particularly responsible and effective Volunteer and was obviously meant to extend the staff function to areas where staff could rarely visit, it was seen by most other Volunteers as a sneaky, undemocratic, potentially traitorous business.

Peace Corps evaluators around the world were given shocking earfuls of what Volunteers thought of the PCVLs in their midst. The evaluators would cringe as furious Volunteers, usually males, would describe with obscene delight the hideous acts they were prepared to perpetrate on the PCVL should he—and it was always a he—ever venture near again.)

Exit Herb Wegner. Enter Mary and Alfred Jones. Alfred Jones was a former foreign service officer who had been stationed in Berlin in the 1930s and who had witnessed Hitler's rise to power. He was also a sociologist—by dint of a Ph.D. from Columbia and a 1941 book on class distinctions in an industrial community: *Life, Liberty and Property*—and a former journalist for *Time* and *Fortune*. This background provided him with the basic instincts and the disciplines to draw him naturally to the Peace Corps in its early stages. His intellectual curiosity about this new social experiment was as passionate as his professional self-interest was dispassionate. As founder and president of his own Wall Street investment firm, A. W. Jones, he had since made himself sufficiently comfortable financially to seek truth and knowledge for their own sakes and to combine such pursuits with a zest for travel.

Jones and his wife, Mary—who had worked for the Quakers during the Spanish Civil War and had since been deeply involved in the work of the Henry Street Settlement in New York—planned to visit several Third World countries in the next two years and they wanted to start out in Latin America, one of the few land masses they had never visited. They expressed their fascination for the Peace Corps; they wanted to see it at work. They had seen other groups at work around the world: missionaries of every denomination and degree of zeal; members of the British Voluntary Service Organization (VSO); the accomplishments of United Nations groups such as UNICEF. And they had seen French, Scandinavian, Dutch, Canadian, and YWCA volunteers at work from the Caribbean to Turkey. The Joneses proposed to operate exactly as did Peace Corps evaluators except they would be doing so at their own expense, with no strings attached, although they would submit their impressions to Wiggins and Shriver. They took their request to Warren Wiggins. He was not only agreeable to their proposition, he was intrigued. Here were two people whose experience qualified them to be uncommonly astute evaluators, yet they would be on their own. Wiggins wasn't worried about setting a precedent that would permit other curious American tourists to closely observe the Peace Corps. How many Americans, after all, were eager to vacation in places that presented risk, discomfort, and stark poverty? The Joneses' willingness to walk with the poor, along with the Volunteers, seemed to Wiggins to bode well. Their original faith in the Peace Corps would not be likely to crumble in the face of grim reality. And since the Joneses were unaware of the interagency rivalry between Wiggins's own empire of PDO (Program Development and Operations) and Charlie Peters's Division of Evaluation, they would give a completely fair account, critical if need be, but no doubt not too critical. So why not Peru?

The Joneses were delighted. They had met the American ambassador, James Loeb, and they knew Frank Mankiewicz's uncle, Joseph Mankiewicz. Two of the sights they most wanted to see in Latin America—Lake Titicaca and Machu Picchu—were in Peru. Wiggins said he would notify Mankiewicz and that the Peace Corps staff in Lima would make arrangements for them to see as many Volunteers as possible. The Joneses were grateful for permission to observe but were skeptical of any real "arrangements," given the fact that they were arriving less than a year after the Volunteers had arrived. The program was still in an experimental stage, and the staff was bound to be vastly overworked with new groups arriving every three months or so. Thus, they were stunned when there at the airport to meet them were members of Mankiewicz's staff, who drove them in a jeep to the Hotel Bolívar in Lima, where they were assured that Frank Mankiewicz himself would soon come to greet them in person. They were skeptical of this, too—this was not, after all, the embassy they were dealing with—but Mankiewicz called on them before the day was out and handed them their schedule. "He told us everything about the program," says Mary Jones. "Where the Volunteers were, what they were doing, what their problems were, which projects were going to survive and thrive, and which might fall apart. He was so candid, we couldn't get over it. But then, how smart of him."

The Joneses called on Mankiewicz the next day in his office in the Lincoln Building on Washington Street, ready to start their visits to the Volunteers around Lima in spite of jet lag, an affliction that no one even remotely connected with the "tough" Peace Corps dared speak of. "Frank provided us with a jeep and a beautiful young Peace Corps Volunteer as our guide," says Mary Jones.

We went to see the Volunteers working in the *barriadas*, introduced ourselves, and helped deliver first aid supplies. All of the female Volunteers in the *barriadas* had had training in first aid, and some had had very advanced training. They did not question our professional affiliations or our personal motives for being there; they just came right out that first day and said what was bothering them. They primarily saw mothers and children in the health stations they had set up. The first question the women asked these Volunteers was, "How can we stop having children?" Always the first question. This was a real problem for the Volunteers, because the Peace Corps had taken a stand that it would not give out birth control information. Yet it was the most needed thing in Peru and in so many other Third World countries. It was painful for the Volunteers to live with these poor women of the *barriadas*, crowded into tiny straw shacks, old before their time, surrounded by masses of hungry, dirty little children.

Out of the two months they spent in Peru, the majority of the Joneses' time was spent in the *barriadas* around Lima "because the most dramatic work that the Peace Corps was doing in Peru was there," says Mary Jones. "Since it never rains in Lima and outside the city there is no irrigation, there is nothing but dust, dust, dust. And the Volunteers lived in these *barriadas* without any of the modern conveniences. But they brought water in, created showers with buckets on the roofs of the straw houses; they set up health stations, built schools and taught in them, ran school lunch programs, got the people involved in crafts cooperatives and credit unions. They were the oasis in the *barriadas*."

"I don't know why we were so surprised by this," says Alfred Jones. "That was the whole point of the Peace Corps, to actually live and work with less fortunate people of other cultures. That's what we had come to see. But I think we were not prepared for the powerful impact the reality would have on us. The Peace Corps grew out of such a generous impulse in the first place, but then to see this rather abstract generosity translated into action under the most appalling circumstances was just so astonishing and inspiring."

The Joneses, although vividly impressed by the work of the Volunteers in the *barriadas*, continued to feel frustrated about the Peace Corps policy that prohibited the Volunteers from actively and openly engaging in birth control education in a place of such extreme need. They were not about to hector Frank Mankiewicz on the subject, nor did they intend to needle Warren Wiggins in their report. They realized full well that no one on earth could seize the first Roman Catholic president of the United States by the lapels and cause him to institute a policy that would require his more devout coreligionist brother-in-law to take the heat for that policy in a Roman Catholic country on a Roman Catholic continent. Indeed, the Joneses could not imagine a time or a set of circumstances in the near future when such a deliberate policy could be set by any American president. But they wondered: Was there anyone in a position of authority in the Catholic church who was even willing to admit to the misery spawned by rampant overpopulation among the poor?

As they boarded the tiny Japanese-built train for the mile trip up to the fourteen-thousand-foot shrine of Machu Picchu, the Joneses were bemused to find that they would be sharing those close quarters for many hours with a Catholic priest, a Maryknoll father from the United States. To bring up The Subject or not: that was the question. They needn't have worried. The priest, once he gathered that the Joneses were in Peru primarily to observe the Peace Corps and displayed neither worshipful nor negative reaction to his clerical collar, unburdened himself of opinions borne of his own long experience in Peru. "This priest told us what he had been seeing in the mountains," says Mary Jones. "He told us that the Indian mother does the plowing and the housework and also takes care of the children while the father is out hunting and fishing. She can't have a second child until the first is old enough to walk behind the plow. If she becomes pregnant and gives birth to another child, they must commit infanticide. The priest told us on that little train that his whole attitude about birth control had changed. He said, 'No one could sanction what those families go through. The church knows about this but can give us no guidelines.' "

Less appalling than the tragic tale told by the Maryknoll priest, but nonetheless disturbing to the Joneses, was a first-hand look at how a group of fundamentalist missionaries from the Midwest related to their "constituency," the Indians who lived on floating islands on Lake Titicaca, the highest water in the world. The missionary group at Lake Titicaca had been contacted beforehand and was glad to receive the Joneses. But the Joneses hadn't even remotely bargained for what they would find. The head missionary family lived on the shore of Lake Titicaca in "an extremely comfortable house," according to Alfred Jones, "and went about their business in a boat that could only be called elegant." Invited to join the missionaries on their rounds, the Joneses were all curiosity. "The missionaries were very proud of what they did. They saw nothing at all hypocritical about it. They went out in their elegant boat periodically and distributed bread to the Indians on these floating islands, made entirely of reeds. To step out on one of them was like stepping on a sponge. The Indians were profoundly thankful for the bread and clearly they needed it. But there was a catch: Before the Indians were given the bread, the missionaries got the scrolls out and made them recite the church creed. In effect, they were required to sing for their supper."

"I was so outraged," says Mary Jones, "I didn't wait. I just handed out bread right and left. These great bags of bread; I've never seen so much bread in my life, but they were making those poor, hungry people *wait* for it, *perform* for it, show themselves *worthy* of it. The missionaries had to know how upset we were but they didn't say anything. That bread was almost the only food these people had, and the missionaries felt they were doing a very good thing by providing it. The only other food consisted of birds, which they caught in nets as they flew over the islands, and fish. Everybody fished. My husband tried very tactfully to find out where and how these missionaries raised their money, but they just smiled beatifically and said that they returned home every two years and raised it. It was simply no problem, they claimed."

The Joneses returned to Lima lamenting the mentality of the "Bread Christians" and reflecting on the stark contrast between what they had just witnessed and the Peace Corps Volunteers back in the *barriadas*. The Joneses had seen enough of the Peace Corps at work, and had gotten to know a number of the Volunteers well enough, to understand that they simply would not tolerate the notion of heroics or saintliness because of how they lived and what they were doing. They saw their jobs in purely practical terms, and they insisted that they got as much out of it as they put into it—that elusive and highly personal thing known as "the Peace Corps experience." Bill Mangin, the deputy Rep of Peace Corps/Peru from 1962 to 1964, and subsequently Rep, says, "Many touching things happened. If a Volunteer in a *barriada* got sick, the Peruvian Indians and/or the squatter settlement people in whose midst they lived would take care of them. They helped the Volunteers set up their houses, or shacks, depending. They would ask about the Volunteers' families, cheer them up if they seemed discouraged. That was one of the best things about the Peace Corps. Maybe *the* best."

Alfred Jones had also noted the bonding relationships that developed between the Volunteers and the people of the mountain villages and *barriadas*. He was very much taken with these apparently spontaneous symbiotic relationships. He was more and more seized during his travels in Peru with the idea that something on the order of a Peace Corps in reverse might eventually emerge out of such an interchange. Jones thinks that he might not have gotten so caught up in this idea had it not been for the "swing" that took him and his wife from observing the Volunteers' total involvement in the *barriadas* of Lima so abruptly up to Lake Titicaca, where the missionaries' patronizing of the "natives" was so blatant, and then quickly back to Lima and the Peace Corps. (Jones pursued the idea of a Peace Corps in reverse with a will in the months to come and found a full intellectual and moral translation for it in a future trip to observe the Peace Corps in India, as noted in the following section on Charles Houston.)

In any case, the Joneses wanted to do something for the Volunteers they had met. Already ultraconscious of the nonefficacy of any "Big Daddy" arrangement, they decided to simply leave it up to the Volunteers. What would they like most? What could they, the Joneses, do to thank the Volunteers for their hospitality, their time? Hoping they would not be resented for such an offer, they were not disappointed: "A hot shower!" was the unanimous and unhesitating answer. "The hotel staff could not figure out what was going on," says Mary Jones. "They couldn't imagine what two people would want with so many towels. We did not enlighten them."

Mangin says that the first Volunteers in Peru were so full of themselves that "they thought they could save Peru better without us." Actually, says Mangin, "that first group didn't know how lucky they were arriving during an interim military government. That meant that we were able to deal directly with communities, schools, squatter settlements, particular offices of the government, bypassing the usual bureaucratic lines. That brief respite from red tape, plus the fact of Shriver's style and Frank's direct access to him, caused things to move so smoothly that some Volunteers got the idea that staff was superfluous. Obviously, quite the opposite was true." Mangin recalls that one Volunteer in Ayacucho during the Cuban missile crisis of October 1962 became so paranoid that he asked the Lima staff to send him a coded message if things got worse and he should head for the hills. The coded message was to have been: "Your trunk has arrived."

"The trouble was," says Mangin, "the kid's trunk—which he had earlier given up as lost forever—did finally arrive in the middle of the missile crisis. Needless to say, we didn't dare tell him."

Of Herb Wegner's and others' flattering appraisal of Mangin's value to the Peace Corps administration in Peru, due to his scholarly and first-hand knowledge of the country, Mangin is not at all displeased, but he is capable of charming self-mockery as well:

One day Frank Mankiewicz, Nancy McNulty, and I were having a meeting at AID headquarters in Lima with an AID official whom I will call Lulu and a Peruvian official I'll call Pedro. The subject of the meeting was how to get our Volunteers involved in a particular feeding program that Lulu and Pedro were dreaming up. Lulu was a woman from Texas married to a Peruvian. Her Spanish was lousy and her Texas accent so thick that few Peruvians knew what she was saying. Pedro was a great survivor of different administrations, a great "expert" on everything except what his listeners wanted to hear. Frank, Nancy, and I did not want to get involved. These feeding programs were okay but often they were just expensive showcase operations using Food for Peace food that often had to be cooked by people for hire. But it was certainly true that these programs looked good. Peace Corps photographers and other photojournalists couldn't resist them. Junketing congressmen loved to see those food kitchens and watch kids eat, supervised by a smiling Peace Corps Volunteer. Mankiewicz used to call that activity groaking. *Groak* is an Irish word for standing around watching others eat. Lulu and Pedro were getting very fired up over their cafeteria plan. The little kids would carry Alliance for Progress trays and cups. They would go down this line and that. In the course of their description it became apparent that the Food for Peace food line and the Food for Peace milk line were going to cross, and I had visions of the multiple collisions: Alliance for Progress trays crashing to the floor, Food for Peace milk in Alliance for Progress cups spilling and splashing all about, Food for Peace cornmeal mush splattering all over the place as ravenously hungry seven-year-olds howled in dismay and confusion. I started laughing and couldn't control it. I tried to suppress it by coughing and talking myself out of it, but I couldn't. I could tell that Frank and Nancy were also on the point of hysteria, but they held on, whereas I had to leave the room. Probably, Lulu and Pedro never realized anything was amiss, they were such jerks. But Frank couldn't resist. After the meeting broke up, he approached me with a sly grin and, in a stage whisper, said, "So much for sensitive cross-cultural anthropological training."

Feeding programs may not have been cost efficient or the best use of a Peace Corps Volunteer's time in Peru twenty-three years ago, but they never failed to mesmerize both believers and nonbelievers—groakers of all persuasions. Mankiewicz and Mangin recall a Volunteer who lived in the mountains four hours from Lima on a bad road. He wrote to his Congressman, Ben Rifle from Nebraska, that the Peace Corps staff was hard-hearted and unmindful. Rifle, true to his name, fired off a missive to Mankiewicz: What were they doing to this poor kid? Rifle warned that he was heading south of the border to investigate his young constituent's charges. This would be a side trip on a "fact-finding tour" elsewhere in Latin America. Mangin was astonished to see the Volunteer in question turn up casually in the Lima office a few days before Rifle was due to arrive. What about that letter? What about these accusations? The Volunteer was nonplussed. He could barely remember the letter. He said he must have written it when he was feeling homesick, had diarrhea, or both. He didn't know that Rifle was actually descending on the Lima staff. "Rifle arrived, disoriented from jet lag and culture shock," says Mangin. "We took him groaking," says Mankiewicz. Mangin adds, "The standard wholesome Peace Corps Volunteer was supervising. The Volunteer from Nebraska in question told Rifle how really wonderful we all were. So much for Congressman Rifle."

◆   ◆   ◆

On Saturday, January 31, 1964, Mankiewicz flew to Washington to testify with Shriver and Wiggins in front of Otto Passman's Subcommittee on Appropriations. Four Peace Corps programs had been singled out for examination; Peru was one of them. Mankiewicz checked into the Claridge Hotel next door to the Peace Corps, a place beloved of all Peace Corps travelers in the first half of the 1960s—and paid his bill for one night in advance: six dollars.

The next morning, February 1, he went out and bought the *New York Times*, which he planned to read until time to meet Shriver that afternoon. "There it was on the front page," he says. "Sarge had been appointed to head up the super task force for the poverty program. They weren't calling it the War on Poverty yet, let alone OEO (Office of Economic Opportunity). This was the preliminary stage. But obviously LBJ wanted Sarge to run the whole thing or he wouldn't have made such a big public gesture. I was stunned, honestly. So I called him up at about 9:00 A.M. and I said, 'Congratulations,' and he said, 'Frank, what do you know about this? Do you know anything about poverty in this country? I said yes—that I knew quite a bit. 'I've read a lot of stuff,' I said. He said, 'Well, what have you read?' I said, 'Well, most important, I've read Michael Harrington's book, *The Other America.*' Sarge said, 'Let's get Harrington in here.' And I said, 'Oh, yes. Definitely.' Well, Harrington was there by nightfall."

Maryann Orlando called Mankiewicz at the Claridge to tell him to meet Shriver next door in his office at 4:00 P.M. Mankiewicz assumed that this was to be their meeting to get ready for their congressional testimony on Peru the following day.

But when I walked into the fifth-floor conference room, there was Kermit Gordon, who was then the director of the Bureau of the Budget [then called Bew Bud by insiders, now known as Office of Management and the Budget, or OMB]. I couldn't quite figure that out. Then in came Walter Heller, chief of the Council of Economic Advisors; then Wilber Cohen, secretary of health, education, and welfare. And behind them came Willard Wirtz, secretary of labor, with Pat Moynihan, assistant secretary of labor, in tow. I was expecting a cozy gathering with Sarge and Warren about community development projects in Peru and how to get around Passman, and instead was getting a Johnson administration cabinet meeting. Huh? And then in came Sarge. Sarge says, "You all know Frank Mankiewicz, don't you? He's my assistant on this poverty task force."

Well, that's Sarge. He liked to pop one on you, send you reeling, make sure you couldn't say no. I think I smiled. Maybe not, though. I might have looked stricken. At 6:00 P.M., in came Adam Yarmolinsky, then assistant secretary of defense under McNamara [for whom Mankiewicz had almost gone to work two years earlier]. Adam was obviously key to this new operation. And finally, Mike Harrington, straight from the shuttle, looking understandably a bit rattled at having been plucked out of relative obscurity onto center stage just a few hours earlier.

With the two summer suits I had foolishly brought from Peru, where it was summer, I stayed a month at the Claridge, until the end of February 1964. Mike Harrington, Paul Jacobs [a West Coast journalist and labor organizer], Pat Moynihan, and I worked on Poverty legislation and the presidential message. That was very, very heady stuff. What we did, basically, was to translate community development as it was then being practiced by the Peace Corps in Latin America to the underclass of the United States.

Poverty had become an uppercase government program as well as a lowercase human condition. As fascinated as he was by the moral, intellectual, political, and operational facets and implications of the War on Poverty, and as much as he had been thrilled to spend every day and night for an entire month helping to invent it, Mankiewicz's heart was in the *barriadas*. As a result of his "heady" exercise, he felt all the more inspired and compelled to carry the torch for community development in Latin America wherever he could—however he could— and if he had to become a one-man Stalingrad in defense of it, he would.

And once again, time was obedient to Mankiewicz's aspirations. Jack Vaughn was sworn in as ambassador to Panama just as Mankiewicz was winding up his work on the Poverty task force and heading back to Peru, thus leaving vacant the job of regional director for Latin America at the Peace Corps. That was a job—*the* job—in which Mankiewicz could hope to bring about his peaceful revolution. And he got it.

CHARLES HOUSTON, M.D.

Charles Houston, M.D., arrived in New Delhi, India, at 5:00 A.M. on October 1, 1962, to take up his post as Peace Corps Representative. Joseph Wheeler, the acting Peace Corps Rep in India (who had succeeded a young woman named Timmy Napolitano as acting Rep, who in turn had taken over from Roger Ernst, special assistant to Tyler Wood, director of the AID mission), met Houston at the airport.

I was taken to the Peace Corps office, which was near the embassy, and shown to a cot in a corner. Joe told me just to lie down and go to sleep. We'd talk later. I took his advice. I was totally exhausted.

The next day, Joe briefed me about Peace Corps/India, and he held back nothing. It was an ugly picture. As I said, I should have *known*, what with all the urgency to get me to accept this post. It seemed that the Volunteers were demoralized. No cooperation from local authorities in the states and villages where Volunteers were located. Little help from the government of India, very poor programs, a succession of temporary Peace Corps Reps before me.

At the end of about six hours, Joe, himself exhausted, announced that he was going to leave India that night. Period. I have never been so deflated. True, it wasn't his fault. He had been summoned back to Washington earlier; Sarge had other plans for him in the NESA regional office at headquarters, which he had helped to set up. He had only stayed to meet and brief me because he knew how hopelessly lost I'd be otherwise.

But there I was, left with the chaos, left holding the bag. I'd inherited one American secretary, Terry Hiepp—a saint, as it turned out—two Indian office workers (one of whom was said to be the fastest typist in India), and Vira Pamar, an Indian journalist of great wisdom and integrity who was to act as my administrative assistant, a man who was to become my best friend.

But after his first thirty-six hours in India, Houston felt friendless.

I was depressed, confused, and angry. According to Sarge, I wasn't supposed to initiate contact with the American ambassador or the director of the AID mission, let alone the CIA guy. Yet an AID officer had been overseeing the Peace Corps program at one point and the only American in India who had the clout to pick up a telephone and call Shriver direct—or even the president for that matter—was Galbraith. I was alarmed enough by the situation to call the American embassy and ask for an emergency appointment with Galbraith. He saw me almost at once. I said, "Mr. Ambassador, I had no idea of what I was getting into. I had only ten hours of briefing in Washington. Wheeler describes chaos here, and now he is gone. I see that this program is in a total shambles. Please send me home before I do irreparable damage to the United States. I am not competent to do this job, and I cannot think of anyone who is. I'll pay my own way back, gladly. Just please get me out of here." [At the time, there were twenty-five Volunteers in India, with another fifty due to arrive in approximately three weeks, in mid-October of 1962.]

Galbraith didn't answer Houston immediately. He pondered Houston's problem, seeing it in no less drastic terms than did Houston. He then spent an hour describing his own problems as a new arrival in India and finally suggested to Houston that he visit as many Volunteers as possible in the Punjab in the next few days. Visit the Volunteers, see what's really going on, and then decide.

Galbraith said that if, after making these trips, I still thought it was hopeless and I wanted to return to the United States, he would support my decision. He understood my predicament, professionally, financially, emotionally. His compassion on this occasion caused me to think that here was a great human being, a great American, and one of the finest people I had ever met. Sarge had been right in describing Galbraith as charming and brilliant, but wrong in assuming that he would try to, and succeed in, dominating me. Maybe that would be so with someone younger and less experienced. But with me, he was then, and ever thereafter, professional, kind, and decent.

Houston set out in a jeep for a tour of the Punjab.

I covered twelve hundred miles in six days. The roads in India are not great. The maps I used were not accurate. The twelve Volunteers in the Punjab were widely spaced. It was not easy to find lodging or digestible food along the way. It was hot, dusty, exhausting, unnerving. I developed galloping diarrhea and a temperature. It was pure hell. I arrived at the first Volunteer site, Nabha, to meet the first Peace Corps Volunteers I had ever met. [Many Peace Corps/Washington officials had never seen a real, live Volunteer by the fall of 1962.] Four of them. I introduced myself as the permanent Rep in India, brought them Shriver's greetings. They showed some interest at first, but basically, they seemed to me to be a suspicious, cynical, indifferent lot. I had expected them to be demoralized; that's what I'd heard, and I could understand that. But instead, these four guys are running around drinking American beer, not offering me any after my long, dusty travels. And they complained a lot. About Peace Corps/ Washington, about the Peace Corps administration in New Delhi, about the Indian government and the Indians themselves, about life in the Third World, about the lack of furniture and motorcycles. They were *rude*. Moving on, I found approximately the same situation in Ludhiana. Complaints, rudeness. But something was different there. A few Volunteers said to me, sensing my alarm and displeasure, "Hey, Dr. Houston; hey, Charlie, don't worry. Things are not as bad as they look. We are doing pretty well here, all things considered. We are surviving. We are not disturbing the peace. We try to do useful work. But we could use more direction, more support. We've had none."

It was that interchange that influenced Houston to embark upon a policy of patriarchal behavior as a Peace Corps Rep, and for that matter, to stay in India and try to make a go of it.

It was apparent, as I departed, that they had been cheered up by my visit and by my concern about their underemployment. They allowed as how they were pleased that a full-time Rep had finally been appointed. They—as was true of all of the Volunteers that I saw on that trip—had been soured by the revolving-door administration of the past nine months. I began to think that Peace Corps/India was *not* hopeless. Once I got into it, once I saw the Volunteers, understood their frustrations and could see what needed doing—and that I could do it—I never again thought about giving it all up and going back to Aspen. India compelled. It was ever fascinating. That's really why I'd gone back, and now I knew it.

As Houston adjusted to temporary bachelorhood in New Delhi— which involved sleeping on a cot in the Peace Corps office, having "miserable breakfasts" in the basement cafeteria of the U.S. embassy, having an occasional "real meal" at the Ashoka Hotel, and looking for a new office and family quarters, he was suddenly called into medical action. A Volunteer in Nepal had fallen off a cliff, damaging his head, and was stranded in an isolated British hospital near the Indian border. Bob Bates, the Rep in Nepal, contacted Houston: Could Houston fly up and get the Volunteer out, treat him, take him back to the States if necessary? The melodrama of it all set Houston's adrenalin to pumping.

I landed on a grass strip in southern Nepal that I actually remembered from my reconnaissance of the south side of Everest with my father in 1950. I was driven by jeep up to the British hospital, brought the Volunteer out, flew him back to Delhi, realized he'd have to get treatment in the States, so we flew back first class—a "first," I am sure, in Peace Corps Volunteer travel arrangements—

and checked him into the U.S. Public Health hospital on Staten Island, flew down to Washington, and checked in with Sarge.

He gave me the same infusion of hope and optimism that I had always gotten from him. He asked me, straight off, how the poultry business was doing in Peace Corps/India. I said, quite honestly, that I didn't know yet, hadn't seen all of the Volunteers, didn't know the details of each one's job. I was struggling to get a grip on the administrative chaos left behind and trying to meet the Indian government officials whose cooperation the Peace Corps desperately needed. Sarge was understanding. But then he asked me when I was planning to go to a town called Nabha in the southern Punjab, because that's where I would see a spectacular poultry experiment that four Volunteers had begun. I was stunned. I said I'd been to Nabha and met the four Volunteers there—the first Volunteers I'd ever met—but there was not a chicken in sight, or any talk of such an experiment, and indeed, I had heard only complaints and negativism from those four.

Shriver could hardly believe what he was hearing. He told Houston that a legendary poultry expert named Manning Grinnan from Dallas, a friend of Betty Harris's, had gone to India before Houston had arrived and had met with four Volunteers from Nabha who told Grinnan that they were doing big things in poultry. They had spoken to Grinnan in the vocabulary of poultry experts. They had claimed to be making their own vitamin B_{12} and their own penicillin from cow dung. They claimed that they were raising chickens with fabulous laying properties and were showing local farmers and youth clubs how to do the same. They spoke with such unblinking authority that Grinnan took them at their word (would Peace Corps Volunteers lie?), returned to the United States, went to the Hill, and read his report on the Peace Corps poultry experiment in India into the Congressional Record. Congress was duly impressed. Shriver asked Houston what he thought about that.

Houston was mystified. "I told Sarge I simply could not understand or explain it."

Shriver barked, "Charlie, get back there and look into it!"

Houston vowed that he would, and "the first thing that I did when I got back to India was to race off to Nabha and confront the four Volunteers, all of whom had had some kind of agribusiness background: 'What the hell is going on here?' "

The Volunteers looked at Houston with shamed faces. "When I told them what had transpired in Washington, what Manning Grinnan had said on the Hill, and therefore what they were now responsible for, they 'fessed up. They told me the truth." The Nabha Volunteers explained to Houston that they had had so little direction and had been so beleaguered by so many visitors—curious tourists and junketing government officials from the United States—that they had gotten sick of it, sick of being treated by the embassy as exotic animals in a zoo, sick of answering stupid questions, sick of being observed and dissected by outsiders while at the same time feeling totally neglected by the Peace Corps hierarchy. Their growing sense of purposelessness and oddness plus the pressure to be perfect angels of peace and convincing advertisements for the vaunted American work ethic had caused them to construct a story that was so logical that it would be easily swallowed, yet so delectably farfetched that it would relieve their boredom. In convincing technical language, they had given themselves giddy satisfaction by their hoodwinking of the Texas poultry expert. Isolated in a village the size of Nabha (five thousand people) in a state the size of the Punjab (sixteen million people) in a country the size of India (over half a billion people), one does not have the perspective to imagine that an antic fib about one's prowess in the matter of poultry raising could reverberate halfway around the world with potentially disastrous implications.

Houston, after hearing the Volunteers' confession, hissed, "Okay. I get the point. But look, are *any* of your claims true?"

The Volunteers humbly said no.

Houston then "tongue-lashed them and threatened to send them home." One of the Volunteers then implored Houston, "You know, Charlie, we *could* get something great going here in poultry. No kidding. We know enough about it from the state poultry farm manager to do it and we'd really like to do it. It would make our lives worthwhile and would help a lot of Indians, which is why I thought we came here. And the local farmers and youth clubs are really interested in it. But we can't do it unless we can get some money to start it up, and some technical help, and I know that isn't the Peace Corps' way of doing things—that it's supposedly taboo—but that's what we *need*. And if we could ever get it, just watch out!"

Houston stayed over an extra day in Nabha and talked further with the Volunteers about actually starting up that heretofore mythical poultry project. He returned to New Delhi with some rule-breaking imperatives in his head: "AID had a poultry man, but in a year he hadn't been able to get anything going. Yet AID had the money. So what was wrong? To find out what was wrong meant that I would have to get very involved with AID, something Sarge was opposed to." But here was a case where it was obvious that AID had something the Peace Corps needed—money and technical know-how—and the Peace Corps had something AID needed—young, eager Volunteers who did not think it was beneath them to live with, and as, the poor, who did not think that raising poultry in the backyard and marketing eggs on bicycles was too humble or inconsequential.

Houston went to Tyler Wood and Jack Fobes of AID and talked them into a poultry loan. He borrowed the AID poultry manual, which had been written by an American poultry specialist. It was ultratechnical and poorly written. Houston, along with his staff and the Nabha Volunteers, rounded up the only two fully qualified poultry Volunteers, Justin McLaughlin and Frank Ziegler, also working in the Punjab; William Stopper, a poultry man in the AID office; and assorted Americans and Indians with broad linguistic skills. Together, the group effort resulted in a brisk, easy-to-follow handbook that was translated into several different dialects spoken in the Punjab, Rajasthan, Madhya Pradesh, Uttar Pradesh, and Gujarat. "We made our own drawings and rewrote the text. And this became the 'poultry bible' of India. An agricultural Volunteer, Bob Gould, was in charge of distributing it all over India. AID provided enough money for us to start some projects, and in six months, we made Manning Grinnan's success story come true. Poultry became the biggest Peace Corps operation in India."

In June 1964, six months before Houston turned over his Repship to his deputy, Brent Ashabranner, and returned to Washington, the Peace Corps had been directly responsible for 540 units containing 150,447 birds, which were laying 96,438 eggs a day. These figures doubled those of six months earlier, and as Houston was packing to leave in November 1964, the count had doubled again. Soon, the Volunteers were assisting five thousand poultry raisers who owned two million laying hens, which were producing about half a billion eggs a year. "At this rate of growth," Houston buoyantly told a general staff meeting at Washington headquarters after he had returned from India, "there will be more chickens than people in India by June 1970."

Ashabranner, while pointing to certain problems with the Peace Corps' poultry enterprises, wrote in his 1971 book, A Moment in History, "In a country of more than half a billion people, half a billion eggs a year may seem a paltry total; but in the areas where the Volunteers worked, it meant a major jump in egg supply" in a country desperately in need of more protein. As to the scarcity of grain for chicken feed, Ashabranner notes that "by making maximum use of grain that had been declared unfit for human consumption and—with the help of AID animal husbandry experts . . . the Volunteers felt they were able to justify their work in terms of the protein the eggs produced." And while many Volunteers were bothered by the fact that they were seldom able to help the poorest Indians, the untouchables, or Harijans—since to get started in poultry one had to have at least some cash (or the collateral to get a government loan)—"here and there a Volunteer, with great persistence or ingenuity, was able to promote a *rupee* grant from some charitable organization and use it to help a few Harijans get a start in poultry."

Houston and Ashabranner, however, saw nothing wrong in the fact that the Volunteers in poultry worked mainly with Indians who "had a little land and a little money, and—when the venture was successful—their efforts helped them to have a little more." Ashabranner recalls visiting a farmer in the Punjab with a Volunteer who had been working with the man for over a year. "The farmer had several hundred fine White Leghorns," wrote Ashabranner, "which he showed me with great pride. He told me that he was now making about a hundred rupees profit a month from his birds." The farmer also told Ashabranner, "I am using some of the money to send my oldest daughter to secondary school," adding, with evident pride, "She is the first female in my family ever to go beyond the primary grades."

"Poultry was big in India. Period!" insists Houston, granting his own initial surprise at how fast the business took off. He originally had known nothing about raising poultry, nor had most of the Volunteers. Suddenly, it was a sensation—a fad, almost. There were no bounds to it. Businessmen and bureaucrats took up the trade in their spare time, some so eager to earn extra money selling eggs that they would tear up a pretty backyard garden and replace it with a chicken house, or poultry unit, as they are more properly called. Indian citizens with white-collar jobs were raising chickens on the roofs of apartment houses. Peace Corps teachers, armed with the "poultry bible," doubled as poultry gurus at their schools. For the self-taught "poultry pioneers" in Nabha, business was booming. (In fact, one of their number, William Donovon of Weymouth, Massachusetts, would join the Peace Corps/India staff after two years as a Volunteer.) They were beseiged by all ages and levels of citizenry to help them get poultry units going. There was gold in them there thatch-roofed huts, and the secret was the deep-litter, close-confinement system, which Ashabranner described in *A Moment in History*:

> The poultry units were all very much the same, small oblong buildings with brick or adobe walls, screened on the long sides, with peaked thatch roofs. The floors were covered with from eight to twelve inches of rice hulls or straw. Every four to six months, this "litter" would be cleaned out and replaced; it then made excellent fertilizer.
>
> [This arrangement] made possible the proper feeding and sanitary control of the birds and provided the best available protection from predators. It was as different as day and night from the tradition of letting the chickens run free, forage for themselves, and take their chances with disease, hawk and mongoose.

The close-confinement system was the one recommended and illustrated in the "poultry bible," and it was also the one taught to subsequent groups of Peace Corps trainees headed for India. The theory was that you could have been raised in Manhattan at 92nd and Madison and never seen a chicken other than dead, dressed, and wrapped in clear plastic at Gristede's and still get a poultry unit started in India if you had precise instruction and a will to do it. The first two groups of Volunteers, known as India I and India II, came from varied backgrounds, some urban, some rural; almost all had college degrees, some from Ivy League schools, some from big state universities, some from small community colleges. A few had been out in the "real world" for a while and had earned a living before joining the Peace Corps. But most had not. Still, it was possible for this disparate, scattered, eclectic but basically privileged potpourri of young Americans to do something quite spectacular, for a while, in an enigmatic, alien culture where the poverty and hunger were staggering. Many of the first two groups of Peace Corps Volunteers followed the "poultry bible," and no matter what their backgrounds managed to create food-production boomlets that lasted as long as there were Volunteers to encourage, advise, and demonstrate. Native American vigor, enthusiasm, and ingenuity were as important as what we would now call "state-of-the-art" poultry-raising methods.

As popular as this method became, and so swiftly, no one stopped to consider for a time that about 40 percent of Indians are vegetarians and would not eat eggs because they contain life. The Hindu religion forbids the consumption of any animal life. Millions of Indians, therefore, would not be buying eggs at all. This presented no hardship for the first two groups of Volunteers, India I and India II, since with the advent of the "poultry bible" and the geometrically progressing poultry projects, they were, if anything, overemployed. They themselves, of course, had no financial stake whatsoever in the poultry business. Financial gain for the Volunteers was the antithesis of the Peace Corps ethic and played no part in Peace Corps life in theory or in practice. In fact, Houston recalls with glowing fondness the remark of Bob Gould, one of his Volunteers working in poultry: "You know what I love about this work, Charlie? I've got nothing to lose because there's nothing in it for me." It was part of the Peace Corps catechism to help poor people to obtain skills that would bring the maximum possible profit and the hope of a better life. Thus, the Volunteers put their eager-beaver minds and glands to work on how to reach the vegetarians. The solution occurred to the Volunteers scattered about India almost simultaneously: Change the image of the egg!

As Houston puts it, "The Volunteers put out the word, and it spread around India with amazing speed, that they were taking the roosters out of the henhouses. The message was clear: The hens' eggs would therefore not be fertilized. The eggs would not contain life. The Volunteers had little difficulty in getting this point across—no doubt largely because many Hindus knew that eggs were an inexpensive source of protein and were glad to have an excuse to buy and eat them. Also, it was a challenge, a game for the Volunteers. Don't worry, folks, the hens keep on laying! In fact, they often laid five- to ten-percent more eggs, it was ballyhooed. And it was true. Since the word had spread far and wide that Peace-Corps-assisted poultry units produced eggs that were twice the size of those of chickens that just ran free, attention was paid. But the best part is this: The Volunteers, all of whom must have been born with some Madison Avenue genes, or at least acquired some by osmosis, furthered the cause of more eggs for India by giving them an irresistible name—'vegetarian eggs.' It took!"

Actually, a key feature of the close-confinement system of poultry raising is that laying hens never come into contact with roosters in the first place. That is part of the plan. Thus, eggs resulting from this system are by design unfertilized and contain no life.

Brent Ashabranner recalls a further public relations benefit from the "vegetarian egg" campaign: "These big, clean, carefully boxed eggs quickly acquired another name in a number of places in India, a name given to them not by Volunteers but by Indians. They were called 'Peace Corps eggs.' "

It was thus logical that the Indian government's Planning Commission would ask for yet more Volunteers to assist yet more Indian farmers in expanding their poultry businesses. As it turned out, almost every state in India had had on paper or in practice some kind of poultry development program, but this fact had not been mentioned to Houston or Ashabranner initially since it did not occur to Indian officials that affluent young Americans would have any proficiency in this field whatsoever—which, in fact, most of them did not. Yet, when the Peace Corps appeared not only to have some proficiency, but indeed to have the Midas touch, the "how" of the miracle was of no interest to Indian officials. Only the curious fact of it mattered. The Division of Training worked out a way to turn an English major into a chicken farmer for a specific area in India even before he left home. Thus, India V was born. Twenty-two-year-old English, history, philosophy, political science, art, and music majors were sent to the University of California at Davis, where there was an emphasis on agricultural programs. They were force-fed the dialects of the states where they would be working, but mostly they immersed themselves in every aspect of the techniques of the close-confinement system, including learning how to debeak and vaccinate the birds when necessary. From Plutarch to poultry in the Punjab in three months. Some of the trainees joked that this branch of animal husbandry ought to be called "the roosters-off-bounds method." Upon hearing this, Houston commented, "The hens may not like their chaste lives, but more Indians get more food."

Ashabranner wrote: "After three months of sharply focused training at Davis, these Volunteers were as ignorant as they had ever been about general farming and animal husbandry . . . [but] they knew one thing reasonably well: how to house, raise, cull and keep healthy a small flock of chickens in India." Performing a useful service immediately upon arrival in a country so vast and complex as India gave these Volunteers an almost unrivaled sense of self-esteem. Their popularity was well deserved. Ashabranner estimates that between 1963 and 1966, "ten of India's seventeen states asked for and received Volunteers to work in poultry development, and all of them asked for additional or replacement groups . . . I am sure that Indian farmers who saw Peace Corps Volunteers sleep all night in a chicken house when there was a disease crisis or a mongoose on the prowl had some new thoughts about Americans."

If poultry is a natural prey of the mongoose, the Peace Corps was the chosen prey of the chairman of the House Appropriations Committee, the wily, reptilian Democratic congressman from Louisiana, Otto Passman. No one at the Peace Corps claimed to be able to understand him as a human being or to pinpoint his exact motives as a politician. Certainly, no one at the Peace Corps who went up to the Hill with Shriver to face Passman at an appropriations hearing ever came away unscathed by Passman's withering sarcasm. Passman reveled in picking on the Peace Corps brass. He seemed to enjoy ridiculing the Peace Corps immensely, yet he also seemed to be fatally fascinated by the program.

Houston had heard about Passman from Betty Harris, who had described the congressman as being "weird, moody, crafty, and powerful—but that's okay, we've always gotten our appropriations. Humor him, I say." While Harris was on business in India and staying with Houston in Delhi, her assistant back in Washington called with the urgent message that Passman was on his way to India and wanted to visit a Peace Corps poultry project. "Betty got practically hysterical with excitement," says Houston. "It's a big opportunity!" she exclaimed. *

"I arranged for him to see one of my better poultry projects twenty-five miles from Delhi," says Houston.

> I rode with him in an embassy car and found him, counter to his reputation, pleasant and conversational, if obviously also a very political animal. He walked through the entire village, talked to Volunteers, made astute observations, asked well-informed questions. He reminisced about his own days as a chicken farmer. It was a very spontaneous occasion; the Volunteers hadn't been briefed. When he got back to Delhi, Passman was positively glowing about his Peace Corps visit. I reported this to Betty Harris, who was

*Harris's Washington assistant at that time was one Richard Celeste, a big, amiable, energetic fellow from Ohio in his midtwenties whose political instincts were as sharp as Harris's. Celeste later became director of the Peace Corps during the latter part of the Carter Administration and is now governor of Ohio.

ecstatic. "Let's send a cable to Sarge," she said. "He'll *love* it." And so we did.

Before Passman left Delhi, he called to say, ever so cordially, that he appreciated my taking time with him and giving him such an enjoyable tour, and he hoped that I'd come up to the Hill and pay him a visit when I returned to Washington. He wanted to hear more about the Peace Corps' progress in poultry. Well! I was very pleased with myself. I thought I had made a convert, pulled off a coup. Betty Harris thought so, too. She was incredulous.

As it turned out, incredulous was the way to be. On my next trip to Washington, Sarge asked me to go up to the Hill with him in front of Passman's committee. I felt confident to do this since Passman had been so effusive earlier and since, by that time, Peace Corps poultry projects had increased in number and productivity. The hearings started amiably with Passman saying nice things to Shriver and to me. He called the meeting to order and suddenly his tone changed. Right off, he started attacking the Peace Corps, attacking Sarge, calling me on the carpet. I did the best I could in my replies to him, and followed Sarge's lead in not losing my temper. But Passman wasn't even paying attention. I suddenly realized he was just putting something on the record to prove to someone that he was anti–Peace Corps, *or*, and this is more likely, that he, Otto Passman, was a force to be reckoned with on the Hill and a man who could not be pushed around by the Kennedys. Certainly, no one was trying. But he was making sure he came across as tough and independent. Wow! What an eye-opener. Now I knew why Betty had first said he was weird and moody. Right after the hearing closed, he came by and patted me on the shoulder and smiled, putting on his amiable act, almost as if to say, "Nothing personal, you understand."

On the way back to Peace Corps headquarters, Shriver said to Houston, very quietly, "Well, Charlie, now you see what we're up against."

It was rumored that Passman owned one hundred silk suits. Houston remembers him as being physically "pale grey all over. His face was grey, his hair was grey, his eyes were grey, his silk suits were grey. He was very folksy when *off* the record. He was compelling when he would drawl on about his deprived childhood and his early days as a chicken farmer. But when he went *on* the record, he was like a snake, with thin, hooded eyes. He would sit there looking as if he were half asleep, asking lazy questions in that syrupy southern way—and then *Bango!* He would suddenly get tough and brutal, threaten to hold back on our money. But as Betty Harris had said, 'Never mind. We always get our appropriations.' "

♦   ♦   ♦

There were "high-risk, high-gain Volunteers" and there were also "high-risk, high-gain projects." Such projects were rarely instituted at Peace Corps headquarters in Washington, where the Murder Board mentality could too easily crush them. Peace Corps/India's Bisauli Workshop was such a high-risk, high-gain project.

Houston says that the Bisauli Workshop project

wasn't programmed, it "just growed." Volunteers from India II got it going— a dozen or so out of the fifty who had arrived in India in mid-October, just three weeks after I had arrived. One of them, Glenn Elkins, an energetic, restless jack-of-all-trades had come as a TEFL [Teaching English as a Foreign Language] teacher, as had his wife, Anne. It was Glenn who got the idea of the workshop and talked me into it. He told me that making farm instruments like hoes and rakes, shovels, small plows, and even water wheels would be a great thing to get going. He envisioned a training program where the locals could learn blacksmithing and eventually have their own business. Since that was precisely what Sarge had in mind when he would constantly say, "The Peace Corps' job is to work itself out of a job," I gave the go-ahead. Glenn just rocketed off and very soon had acquired a huge, old, deserted brick building— albeit of basically graceful Muslim architecture—filled with debris, manure of all sources, rats, and vermin. He and about fifty locals cleaned the place up, collected some primitive smithy instruments, turned it into a reasonably good forge, and had a going concern within several weeks. And that is *speedy* by Indian standards. I visited Bisauli [a town approximately seventy-five miles northeast of Delhi in Uttar Pradesh] several times during this period and I was very impressed. His wife, Anne Elkins, kept the workshop's books in addition to teaching.

The Elkinses further wowed Houston by mounting a full-scale opening gala. "The first Peace Corps tea party, I'll wager," says Houston. "They had bought several hundred clay teacups, which are cheaper than paper in India, made vats of milk-tea, wangled assorted cooks to provide trays of *pakorra* (little fried meat cakes), had a band, puppet shows, and jugglers. About two hundred townspeople came, including local dignitaries, and of course, the Delhi contingent. I drove up with Ty Wood of AID in his big, black car. It was a huge success and, I felt, a splendid omen."

A promising period of production followed. The shop flourished. Other Volunteers in the India II group, both teachers and agricultural extension workers, got involved in the project. Then came the first crisis: Professional makers of farm implements within a radius of fifty miles, upon discovering that the Bisauli Cooperative Workshop could make products of higher quality and undersell the competition by half, undertook a series of subtle harassments involving licenses, taxes, and permits. These unfriendly ploys did not stop production, but they siphoned off the time and energy of Elkins, who was still the guiding force behind the workshop. Elkins sought the intervention of Houston, who says, "I went with Glenn to argue with the local authorities. We got promises but no results. We went back again, and this time I exerted some pressure on one Block Development officer whom I had befriended and got things straightened out." The harassment stopped— for a while.

But suddenly, Elkins, not only the director of the workshop but also its chief "buyer," could not obtain steel from nearby markets. The workshop had to have steel for much of the equipment that it produced. Elkins asked Houston for permission to travel to Allahabad, a city five hundred miles southeast of New Delhi on the Ganges River, to buy. Permission granted. "There in Allahabad, Elkins met a plausible, credible man who gave him a very good price. Elkins felt he had no choice but to trust him, and so paid him in advance—and that was the last he saw of the money or the steel. Glenn told me about this swindle immediately and we tried everything we could to trace the crook, but got nowhere. Glenn was out more money than I care to think about, and we had almost no steel at Bisauli."

The Bisauli Cooperative Workshop limped along for several days, its finances depleted, its supply of steel nearing zero, its morale plummeting. The future suddenly looked bleak if not hopeless. At this point, in late January of 1964, Charlie Houston received a telephone call from an elaborately polite, articulate man named Alfred Winslow Jones. Jones was calling from the Ashoka Hotel in New Delhi. Jones explained that he had met briefly with Sargent Shriver weeks before, and at more length with Warren Wiggins, at Peace Corps headquarters in Washington. He, Jones, assumed that Houston had received an introductory letter from Shriver or Wiggins some time ago asking that Houston welcome Jones, and in effect, plug him into Peace Corps/India. Houston had never received such a letter, and said so quite curtly. (Houston was suffering from an affliction that no other early Peace Corps Rep ever suffered: an onslaught of American tourists who had made the dissection of India a kind of hobby. This familiar breed called Houston at home as well as in his office asking to see that unfamiliar breed, the Peace Corps Volunteers. These visitors arrived, nine times out of ten, without prior warning or introduction and were often industrialists or movie producers who claimed to be friends of Old Joe or of another Kennedy relative who had contributed stunning amounts of money to JFK's campaign.) Houston had his hands full simply accommodating congressmen and evaluators. He had notified Shriver that he could not and would not receive any other than official visitors, and only then if given fair warning. Jones's call therefore irritated him. But he was intrigued by the man's courtliness and fearful that he might be making a mistake to dismiss him. Houston let him continue. Jones said that he had a copy of Shriver's letter of introduction in his briefcase, and further, copies of previous correspondence with Warren Wiggins months earlier, when Jones and his wife, Mary, had visited Peace Corps Rep Frank Mankiewicz and his flagship program in Peru. Since Jones remained calm and civil, so did Houston. Houston realized that it was almost impossible that Jones could make up such a story. He thus agreed to see Jones. He had to check the situation at Bisauli anyway in a couple of days, and with just a tincture of resignation in his voice, invited Jones to accompany him. (An enthusiatic, flattering letter from Shriver to Houston, introducing Jones, arrived a day later—delayed, as mail so often was in India.)

Houston took to Jones immediately. These two Harvard men (Jones, class of 1923; Houston, class of 1935—something they did not discuss) had more in common than either of them could have ever guessed. The two discovered, alternately, that Jones was a close friend of Louis Fisher (who had written the definitive biography of Gandhi), that he and his wife had traveled extensively in India before, and that they were also close friends of Rajeshwar Dayal (formerly High Commissioner to Pakistan, soon to become India's ambassador to the United Nations) and his wife, Susheela. In addition, the Houstons and the Joneses were both friendly with outgoing ambassador Galbraith and incoming ambassador Bowles and their wives, as well as with Carol Laise, a senior Foreign Service officer with a legendary knowledge of India, who would soon become ambassador to Nepal. They also shared a friendship with Kusum Nair, author of *Blossoms in the Dust*. Houston marveled that Jones, like himself, had also made a precipitous career switch in early middle age—in Jones's case from journalist to founder of Wall Street's most successful hedge fund, A. W. Jones & Co. Jones marveled that Houston, about whom Jones knew a great deal in advance of his India trip, thanks to Shriver, had sacrificed a chance to make medical history, thereby becoming rich and famous, as the perfecter of the artificial heart only to follow the more elusive grail of Peace Corps service. Houston and Jones were, as they arrived in Bisauli, at their respective ages of fifty and sixty-two, exactly where they wanted to be spiritually and intellectually just at that moment in their lives. Bisauli was only a common metaphor.

Houston later wrote a memorandum to the files, witnessed by Brent Ashabranner and Vira Pamar, dated November 15, 1964:

> On February 2, 1964, Mr. Alfred Jones accompanied me on a visit to the Bisauli Workshop. I spent most of the day examining their accounts, and concluded that their financial position was precarious. That was due to several factors: . . . District officials had greatly reduced their original commitment to purchase a large number of water lifting devices . . . It was necessary to purchase metal [steel] for these devices at higher than normal rates [which refers to the games being played on the workshop by its competitors, not the swindle which Houston declined to put in writing] . . . District officials delayed payment for delivered devices . . . [and after] payroll and purchases . . . the workshop exhausted its meager reserves and on February 2 was in danger of closing within a few days unless a considerable sum was found immediately.

"After reviewing this gloomy picture," says Houston, "Jones and I discussed the matter in detail. We agreed that the workshop must not be closed, because Peace Corps prestige would suffer, the American image in the Punjab would suffer, the Volunteers who had put an enormous amount of effort into the project would be seriously demoralized, and the funds already invested in the program would be lost."

Houston included in his memo the fact that "during the journey back to Delhi, Mr. Jones generously offered a loan of Rs. 20,000.00 repayable at the end of 1964 to keep the project alive. On Monday morning, February 3, Mr. Jones cashed a personal check drawn on the Chemical Bank New York Trust Company for $4,226.72, converting this immediately to Rs. 20,003.00 at the First National City Bank in New Delhi. This money was transmitted immediately by bank draft to the Bisauli Workshop."

With the infusion of Jones' contribution, the workshop's "growth chart" again headed up. "Glenn and Anne Elkins were real tigers," says Houston. "Under their dogged, dedicated management seven days a week, and with the Jones loan, the shop again thrived." In a letter of June 2, 1964, Houston was thrilled to be able to report to Jones, who had by then returned to New York after three months in India, that the workshop "ended its current season with money in the bank. After paying all loans, including a reserve set aside for you, they have [enough] to continue operations. Your timely help saved the bacon, and the bacon is now cooked and ready to serve." Jones replied that he was "overjoyed" with this news and would soon be sending Houston his report on his observations about Peace Corps/India.

Houston concluded his June 2, 1964, letter to Jones by noting, "We are now in a very strenuous period with the arrival of India VI, termination of India II, and program site visits for India VII, VIII, IX, and X."

Glenn and Anne Elkins, members of the soon-to-depart India II contingent, had set about doing what they intended to do: start a business, teach a few interested Indians the manufacturing and management skills necessary, and then let them take it over. Glenn Elkins had found a promising young Indian to replace him as majordomo, and he gradually stepped aside, acting as chairman of the board, in effect. Anne trained an Indian bookkeeper and went back to teaching full time. During their last few weeks, the Elkinses acted purely as advisers to the workshop. Mission accomplished, theoretically.

In practical terms, however, the local man whom Elkins had trained lacked advantages that Elkins (and most other Volunteers) took for granted: a college education, a natural bent for entrepreneurship, the built-in conviction that hard work pays off, and the support of an authority figure who could exert pressure on the opposition if necessary. "He did not have the Elkinses' status or intrepid administrative track record," says Houston. "He had no political skills. He had trouble resisting the inroads from other fabricators and the Indian bureaucracy. In any case, the Bisauli Workshop was sold at least once shortly after I left India. Greg Brown, a Peace Corps Volunteer who had helped get the workshop started, and who had had a bountiful poultry venture going in Bisauli at the same time, went back years later, full of curiosity and hope, only to find the workshop building abandoned, returned to its original derelict state, and his poultry houses leveled, his chickens sold. It turned out that just over a year after he had left, the rumor went around that all poultry houses were to be taxed. It was a false and malicious rumor." But the panicky devastation had happened quickly, irrevocably.

As to the concept of "high risk, high gain," the Bisauli Workshop burnt the candle at both ends. But it could not last the night.

◆   ◆   ◆

The exertions and melodrama attendant to Houston's responsibilities as the first full-time Peace Corps Rep in India could have consumed him utterly without any other intrusions. But to live in India is to be intruded upon. Three generations lived under one roof. Except among the most privileged segment of Indian society, privacy is not sought or cherished. Order in the streets is apparently not valued and therefore not observed. Houston found himself bleating the time-honored bleat of newly arrived westerners in India, even though he had been an entranced visitor years before. In one of his first letters home (he usually sent mimeographed copies to several of his friends, begging their forgiveness for the mass-produced format), he cries out. "People—people—everywhere!" He was intensely frustrated by the traffic in Old Delhi, feeling that "traffic" was too rational a description of what he encountered:

> Driving manners are awful. Horns blow constantly. People stand, sit, even sleep all over the roads. Cyclists swerve crazily through the bullock and buffalo herds, the camels and dogs. Bicycles outnumber cars twenty to one and sometimes they seem to outnumber people. They pay no attention to the horns of the cars, which compete with each other for speed, although speed is fortunately impossible since the roads are terribly rough, being hand laid and hand patched. The women who mend the roads wander in and out of the gridlock draped with their entire fortunes in silver on their ankles and wrists, some with nose rings, carrying tarred gravel

in flat baskets on their heads. An emaciated horse bedecked with ribbons and bells draws a tonga [a glorified covered cart] slowly through the masses carrying twelve people ranging from the ages of newborn to ninety. A ramshackle "Public Carrier" truck, badly overloaded with bales of jute, careens down the middle of the road, horn blasting, scattering the people. These trucks are a terrible hazard and frequently overturn. On their tailgates are gay designs and the message "Please Use Horn."

Houston was seesawing between a state of exhaustion and exhilaration throughout his first week in India. Vowing to leave behind his lumpy cot in the original Peace Corps office in New Delhi at the first possible moment, he enlisted the help of his inherited administrative assistant, Vira Pamar, to guide him through a house-and-office hunt. His wife, Dorcas, and his two sons, David and Robin, would be arriving in mid-December 1962. His daughter Penny would be joining them in May 1963, upon graduation from Milton Academy in Massachusetts. Houston and Pamar set out in a jeep to look. Houston, with the "Peace Corps Image According to Shriver" lurking guiltily in his mind, asked Pamar to take him to the Delhi slums. Pamar was puzzled, then alarmed when he began to realize that the immaculate Dr. Houston was actually contemplating setting up shop there. But Houston was quickly cured of such a notion when encountering their appalling reality, and both he and Pamar were relieved to turn the jeep in another direction. Pamar showed Houston a housing project that was considered upper-middle-class by Third World standards. The house that Houston was first shown was both large enough and plain enough for his purposes; it could contain both his family and his office and would not betray the Peace Corps image. Eager to be done with the matter of real estate and eager to get back to work, Houston signed a lease and breathed a sign of relief, as did Pamar, who would act as office manager and troubleshooter for the Peace Corps operation. (Pamar had worked for American agencies in India for twenty years and was looking forward to his new role as an important functionary in the Peace Corps' head office in New Delhi: 61 Sunder Nagar, a dwelling much to Pamar's liking.) At the ground level, according to Houston, was "a very small front yard, a medium-small backyard where you hung out the laundry, a living room, three bedrooms, and a small kitchen. That was family living quarters. The second floor was identical in layout, and that was the office. The stairs were outside, so theoretically one unit wouldn't bother the other. At first, the house seemed airy, even big, after the tiny Peace Corps flat near the embassy. But today, I could only say a qualified 'nice' about it. As time went on and more and more Volunteers arrived, and as the staff grew, we never had enough space or privacy, to put it mildly. Visiting firemen were in and out, as were Volunteers, all of the time."

Once the lease at 61 Sunder Nagar was signed, Pamar told Houston that he would not only feel privileged to serve his administrative needs but would also be glad to oversee his domestic staff, as well. "Domestic staff? *What* domestic staff?" bellowed Houston. "I've never had a domestic staff and I certainly don't mean to start now. In the Peace Corps, of *all* places." Pamar looked stricken. He explained, very gently, that this type of housing in India automatically came with servants. No fewer than one, certainly. It was usual. It was expected. Houston's retinue, Pamar explained, would in any case be far more modest than that of other ranking American officials. Not highly skilled, not formal or uniformed. Surely the good doctor would not dismiss people who so desperately needed work, who might well starve without this job. And further, Pamar advanced, how could Houston expect to travel sixty thousand miles a year on Peace Corps business during his tour as Rep, as he felt he must do, without a strong support system at home? How could he feel comfortable about leaving his wife and children behind in a strange and complex culture with no protection or assistance? How would they cope? Besides, said Pamar, most of the servants were included in the rent. That was just understood.

Houston, chagrined at how far he had edged away from the "holy" Peace Corps image and Shriver's admonitions about the embassy in general and Galbraith in particular in so short a space of time, nonetheless could not fault Pamar's logic. And in fact, he was going to be living simply compared to the majority of Americans in India. Galbraith lived regally. It was all relative. But he had to swallow hard when Pamar outlined his domestic situation: a laundress, a gardener (called a *mali*), a part-time sweeper, a cook, and a driver. (An Indian driver in India was an absolute necessity, as Houston had already come to see, and as is described by former India Volunteer Alan Bradford in Chapter 9.) The cook, who was to be a "live-in," would occupy one of two tiny rooms over a garage that was detached from the house. These rooms were no more than eight feet square and six feet high, but the cook, who will be called R. B., seemed satisfied, even grateful. Houston concluded that it was a good thing to have a cook whose morale was so easily boosted. His cook's gratitude made Houston feel better about the entire setup. It *would* be cruel to deprive these people of work, and in some cases, shelter.

However, as Houston returned one evening after a field trip, he found his household staff "downcast, not talking. Something was obviously very wrong. Pamar spoke for the group: 'Sahib, R. B. a very bad man.' I asked what he had done and why everyone was looking so frightened.

"He said, 'Sahib, remember you have been complaining about noise at night? People coming in late, laughing, and slamming the gate?' I said, yes, that had been going on for some time. I assumed it was uncustomarily noisy Indian neighbors. What had this to do with R. B.? Pamar said, 'R. B. and his brother (long pause, as the servants cower and shake their heads)—they keeping two girls in that room, and (another long pause, as all shudder)—many men come to visit. It is these men who are opening gate and making noise at night.'

"Well, it turns out that my cook and his brother were in fact running a two-girl whorehouse above my garage, and it was their clients who were coming and going at all hours, laughing, banging the gate, waking me up. So I told Pamar, 'Just get them out of there. Tell them to *go.*'

"'Sahib, you don't understand,' said Pamar. 'R. B. very bad man, *very* bad man, has *many* friends. If R. B. knows we have told about him, he will be sending men with knives and they will *kill.*' "

With a wave of his hand, Houston tried to dismiss the stated risk: "Oh, look, this is a good section of Delhi. We're not going to have any of that here, I feel sure."

Pamar pleaded. "*Please.* Bring the police before you tell R. B."

"So, in order to placate Pamar and the domestic staff, who were really very frightened, I sent for the police. The police came. I sent for R. B. and confronted him. He was extremely angry and denied everything. The police then went up to his little room over the garage, and pretty soon, two bedraggled girls carrying shabby bedrolls stumbled out and disappeared through the back gate of the compound. That was it. I paid R. B. his wages and sent him off. A policeman guarded my property for about a week, but there was no reprisal."

A few days before Christmas 1962, Dorcas Houston arrived with the Houston's two sons, Robin and David. He wonders now why his wife did not leave him abruptly, given what awaited her. Innocently enough, Houston had earlier planned a pre-Christmas get-together at

61 Sunder Nagar to welcome his family and to introduce them to the staff, a few people on the American "country team," and a handful of new Indian friends. In addition, Bill Moyers and Betty Harris had come their separate ways to India for a few days and would be departing the next day. It seemed like the perfect time for a simple, cozy celebration. Houston had not invited any Volunteers on the wise assumption that as a matter of protocol you couldn't ask one and not ask all, and if you asked one, all would show up, no matter how expensive, difficult, or ill-advised the trip to Delhi might be. There were seventy-five Volunteers then in India. They could not be accommodated as to food or lodging by any stretch of generosity or the imagination. As it was, he knew he had taken on a challenge just in trying to do right by the twenty people—including his own family— who were expected. He felt a bit like Scrooge in the matter of the undoubtedly homesick Volunteers. But what could one do? Houston took the precaution—to spare his newly arrived wife any chores while she was recovering from jet lag and just settling in—of having his new cook (successor to the naughty R. B.) bring in an assistant. In India, there was *always* someone to assist.

Alas, what Houston thought would be a fitting welcome to India for his wife and sons turned into a nightmare for his wife and a bahhumbug pre-Christmas for his sons. Word had spread among the Volunteers all over India that their Rep was hosting an "open house" in New Delhi. And indeed, they had cabled home for money, committed their last dime, borrowed the difference, rolled up their sleeping bags, and flocked to New Delhi by a variety of transport. A horrified, embarrassed Houston stopped counting guests when they reached ninety. Dorcas Houston, normally an immensely cool, calm, unflappable woman, ran frantically back and forth between the stove of the small kitchen, where two harassed Indian cooks were trying to keep up with the constantly arriving hungry mouths, to the front door in order to properly greet the people who now constituted her husband's personal and professional circle. "We ran out of food after about sixty people had eaten," Houston recalls. "It was chaotic. It was wild. And it was far too much culture shock for Dorky to go though just twenty-four hours after arriving in India." Almost inaudibly Houston adds, "I later heard that Bill Moyers got nothing to eat."

Thus began a year, 1963, of what Houston described in a letter to friends in the United States as "terrific excitement and near collapse. For Dorky, running a house that is more like a hotel is neither fun nor simple in India. Servants may sound great to you, but the problems they present can be worse than the help they provide." Citing the myriad colorful, seductive aspects of India, Houston went on to say, "Although none of us has been really ill, we have had many alarms— and in a country like this you can't dismiss a fever as the 'bug that's going around.' It could be dengue, malaria, encephalitis, cholera. Boiling *all* the water, soaking *all* the fruits and vegetables, or seeing that this is done exactly right, is exasperating.

"Dorky suddenly realized that in one month alone, she had served an additional fifty meals. We thus sharply reduced our Volunteer hospitality and went out on the road more. We slept on a lot of Volunteers' cement floors and traveled in some weather that you cannot possibly imagine.

"I don't know which was worse, the monsoon or premonsoon. During the dry season, the dust would build up and the air would get dryer and hotter and then there would be a tremendous wind. You could hear it coming, and then see it coming, and everything would blow like crazy. And the next day, without a drop of rain falling, the air would be crystal clear and almost cool. The temperature would drop from 110 degrees to around 80 degrees. The wild dust storms in contrast to the cool, clear air afterward were phenomenal. Once the monsoons begin, the atmosphere switches from a dry, baking heat like Death Valley, to a sodden, wet heat, with the rain coming down as if from open faucets. It stayed as humid as a Florida swamp in August."

Needless to say, the question of air-conditioning quickly arose in the Houston's household. Dorcas Houston discussed the subject with her husband—no pun intended—heatedly. It was agreed that, yes, the weather was oppressive for five months of the year; yes, they were all working like demons; yes, the combination was debilitating, and surely they could both do more and better, as could the office staff upstairs, and with better humor, if they could have air-conditioning at 61 Sunder Nagar. "But Sarge had issued a directive saying that Peace Corps staff could not have air-conditioning because it was bad for the image. I must say," says Houston, half laughing, "my instinct was to rebel against this directive, but I knew how terribly seriously Sarge meant it, so I refrained. Dorky, however, was far more angry than I was, and at some expense sent a telegram directly to Sarge. It said, in effect, that if the Peace Corps Rep in India couldn't have air condi- tioners in his home and office, the Rep would soon be dead, or at best, his wife would leave him. Within twenty-four hours I got a telegraphed reply from Sarge, dated February 12, 1963, which implied that we could have air conditioners: 'TOO FEW HEART SPECIAL-ISTS IN WORLD FOR US TO RISK YOU BUT WIRE UNCLEAR WHETHER PRESENCE OR ABSENCE AIR CONDITIONERS MOST CONDUCIVE TO MENTAL PHYSICAL HEALTH OF MY ESTEEMED DIRECTOR OF PC IN INDIA. SARGE.' "

Having obtained this magnificent concession, the Houston's hunk-ered under and asked not. Dorcas Houston successfully closed her eyes to 90 percent of the ineptitude and odd habits of her domestic staff. Houston recalls that his wife did a lot of the cleaning herself, to the amazement and dismay of her Indian staff. However, laundry for a husband and two young sons in both the soggy and dusty seasons was a rigorous task, since nothing could be worn twice and there were no washing machines. Thus, when it came to the seemingly endless baskets full of white shirts, sheets, and her husband's white duck trou-sers, Dorcas Houston was resigned to having it done the way it had been done in India through the ages. The laundress carried it away to be washed in the Ganges River. "For an American, that is really a sight," says Houston. "All of these people scrubbing the clothes in this muddy, filthy river into which everything is dumped, from garbage to dead bodies to ashes of dead bodies, and then beating the clothes on rocks or slanting boards. They didn't use soap much. Then they'd spread out the clothes on the grass—which had been cropped short by the grazing animals—in the sun, and then bring them back to be ironed. Not such a bad idea, since the grass is saturated with urine, and as the heat of the sun and the moisture of the clothes break through, the ammonia from the urine acts as a powerful bleach, so that white clothes do come out amazingly clean. Maybe it's a better way than our commercial system here, but I was certainly never able to convince Dorky of that."

The clash of cultures under the Houston's roof was constant, as it was bound to be. The Houstons spoke no Indian dialect, and did not need to. Everyone with whom they did business or saw socially spoke English. But the Houstons' domestic staff, unlike the polished professional retainers at the U.S. embassy, spoke either no English at all or just a smattering, a fact that led to some melodramatic misun-derstandings.

The second Christmas the Houstons spent in India, 1963, was going to make up for the previous one, which had come on the heels of their arrival and the chaotic, cacophonous 1962 "open house."

This, they all vowed. Tree, turkey, and presents with all of the trimmings on each. Finding that one could not buy a cut Christmas tree in India was a disappointment, but with some hunting, they located an eight-foot cedar tree planted in a giant tin can. It was extremely cumbersome and heavy, but Houston and his sons finally managed to get it into their living room. They covered the ugly tin can with white sheets—white as snow, thanks to the Ganges River method—and decorated it with old family ornaments sent from Aspen. The domestic staff eyed the giant tree, and the exuberant fuss that was made over it by the Houston family, with awe and bewilderment.

The Houston's gardener, the *mali*, was especially intrigued with the tree but also leery of it. Houston describes him as "a little wizened-up man with a white turban and a white sheet draped around himself, little spindly legs, long white moustache. He spoke no recognizable language and mainly occupied himself by puttering around the garden. His characteristic pose was to stand with his head cocked to one side, hand on hip, motionless, for fairly long periods of time, contemplating some plant. Then he'd squat down, work furiously for about two minutes, then stand up and look again. Dorky wanted to fire him at first because she just didn't think he worked, but after a while, like me, she got attached to him, found him beguiling. After Christmas, Dorky decided we ought to plant the tree in our front yard. It was a big, handsome tree; it reminded us of Aspen; why waste it? She called the *mali* in and indicated by elaborate gestures that she wanted him to plant it. He got very agitated and said quite clearly, 'No, no, no!'

"But *why* no? We got a translator in. Through the translator, it became clear that the *mali* wasn't going to lift a finger to plant that tree because he was utterly convinced it would die. We all argued with him for a week, grunting and using sign language. No go. So I got Robin, David, and the sweeper and together we hauled the huge tree in its mammoth tin can out on to the porch, down to the lawn, huffing and puffing. We set the tree down and the boys started to dig a hole. The *mali* appeared around the side of the house. He looked horrified and quickly retreated. Suddenly, he came steaming out, brushed everyone aside, and with a force and deftness we never knew he possessed, he dug the hole himself. He filled it with water, aggressively directed its planting, and henceforth it became his. He lavished it with care, watched it like a hawk, and it took!" (Houston, on a visit back to India in 1965, called on the *mali* at 61 Sunder Nagar. "The *mali* greeted me warmly, hung a garland of flowers around my neck, and took me into the front yard to show me our 1963 Christmas tree, which had grown a full two feet since we left India. He took me around to the back where he had planted several seedlings of the tree, which were four inches high.")

As time went on, Houston ceased writing his friends back home laments such as "The *masses* of people weigh you down" and "Five or ten thousand years of war, starvation, disease, oppression, heat, floods, famines, and droughts, plus all the evils that man can invent, have left these people drained and tired beyond death." More and more often, positive comments predominated in his letters and journals: "Life here has a fascination that makes it very hard to return to the U.S.A. The pageantry about you is addictive and hypnotic. Driving back to Delhi the other day, I fleetingly observed a lady in a brilliant indigo sari bending over a kelly-green rice paddy, spotlighted for a moment by a ray of late-afternoon sun breaking through heavy clouds." And he began to speak not of the average Indian's misery but of the "hospitality and kindliness of the villager." Of a field trip to Darjeeling (to look at schools that wanted Peace Corps teachers) in September 1964, three months before he left India, Houston wrote, "It rained— eleven inches in ten hours [New York gets twenty-three inches a *year*]—and huge landslides blocked two miles of road. [Therefore] I went up the back way, on a narrow road that spirals over itself like a staircase, through ten-foot ferns, tea plantations, and bamboo forests into silent evergreens. Wispy clouds filled the valleys [and then] up over the [Tista] gorges and further up to terraced slopes to the bright sunlight of Kalimpong. What pictures that name evokes for the mountaineer! Only a score of miles from the Tibetan border, it has been for centuries the main trading post on the great Indo-Lhasa caravan route." (Houston was constantly seeking news of the Everest expedition on the newly attempted West Ridge, of which Willi Unsoeld, the deputy Rep in Nepal, was a member. The news continued to be good, Houston wrote his friends in the United States. "How I envy them!")

The Indian attitude and pace that Houston at first found both bewildering and frustrating—as do most westerners who do more than just brush up against the culture—ultimately provided Houston with new insights: "The Hindu mystique is such that *things* don't matter. Life is here, life is today, life is a gift. Why fear tomorrow? Why desire more?" Since so many Indians feel that way, wrote Houston in October 1964, after nearly two years there, "the question naturally arises 'Why help India?' In the last analysis we help India because we must. The morality involved is really the deep reason. In our fat plenty, we cannot conscience the needs of starving people. We have to help India because of what we have and of what we believe in. There isn't any better reason."

But Houston also came to see that unilateral giving contained spiritual flaws. After discussing this quandary earlier with Alfred Jones, who in the course of observing the Peace Corps program in Peru had become devoted to the notion of a reverse Peace Corps, Houston found himself ever more preoccupied with the moral symmetry of Jones's notion. (Harris Wofford had been likewise seized by the wisdom of this concept. President Kwame Nkrumah had suggested such an arrangement in the spring of 1961 when he first met with Shriver. The idea had earlier occurred to Shriver independently, but he believed it to be premature.) The peace corps idea, *extended*, produced many different imaginings and imperatives. Wofford, as the first Rep in Ethiopia, had been able to convince some Ethiopian students who were being taught by Peace Corps Volunteers that they, too, should go out in the course of their educations and do menial work in provincial posts, to work for their fellow man. "That was no easy trick," says Dick Elwell, who had evaluated Wofford's program. "The educated elite in developing nations do not do certain kinds of labor at all. They are very conscious of their status and caste." For Houston, as for Jones, the priority was "to find ways to let India help us, a two-way pattern of giving that restores their pride, lets them accept gracefully what we give, since they are paying in the same coin. To me, this should be the aid pattern of the future—one I hope the War on Poverty will examine and use."

Alfred Jones, who had given more time and thought developing the idea of a reverse Peace Corps than anyone else, extended his theory and written exposition into actual practice the following year. His plan was anything but utopian; it was practical and thought out down to the last detail. In 1965, he returned to India with a specific blueprint for negotiating a pilot-project reverse Peace Corps with the Indian government, with Peace Corps/India and Peace Corps/Washington serving as catalysts and advisers. Jones consulted in Washington with Houston, who had returned from India in January 1965, and in New Delhi with Brent Ashabranner, who had replaced Houston as Rep in India. Houston, Ashabranner, and Indian government officials cooperated in selecting five well-educated, experienced social workers to go to the United States to work in settlement houses in New York and

Philadelphia. (Jones and his wife had extensive knowledge of how settlement houses functioned, having been active for twenty years in the shaping of policies and initiatives of the Henry Street Settlement on the lower east side of Manhattan.) Such a selection process and plan might ordinarily have taken months to implement and find official agreement in the notoriously complicated and sluggish bureaucracy of the Indian government. But since Jones had planned it in such fool-proof detail, and since he himself was willing to pay for the five Indians to travel to and from India and to provide their living allowances in the United States for a year through his own private philanthropy— the Foundation for Voluntary Service—there was no red tape and no stalling. The five Indian social workers were ecstatic to have been chosen as "guinea pigs" for such a novel experiment. They understood their mission and their responsibility very well. Even so, Jones did not let it drop there. He and his wife, Mary, shepherded them into their training program at the Columbia University Graduate School of Social Work, where they would train side by side with VISTA Volunteers.* The Joneses entertained them, kept in touch with them by letter and by telephone, and gave them cultural tips and moral support whenever it was required, keeping in mind the salubrious results Charlie Houston had gotten by "foster-fathering" (as Jones put it) the American Peace Corps Volunteers in India.

"We are the Peace Corps in reverse," announced Mrs. Satwant B. Singh proudly to Joan Larson, acting director of VISTA's Community Relations department. Larson had been alerted to the brief presence in Washington of the five Indian VISTA Volunteers by Glenn Ferguson, then the head of VISTA and formerly Peace Corps Rep in Thailand. "This is a unique situation," said Ferguson. "These people have been hand picked and privately sponsored. Technically, they are VISTA Volunteers, but they think of themselves chiefly as a reverse Peace Corps. Let's get a story for the VISTA magazine, and if possible, place one in the *Washington Post*, too." Larson was astonished to confront the elegant, articulate, self-possessed, sari-clad Singh, a forty-

*VISTA stands for Volunteers in Service to America. VISTA was one arm of the Office of Economic Opportunity (OEO), which many people persisted in calling the War on Poverty, just as they persisted in calling VISTA "the domestic Peace Corps." Other arms of OEO were Operation Head Start, the Job Corps, Community Action Program (CAP), and Legal Services. These programs found full force and funding under President Lyndon Johnson, whose "creatures" they were. Under President Richard Nixon, many of them were dissolved or drastically minimized.

six-year-old widow with a master's degree in social work from the University of Delhi. "Hardly your prototypical hot-eyed, twenty-one-year-old bearded male VISTA Volunteer from Seattle," says Larson. "This woman was a 'bluestocking' from another culture. She told me that she had packed twenty-five saris to bring to the United States, and that she planned to wear them on the job at Henry Street Settlement in her work with day-care centers and rehabilitation for the aged." Singh, who was the senior member of the five-person reverse Peace Corps from India (the other four being men in their thirties who also had advanced degrees in social work and who were working in Philadelphia settlement houses), ruminated frankly about poverty at home and in the United States. "Compared to India," maintained Singh, "poverty here is a luxury," adding that "your poverty problems are vastly different from ours. But we can learn much from you. We have a greater problem with overpopulation and education. Our young people want only white-collar jobs. We must train them for many kinds of jobs needed in India today. We don't have the problems with older people you have, however. Our family system takes care of them."

The five Indians cooked Larson a multicourse Indian dinner in her apartment and repaired to their respective assignments. "I adored them," says Larson. "And I adored the reverse Peace Corps idea. Everyone did. But I just knew the thing couldn't be sustained. It was privately funded, and while brilliantly conceived and successfully implemented, it was still an experiment. That it worked didn't really crack any ice in the end. It proved Alfred Jones's point, but clearly he couldn't go on and on funding it. It was too expensive and sophisticated an idea for most developing nations to grab onto. And here in the United States, you need a constituency, someone who is going to fight for it, make it their cause. You need congressional support. Now, that might have happened in the second year of the Peace Corps, in 1962, because the Peace Corps was still a novelty and had no competition. But by October 1965, when the five Indians arrived here, there were just causes galore! And everyone was taking their pick and aligning themselves."

Larson refers, of course, not only to the Peace Corps and OEO, but also to the yeasty civil rights movement while Dr. Martin Luther King, Jr., was still alive, and to the growing and increasingly well organized antiwar movement. "And if none of that appealed to you—Peace Corps, OEO, civil rights, or antiwar—you could always just 'drop out.' Flower-child communes were flourishing from coast to coast. There were already too many options," concludes Larson. "People could not really absorb another heavy philosophical concept."

Before, during, and after the advent of the pilot-project reverse Peace Corps, Alfred Jones kept in touch with Shriver, Wiggins, Houston, and Ashabranner in an exchange of correspondence that made for a rich dialogue about Gandhian principles: "It is impossible to exaggerate the receptivity of Indians to the Peace Corps," wrote Jones to Shriver and Wiggins, with copies to Houston and Ashabranner.

> For India, and no doubt for the rest of the world, Volunteers have three outstanding attributes: (1) A lack of status consciousness, in fact a preference for helping the poor and lowly; (2) eagerness to go into the countryside, towns, and villages, to work with their hands, to demonstrate the dignity of labor; and (3) nothing but loyalty to the general interest of the host country—no selfish motives at all, not even the enlightened self-interest that one may hope brought them to the Peace Corps in the first place. These three are Gandhian qualities.

> Gandhian influence of another sort came to the U.S. to help form the strategy of passive resistance in the movement for Negro civil rights. It would be one of the gentlest ironies of history if, back from our "self-seeking, capitalist, materialist" culture, there should be returned to India the Gandhian tradition, in the persons—numerous enough to have a real impact in this enormous country—of our Volunteers, practicing the virtues that Mahatma Gandhi tried so eagerly to inculcate in his people.

Referring to a group of young people in Bombay who on their own were trying to start up a reverse Peace Corps after having got the idea from Houston, Jones—who visited the group—observed: "With the help of a powerful and large enough American Peace Corps [such a movement] could spread like wildfire. It would become the most sensational of all the present and future Peace Corps achievements in India, providing the ultimate in multiplier-effect on a mass scale. And from it would come the leaders of the recruits for a Peace Corps in reverse."

Jones simply saw no limits to the uses of the American Peace Corps. He advocated to Shriver and Wiggins that Peace Corps/India grow and grow while retaining Houston and Ashabranner at the top of the hierarchy, writing: "If there ever were Peace Corps/India staff deficiencies, they do not now exist except for the deplorable lack of funds for secretarial help. The staff is mature, responsible, and conscientious in dealing with the Volunteers whose morale as a consequence must be as high as that of any Peace Corps contingent anywhere." Houston concluded by suggesting that the Peace Corps "give more attention to its Indian public relations, utilizing the extraordinary receptivity of India to the Peace Corps. Indian newspapers in English are of excellent quality but are too poor to buy much from the wire services; they would welcome material from the Peace Corps." In both cases, Jones got half of his wish. The Peace Corps in India grew from approximately two hundred Volunteers in August 1964 to 715 just over a year later. "This figure would pale in September 1966," wrote Kevin Lowther and C. Payne Lucas in their 1978 book, *Keeping Kennedy's Promise*, "when the peak of sixteen hundred Volunteers was reached." Houston would return to Peace Corps headquarters in January 1965 at Shriver's insistence to attempt to form an all-Volunteer doctors' program (an idea that was as bureaucratically doomed as it was philosophically pure). Ashabranner would replace Houston as Rep. And the Peace Corps would attempt a one-man journalism experiment in India through the person of Volunteer Alan Bradford (see Chapter 9).

By the end of 1964, Dorcas Houston let it be known that she would be less than heartbroken if the family returned to the United States. As Houston wrote in his last letter from India, dated November 20, 1964, "Dorky has had all the work and little of the variety I have had." The three Houston children had traveled all over India, from Kashmir to Calcutta, from the caves of Ellora and Ajanta to the island of Goa in the Arabian Sea. They had been enthralled but were sated. Shriver was constantly pestering Houston to come home and start working on his utopian dream of an all-Volunteer doctors' program. Houston alone within the family unit would ache for India; that he knew. But he happily reviewed his two years in India: "Seventy-five Volunteers have completed their service and gone home; 240 more have arrived; the program will expand to more than 600 in early 1965. One Volunteer was bitten by a deadly scorpion; the scorpion died. Two more were licked by a rabid dog; the dog died. The Chinese threatened to overrun India, then backed out. Experimental television came to Delhi. Russia changed leaders [from Khrushchev to Kosygin and Brezhnev] as did many nations of Asia and Africa. Last year America lost violently one of our greatest presidents and this year India lost her magnificent leader, Jawaharlal Nehru . . . By not wearing the hair shirt too obviously we have gotten along well with the embassy, AID, and USIS staffs at all levels. By watching us work like the devil and do without the special privileges, the Indians have come to like and admire us more, I believe, than they do the privileged groups. There is no sense in pretending that all our Volunteers are Tom Dooley, Albert Schweitzer, Thomas Edison, or Bernard Baruch. Mostly they are just American kids with a fuzzy feeling that they can better the world, and themselves, by spending two years in the Peace Corps. After two years here, I'm certain of it."

Dorcas and Charles Houston and their two sons, Robin and David (Penny Houston had since entered Radcliffe, where she was majoring in Eastern studies), were preparing to board a flight from New Delhi to Athens on December 1, 1964, when into the airport rushed the *mali* from 61 Sunder Nagar, toddling along at high speed on his spindly legs, heading straight for the Houstons. Draping each one with a garland of flowers from the garden of the Houston's first home in India, which he had tended, he made the universal signs of farewell. The Houstons simultaneously swallowed hard and unsuccessfully tried to fight back the tears.

"Damn it," snuffled Charles Houston, M.D., as he buckled his seat belt in preparation for takeoff a few minutes later, "I wept my way over here. I'm just *not* going to weep my way back. What am I? A man or a mouse?"

"Think of something funny, Charles," suggested his wife. "Because you know, many, many funny things happened to us in India. When you stop to *think* about it . . ."

"Ahhh," Houston interjected, brightening. "Did I ever tell you about the chicken farmer from Brooklyn?"

"No, Charles, you didn't. You never told me about any chicken farmer from Brooklyn. But please do."

"Well, well. His name was Ronnie Amend and he had never seen a chicken outside of a supermarket before. One of those. Then some other Volunteers got him interested in the AID 'poultry bible,' showed him he could do it. Against all odds, really, he got hooked on it and became a very hard working, enthusiastic poultry worker. Ronnie, by the way, lived all alone in one of the bleakest, coldest, hottest, flattest, sandiest parts of the Punjab about forty miles north of Delhi. It was desolate, I'll tell you. But he never lost his sense of humor. The second time I visited him, he told me this story: 'Charlie, I woke up the other morning and my head was hot. The fact is, I was *sick*. I had a raging fever but I didn't know it. I looked up and there was this old lady sitting by my bedside. She looked like an old witch. I looked out the door behind her and what did I see? Nothing but sand, sand, sand— and camels, yet, walking across the sand. Gee, I thought, what a weird place to live. Thank God it's only a dream.' "

President Kennedy's funeral procession.   AP/WIDE WORLD PHOTO

Frank Erwin

Four who ran the "talent search"
for Shriver: Nan McEvoy,
Bill Wister, Jay Rockefeller,
and William Warner

Thomas Quimby

Donovan McClure PHOTO BY JOE ROSENTHAL, *San Francisco Chronicle*

Frank Mankiewicz in 1963

A barriada outside of Lima; it was here that Mankiewicz believed the Volunteers could bring about a peaceful revolution

Mankiewicz's Deputy Rep in Peru William Mangin (left) and Associate Rep Emory Biro, who ran the Arequipa office. The volcano El Misti is in the background

Houston visits a Peace Corps Poultry Project in the town of Palempur in the Punjab. He is accompanied by an Indian government official, Gosal Singh (in tie)

U.S. Ambassador and Mrs. John Kenneth Galbraith admire a "vegetarian" or "Peace Corps" egg in Nabha, where the idea was first hatched

The Bisauli Cooperative Workshop

Paul Tsongas in Ethiopia

*Christopher Dodd in the
Dominican Republic*

Maureen Orth and Brenda Brown with Lyndon Johnson

David Gelman PHOTO BY MAGDA JONES

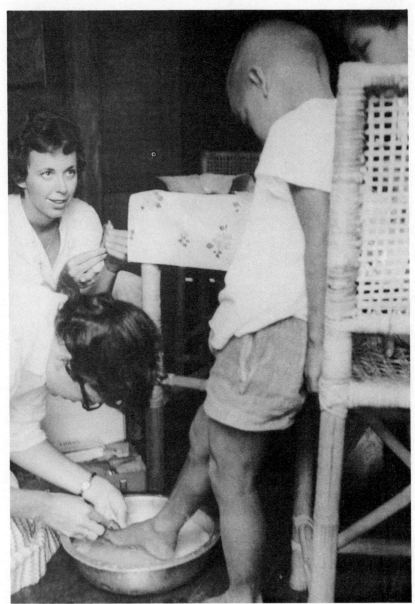

Maureen Carroll in the Philippines   PHOTO BY H.A. FIGUERAS, *Black Star*

Tom Scanlon sails for Chile

Loren Jenkins in Sierra Leone

Allen Bradford with Indian journalism students interviewing villagers

Carol Bellamy in 1985

Julia Chang Bloch being sworn in at the State Department as assistant administrator for Food for Peace and Voluntary Assistance in the Agency for International Development in September 1981. Her father holds the Bible as her husband, Stuart Marshall Bloch, looks on AID PHOTO

David Richards in 1983 PHOTO BY ROBERT BOWDEN

Shriver visiting Pokhara, Nepal, where Peace Corps architects had designed a number of buildings. The Annapurna range of the Himalayas is in the distance

CHAPTER 9

HELLO, THIRD WORLD

"**Y**ou'd certainly be taking a chance on a thing like *that*," said a dean at the University of Colorado when senior classman Bill Robinson came looking for Peace Corps literature and an application form in May 1963. The dean had no Peace Corps material to give Robinson. Robinson was stunned. Just the week before, Peace Corps Director Shriver had come to the university to participate in World Affairs Week and had personally recruited Robinson who was his escort. "Your father's business, graduate school and the military can wait. The Peace Corps is the thing to do *now*," Shriver had told Robinson and several hundred others who had political and internationalist leanings. Robinson had just read in the *New York Times* that the Peace Corps would have nearly seven thousand Volunteers in training and working overseas in forty-eight countries, and yet here was a dean of the university warning him against Peace Corps service, the clear implication being that it was unproved, unsafe and unsound.

The dean wasn't the only one voicing doubts. Many parents of the first Volunteers were wary as well. Mothers worried that daughters would throw away their prospects for marriage by appearing ultra-liberal and bohemian. Fathers fretted that no bank would want to hire a young man who had entered into such a crazy caper directly upon graduation from college. But those who were determined to join the Peace Corps did, over all objections. Robinson got his Peace Corps assignment for Nepal the week after President Kennedy was assassinated. He thus felt the hand of fate upon him.

Bob Gale had invented blitz recruiting in April 1963 and had tried it out at the University of Wisconsin and the University of Michigan. It worked like magic. Within just a few months, no major American campus would have failed to feel the Peace Corps presence. By the end of the year few if any deans existed who were without information or enthusiasm for the Peace Corps.

Over 120,000 Volunteers have served in seventy-two countries since 1961 when the Peace Corps was formed. Far from being a hindrance to future "establishment" employment, Peace Corps service has increasingly proved a boon to the resumé. Banks, particularly the mighty ones such as Chase Manhattan Bank which have large and

important international divisions, rate Peace Corps service as a spar-
kling asset. Not surprisingly, overseas development work has claimed
the greatest number of former Volunteers. There are 682 of them
presently employed by the Agency for International Development (AID)
both in Washington and overseas. In fact, Peter McPherson, a former
Volunteer in Peru during the mid-1960s is now the administrator of
AID. Thomas J. Scanlon, a Volunteer in Chile I, is now president of
his own overseas development firm, Benchmarks, Inc. Before any
Peace Corps Volunteers had completed service and returned to the
United States, Scanlon was the embodiment of the new species. A
letter from him to the Peace Corps headquarters beginning "Hello,
Everybody" and describing his life in Chile as a community development worker, was used as the opening portion of the agency's
Congressional Presentation, FY 1963. Those congressmen still cool
to the Peace Corps idea tended to melt. When Father Theodore Hesbergh, president of Notre Dame (where Chile I had been trained),
stopped by to check on Scanlon in Rio Negro, Chile, in April 1962,
Scanlon mentioned that he had just been up in the village of Catrihuala
talking to the *campesinos* who sold lumber for a living, and he was
distressed because the Communists were exploiting them, buying their
wares at the lowest possible price and then marking them up for resale
by 300 percent. Scanlon was trying to persuade them to go for a better
deal through a cooperative. The Indian leader in Catrihuala said to
Scanlon, "Why don't you come up here in the winter when we are
snowed in and have time to talk?" The leader explained that the
Communists were always willing to come up during the snows. "You
will have to park your jeep and then walk twenty miles." And so,
Scanlon told Hesbergh, "I'm just waiting for the snow."

Hesbergh, ideologically all aglow, repeated this story to Eunice
Shriver. She used it in a speech in California soon thereafter to salubrious effect. Shriver picked up on it and pressed it into frequent
anecdotal service. Finally, President Kennedy himself latched on to
it, most notably in a speech to four thousand college students working
as summer government interns on June 20, 1962, which was in turn
reported in the New York Times the following day with Scanlon prom-
inently mentioned. On June 21, 1962, Scanlon became for at least a
day *all* Peace Corps Volunteers, combatting Communism south of
the border, the epitome of one of the few good guys in *The Ugly
American.*

Bill Haddad used to kid Kennedy aide Kenny O'Donnell that the presidential candidate in 1964 would be Shriver, not Kennedy, because by then there would be a former Peace Corps Volunteer in almost every precinct in America who would organize for Shriver. Former Peace Corps Volunteers as a united political force never materialized although it appeared that a majority of them supported the McGovern-Shriver presidential ticket in 1972 and station-wagon-loads of them showed up for Shriver's announcement as a presidential primary candidate in 1976 at the Mayflower Hotel. They packed up their young children and drove to Washington from all over the country. Love and admiration for their former leader abounded but no viable political muscles were flexed. Still, two former Volunteers did become United States Senators: Paul Tsongas (D-Massachusetts) from the first Peace Corps contingent in Ethiopia (who has since retired due to ill health); and Christopher Dodd (D-Connecticut) who served in 1965 in the Dominican Republic. Several others have been elected to the House of Representatives down through the years. Parker Borg, who served in the Philippines, became ambassador to Mali. Robert Haas, a former Volunteer in Panama, became president and chief executive officer of Levi Strauss & Co, the world's largest apparel manufacturer. Leonel Castillo of Philippines I was appointed Director of the U.S. Immigration and Naturalization Service by President Jimmy Carter. And of course, President Carter's mother, Lillian, served as a Volunteer in India when she was in her late sixties. Loren Jenkins, a member of the most precocious early group, Sierra Leone I, won a Pulitzer Prize in 1982 for his coverage of the refugee camp massacre in Beirut, Lebanon, for the *Washington Post*. Michael McCaskey, who served in Venezuela, is president of the Chicago Bears. Noted travel writer and essayist, Paul Theroux, a Volunteer in Malawi, 1963–65, wrote of his exceptionally fractious activities there, including being an inadvertent minor operative in a plot to kill Prime Minister Hastings Banda, in *Sunrise with Seamonsters*.

Maureen Carroll, a veteran of Philippines I and a former deputy chief of Evaluation, is corporate vice president of the University Research Corporation in Washington, D.C. A fellow Volunteer of Carroll's in the Philippines, Brenda Brown, is a top level Foreign Service Officer in Tunisia. Tom Dine, another Volunteer in the Philippines, is Executive Director of the American Israel Public Affairs Committtee. Maureen Orth of Colombia I is an editor of *Vogue* magazine. Penelope Roach of Ghana I is a Professor of Sociology and Anthropology at Marrymount College in Tarrytown, N.Y. Donna Shalala, a former

Volunteer in Iran, is president of Hunter College. The careers of Carol Bellamy (Guatemala) and Julia Chang Bloch (Sabah, Malaysia) have been nothing short of spectacular and would be considered so within any group of successful men. (The Peace Corps experiences of Bellamy and Bloch are related in this chapter.)

The dean at the University of Colorado who in 1963 told Bill Robinson that he'd be taking a chance if he joined the Peace Corps was philosophically wrong but semantically right. The element of chance was what made it attractive in the first place; the reality of great personal growth made it worthwhile in the last. But the independence that the Peace Corps seemed to offer was what beckoned most seductively. "Everyone who joined the Peace Corps at the beginning was a bit eccentric," says Loren Jenkins of Sierra Leone I. "I mean, why else would you join it? You weren't going to fit into usual bureaucratic, authoritarian situations. You did it because you had a different concept, a different way of reacting to things, but you still did your job." Even after Peace Corps service, Volunteers fiercely maintained their autonomy and special identity. When in 1964 the General Counsel's office of the Peace Corps formally and legally objected to nomenclature and the rhetoric of a group called Former Peace Corps Volunteers Against the War, which was led by Jenkins, Jenkins and Company replied, "You can't say we can't use the words 'Peace Corps.' You are not the Peace Corps. We are the Peace Corps.' "

Paul Theroux wrote in an *op ed* piece in the *New York Times* on February 25, 1986, "When I think about those years, I don't think much about the Peace Corps, though Malawi is always on my mind. That is surely a tribute to the Peace Corps. I do not believe that Africa is a very different place for having played host to the Peace Corps— in fact, Africa is in a much worse state than it was twenty years ago. But America is quite a different place for having had so many returned Peace Corps Volunteers, and when they began joining the State Department and working in the embassies, these institutions were the better for it and had a better-informed and less truculent tone."

Theroux says that he would do it again. "The Peace Corps always allowed me to be myself . . . I learned that you make your own life."

Or as Jay Gatsby put it, "In any case, it was just personal."

ALAN BRADFORD

Alan Bradford, a soft-spoken, courtly, idealistic young man from Auburn, Alabama, felt the full force of the Kennedy years. He had been tracking Kennedy's political moves since the 1956 Democratic National Convention when Kennedy had come so close to getting the vice presidential nomination. By 1959, when Bradford graduated from the University of Missouri School of Journalism, it looked as though Kennedy might well be the presidential nominee in 1960. Bradford had just finished his course work for his masters degree in foreign affairs at George Washington University in Washington, D.C., in May 1960 when he heard that it was possible to get in on the Kennedy campaign that summer as long as he didn't mind working as a lowly "gofer." Bradford, now assistant national editor for the *Washington Times*, laughs. "I worked in Records and Lists, but even that was exciting because everything about that campaign was exciting. And *then*, I got asked to go on the whistle-stop train tour through the south with Lyndon Johnson. That was in late September, just after Kennedy's first debate with Nixon on the twenty-sixth, and the momentum was really building. Several of us on that train were in charge of creating the hoopla at every stop. We'd jump off before the train came to a halt and start handing out Kennedy buttons and balloons. We came down from Washington, and the first actual whistle-stop along the way was in North Carolina. We proceeded through South Carolina, Georgia, Alabama, Mississippi, and ended up in New Orleans.

"Lyndon Johnson made fun of Nixon at every stop along the way. He'd tell the crowds that Nixon was the first candidate in history who had a makeup problem. Lyndon was very good at ridicule, which is the weapon he used against Nixon."

The Democratic National Committee chartered a plane for Kennedy's closing rally in Boston. The volunteer campaigners, such as Bradford, were flown up for the event, just as were the paid campaign officials. "That was when I just *knew* Kennedy was going to win," said Bradford.

If you could have seen that magic, that charisma, that interaction with the crowds. And the polls, too, as election day got closer and closer, were getting better and better for Kennedy. It was a wild, happy time, and I met John Kenneth Galbraith at the closing campaign rally. I knew very well who he was, this famous six-foot-six Harvard economist. I'd studied economics at college. I'd read his articles and his book *The Liberal Hour*. I'd seen him on television. When you're young and from another part of the country, you never think you'll meet anyone like that. Obviously, I couldn't guess that he would become Kennedy's ambassador to India or that I would become a Peace Corps Volunteer in India in just over a year. Who could imagine anything like that? But I did meet him again at an embassy reception for our group, India II, when we arrived in Delhi in October 1962. It was right in the middle of the Cuban missile crisis. It was a terrifying time, a melodramatic time. So I was emboldened to say to Galbraith, "Oh, we've *met*, Mr. Ambassador." But of course he didn't remember me. I mean, they *don't*.

To regain solvency after the campaign and to keep busy while awaiting news from the Peace Corps, he took a job in Washington at United Press International (UPI) "working the phones on the foreign desk." He realized that joining the Peace Corps before it had actually taken shape could mean career suicide, but today he ascribes his willingness to take a plunge into the unknown as a symptom of the heady idealism that was in the air at that time. "It was far more a great feeling than a scary one," says Bradford. "One did not too much weigh the risks."

And then one day, the call came. "I was told by a woman at the Peace Corps that I had been selected to be a teacher of journalism at Osmania University in the city of Hyderabad, India, in the state of Andhra Pradesh, and that I should report to the University of Illinois at Urbana for training in early August 1962." The only person who tried to discourage him from doing this completely unprecedented thing was his boss at UPI, who said, "Look, if it's travel you want, you can travel for UPI. Just give it time." But Bradford quit on the spot, explaining as he ran out the door that travel was not all he wanted, thanks, and good-bye. He spent two of his last ten dollars taking a cab to the Library of Congress on Capitol Hill to seek knowledge of this place called Hyderabad in India. Halfway across the world? Something like that.

Some of our group worked in agricultural extension; others taught math, science, and English. I was the lone journalist. The fifteen of us going to Hyderabad were put on a train after a few days of orientation in New Delhi, where we were given a crash course in not drinking the water and so forth. It was a long, long trip—three days and two nights. By day we sat on wooden benches. By night we slept in our sleeping bags in wooden bunks in what was called a "third-class sleeper." We each carried a suitcase, a sleeping bag, and our own boiled water. It was a great way to be introduced to India—through the windows of a slowly moving train. The light is different in India. The colors are different. The smells are different. We'd get off at every stop for twenty minutes to stretch our legs. There were always people at the stations selling tea in clay pots, which you'd just throw away afterward. The thing that struck me right away was the *people*—you could never get away from people.

Having issued forth the westerner's standard stunned lament about India within hours of his arrival, the usually patient, optimistic Bradford was in for another surprise. Not only would he never be able to get away from the masses of people in India in general, but he would never be able to get away from his students or his confreres. He and four other male Peace Corps colleagues were housed in a two-story dormitory built around a courtyard in the midst of 150 Indian students, usually two to a room. This had been the idea of D. S. Reddi, the vice chancellor of Osmania University, who thought that the Volunteers, being foreigners, would benefit from getting to know both the undergraduates and graduate students who ranged in age from seventeen to twenty-two. The vice chancellor's reasoning was that the schoolroom atmosphere was so formal and the British syllabus-bound lecture format was so strict that what was to be a cross-cultural experience might not amount to anything very significant if there was no contact beyond the classroom. However, Bradford found this arrangement odd. On the one hand, an Indian official was saying, "Get to know each other—that's what the Peace Corps is all about," but on the other hand the British system, which was the predominant one in India, deliberately discouraged any sense of equality between teacher and student.

There was a great chasm between student and teacher in India, yet there we all were, living practically cheek by jowl in the same building. It was a tricky situation, a contradictory one, and it made everyone nervous at first. But we solved the problem of awkwardness by encouraging the students to visit us in our offices at the university, American style. We'd rap. We'd talk about all kinds of things: what the United States was like, about Kennedy, the bomb, English literature, Faulkner, Hemingway, just anything. This, they loved. In retrospect, I guess having us in the same dorm was a good idea. At least they knew how we lived, knew that we were human and not ultra-elitist or Godlike. Certainly, we were satisfying the Peace Corps image: cold showers, no screens on the windows, a lot of mosquitoes, and a lot of mosquito netting. We had simple desks and metal beds just like everyone else.

People would ask me later, what was the high point of my Peace Corps experience in India. I knew they wouldn't understand, so I'd usually say, "Oh, meeting Prime Minister Nehru," and they'd just *flip*, of course. Actually, I *did* meet Nehru, and alas, it was far from being the high point. Funny how life is. All of us, my group, the fifteen of us in Hyderabad, met him when he came to visit the president of India, S. Radhakrishnan, who had a home in Hyderabad. Nehru was on vacation there. I recall that Charlie Houston arranged that meeting at the president's house for us through [ambassador] Bowles. But Nehru was not the fiery, inspirational leader of independence anymore. He had a kidney problem and was on drugs to relieve the pain. He was sedated, slowed way down. He was wearing his signature outfit, the white "Nehru coat" and the small red rose. He just answered our feverish questions very blandly. All he could do. Oh God, it was a great honor, of course. But not the high point. And at that time, in early 1964, no one was predicting that his daughter, Indira Gandhi, would *ever* come to power.

For Bradford, one of the high points of Peace Corps life in India was his contact with Charlie Houston. "Having a man who was a distinguished scientist and a well-known mountain climber as your Rep, there was glamour in that. It was great to have an authentic hero as your leader. In a country like India, which is centuries and centuries old, and so burdened by all of those centuries, it's good when you have someone dynamic pushing you. Otherwise, those centuries can really nibble away at you." Just as they were nibbling away at him most insidiously, says Bradford,

Charlie would roar into town in a jeep, full of energy and ideas and stern advice, with his Indian driver, Francis, at the wheel. What a welcome sight it always was!

No one resented Charlie's arriving in a jeep with Francis driving. To have an Indian driver was very wise in his position. Because if you had an accident, you could be in serious trouble as a westerner. Anybody in a car, a crowd is going to be against: the guy on foot—the victim—versus the rich person who is in the car. It's much worse if you are a westerner who hits someone, however innocently. An Indian driver can get out of the situation. But the westerner—the crowd could set upon him. It could. It had been known to happen. The embassy issues instructions to new people in India. If you are in an accident, they tell you: "Leave the scene." Something you would never do in the United States. But in India, you are told—leave the scene of the accident at once and go to the nearest police station to get help. If there's no police station, so be it. So that's why Charlie and other staff members in Delhi had Francis.

Bradford was astonished to learn later that Houston had been criticized in Washington for being "too paternalistic" a Rep, too coddling and pampering of the Volunteers. "Charlie *was* paternalistic," says Bradford, "but never coddling. Charlie listened. He wanted his Volunteers to succeed. He hated it if you didn't. If you wrote a letter to Peace Corps/New Delhi saying you had problems, Charlie might very well get on the next plane and fly down. He was that sort of person. You always got a response out of Charlie and you knew that he would back you in a project if he thought you had any chance of success. But he never pampered anybody," says Bradford, laughing. "Indeed not. Charlie was a Dutch uncle."

The low point of Bradford's time in India as a Peace Corps Volunteer was on November 22, 1963. He was grading papers in his dormitory room when his students started lining up at his door. He was taken aback. There was an unspoken rule that they call upon him only in his office. But Bradford could see immediately that they were shaken to the core. "Asians kept their emotions in check, but these boys were very, very upset. They started offering me their condolences. Condolences for what, I wondered? They asked: Didn't I know that President Kennedy had been killed? I said, 'Oh, *no*. You must be mistaken.' They said, no, they had heard it on the Voice of America. They assumed I knew. I immediately tuned in the Voice, and there it was, and I couldn't believe it. You know? And the students just kept coming to pay their respects to the Kennedy family, and to America,

through me. I went into shock and stayed in shock for some time."
Bradford spent

three extra lonely months after everyone else in India II had gone home, finishing up a study with my journalism students. The point was, get the students into the villages of India, find out how much news trickled down to a native village. What the village people knew. What they cared about. How they heard it. I pointed out to my students that the head man in the village got a newspaper, as did the milkman, from the city, both in the local dialect. And there was a radio in the village that was centrally located so that any villager could come and listen to it. The basic idea was that New Delhi would educate the villagers, tell them what was going on in their government, in the world. But the untouchables, the Harijans, were not encouraged to listen to the radio, nor were they interested in world news. People at the bottom of the social ladder just aren't—anywhere. But they are interested in local gossip. That's what's news to them. So I took my students into village India, and we camped out. I told them, get out there and find out what's going on in this village, idle gossip and all. Figure out the whole system of communication here. And so my students went forth. But the villagers were baffled. Who were these people and why did they want to know these things? No one else had ever done this before and my report caused repercussions all the way to New Delhi. It was picked up by all of the major Indian newspapers and one item in it—that a number of Indians didn't know who Nehru was—was picked up by *Time* magazine. For *Time* to have emphasized that fact wasn't fair, because there are people in the United States who don't know who their own president is at any given time. But my students understood that such an item makes better news if it comes out of a Third World country, and they also learned how easy it is to point a finger in journalism.

Some of Bradford's students joined UPI after they graduated. One joined the premiere news agency, Press Trust of India (PTI). Others went to work on newspapers, English-speaking and otherwise. Bradford himself expected to return to the United States and resume his own journalism career once the village news experiment was completed. But as he prepared to leave New Delhi in the fall of 1964, having already said good-bye to his friends at Osmania University in Hyderabad, he ran into the press attaché from the American embassy, who was famous for his open-house Sunday brunches, and he invited Bradford to his next one. There, Bradford met Dean Brelis of NBC (who is now a reporter for *Time*). The press attaché mentioned that Bradford had been in India for two years teaching journalism at the university level and had "really been around." Brelis promptly hired Bradford as a stringer to help cover Pope Paul's upcoming visit to Bombay. Bradford was thrilled, but still planned on going home immediately after that assignment. "But then came the India-Pakistan war and I was also hired as a stringer for *Time-Life* to cover that, which of course was irresistible, a great opportunity. Except that something happened at that point that is very painful for me to remember.

I had gone over to Lahore, Pakistan, which is on the Indian border, with the idea of briefly viewing events from that angle. I was told in Lahore that I would have to get my passport renewed. I sent it through the American consulate officer to Karachi, which was then the capital of Pakistan. It was a chaotic time, and by the time my passport got back to me, the war had begun. And I was on the *wrong side* in terms of all my contacts for reporting the war. I was ordered not to leave. I was trapped in Lahore, on the border, and oh, God, *unable to get the story out!* It was a nightmare. Well, it was a short war, nineteen days as I recall, but I ran out of money meanwhile, trying both to survive in and get out of Lahore. I had to borrow money from somebody in the consulate, which was humiliating. Finally, when I got my passport I just raced back to Delhi, cabled home for money, and *left*. I have always hoped that that was one story my Indian journalism students never got!

CAROL BELLAMY

On Tuesday, February 12, 1985, Carol Bellamy, Democrat and then president of the city council of New York, announced her candidacy for the office of mayor. No one was surprised, and certainly no one was disappointed. That she would be making her ongoing feud with Democratic Mayor Edward I. Koch an even more open one than it already was, caused New Yorkers to rub their hands together in glee. Bellamy, a woman who seems to be scared of nothing, marched into battle armed with taunts and jibes enough for any political season, assuring New Yorkers of the kind of campaign they love: sassy, insulting, colorful. A fairly mild example of what it's like when Bellamy and Koch square off was recorded in the *Washington Post* on Sunday, May 27, 1984:

> City Council President Carol Bellamy called a news conference a few weeks ago on the edge of a Brooklyn pothole 4 feet wide. The condition of the streets, she said, showed that Mayor Edward I. Koch was "not interested in improving services."
>
> Koch replied . . . that Bellamy should "hold her tears" since "a major citywide street-repair initiative" would be announced soon.
>
> Bellamy countered that she was "glad the mayor has finally awakened to the need to improve city services. Perhaps this means he'll devote the same energy to fixing up the city as he has to peddling his book, *Mayor*."
>
> The street fight over potholes between the city's two most prominent politicians was evidence of what promises to be a long and bitter battle between Koch, who will run for a third term in 1985, and critics (such as Bellamy) positioning themselves as possible opponents.

Both print and television journalists referred to "the smell of blood in the air" as Bellamy needled Koch for his buffoonery, adding "phony" and "fraud" to her charges, and Koch needled Bellamy about her "shrillness," labeling her a "disaster" on at least one occasion. But the advantage was always Koch's. He is a man, he is the mayor, he had the money. He also had the book and he had the Broadway play based on the book. He began the race in early 1985 with campaign coffers already in excess of $2 million in comparison to Bellamy's $125,000. Still, Carol Bellamy played to win. Carol Bellamy ran hard. The question is, given the odds, what made Carol run?

Bellamy grew up middle class in Scotch Plains, New Jersey. There was never any "extra money." Her father, Lucius Bellamy, was an installer for the New York Telephone Company and her mother, Frances, was a registered nurse. She was never hounded by a sense of family destiny, as might be the case with a Rockefeller or Kennedy. And when she entered her senior year at Gettysburg College—an institution of solid if not elegant repute—she had no further thought than to take a masters degree in social work somewhere, and then see what happened. "The thought of a political career never occurred to me. Elective office? It never entered my mind. I was not even thinking about government service then. Maybe I would become a social worker. *Maybe.*"

Until the Peace Corps, that is. "I don't know exactly what motivated me to apply. I think such decisions are made for lots of reasons, ranging from wanting to save the world to wanting to have some excitement. There's the altruistic and the personal. I must say, graduating from college in June 1963 at the height of the Kennedy years made a big difference. He was still alive. He had given us the sense that each individual could do something about the world's problems. It was a very exciting time."

It was during Bellamy's fall 1963 training period at New Mexico State University in Las Cruces that Kennedy was killed. Bellamy's group, Guatemala III, was devastated, "but nobody dropped out on account of grief. We were determined to go on." They were even able to make jokes about their preparation for this mission. "Not too many people there seemed to know anything about Guatemala. But they knew about Mexico. The idea was, well, they do it this way in Mexico, so we assume they do it this way in Guatemala." The fifty Peace Corps Volunteers of Guatemala III were deposited in the country in January 1964. "Forty-eight were sent south where the mountains and most of the people are. Two of us were sent north, which is mostly rain forest and is sparsely populated. Most of us were in that amorphous category called community development—liberal arts graduates who were not very qualified to do anything but people who really wanted to do *something.* There were no roads to where the two of us lived on the shore of that little lake, Lake Flores. You had to fly in there and land in a clearing or walk several miles up a cracked creekbed." (The only person from Peace Corps headquarters to visit Bellamy's site was Frank Mankiewicz in late 1964, a few months after he had become regional director for Latin America. "I walked," says Mankiewicz.)

"At first," says Bellamy, "we shared a hut. There was no electricity. It was beautiful, though. It was the jungle. In time, I moved into my own little hut. Meanwhile, we had a good arrangement. I'd kill the spiders and he'd kill the snakes." The "he" living in a jungle hut with the possible first female mayor of New York was Tim Kraft, who would, fourteen years later, become President Jimmy Carter's appointments secretary. "At first, Tim and I did some work with the CARE people on their school lunch program. He then went on to work on housing projects and in physical education. I continued on in child nutrition and health care—issues I dealt with in city government. But we didn't have your seven green leafy vegetables in Flores, Guatemala. You can't grow things like that in the jungle. So I concentrated on oranges and grapefruit, which were available. Nine thousand ways to use an orange. Boil the water. Boil the milk. Get the immunizations. I even got into poultry raising about which I had originally known nothing. Protein mattered, so you learned. In the Peace Corps, you learned. Peace Corps Volunteers got a lifetime of experience in two years in those days. You couldn't *pay* for that kind of experience."

Ultimately, Bellamy was broadcasting. "The people I had encountered were basically illiterate. But they had radios and they listened. The town of Flores had a generator which produced two hours of electricity a day. I went on the air with some Guatamalan teachers and spoke of basic nutrition. In Spanish. I didn't speak Spanish before Peace Corps training. But then, it was a lot easier than Mayan."

What struck Carol Bellamy at that time was "the overwhelming poverty of these people. Without strong government support, how could they ever hope to climb out of it? It was there that I decided that I wanted to go work in government. Not politics. Not running for office. But working for change within government. This had not occurred to me before I got to Guatemala with the Peace Corps. My next thought was, if you were a woman and you really wanted to do a *good* job in government—and I knew that I would want a job where I had something to *say*—then getting a law degree would be very helpful. It would give you legitimacy."

Carol Bellamy's official press release from city hall ticks off her astonishing progression: After Peace Corps service, she entered New York University Law School, passing the New York Bar in 1968. She joined the prestigious Wall Street law firm of Cravath, Swaine and Moore, where she specialized in corporate finance and securities law. In 1971 she was named assistant commissioner in the New York City Department of Mental Health and Mental Retardation Services. Elected to the state senate in 1972, she served as ranking Democrat of the Cities Committee, and chaired the Senate Democratic Task Force on the City of New York. In 1975 she was tapped for a fellowship at the Institute of Politics at Harvard.

At the time she announced her candidacy for Mayor, she was serving her second four-year term as council president, the second highest office in city government. She was reelected to the post on November 3, 1981, with 79 percent of the vote. She is the first woman to hold citywide office in New York.

Even though Bellamy lost the election to Koch, there is no chance she will fade away. She has come too far, too fast, with too fierce a will to be moved off center stage of New York politics for very long. Harvard has acknowledged her importance, as have *Newsweek*, in proclaiming her one of the "New Faces for the 1980s," and *Time*, by including her in its "Fifty Faces for America's Future." She is only forty-five and success has not spoiled her. (She is now a vice president of Morgan Stanley & Co.)

Of her Peace Corps tour in Guatemala, Bellamy states unequivocally and in ringing tones, "Those were two of the most important years of my life. It was a time of space, a time of challenge. You had to be as self-reliant as you could possibly be. You had to learn to accept failure. Because there were failures. And you were often the only person to enjoy your own successes. People speak of the brilliant staff that Shriver assembled in those early years. But historically, the greatest impact on the Peace Corps were the early Volunteers. And they were all *different*! I was strictly East Coast. I'd never known people from the South, the West and the Midwest before. People from California beach communities, people from Kalamazoo, Michigan, people from Berea, Kentucky. It was an eye-opening experience."

Asked if she would agree with the assessment of Dr. Carolyn Payton, a black psychologist who was a director of the Peace Corps (1978–80), that Peace Corps service at its best was equivalent to having had successful psychotherapy, Bellamy almost bellows: "I don't know what therapy means. But I do know that if I had to pick people to be stranded on a desert island with, I would pick those Peace Corps Volunteers I knew in Guatemala. They were the most terrific, smartest, neatest people I've ever met!"

Thank you, Madame President.

JULIA CHANG BLOCH

The University of California at Berkeley was "the Peace Corps school to end all Peace Corps schools," according to Bob Gale, director of recruiting from 1963 to 1965, and inventor of the "blitz." "No matter how many times Frank Erwin and I went out there, or sent other Peace Corps staff out there to recruit during the Shriver years, we always got more applicants than from any other school. And they almost always made outstanding Volunteers." Julia Chang was one of them.

I was not directly recruited by any particular Peace Corps person, but there was tremendous awareness of the Peace Corps at Berkeley. Peace Corps recruiters had made quite a splash when they came out in October 1963. Then, just a few weeks later, President Kennedy was assassinated. I could still hear him saying, "Ask not what your country can do for you; ask what you can do for your country." That call to service hit a responsive nerve with me from the first. I am an immigrant, a first-generation Chinese-American. My family came to the United States in 1951 from Shanghai, and my father believed very much in public service, and we all felt that this country had been very good to us. I was a senior in college at the time. So the Peace Corps seemed just the right thing. Since I spoke Spanish, I was very concerned that they would send me to Latin America. But I made it very clear on my application that I wanted to go to Asia.

And Asia it was. Chang was assigned to a group labeled Sabah and Sarawak IV. At the time that the Peace Corps agreed to send Volunteers there in 1962, Sabah—earlier known as North Borneo—and Sarawak were British Crown Colonies situated side by side on the island of Borneo, southwest of the Philippines. Sabah's crooked coastline borders both on the Sulu Sea and the South China Sea, due south of Hong Kong. By 1964, the British had all but pulled out, and Sabah and Sarawak joined Singapore and Malaya to form a new independent nation, Malaysia. Julia Chang was slated for Sabah.

We trained at the Peace Corps' Outward Bound camp in Hilo, Hawaii. Thank goodness they didn't make us rappel down dams as they did in the Puerto Rico camps, or I wouldn't have survived. I am not athletic. But Hilo was physical enough—hiking, mountain climbing, making us practice living like peasants. This was of no use when I got to Tenom, Sabah, to take up my teaching assignment in a secondary school. What greeted me was no mud hut, but a standard house for middle-level civil servants and a cheerful Peace Corps Volunteer roommate who had baked me some chocolate chip cookies as a welcoming gesture. She showed me her all-electric kitchen and western toilet. Everything was screened in and I had my own room with a fan. When I saw this, my mouth just dropped.

But the good living conditions cut out what I had anticipated would be a difficulty and allowed me to concentrate internally on what I was there to do. There is no reason for teachers in a semi-urban setting to go through complete deprivation. That is counterproductive. And for those who ended up with primitive living conditions, well, I would say that it deselected many people who would have made wonderful Volunteer teachers but did not have the will or were not physically able to adjust to mud huts. On the other hand, I know that some people joined the Peace Corps just *for* that. But it didn't work for a teacher. Teachers have considerable status in most of the Third World countries, and if a Peace Corps teacher lived or acted peculiarly different from other teachers, that teacher's credibility would be damaged. To me, it's not the physical apparatus. It's the Volunteer and what's inside.

For Julia Chang, going to Sabah was like going back to her roots. She had only Chinese students. She was befriended by Chinese store owners in Tenom as well as by young Chinese professionals who lived nearby. "I even had a date with a very nice young Chinese man who brought his brother as chaperone. I figured that I had made it as an acceptable Chinese woman at the social level, yet I didn't have to act like a Chinese woman at a professional level. Chinese women were supposed to be wives and mothers, period." (Chang had virtually no supervision. She had almost no dealings with the overall Rep in Kuala Lumpur, Malaysia, who was stationed miles to the west on another land mass. Chang reported to Roger Flather, who was regional director in charge of Sabah. But he, too, was rarely accessible, being five hours away by rail car in Jesselton, Sabah's capital. This was of no concern to Chang, but it was a source of amazement to her Chinese friends in Sabah.)

In addition to teaching English as a second language (a method called TESL in the United States), Julia Chang took on another job teaching history at her Peace Corps roommate's Catholic school nearby. She studied her own first language, Chinese, "because it was useful in that environment" and because she had lost a great deal of it growing up American in San Francisco. She worked on Saturdays, and she spent most of her "free" time with her students. Such industriousness, for which the Chinese are famous, was joined in the person of Julia Chang with a natural exuberance, for which young Americans are noted, to make her the kind of Peace Corps Volunteer about whom myths were made. (Charlie Houston, the first Rep in India, used to call such buildups by Peace Corps/Washington "Immortal Volunteer Stories." And Shriver, with no guile whatsoever, believed them and perpetrated them.) There was the chic, petite Chinese-American, Julia Chang, she of the soaring I.Q., striding through the jungles of Sabah, Malaysia, surrounded by her adoring students, as native guides whacked away at the dense, tangled foliage with machetes to make them a path—sleeping in tents or in thatched-roof huts in serendipitous jungle villages, bathing in rivers, climbing spectacular waterfalls.

And in Chang's case, it was all true. But she did not bask, then or ever, in compliments. She saw the irony of her particular situation: She was an Oriental female by birth, who had become an American woman in every respect and who had, in addition, become an intellectual and a politically aware human being who was returning to the culture of her birth to offer friendship and render a basic service. Chang was in a unique position to ask questions of her students that other Volunteers could not ask, or would not ever think to ask. Reciting the litany of hundreds of Peace Corps Volunteers and staff around the world who were apprehending societies just emerging from British colonial rule, Chang says,

> Teaching was by rote. You repeat, repeat—essentially memorize out loud. As an American, you are frustrated by this system and you will jump at any chance to introduce deductive thought, *reasoning*, into the process. I was teaching adjectives one day, so I asked my class to make two columns—one column to describe Malays, another to describe Chinese. In the Chinese column, they inevitably wrote, "diligent," "clean," and "good." And for the Malays, "lazy" and "dirty." I asked, "Are *all* Chinese this way? Are *all* Malays this way?" One little kid looked up at me quickly and I could tell that he knew what I meant. If all Chinese were alike, and I was Chinese, they could not truly say that all Chinese are alike. They looked around at each other. The kid who had just looked up was in fact Malay, the only Malay I taught in any class—and the *only* Malaysian or Sabahan who now holds an advanced fisheries degree—raised his hand: "Most Chinese are

like this," he said tentatively. I said, "Go on. Not all people are alike, are they? And you can't characterize people by racial types, can you?" He wasn't ready to accede that point, so I said bluntly, "Am I like all Chinese girls or women?"

The class was really stumped for a final answer on this. The boy who had broken through to speak in the first place suddenly said in an awed tone, "Miss Julia, no, you're not like a Chinese girl. You're like a Chinese boy".*

As advanced and emancipated as Julia Chang must have seemed to the citizens of Sabah, Malaysia, she was soon to feel the sting of the heavily male chauvinist thinking that existed at Peace Corps headquarters. With a dazzling record as a Volunteer, she returned to the United States and added another impressive credential to her resume, an M.A. from Harvard in government and East Asian studies. She then applied for a Peace Corps staff job overseas. "I wanted to go back to Asia, but they indicated that Asians would look askance at Asian-American women in a very obvious position of authority. I argued about that, but to no avail. I asked what else was wrong with the idea of sending me back as an associate Rep or a regional director, since many of my male colleagues in Sabah had been immediatly reassigned to such jobs." Officials of EAP (East Asia/Pacific) then vaguely mentioned the possibility of Chang's being an administrative assistant overseas, just a notch above secretary. The gist of it was, the men who ran EAP really did not want to send a female overseas in that region in any responsible staff capacity. "They came up with these reasons, finally," says Chang. "I didn't drive a jeep, and even if I did, Asians would be offended: I was too young and *I was a woman*. End of debate. They gave me a job in Washington as a lowly training officer." (The glory days of being a training officer were gone by 1968. Padraic Kennedy and Al Meisel, the first two training officers in 1961, had had the best of it, autonomously planning and monitoring the first groups' training programs and then acting as their escorts to the Peace Corps' first ports of call in the Third World. It had been a glamorous,

---

*While a young Malay student understood very well Julia Chang's special place in that community, a British district officer in Sandakan, a town due east of Jesselton, missed it completely. As Chang discussed with him arrangements for a boat trip for her students, the D.O. remarked in some amazement, "My, but you speak good English. What a little education can do for people."

creative, nonbureaucratic job at the beginning—a labor of love and surprise.)

Soon enough, however, the talented, motivated Chang was plucked out of the Training Division and assigned the intellectually rigorous and prestigious post of evaluator, where she traveled to and reported on Peace Corps programs in the Dominican Republic, Philippines, Malaysia, and India. In 1968 she married Stuart Marshall Bloch, a Washington lawyer, a partner in the law firm of Ingersoll and Bloch. After a year's sabbatical with her groom (who had objected to her relentless traveling for the Division of Evaluation), Julia Chang Bloch joined Senator Charles Percy's Senate Select Committee on Nutrition and Human Needs in 1971, becoming its chief minority counsel in 1976 before leaving a year later. ("They did away with my Committee, see?") She then joined USIA as deputy director for Africa. When you are rising in government—state or federal—at the rate that Julia Chang Bloch was rising in the mid- to late 1970s, you will be of interest to the Institute of Politics at Harvard, whose vaunted fellowship program is forever on the watch for potential "movers and shakers" in either political party. Julia Chang Bloch got a fellowship.

Shortly after Ronald Reagan had been sworn in as president on January 20, 1981, Julia Chang Bloch was sworn in as assistant administrator for Food for Peace and Voluntary Assistance. (Food for Peace began in 1962 as a separate agency under the wing of the White House with the then-to-be senator and, ten years later, presidential candidate George McGovern as its head. It is now a part of the State Department.) At thirty-nine, Julia Chang Bloch became the highest ranking Asian-American in the Reagan administration.

For Bloch, the impact of her Peace Corps experience has never diminished: "I think of my Peace Corps roommate in Tenom, Sabah. She was also a Californian. She's now a tenured professor of anthropology at Tufts. She studied Chinese. She became what she is today because of the Peace Corps. Certainly the Peace Corps was the first step for me in my finding a career in overseas aid and development. When I was an undergraduate at Berkeley, I had thought I might be a journalist, having majored in communications and public policy. But there are several hundred like me that I could point to. If you look at some AID missions around the world, particularly in Africa, you would find that almost all of them are former Volunteers. In my day, however, Peace Corps and AID looked at each other very warily. Now, a former Volunteer, Peter McPherson, is running AID."

Julia Bloch returned to Sabah, Malaysia, in 1983, sixteen years after she had completed Peace Corps service. As she and her husband rode on a little train down from Kota Kinabalu (as Sabah's capital, Jesselton, had since been renamed—although the travel time, five hours, was the same as ever), Stuart Bloch remarked more than once, "You didn't tell me that this was the *jungles*." (Julia Bloch had learned through letters and the Peace Corps grapevine that many of her students had emigrated to Taiwan, Hong Kong, even England, but several of her former students had shown up at the airport when she first arrived. Most of them now lived in Kota Kinabalu.) Once back in Tenom, Bloch didn't want to look too closely for changes in the people she had taught and known. She held to the cautious attitude that was and still is prevalent among former Peace Corps Volunteers: "People always ask, what did the Peace Corps *do*? They ask you to quantify what happened in terms of your Peace Corps service, as if you could, as if it was something like strategic bombing. You usually can't trace direct cause and effect in the Peace Corps. It does not lend itself to statistics. But one thing I did notice upon my return: Among my girls, none of them had more than four children and they all had come from families of seven, eight, nine, and more. And all of my boys now have wives who work."

DAVID RICHARDS

David Richards grew up consumed by three passions: the French language, the theater, and newspapers. Today, at forty-five, he is the drama critic of the *Washington Post*. "I often say that the job I probably should have gotten, the only job that would satisfy the three, would be drama critic of the *Herald Tribune* in Paris. But that position has long been filled by another." He acknowledges with a quick nod and a slight smile the suggestion that he has got, nonetheless, one of the best jobs in the world. "Ah, but the French side languishes."

It is difficult to account for Richards' francophilia, since he was born in Concord, Massachusetts, and brought up in neighboring Lexington, an area steeped in Revolutionary War lore, awash in early Americana. It is still harder to understand when one learns that Richards spent his adolescence in Spanish-tinged, western-frontier-oriented

Scottsdale, Arizona, "when it was a little town of two thousand people and the horses had the right of way." None of that particular culture rubbed off on Richards, either. "I had pictures of French châteaux on my bedroom walls."

Richards got his first "break" while an undergraduate at Occidental College in Los Angeles in spending his junior year in France through the auspices of Hamilton College in upstate New York. His passion for the country and the language deepened with the reality of living there. He graduated from Occidental in 1961 with a major in French, hove off to Middlebury College for a masters degree in French, and then back to France. "I was *very* aware of Kennedy, of course. Who at that time was not? Still, the notion of coming back to the United States just at that point did not appeal to me at all. On the other hand, I was in the mood for adventure—was it in the air?—and the Peace Corps sounded exciting to me, though not for any political reasons. What I wanted, above all, was to remain in a French-speaking culture." That, plus the pull of exotic travel and personal challenge, added up to French-speaking Africa and the Peace Corps.

Richards arrived at Oberlin College in Ohio in July 1963 to be trained as a Peace Corps teacher in the Ivory Coast, West Africa. "What astonishes me now, in retrospect, was the colossal naiveté of it all. I remember taking a test when I first got to Oberlin. We were given a map of Africa and told to fill in the names of the countries and the capitals. God, if you *knew* them. Some of us came up with two or three countries at best—at best." (Richards's fellow Peace Corps trainees felt less ignorant when, upon arriving in the newly independent Ivory Coast—*Côte d'Ivoire*)—they were asked by their students where in France the United States was located.) Richards was assigned to teach English as a second language in the secondary school (*l'école secondaire*) of Aboisso, a town of 800 people miles from the capital city, Abidjan, which is on the coast. The predominant tribe in and around Aboisso, the Ibo, had caught independence fever and had rebelled with the intention of forming a new nation, which would include an area just over the border in Ghana, where others of the tribe resided. "The rebellion was quelled," says Richards, "with the result that the border with Ghana was sealed off. Thus, what little fame and usefulness had accrued to Aboisso as a jumping off point for Ghana had now evaporated. It had no real reason for being anymore. It was sort of the end of the world."

David Richards, twenty-three, late of Scottsdale, Arizona; Middlebury, Vermont; and Paris, France, sought to accommodate himself to this apparent nonplace. He was the only Peace Corps Volunteer in Aboisso and the only American. He was teaching English as a second language to young black Africans who were at first as baffled by his presence among them as he was. He lived in an apartment over a garage that had been converted to a kindergarten, next door to a Catholic church whose bells pealed at length each morning at 6:00 A.M. like some infernal Third World alarm clock. He was cut off from everything familiar: He had no radio, no television, no newspapers. "But I had my Peace Corps book locker, which I quickly read through twice. It is strange to read Thurber in that environment." He also had running water, low-voltage electricity, and a kerosene refrigerator, the mention of which sets him off twenty-three years later: "Ask any Volunteer in West Africa about those things—they were a curse! They actually burned kerosene and you had to adjust the flue absolutely perfectly in order to get the chilling effect. After tinkering with that damned thing for an entire week, I finally got it to draw correctly and produce ice cubes. You kept doing it until you got it right," he says. "In the Peace Corps, if you didn't do it, no one else was going to do it. There was nobody to help you. That was one of the extraordinary things about the Peace Corps, and I remember feeling that fixing that refrigerator was one of the greatest accomplishments in my life up to that point. But you were playing with fire and matches, curiously enough, to get a refrigeration effect and there were cases of them exploding and people being shipped back to the United States covered with burns. They were pretty lethal little instruments."

To get to Aboisso in 1963, it was necessary to travel by hand-cranked ferry across two lagoons from Abidjan, a trip that took three hours. Richards was, as noted, isolated. "My day was pretty much regimented by the fact that I taught. The school was on the top of a hill, and I would go up early in the morning, teach until 3:00 P.M., correct papers, and prepare lessons for the next day. That was the basic framework. But very early on, I found myself devising all sorts of ways, frankly, to keep my sanity. I wrote a series of articles about life in Africa for the *Cape Cod Standard Times*. I started a garden, got myself a dog, staged plays in French with my students and fellow teachers in the local cinema house. My most popular effort was a medieval French farce about the tricker getting tricked." Richards also took in a boarder:

One of my students lived with me the first year I was in the Ivory Coast. This was the result of a government effort to encourage bright children, mostly male (only one-quarter of females got beyond the primary grades) to go to schools in areas other than their birthplaces. They were sending them out hither and yon with the idea of combatting residual tribalism, to shuffle the deck so that these kids would begin to think of themselves more in terms of a national identity, more as being Ivorians, as opposed to being members, say, of the Baoule tribe. * The student who came to live with me—Guetta Emolo was his African name, Samuel was his Christian moniker—walked into town barefoot and with very little money. He was a bright, bright kid. I had occasion to use a jeep now and then, and I made it a point to drive him the eighty miles to the ocean, which he had never seen. And the wonder in his eyes!

Richards remained in Aboisso for a year. He was aware that his students desired above all else to become government *fonctionnaires*. "This was seen as a cushy and plush job," says Richards, "and most of my students were bent on getting there." But these students were primarily citizens of Aboisso; they thought of themselves as Ivorians; they were not tribal boys. What would become of Guetta Emolo Samuel, Richards wondered. He was kind of a wild card. Samuel invited Richards to sample some tribal hospitality. They traveled three hundred miles upcountry to Koffikro. "This was traditional Africa," says Richards, "and as isolated as I felt in Aboisso, I had really never seen the 'real thing' before." It was a *National Geographic* cover story come to life: "Mud huts, thatched roofs, no electricity, and a tribal chieftain who presided over the village. I was given my own little hut and the town religious band played an odd but exuberant tune for me outside my hut. We had communal meals with Samuel acting as an interpeter, translating the tribal dialect into French. An incredible experience." Richards mused that the Peace Corps was a great invention, second only in its special magic to the French language, and that the two had fused at that moment to bring together a privileged blond college boy from America and an African tribal son and his family.

Richards could not help but look forward to the Peace Corps reunions that were held every four-to-six months in Abidjan. Vol-

*Martin Meredith writes in his book on Africa since 1945, The First Dance of Freedom: "Once the momentum that nationalist leaders had achieved in their drive for independence began to subside, so old tribal rivalries and ambitions came thrusting to the surface . . . 'We have all inherited from our former masters not nations but states,' remarked the Ivory Coast's president, Felix Houphouet-Boigny, 'states that have within them extremely fragile links between ethnic groups.' "

unteers from all over the Ivory Coast were summoned to the coastal headquarters for three days of lectures, booster shots, medical exams, and, generally, a rousing good party. The Peace Corps Rep, Henry Wheatley, a prominent native of the Virgin Islands, was indulgent on that point. "We'd pile in from different corners of the country, and I have to say that, while I've never been a team player and have always been very much a solitary individual, this was one time in my life when I have felt solidly and warmly a part of a group. I have never experienced such a sense of fraternity or brotherhood so vivid as being with my fellow Americans at these times," says Richards.

That sense of fraternity and brotherhood was severely if temporarily shaken on November 22, 1963. "A student came to my apartment and said very simply, *"Monsieur, votre président est mort."*

"I couldn't fathom it at all. I thought it was utterly, utterly improbable. The only radio I had access to was at the post office, so I ran over there. And, well, indeed Kennedy had been assassinated. We didn't know what assassination meant back then. That news that was unreal to everyone all over America was doubly unreal to me in the context of Aboisso, Ivory Coast, West Africa. A curious thing happened. My students, fellow teachers, friends in the town—assuming that I was a close friend of Kennedy's and that we all knew one another in the United States—all descended on my apartment and insisted on staying there through the period of mourning. I was able to cut it short after about five or six hours of sardine-packed grieving. Otherwise, they would have been there for days."

Months later, the people of Aboisso and Richards reconvened as if to complete the mourning process. Somehow, a print of a documentary film about the Kennedy administration and its tragic denouement, *Years of Lightning, Day of Drums,* found its way to Aboisso. "There was no secret about USIA's being responsible for the movie theater's being there, and the owner was a Lebanese who was very sympathetic to the United States," says Richards. "So it was probably a combination. The townspeople, who had all along had in their little houses pictures of Kennedy and Martin Luther King on the walls, came to pack the place that evening, some with clothes on whose fabric was emblazoned Kennedy's likeness. I've heard that was not uncommon in Third World countries. I just remember that I came away from that event absolutely shaken."

◆　　　◆　　　◆

After a year in Aboisso, Richards was reassigned to the capital city of Abidjan, which seemed to him, compared to Aboisso, "the Paris of black Africa." "But that's what Abidjan is called now. Actually, Abidjan in 1964 was a sleepy little postcolonial town." Richards had four jobs there: working for a government radio station as a "second voice" accompanying that of a woman from AID; broadcasting a fifteen-minute English segment that went to Ghana and Liberia; teaching English as a second language at two Catholic schools; and teaching English to the waiters at the Hotel Evar, for its time a supersleek modern hotel symbolic of the Ivory Coast's ambitions. "It was just opening in 1964 and the owners and government officials wanted the staff to have a few rudiments of English." Richards's work there carried a prerequisite almost surely unique in on-the-job Peace Corps experience at that time: the chance for a dip in the hotel pool after class. It was *hot* in sub-Sahara Africa, and Richards reasoned that only a terminal masochist would turn down such an opportunity at 3:00 P.M. on a sodden, blistering afternoon.

One day, after giving his English lesson to the waiters, Richards dove into the blessedly cool water and was doing his laps when there appeared at poolside "a chic, 'New Yorky' looking woman with her hand on her hip, obviously come to give me hell." It was an evaluator from Peace Corps headquarters, whose name Richards cannot recall in spite of her dramatic appearance in his life. He does recall, however, that "her reputation as a terror had preceded her. She told me that if word got back to the United States that I was swimming in this posh pool, the whole Peace Corps effort would be jeopardized worldwide, and that she was going to see to it personally that I would be forbidden forever after to swim in that pool. Boy, did I hate her." (Richards wondered if this evaluator ever saw him years later in a cameo role as a cameraman in a French film, *The Gentleman from Kokodie.* "I hope so, because the scene I was in was shot at the Hotel Evar pool! Kokodie was a fancy residential section of Abidjan where most of the diplomats lived. The main character, a diplomat, was played by Jean Marais, then a very big French stage and movie star. It was one of those mad, slightly tongue-in-cheek, chase films; the chase took place all over the Ivory Coast—which is very photogenic, just beautiful—and the scene consists of an irate girlfriend pushing Jean Marais into the pool in front of a bunch of journalists and cameramen." Richards might have missed it himself had not the *Washington Post*'s television critic, Tom Shales, awakened him at 2:00 A.M. with this message: "The film we have all been waiting for is being rerun on WTTG.")

David Richards formed an opinion of the Division of Evaluation based on that and other experiences that he heard about from Volunteers and staff during his two years in the Ivory Coast. "The evaluators. They always killed you. They had no notion of what was going on, no idea of what you were doing."

♦   ♦   ♦

Richards returned to the Ivory Coast in 1978, fifteen years after he left it as an outgoing Peace Corps Volunteer.

> I flew from Kennedy to Monrovia, Liberia, and then puddle-jumped over to Abidjan. Abidjan! It was by that time a roaring, traffic-clogged metropolis. Skyscrapers, cloverleafs. I went up to Aboisso over new bridges and slick highways. Aboisso was making its way into the twentieth century. People were watching television. I looked up Guetta Emolo Samuel while there, of course. It turned out he was working in Abidjan, in a government office. He was married and he had four children at the time, with another one on the way. He drove to work in a car he was paying on. He complained about the high price of gasoline. He got caught in traffic jams. And here is someone who walked out of the bush barefoot fifteen years ago, and I mean he had literally bolted two hundred years ahead in a brief period of time. It was *staggering*.

Samuel took his former landlord and teacher back to his tribal village, which had not changed at all. The chieftain, by then almost one hundred years old, welcomed him back, apologizing that the same band that had greeted Richards fifteen years before had been dissolved. Again, Samuel translated the tribal dialect into French.

"Sitting out under the starry African sky," says Richards, "which is as vast as any I've seen, and eating out of a communal pot, I was again overcome by a sense of kinship that I can't explain to this day. I had absolutely nothing in common with these people. I did not speak their language. I certainly came from a different socioeconomic status. My experience had nothing to do with theirs. Corny as it may sound, I think I realized in my gut, in a way that I have never realized since— that we are indeed all brothers under the skin." As if reading Richards's thoughts, Samuel said to him in French, "If my next child is a boy, I will name him after you." Richards was touched, but thought no more about it until he received a letter from Samuel two months later in Washington, D.C., where he was then a reporter on the now defunct

Washington Star. "It said that his wife had given birth to a boy, and in the African fashion of putting the family name first, this little child had been baptized Guetta David Richards."

Before leaving the Ivory Coast, Richards paid one last visit to Aboisso. I went and just stood in the courtyard at the secondary school where I had taught and let the memories come. Strangely, I thought about Kennedy. I thought about him in a way that I had not thought about him when he died. I thought of the profound effect he had had on my life, certainly as no other president has or ever will. I can clearly say that he had a direct, personal effect on the course of my life, the way I look at the world. And there, fifteen years later, I started to cry. The tears were just pouring down my face. Why had it taken fifteen years to truly lament his death? Maybe it takes time to find out what impact certain people have had on you, how they have changed your life. But he sure changed mine."

CHAPTER 10

WHEN JOHNNY COMES MARCHING HOME

"The Kennedy assassination was the most shocking public event since the bombing of Hiroshima."

This statement, perhaps more than any other, does justice to the trauma of November 22, 1963. It was made with glum finality by Mark Harris, author of *Bang the Drum Slowly*, *Mark the Glove Boy*, and *Twentyone Twice*. Published in 1966, *Twentyone Twice* is a bemused account of Harris's encounter with the Peace Corps as an evaluator, he being one of those authors most sought after by Shriver, Peters, and Haddad—an author through whose strictly masculine perspective they wanted to sift the Peace Corps experience. Harris had arrived at Peace Corps headquarters on July 28, 1963, two months before Haddad left and four months before the assassination. He thus caught the Peace Corps at full throttle, awash in euphoria, head over heels in love with itself. He also caught "founding father fever," not to mention Potomac fever. He was put through the requisite number of interviews even though he was slated to be only a "consultant," partially because many staff members had lobbied Peters to meet him and partially because he indicated that he was vaguely job hunting (writers are always vaguely job hunting). Who knew? He might be a candidate as a full-time evaluator. (This was a foolish notion on the part of Harris and everyone else. It soon became clear that Harris was far too imprudent a cause-seeker to work in a bureaucracy, even the most unbureaucratic bureaucracy in the world, which the Peace Corps prided itself on being.)

Harris, at the end of a day of many interviews, went in to meet Shriver, and typically, he was overwhelmed by the man. He loved it when Shriver described the Peace Corps as being like yeast: "It's not sensational, it requires time." Mark Harris described Shriver as one who "bubbles with enthusiasm and recognizes no obstacles, looking upon everything as possible until proved otherwise. On his walls many signs are hung, usually framed, as a man does who is not himself so much a man of words but who admires eloquent definitions of his ambition—his, to use a word frequently with him, 'dream.' " Shriver, thought Harris, was "a front for all dreamers, giving confidence to the anti-dreamers because he doesn't himself appear to be a dreamer." Harris noticed a banner on the wall that no Peace Corps staff member could ever forget; it read, "There is no place in this club for good losers." Another made him think of Kennedy: "Those who would carry on the great public schemes must be proof against the most fatiguing delays, the most mortifying judgment of the ignorant on their designs."—Edmund Burke. Harris also noticed on the wall a quote from Volunteer David Crozier, twenty-two, of West Plains, Missouri, killed in a plane crash in Colombia: "Should it come to it, I had rather give my life trying to help someone than to have to give my life looking down a gun barrel at them." Harris found it charming that "on the floor, not yet hung, lay many honorary degrees he has received, and all sorts of citations." (Shriver's Washington law office today looks much the same, as did his office at OEO when he was "Poverty Czar.")

Shriver spoke to Harris of "the American fascination with cannons and home runs as expressions of power, whereas it was his opinion that the true expressions of power ought to be *moral* power, *spiritual* power, the power to *heal* and *improve*." Harris added, not without awe, "And he is very handsome."

Thus bewitched, Harris happily accepted certain "homework assignments" required of him. He read dozens of training and overseas evaluations and discussed them with the evaluators. He studied the "cable traffic" to learn how headquarters and the field staff communicated. He filled out many maddeningly long and convoluted government forms, not the least of which was a prying document used to "run" security clearances on incoming staff. He hated this one with a passion, but so did everybody, he was assured. But how was it, he queried, that he was not only allowed but encouraged to read material labeled "Authorized Eyes Only" without a security clearance but not allowed to go to Africa and talk to a few Peace Corps Volunteers. "Don't ask," he was advised, "because there is no answer."

The abnormally hot summer of 1963 came to a close in mid-October, when the temperature in Washington finally began to drop below eighty. Harris had become a fixture around Peace Corps headquarters, but still no security clearance. No one mentioned it so Harris continued blithely to read classified documents. He was enjoying his life at 806 Connecticut Avenue. He looked forward to lunching often with evaluators Tim Adams, Phil Cook, Kevin Delany, and Gardiner Jones at Chez François (where poached salmon with sauce *verte* was

$1.75), the Hay Adams, and the Black Steer, and occasionally at the new ultra-establishment luncheon haunt, Sans Souci, where one could gawk at cabinet members, Supreme Court justices, congressmen, senators, television news personalities, legendary political analysts, White House aides, and a smattering of the more politically hip elements of "social Washington." The attorney general, Robert Kennedy, brought his big shaggy dog, Brumus, right into these elegant precincts; no one dared to object. Brumus slept at his master's feet while the third Kennedy brother joked with columnist Art Buchwald at his special banquette against the right-hand wall. The food at Sans Souci, which had the atmosphere of an English country manor house, with dark paneling and subtle chandelier sparkle, was good but irrelevant. In Washington, Harris had come to understand, politics was *all*. And the late Paul deLisle, the courtly and politically astute maître d', was made in heaven for the place.

Harris continued to live at the Claridge Hotel, which the Peace Corps called its own, as the weeks and finally months wore on. At $6.00 a day—a bargain even by Great Depression standards—he could not complain. He often took breakfast at the Hot Shoppe around the corner. He had no need to leave that block, it seemed. For thrills, he could see the White House as he walked either out of the Claridge and into the Peace Corps or out of the Hot Shoppe and into the Peace Corps. Another, more spectacular view of it came with Charlie Peters's territory on the eleventh floor. One morning Harris decided to explore further. He came upon the house where Lincoln had died and a barbershop of the famous, Ewell's Barber and Manicure Shop, "which had eighteen chairs." My barber told me this: "Barbers go directly from this shop 'up into government,' and that the man who formerly worked at the chair next to him has, for example, cut the hair of John Kennedy and Chief Justice [Earl] Warren." Indeed, power was *all*.

Harris was getting spoiled, he thought, and he was also beginning to wonder seriously: Has something gone wrong? Why has my security clearance taken nearly five months? Was the FBI *that* inefficient? Did J. Edgar Hoover not like the cut of his jib? All during this delightful but rather unreal period, Harris had been hearing that FBI agents had been "asking questions about me all over the country, ranging from Ben's and Bea's Friendly Market to my Aunt Leah in Mount Vernon, New York, and points between in all the places I have lived in the last twenty years." He did not like this at all but was told not to worry, nobody does. He went to see a friend at the Peace Corps, Robertson

Upp, who facilitated such matters. Upp conceded that Harris's security clearance had indeed taken an unusually long time to come through. Harris stated unhesitatingly that he had "a clear conscience and no mental reservations." He meant it. But he then told Upp, just as forthrightly, that, well, Mr. Hoover *could* be scratching his head over this Mark Harris because "I had opposed the execution of the Rosenbergs in 1953, voted for Wallace in 1948 when I was a student, . . . and had gone to some meetings of the Soviet-American Friendship Society."

Upp groaned.

Undeterred, Harris threw in as an afterthought: "Oh yeah, and I've been fairly active against the House Un-American Activities Committee over the years."

"That'd make their eyeballs roll," said Upp, rolling his own.

But finally, miraculously and mysteriously, Harris's clearance materialized. Upp was frankly surprised and said so, indicating that lesser "crimes" that those Harris had committed had been cause for withholding security clearances. Upp figured that "Mr. Hoover and his gumshoes" had concluded that Mark Harris was an innocent fool who knew not what he did.

While his security clearance arrived as something of an anticlimax, Harris was nonetheless elated. Off to Africa, at last. After all, that's what he'd come for. While he was packing in the Claridge, he heard of the assassination via agonized shouts in the hall. He was due to have lunch with Joe Colmen right next door at Chez François, Friday luncheons at "Chez" were always especially festive, celebratory, late, and long and he was looking forward to a cheerful send-off by the witty director of research. Instead, he stopped packing abruptly and staggered, stupefied, into the Peace Corps building a few doors up the street as if drawn by some unknowable force. There, mirrored in the faces and body language of his new friends and colleagues, was the shock, disbelief, horror, and nausea he himself felt. No Darkest Africa today, he thought, or maybe ever. Which is fine, he thought. I mean, why bother now? Peace Corps people—and Mark Harris had quickly become one—took some kind of grisly pride in believing that they were the most wounded organizational body in America. It ran on New Frontier fuel. Now what would it run on?

As paralysis set in and the staff skulked away uncharacteristically at 5:00 P.M. to curl up morbidly with a stiff drink or two and a television set, a rumor circulated that Shriver had been tapped to organize the funeral. Oddly, that provided some kind of macabre consolation. The Peace Corps, through the person of Shriver, was still central to history.

When the terrible news came, Shriver himself was having lunch with his wife, Eunice, and their four-year-old son, Timmy, at the Lafayette Hotel (now vanished) two blocks away, off Farragut Square, across from the Army-Navy Club. Eunice Shriver was expecting her fourth child in February and had just come from the office of Dr. John Walsh, a famous and distinguished obstetrician who practiced at Georgetown Hospital and had delivered many a Kennedy baby. (Ironically, Walsh's chief assisting nurse was Elaine Gelman, whose husband was head of Special Projects and a former ghostwriter for Eunice.) During lunch, Shriver was summoned to a phone, which was hardly unusual. According to William Manchester in *The Death of a President*, "Shriver returned to the table and said to his wife, 'Something's happened to Jack.' Eunice asked 'What?' 'He's been shot,' Shriver said. She asked if her brother was going to be all right. 'We won't know,' her husband replied. Eunice thought a moment and then said, 'There have been so many crises in his life; he'll pull through.' Here were two people in conspiracy against reality. They calmly studied the menu and ordered lunch. Eunice ate the bread and drank a cup of soup before a second telephone call destroyed their fragile facade."

The Shrivers hastened to Peace Corps headquarters. Shriver's unerringly poised secretary, Maryann Orlando, looked distraught, confirming the awful truth. At this point, the Peace Corps' Chief of Psychiatry, Dr. Joseph English, and the head of the Medical Division, Dr. Joseph Gallagher, converged on Shriver's office. Not knowing that Eunice Shriver would be on the premises, they were filled nonetheless with grave concern about her physical and emotional well-being in her advanced months of pregnancy, as she was over the age of forty and especially close to the president. They had come to Shriver's office as a flying wedge of support.

Charlie Peters was in the Division of Public Information talking to its director, Douglas Kiker, in front of the teletype machine when the calamity was tapped out. While shocked, they and others in the room told each other that Kennedy would be all right. Any other outcome was unthinkable. They did not wait for an elevator when the unthinkable was confirmed. They ran like crazed jackrabbits down the two flights of stairs to the fifth floor and ran headlong into the Shrivers and Drs. English and Gallagher emerging from Shriver's office. "The men looked grim enough," says Peters, "but Eunice was pulverized. *Pulverized*. Oh God, she was *shattered*."

◆　　◆　　◆

Finally, on January 7, 1964, Mark Harris repacked his bags and set off for New York to embark on the trip to Africa—long planned and long delayed. He had the weird, unsettling sense that this was not the same world he had once known. Not the same Peace Corps. It was definitely a different year and undeniably a new era. He was depressed in a way he could not put words to and yet he wanted to go on. Go to Africa. See the Volunteers. Soak it up. Make it all real and meaningful again. He went up to the eleventh floor to say goodbye to those whom he now considered his fellow evaluators. He shook hands with Charlie Peters and Phil Cook. As he was boarding the elevator, Tim Adams rushed by, exhorting him to "take plenty of gamma globulin." Downstairs, on the sidewalk, while hailing a cab, he ran into Kevin Delany, who "smelled excellently of shaving lotion," which was the last civilized scent that Harris expected to inhale anytime soon. He arrived at Idlewild three hours later. But no. It wasn't Idlewild any more. It was Kennedy. Harris felt sickened by the reality of that "dismally hideous airport named for a young assassinated president, his name itself reduced to initials scrawled on baggage checks. He's an airport now," thought Harris bitterly. "A baggage destination."

◆　　◆　　◆

Aside from members of the Kennedy family, their close friends, and longtime political associates, few people's lives would be so altered by the fact of the assassination as that of Jack Vaughn. Other than working for Shriver and having found his respect, Vaughn had no relationship with the Kennedys or their intimates. He had met Lyndon Johnson only in a receiving line and did not know Moyers particularly well. In fact, he and Moyers were rather alike in that they both seemed chummy when in fact they were not. Both marched to the beat of his own drummer and operated with a certain shrewd, cool independence. However, the curious interlacing of these powerful people's styles, personalities, and political fortunes was to act as a poltergeist in Vaughn's life, little by little upending it until Vaughn was living a life he could not possibly have anticipated or even dared hope for.

At the time of the assassination, Vaughn was director of the Peace Corps' Latin America Regional Office. He was uniquely suited to that job, he loved it, and he coveted no other job inside or outside the Peace Corps. For him, the assassination was a monumental tragedy— ugly and bewildering—but not something that would intrude permanently into his own life. Still, Vaughn had experienced the assassination under singularly grotesque circumstances, what he calls "a hellish metaphor":

I was in San José, Costa Rica. A nearby volcano had been erupting for over a year and had spewed untold inches of gray ash over that high valley. Vegetation had been killed, roofs had actually collapsed because of the accumulating ash. Everything was gray. I had just entered a restaurant with some Peace Corps staff and Volunteers. We had been padding around in this junk and every time we'd take a step, we'd send up puffs of ash and be covered with it. It was really offensive and grim. We were having lunch about four blocks from the U.S. embassy, and when we heard a fire siren start to wail—it was an awful sound and it kept going— I said, 'Listen, I'd better check this. Some calamity has occurred.' I ran over to the embassy and by the time I got to the door, people were running around just screaming and waving their arms. The ash was flying everywhere. You could have choked to death on it. I tried to get through the door of the embassy but they were just closing it. Bam. That was it. All of a sudden I was surrounded by about fifty people—charladies, paperboys, vendors—who were all falling to their knees in front of the U.S. embassy on the sidewalk, praying and crossing themselves and moaning. It was mad. It was ghoulish. It was out of Dante. I just stood there, frozen, at the door of the embassy. But now I knew. Kennedy was dead.

It was very, very emotional, and it got worse before I left the next day. Swarms of people were paying homage to Kennedy at the Peace Corps office, crying, carrying on, and for blocks and blocks there were people waiting to send a telegram to Mrs. Kennedy.

Kennedy had visited San José, and today, all those years later, there are still pictures of Kennedy in windows all around San José. Many hundreds of them. Where they would have typically put up something like, "This is a Catholic home. We resent the Protestant invasion," instead they have a picture of John F. Kennedy.

When Vaughn returned to Peace Corps headquarters two days later, Monday morning, November 25, 1963, he found the place transformed. The usually bustling Bugs-Bunny-ish halls and offices—busy even on weekends—were hushed and empty. About seventy-five staff members had instinctively gone to the eleventh-floor parapet of the Maiatico Building, crowding the side overlooking Lafayette Park and the White House. As the funeral procession moved down Pennsylvania Avenue from the Capitol and wound around the semicircular White House driveway, the Peace Corps staff for the first time saw the casket and the riderless horse and heard the dirge and the drums up close, and they wept as one.

The Peace Corps staff was despondent for many weeks. People who had been vivacious or even boisterous were subdued. As the staff arrived in the morning and left in the evening, they came face to face with a large picture of John F. Kennedy in the lobby. Under the picture was a quote from his inaugural address: "Let it be clear that this administration recognizes the value of daring and dissent—that we greet healthy controversy as the hallmark of healthy change. Let the public service be a proud and lively career." They would stare at it for a moment, then look down abruptly and move on. Visitors to the building noted that the Peace Corps' gloom was as contagious as its bubbliness had been. Gloom soon turned to just plain surliness. Seeing Bill Moyers's office empty put people in a bad mood, partly because it reminded them of the riderless horse and partly because the Shriver-Moyers team had been so perfect. However, no one begrudged Moyers's having returned to his old boss and mentor in the latter's hour of maximum need. The most politically attuned citizens had realized it was going to happen when they saw Johnson—*President* Johnson—get off *Air Force One* at Andrews Air Force Base on the night of November 22, 1963, on their television sets. Right behind him was Moyers, his young, bespectacled, keenly intelligent face framed over the president's left shoulder. And indeed, Moyers never returned to the Peace Corps. Never. Moyers had managed to have a note delivered to Johnson aboard *Air Force One* just before it took off from Dallas after having himself chartered a plane from Austin when he heard of the assassination. It read, "I'm here if you need me." Johnson needed him desperately. As Adam Yarmolinsky was often heard to say to political neophytes with weary patience, "The first rule of politics is to *be there.*"

The less politically attuned Peace Corps staff members concocted worst-case and best-case scenarios ("scenario" had just entered the political vernacular): (1) Shriver would never leave. "In, Up & Out" could not possibly apply to him. But if it did, the only possible replacement for him was Moyers; (2) Moyers would definitely come back, would replace Shriver in the fullness of time; he would, because he had been hinting to members of the press that that's what he wanted to do; he had written to Charlie Houston that that is what he wanted to do *above all else*, and he had given other Peace Corps staffers the same distinct impression; (3) Even if Moyers did not return, either because Johnson absolutely would not release him this time or because he had become understandably "high" from deep inhalations of raw power, that would still be all right. For at twenty-nine, Moyers was being called "deputy president," since until the November 1964 election—almost a year after the assassination—Johnson would not have a vice president of his own.

Moyers's influence with Lyndon Johnson did not derive from Johnson's lack of an official vice president; it derived from his original relationship with Johnson from college age, his astonishing political acumen, his immense personal charm, and his seemingly effortless diplomatic skills. Moyers was almost magical. Moyers would somehow make it right for the Peace Corps. The political neophyte, Charlie Houston, who wanted to believe more than almost anyone else the myth that Moyers would actually give up his awesome power at the White House and return as director—as it became increasingly obvious that Shriver was of necessity easing himself out—was soon throwing cold water on the notion. Houston had become all too quickly a sadder but wiser man upon his return from India to Peace Corps headquarters, where he thought he detected the mentality of a lynch mob at times as the agency lurched on, leaderless, and the staff meetings became ever more confrontational. "Better forget it," the good Dr. Houson was saying, in effect, "you with the stars in your eyes."

But surely, the brethren thought, Moyers would pull some strings. Moyers was pulling them. It just wasn't obvious at first. An early major foreign policy recommendation Moyers made to Johnson was to elevate Jack Vaughn to the post of ambassador to Panama in March 1964. Vaughn was fluent in Spanish and French. He had worked for two years as a college professor and ten years in the foreign aid bureaucracy in both Central and Latin America, including four years in Panama. (He had met Shriver in Senegal, West Africa, however, when he was setting up programs for ICA programs in Senegal, Mali, and Mauritania.) He had known heavy combat duty as a marine officer on Eniwetok, Guam, and Okinawa in World War II and had been decorated. He had a way of deflecting panic and crises with calm, dry wit and even gallows humor. He was "mellow" and "laid back" before it was fashionable. Moyers was impressed. He thought Vaughn just the right man for the immediate Panama crisis. Vaughn describes it: "Panama had broken diplomatic relations with us and some Panamanians were out to kill Americans because we had killed twenty-six Panamanians when they tried to storm the Canal Zone. Moyers called me to come over to the White House from Peace Corps—that minute—to discuss the situation with the president. The president offered me, point blank, the ambassadorship."

Vaughn had heard rumors the week before that the idea of his appointment had been floated around the State Department. He had also heard that it had been rejected at the highest levels: "Dean Rusk (secretary of state) didn't want me to go, and George Ball (undersecretary of state) didn't want me to go. Thomas Mann (the assistant secretary of state for inter-American Affairs, a job that Vaughn would soon have himself) did not want me. Nobody wanted me—nobody. These State Department people, they were just very, very hostile. All the pros in the State Department thought it would be a form of madness to send an amateur to Panama at that time. They were saying, 'This is a tough situation. We need a professional diplomat. We don't need a joker like Vaughn. In the end, I think maybe even Johnson was doubtful that he had made the right choice. But Moyers was persuasive and Johnson stood by me." (Moyers also had been persuasive and Johnson had stood by the Peace Corps in May 1961, when the infant Peace Corps was about to be abducted by AID.)

Johnson called Vaughn over to the White House before he left. He said to Vaughn, "You've got to be very careful. We don't want you to get crosswise with those university students who are mad at the Americans. No incidents. No incidents. Keep it smooth. Low profile. Just kind of sneak in there and get things back in shape."

Vaughn replied, "Mr. President, I've always just snuck in before. I'll just sneak in again and be very low key."

Vaughn arrived in Panama City at 2:30 A.M. on the Pan Am DC-6B milk run in a driving rainstorm.

Nobody knew I was coming except the chargé d'affaires at the U.S. embassy, and he knew the importance of low profile in this case. He was in virtual exile himself. He wasn't even living in Panama;

he was living in the Canal Zone. So as my plane taxied up to the terminal in a torrential rainstorm, I was relaxed. Then I looked out the window through the driving rain and I said out loud, "Oh, Jesus Christ!" There were about fifty Panamanian men—all people I'd worked with in the 1950s—looking like drowned rats, holding up a sign about one hundred feet long, reading "Welcome Jack." I knew then that there would be no big problems.

I was there about nine months. I got all the credit for reestablishing relations, but I didn't do anything brilliant. It was just like a lovers' quarrel in which you reach a point at which you realize that the pouting and vituperation don't accomplish anything, and you decide to get back together and go on. I arrived in Panama just when they were ready to kiss and make up.

Vaughn is too modest. The Panamians loved him and called him the "*campesino* ambassador"—the people's ambassador. No other American ambassador had ever been named so affectionately. Vaughn had succeeded by doing what comes naturally—to him. This fact was not lost on President Johnson, who had gone against the wishes of the State Department to appoint Vaughn, strictly on the word of Moyers. Now that Moyers's judgment on such matters had been vindicated with Johnson, and Johnson's with the top people at the State Department, there were no objections when Johnson tapped Vaughn in March 1965 to be assistant secretary of state for inter-American affairs, again at Moyers's suggestion. (Vaughn was replacing Thomas Mann, a favorite of Johnson's from Laredo, Texas, who was being promoted to undersecretary of state for economic affairs.)

Vaughn remained in that job until February 1966, when he received a strange telephone call in a Georgetown bar.

◆   ◆   ◆

Paul Conklin, the official Peace Corps photographer from 1962 to 1965, traveled with Shriver, Walter Ridder (owner of the Ridder newspaper chain, now known as Knight-Ridder), and Dick Goodwin to record an odyssey of great geographical sweep and historical drama. The trip, which was planned before Kennedy's assassination, was to have taken the group to see Peace Corps Volunteers and staff in Turkey, Iran, Afghanistan, Nepal, India, and finally to Thailand, where Shriver was to receive an honorary degree from Chulalongkorn University. Conklin keenly looked forward to the trip despite the renowned rigors of traveling with Shriver and the reported high-handedness of Goodwin. The itinerary would provide incomparable opportunities for a photographer.

The trip would also provide an ideal opportunity for the American government to display continuity. Shriver was a well-known entity to leaders of the Third World. In his role as Peace Corps director he was a neutral rather than a political entity, but he was still the brother-in-law of John F. Kennedy. He would be welcomed as an emissary of the Kennedy family. And since President Johnson liked and admired Shriver immensely and had named him to head the Poverty task force, Shriver would have yet another role as a diplomatic representative of the new administration. And so the trip ballooned in importance. Shriver would be meeting with, and carrying official messages to, prime ministers and presidents at every stop; and stops were added—the most important being those in Israel (where he would meet with David Ben-Gurion and Golda Meier) and Jordan (where he would meet with King Hussein). And since Pope Paul would be in Jerusalem at that time, yet another portentous encounter was scheduled.

The latter three encounters took place where no Volunteers were posted. This fact, and many others that accumulated on that trip served to remind Conklin that Shriver was no longer "merely" Peace Corps director. A chapter was coming to a close. Conklin was feeling nostalgia before the fact as he watched Shriver fill new roles. "For one thing, there was a lot of cable traffic between our planes and Washington. It was mostly about the poverty program. It was definitely diverting him from Peace Corps matters. The Volunteers were often secondary. But obviously it couldn't be helped. I couldn't imagine how long he would be able to juggle the two. I never dreamed it would be almost two years." There were other uncommon diversions. Others who had traveled with Shriver had complained that he would never stop anywhere, even briefly, "just for fun." But on the leg to Istanbul, Turkey, via Athens, Shriver discovered Lillian Hellman was on the same plane. "Sarge, Dick Goodwin, and Walter Ridder all knew her," says Conklin. "When she suggested that she take us all to a quaint little restaurant in the shadow of the Acropolis after a proper pilgrimage, Sarge happily agreed. When Lillian had trouble negotiating through the broken stones of the steps of the Acropolis in her high heels, the three men jovially picked her up and carried her. Then we had this festive lunch at the little restaurant. Lillian reached for the check grandly, but when she read it, she blanched. I could see that it was a long stretch of numbers. I'd heard that Sarge never carried money, and I figured Goodwin didn't, so I guessed Walter Ridder would grab the check.

But no, Sarge came right up with it, peeled off several hundred dollars."

Conklin recalls that, otherwise,

Sarge did all of the things he was famous for. Slept under the seats of the planes. Fell asleep in an incredibly noisy Israeli army helicopter. Jumped out of jeeps to shake the hands of the likes of wandering herdsmen in a long camel chain near the Khyber Pass. Drove through the Khyber Pass at night. Now, nobody does that, but we did. Cheated death in a small plane in the middle of nowhere up in northern Iran: We took off in a sandstorm and were just off the ground when my seatmate, Bob Steiner, the Rep in Afghanistan, who was traveling part of the way with us, said, "Something's wrong." He'd been a pilot in World War II and *knew*. Sure enough, one of the engines of this two-engine Convair simply quit. The pilot had just enough forward motion to make one circle as we dodged camels and somehow landed without hitting anything. Plenty of drama in Iran. One day Sarge just tore up the schedule and said, "Let's go up to Persepolis." There he gave us a full lecture on the Persian dynasty. He knew more than Goodwin. When we went to meet the Shah in Tehran, I was almost jumped by the Shah's bodyguards. They surrounded me. Seems that very recently the Shah had almost been assassinated by a man posing as a photographer. That Sarge had introduced me as his personal photographer did not help.

Once in Nepal, when we were walking from a village in the Ganges plain several miles to our airplane, Sarge decided to hitch a ride on a horse-drawn cart. Dust came swirling up and encased him in dirt. This amused me because he's always so immaculate. Off we went to Katmandu, where we kept a staff and a bunch of very eager Volunteers waiting for over an hour because Sarge had exhorted the pilot to "fly closer to Everest."

Shriver was the kind of guy who, when you traveled with him, would all but loan you his toothbrush. He would make you feel like a part of his inner circle. But when you'd come back—well, I remember he drove off at the airport and left me standing there with my baggage and camera equipment.

In summer of 1964, the poverty legislation was passed in Congress, the Office of Economic Opportunity (OEO) was officially established, and Shriver spent half of each day at OEO headquarters. By the time

Conklin left the Peace Corps in spring of 1965, Shriver was spending just over one-fourth of his time at the Peace Corps. During the last eight months of his five-year tour as Peace Corps director, he came to his Peace Corps office only one day a week. The chief of Special Projects, David Gelman, was one of the few who felt free to rib Shriver. He penned this limerick and sent it on memo paper:

Washington's number one resident,
Without seeming overly hesitant,
Said, "I hate to deprive yer
Of R. Sargent Shriver,
But Poverty needs its own president.

No reply.

When Gelman would run into Shriver in the hall during the latter part of Shriver's two-hat period, he would ask pleasantly, "To what do we owe the pleasure of this visit?" Shriver would chuckle nervously. Another time, Gelman met Shriver on a crowded elevator. Since the staff rarely saw Shriver anymore, they were staring at him open-mouthed but speechless. Shriver, obviously uncomfortable, looked relieved to see Gelman, someone who was not feeling orphaned or intimidated. (Gelman, who had no intention of working in a Shriverless Peace Corps was openly job hunting in New York.) Gelman, slyly noting Shriver's relief, said, "Oh God, Sarge. Say it isn't so."

"Say *what* isn't so?"

"That Vince Lombardi is your successor."

The inhabitants of the elevator gasped. As Shriver got off the elevator at the fifth floor, he said to Gelman in mock amazement, "Dave, how in the hell did you ever find out?"

"Sometimes Sarge enjoyed playing that game and sometimes he didn't," says Gelman. "He knew the whole place was frantic wondering who would take over. But I began to sense that Sarge had gotten to like the idea of being the only guy in town who was running two agencies."

When the Poverty task force was announced the first weekend in February of 1964 (at which Mankiewicz was surprised to find himself an involved onlooker, having come up from Peru on Peace Corps business)—and even as Conklin mentioned to Peace Corps colleagues that quite a bit of Shriver's time on his just-completed round-the-world trip was taken up with "poverty business"—most people at the Peace Corps didn't want to believe it, refused to acknowledge it. First Kennedy had been killed. Then Moyers had been snatched away. And now Shriver was giving birth to another novel social program. And right on the premises.

Adam Yarmolinsky was on leave from that famous den of "whiz kids" at the Pentagon to act as Shriver's deputy and was sitting—where?—but in Bill Moyers's former office in the executive suite across from Shriver. Hyman Bookbinder, special assistant to both Shriver and Yarmolinsky on the Poverty task force, was sitting down the hall in Haddad's former suite of offices. Word quickly got out that Yarmolinsky and Bookbinder's secretaries answered their telephones with one word: "Poverty." The Peace Corps staff found that alternately amusing, peculiar, and grotesque. As more and more "poverty-ites" moved into other offices at 806 Connecticut Avenue, the Peace Corp staff coined the phrase "Po' Co' " and looked upon them as Martians, mutants, and of course, profoundly unwanted siblings.

However, when the poverty legislation passed in June 1964, Shriver, Yarmolinsky, and Bookbinder moved into temporary offices at 17th and Pennsylvania on the top floor of the Renwick Gallery, one of the Smithsonian's most handsome and unique buildings. "Shriver was under one cupola, I was under the other, with thirty-foot ceilings, with Bookie in between," says Yarmolinsky. (Shriver was then spending half of every day at the Peace Corps. Soon, the entire "Po' Co' " moved to permanent quarters at 19th and M, a more suitably proletarian environment.)

In addition to the "Vince Lombardi scare" that Gelman and Shriver gave a few staff members, other wild rumors rumbled through headquarters for over a year. While Warren Wiggins had been named acting director in January 1965, and ran the agency smoothly and evenhandedly (and clearly hoped to replace Shriver officially), nobody thought that would happen. Wiggins simply did not have enough charisma, it was argued, and the Peace Corps had been weaned on charisma. Besides, many thought that the general counsel, Bill Josephson, had too much influence over Wiggins, and Josephson simply had too many detractors. A very strong rumor was floated (and therefore those with the most sensitive political antennae, such as Charlie Peters and Frank Mankiewicz, briefly believed that Shriver or Moyers had deliberately floated it) that the top candidate was Donald Petrie, then president of Avis Rent-a-Car. On that one, a howl went up. "Oh God, no! Not a *businessman*!" (Those howling seemed to forget that Shriver had been first a businessman.)

A few people thought briefly that, in the end, the job might fall to Mankiewicz because of the charm factor alone. But no, on immediate second thought, Mankiewicz was too much of an idealogue, too hooked on bringing about peaceful revolution in the shantytowns of Latin America, too sure that it could be done in his lifetime and that Peace Corps Volunteers could do it. Too many others knew it could not. Yes, Mankiewicz could *inspire*, but Mankiewicz could not dot the i's or cross the t's. Scratch Mankiewicz. But what about Harris Wofford? Wofford after all, was the man Shriver knew best on the Peace Corps staff. Wofford, in 1965, was associate director of Planning, Evaluation and Research, which, like Haddad before him, gave him maximum propinquity to Shriver. And Wofford had been the first role-model Rep in Ethiopia. He had worked intensively with Shriver on the civil rights section of the 1960 campaign. Wofford and Shriver were philsophically, intellectually, and socially compatible. The most significant factor in considering Wofford as the heir apparent was the fact that Wofford was now riding to work every morning with Shriver (both lived in the Maryland suburbs). It was assumed that Wofford was successfully lobbying his own case with Shriver. But on third thought, it was assumed among compulsive heir-watchers that Shriver must have known that Wofford would not be a popular choice with the Peace Corps staff. Wofford was too much the gentleman mystic, the dreamer, and a majority of the senior staff had made it clear in staff meetings that they could not communicate with him. Charlie Houston, as blunt a man as Wofford was vague, once said, "When I am talking to Wofford, I always feel as if I am speaking to an intermediary who will soon transmit my message to Mr. Wofford, wherever he might be." Betty Harris used to say that Wofford would have no trouble finding a job when he left the Peace Corps because "he can always open a Rent-a-Grail service." When Wofford suggested that the Peace Corps was really a "university in dispersion," George Nicolau, deputy director of Special Projects, replied, "Then why don't we just call it the "dispersiversity." There was one more worry: If Wofford could not sell himself to Shriver, he might be able to sell Father Theodore Hesbergh of Notre Dame as "a beard." (Hesbergh, it was said by the ever-gossiping Peace Corps staff, after two Bloody Marys at Chez François had the four C's that enchanted Shriver: Catholicism, Courage, Constituency, and Charisma. Shriver never said that; it was only imagined that Shriver *thought* that.)

Charlie Peters, who in those days was much too puritanically workaholic to indulge himself in these bibulous luncheon wonderings, was nonetheless keeping track of every rumor and of every source theory about every rumor. One day, over a rare coffee break in his office, he blurted, "Why does everyone assume that Shriver can make this decision? Shriver is a lame duck. He's got another job. So forget all those people that Shriver is supposed to be appointing. Only the White House can appoint. And that means Moyers. Because who else at the White House has the interest or the power to appoint a new Peace Corps director? Moyers won't appoint anybody on our present staff. He knows that would tear the place apart. And who keeps saying publicly and privately that all he wants in life is to be director of the Peace Corps? Moyers. I think he is really tied up in knots of ambivalence about this. But let's face it: *Moyers isn't coming back.*"

◆　　◆　　◆

On February 16, 1966, Jack Vaughn was sitting at a bar at 12:30 P.M. on M Street in Georgetown. He was exchanging mellow, macho memories with Johnny Johnston, a former AID mission director in Cuba just before Castro made his revolution. Vaughn relished his occasional rendevous with the personable, voluble, opinionated Johnston, who had, in addition to leading an otherwise very colorful life, been a close friend and fishing/drinking buddy of Ernest Hemingway. Johnston and Hemingway had moored their boots side by side in the Havana harbor in the 1950s and had hoisted many a margarita together at the La Floridita bar. Vaughn and Johnston were vaguely thinking about sitting down to lunch after a couple of margaritas themselves when the bar telephone rang. "Is there a Mr. Jack Vaughn here?" inquired the bartender nervously. Vaughn identified himself.

"Mr. Vaughn," said the bug-eyed bartender, "it's someone who says he's the president of the United States."

"Wait until I finish my drink," said Vaughn. He threw back what remained of his second margarita. He picked up the telephone. "It wasn't a receptionist. It wasn't a telephone operator. It was LBJ himself."

"Vaughn, how'd you like to be director of the Peace Corps?"

"Mr. President, I thought you'd never ask."

INDEX

Adams, Timothy, 124, 155, 210, 388; Public Information Office, 84, 121
Afghanistan, 399
Agency for International Development (AID), 38, 121, 174, 213, 294; cooperation with in Peru, 304–5; as employer of ex-Volunteers, 358; and India program, 307–8, 313–14; Shriver on contacts with, 92
AID. *See* Agency for International Development, ICA
Alexander, John, 74, 222, 258
Alliance for Progress, 304–5
Ambassador to: Denmark, William McCormick Blair, 11; Ethiopia, Arthur Richards, 162; Great Britain, Joseph Kennedy, 67; India, John Kenneth Galbraith, 92, 308–9, 322; Mali, Parker Borg, 359; Nepal, Carol Laise, 323; Nigeria, Joseph Palmer, 120; Peru, James Loeb, 52, 299; Tunisia, Francis Russell, 181
Apter, David: initial training for Africa, 79
Ashabranner, Brent, 89, 313–14, 317, 323, 334
Ashanti: A Proud People, The (Robert Lystad), 79
Atlanta Constitution, 229
Azikiwe, Dr. Nnamdi (governor general of Nigeria), 140

Baird, Eugene, 265, 297
Barriadas, slums in Peru, 292, 299–301
Bates, Robert, 85–87, 310
Bayley, Ed, 75, 83, 152, 229; on Burma, 143; in Public Information, 49, 139; trip to Africa and Asia in April 1961, 143–44
Belize. *See* British Honduras
Bell, Darwin (associate director for Management, Peru), 264, 288; in Costa Rica, 289
Bell, David (ICA): and Peace Corps under AID umbrella, 39
Bellamy, Carol: Volunteer in Guatemala, 367–71
Billings, Lemoyne, 75–76
Biro, Emery (associate director, Arequipa, Peru), 289
Bisauli Workshop, 320–25
Blitz recruiting, 239–42
Bloch, Julia Chang: Volunteer in Sabah, 371–77
Bookbinder, Hyman, 401
Boubion, David, 265
Bowles, Chester, 88, 135, 141, 180, 323
Bowles, Sally, 36–37, 77, 89, 94–96, 112, 124, 241; deputy director, Division of Volunteer Support, 96
Boyce, Gordon, 201; Division of Private Organizations, 74
Bradford, Alan: Volunteer in India, 361–67
Braestrup, Peter, 34–37, 39, 41

Bread Christians: in Peru, 302
British Honduras, 211–12, 289
Butterworth, Blair, 154
Byers, Marjorie (*Life* reporter):
  Michelmore incident, 123

Campesino ambassador, 397
Campesinos, peasants in Chile,
  358
CARE, 369
Carrington, Walter, 84, 266,
  268–69
Carter, George, 77, 125
Celebreeze, Anthony (Secretary of
  Health, Education and
  Welfare), 66
Celeste, Richard (director during
  Carter administration), 318
Challenge: competition among
  service options, 336–37
Chang, Julia. *See* Bloch, Julia
  Chang
CIA: Nkrumah's comments, 137;
  Shriver on contacts with, 92
Civilian Conservation Corps
  (CCC), 38; and case for
  independent agency, 41; and
  Outward Bound camps, 116
Coffin, William Sloane (director,
  Outward Bound camp), 58,
  116; Michelmore incident,
  123–24
Colmen, Dr. Joseph (director of
  research), 117, 158, 163, 175,
  204, 206, 390; East Africa trip
  in October, 1962, 158–60,
  163–64
Colorado State University: report on
  Reuss proposal, 29
Come as you are: Mathews, Tom,
  48
Conklin, Paul (official
  photographer), 126, 397

Connolly, Cyril, 3
Cook, Philip (evaluator), 210, 214,
  388
Cowan, Gray (professor of African
  studies): Columbia University,
  79
Crichton, Victor (assistant to
  Haddad), 117

Davies, George: Ministry of
  Education, Sierra Leone, 274
Dayal, Rajeshwar (Ambassador to
  the United States), 322
Death of a President, The (William
  Manchester), 391
Delano, William, 88–89
Delany, Kevin Francis Xavier
  (deputy director for the
  Asian Operation), 212, 213,
  388
Dennis, Larry (associate director,
  Office of Peace Corps
  Volunteers), 78, 94
Discrimination by sex: in
  appointing evaluators, 214; in
  education, Ivory Coast, 380;
  and first anniversary
  celebration, 155; Harris
  appointment to deal with,
  94–95; and Julia Chang,
  375–76; overcoming, associate
  director, Peru, 290; in policy
  determination, 112; pregnancy
  and related problems, 96–98;
  in selecting Reps, 263;
  successful women, 360
Dodd, Christopher (Senator from
  Connecticut), 359
Dog boxes: Public Health in Peru,
  291
Drake, Sinclair (professor of African
  studies): Roosevelt University,
  79

Dungan, Ralph, 38, 40; AID, 53; reorganization of foreign aid programs, 27–28, 38–42

Ecuador, 288
Education: British system, 140, 274–75, 363; learning by rote, 374–75
Elwell, Richard, 210; evaluation, British Honduras, 211–12; evaluation, Ethiopia, 334
English, Dr. Joseph (Chief of Psychiatry), 98, 112, 391
Ernst, Roger: AID, acting Rep in India, 307
Erwin, Frank (deputy director of Selection), 239, 372; recruiting Volunteers, 254–57
Ethiopia, 159–63
Evaluation, 199–218, 382; a language for the Division, 215; by volunteers Mary and Alfred Jones, 298; Houston on leaving India, 338–39; long-term effects, 377; nature of, 203; rationale for, 205; as reason for Shriver October 1961 trip, 206; of training program, 61
Experiment for International Living, 74

Family of Man, The, 221
Favelas, slums in Brazil, 292
Feminine Mystique, The (Betty Friedan), 112
Ferguson, Glenn, 51; recruiting head, 52; Reverse Peace Corps, 335–36; Talent Search (hero hunt), 263
First Dance of Freedom (Martin Meredith), 380
Five Miles High (Houston and Bates), 87

Five-year flush. *See* In, Up & Out policy
Flather, Roger (regional director for Sabah), 373
Florence Crittenden Home: caring for unmarried mothers, 97
Food for Peace, 304–5, 376
Foundation for Voluntary Service, 335
Freetown Daily Mail, 283–84
Frost, Robert: inaugural poem, 29, 141
Fulbright, William (Senator from Arkansas): 1961 legislation, 147
Fuller, Captain Frederick: Outward Bound School at Aberdovey, Wales, 115; Outward Bound, Arecibo, 116

Gale, Robert Lee, 126–27, 215, 221–59; blitz recruiting, 357; director of recruiting, 236
Gallagher, Dr. Joseph: head of Medical Division, 391
Gandhi, Mahatma: peacekeeping and service, 141, 337
Gavin, General James M.: and peacetime alternative service, 14–18
Gehrig, Dr. Leo: arrangements about overseas pregnancies, 97
Gelman, David, 27, 59–70, 163, 199, 204, 215, 400; and Eunice Shriver study, care of retarded, 62–70; evaluation, Somalia I, 61, 168–71, 207; evaluation, Tanganyika, 178–79
Geren, Paul (deputy director), 146, 157; on women's issues, 95
Ghana, 79–81; acceptance of Volunteers, 91; Africa and Asia

trip in April 1961, 137; first
request, 6; welcomes first
Volunteers, 80
Gilbert, Alice, 112
Gold Coast in Transition (David
Apter), 79
Goldwater, Barry (Senator from
Arizona): 1961 legislation,
147
Golpe, military coup, 288
Gore, Albert (Senator from
Tennessee): 1961 legislation,
147
Gore, Nancy, 36–37, 77; assistant
to Moyers, 216
Graham, Dick, 211
Greenberg, Howard (director,
Office of Management), 224;
on recruiting Volunteers, 233,
235–36
Greene, Jerry (deputy to ambassador
to Nigeria), 120
Grinnan, Manning: on poultry
farming in Punjab, 311–12
Groak, adapted Irish term: and Peru
feeding program, 304–5
Grothe, Peter: and 1960 legislation
for peace corps, 146–47
Guatemala, 369–70
Guskin, Alan and Judy, 12–14

Haddad, William F. (Bill), 8, 26,
28, 36, 39, 48, 52, 55, 59, 61,
114–17, 204, 210, 216,
221–22, 236, 258, 266, 358,
387; associate director for
Planning, Evaluation and
Research, 48; In, Up & Out
policy, 129; internal politics,
224–25; and *New York Post*,
11; origination of
self-evaluation, 199; and
Peace Corps under AID

umbrella, 39; on State
Department suggestions, 114;
Talent Search (hero hunt),
263; task force on peace corps
concept, 26
Handwerger, Gretchen (director,
eastern region, Latin America),
57
Harijans, untouchables, 314, 366
Harris, Elizabeth Forsling (Betty),
93–98, 111–12, 124, 288,
329, 402; on appointment of
women evaluators, 214; deputy
associate director, OPCV, 96;
Michelmore incident, 122; on
Passman and India program,
318–20; on Shriver, 93, 148;
women's division, Peace
Corps, 94–95
Harris, Mark (evaluator), 387–92
Hayes, Samuel (University of
Michigan): and report for
Peace Corps task force, 29
Heart of the Matter, The (Graham
Greene), 269
Hernandes, Andres, 265
Hesbergh, Father Theodore
(president, Notre Dame): visit
to Chile, 358
Hiepp, Terry (secretary to Houston
in India), 308
Hindi, language of India, 142
Hollings, Ernest F. (Senator from
South Carolina): peacetime
alternative service, 15–16; on
staffing for Peace Corps, 28
Houston, Dr. Charles, 86–93, 130,
265, 307–40, 374, 395; as
described by a Volunteer,
364–65; on In, Up & Out
policy, 130; medical
emergency in Nepal, 310;
meeting with Ashabranner, 90

Humphrey, Hubert (Senator from Minnesota), 147, 221; legislation for a peace corps, 7

Ibo: Ivory Coast ethnic group, 378; Nigerian ethnic group, 140
ICA. *See* AID, International Cooperation Administration
Idealism: appeal in India, 140–42; and asceticism, 182–83, 242–43, 363–64; Chang on, 372; David Richards on, 380; and elitism, 272, 277–78, 373; expressed by Houston, 333–34; expressed by returned Volunteers, 360; expressed by Shriver, 388; expressed by Volunteer, 316; and first anniversary celebration, 155–57; Gandhian principles, 337; Houston and ascetic image, 327; Meisel on, 118; and Peru program, 287–88, 300, 302–3; and salary, 37; service motivation, 31; Shriver's standards of, 164
India, 140–43, 309–18, 320–33; program at Osmania University, 362–66; Punjab, site for first Volunteers in, 142
In, Up & Out policy, 286, 395; origin as antibureaucratic measure, 129; self-imposed, 256–59
Institute of International Education, 74
Institute of Politics at Harvard: fellowship for Carol Bellamy, 370; fellowship for Julia Chang Bloch, 376
International Affairs, Center for, at Harvard: Bowie, Robert, 16
International Cooperation

Administration (ICA), 30; Ashabranner, Brent, 89; Bell, Darwin, 288; as source of Peace Corps staff, 201
Ivory Coast, 379–84; Guetta Emolo Samuel, student, 380; long-term effects of program, 383–84

Jacobsen, Dorothy (personnel director), 37, 97
Jamaica, 289
James, William: Moral Equivalent of War, The, 38
Jenkins, Loren: Former Peace Corps Volunteers Against War, 360
Johnson, Lyndon Baines, 6, 11; and Peace Corps under AID umbrella, 39
Jones, Alfred W.: in India, 321–24; in Peru, 298–303; Reverse Peace Corps, 137, 334–36
Jones, Gardiner, 388
Jones, Mary; in Peru, 298–303
Joseph P. Kennedy Foundation, 68
Josephson, William, 31, 46, 88, 144; internal politics, 201–2

K-2: *The Savage Mountain* (Houston and Bates), 87
Kauffman, Joe, 158, 163, 175, 206
Keeping Kennedy's Promise (Lowther and Lucas), 294, 338
Kelly, Bill (director of contracts), 217
Kennedy, Ethel (Mrs. Robert): on pregnancy and childbirth among Volunteers, 113
Kennedy, John Fitzgerald: as ideal in Ivory Coast, 381; impact of assassination on Peace Corps, 391–94; Senator from

Massachusetts at 1956
Convention, 9; at University of
Michigan, 3
Kennedy, Padraic (Pat), 75–81,
148, 235, 375; director,
Division of Volunteer Support,
81, 96; Division of Training,
78; recruiting at University of
Wisconsin, 75, 230
Kennedy, Robert, 9
Kiker, Douglas (director of Public
Information), 229, 391
King, Martin Luther, Jr., 381
Kittell, George, 156
Klein, George (associate Rep,
Tunisia), 181
Knebel, Fletcher, 55
Krio, language in Sierra Leone, 268

Labouisse, Henry: and AID
umbrella, 39
Landrum, Roger: Returned Peace
Corps Volunteer Association,
124
Lausche, Frank (Senator from
Ohio): 1961 legislation, 147
Liberal Hour, The (John Kenneth
Galbraith), 362
Life, Liberty and Property (Alfred
W. Jones), 298

MacArthur, Diana, 112
McCarthy, Eugene (Senator from
Minnesota), 8
McClure, Donovan, 81–86, 130,
152, 155, 176, 184, 206,
266–86; campaign reporter,
1960, 19; East Africa trip in
October 1962, 158–60; in
Office of Public Affairs,
285–86; in Public
Information Office, 83;
San Francisco Chronicle,

81; on wisdom of In, Up &
Out policy, 130
McCone, Mike (deputy to McClure
in Sierra Leone) 271–76
McEvoy, Nancy Tucker, 112, 243;
deputy director, Africa
Regional Office, 153;
recruiting Volunteers, 239; and
Talent Search, 153, 263
McGuire, Mick (evaluator), 213
McNulty, Nancy (associate director,
Peru), 289–90, 304
Macy, John (chairman, Civil
Service Commission): In, Out
& Up policy, 131
Making of the President, The
(Theodore H. White), 7
Malaysia. See Sabah, Sarawak
Mali, gardener, in India, 332
Mangin, William, 264, 288, 295;
deputy Rep, Peru, 288, 290;
on Peru evaluation, 304
Mankiewicz, Frank, 49–59, 52–53,
55–57, 72, 78, 84, 116, 264,
286–307, 322, 369, 401; aide
to Shriver at OEO, 306–7;
on Outward Bound camp,
Arecibo, 116
Marin, Muñoz (governor of Puerto
Rico): Outward Bound camps,
116
Marshall, Justice Thurgood, 71
Masai: in Tanganyika, 136, 175–76
Massachusetts Institute of
Technology (MIT): Millikan
report on Peace Corps
structure, 29
Mathews, Tom, 57, 61, 81,
121–23, 155, 157, 204, 229;
deputy director of Public
Information, 49, 57, 121;
director of Public Information,
83; at San Francisco Chronicle,
47–49, 81–82

Medical care: comments by Houston, 338; decisions in 1961, 111; emergency in Nepal, 310–11

Meisel, Al, 77, 375; on Shriver administrative style, 148–51; training officer, 118

Mende, language in Sierra Leone, 268

Meyers, Tedson J., 8–9

Michelmore incident, 118, 121–24, 128

Michigan, University of: Hayes report on Peace Corps, 29

Millikan, Max (MIT): task force on peace corps concept, 26–27

Milwaukee Journal, 139

MOM and POP memos, 97, 111–14

Moment in History, A (Brent Ashabranner), 313–14

Moral Equivalent of War (William James): as inspiration for Peace Corps, 38

Morris, Dr. Ralph, 185; Peace Corps doctor in Tunisia, 181

Moyers, Bill D., 40–41, 154, 203, 216, 225, 242, 286, 329; associate director for Public Affairs, 145–46; and Lyndon Baines Johnson, 41, 394–95; on obtaining legislative support, 145; and AID umbrella, 40–41

Mutual Security Act of 1954: authority for executive creation of Peace Corps, 32

Mydans, Carl (*Life* photojournalist): Michelmore incident, 123

Napolitano, Timmy (acting Rep in India), 307

Nashville Tennesseean, 213

Nehru, B. K. (Ambassador from India), 136

Nehru, Jawaharlal, 136, 364

Nelson, Charles, 74, 77

Nelson, Dick, 154, 203; internal politics, 203–4, 225–26

Neuberger, Richard (Senator from Oregon): 7

New York Herald Tribune, 210

New York Post, 8, 11, 27, 52, 58, 60

New York Telegram, 212

New York Times, 25, 34, 152

Nicolau, George, 402

Nigeria, 90, 111, 118; Africa and Asia trip in April 1961, 136, 139; assignment at University of, 125

Nkrumah, Kwame: on American influences, 137; initial acceptance of Volunteers, 90

Nu, U (premier of Burma), 143

Nyerere, Julius (president of Tanzania), 135

Objectives, 320; original report, 34; political, 6

O'Donnell, Kenneth, 12, 215–16, 358

Office of Economic Opportunity (OEO), 305, 335, 399

Of Kennedys and Kings (Harris Wofford), 139–40

Olson, Ruth (deputy in Personnel), 97; Michelmore incident, 122

Opposition: Bob Jones University, 239; to community development program in Peru, 293–94; Daughters of the American Revolution (DAR), 33; Eisenhower, Dwight D., 33, 128; Ghana sensitivity, 125; hostility to Volunteers, Nigeria, 125; Nixon, Richard, 33; Nu, U, 143; Ruark, Robert, 33; *Wall Street Journal,* 33

Organization: Division of
Evaluation, 299; Division of
International Organizations,
74; Division of Private
Organizations, 74; Division of
Special Projects, 222, 224–235;
Division of Training, 78;
Division of University
Relations, 74; Division of
Volunteer Support, 81, 96;
independence from AID, 143;
Office of Management, 224;
Office of Peace Corps
Volunteers (OPCV), 78, 94,
96; Personnel, 37, 97;
Planning, Evaluation and
Research, 48; Program
Development Operations, 74,
299; Program Development
Overseas, 74; Public Affairs,
145–46; Public Information
Office, 49, 83, 121, 139, 241;
Selection, 239; Staff to
Volunteer ratio, 295; and State
Department recommendations,
114
Origins, 3–21; as alternative
service, 14; christening at
Arthur D. Little Co., 17;
developing independent status,
25–42; first mention as
organization, 12; growing
pains, 111–31; Mallina,
Mitzi, first employee, 37;
recruiting, 45–98; task force
on peace corps concept,
26–30
Orlando, Maryann, 55, 77, 158,
222, 245, 391
Osagyefo, honorific applied to
Nkrumah, 137
Other America, The (Michael
Harrington), 306
Ottinger, Dick, 55, 294

Outward Bound: at Arecibo, Puerto
Rico, 55; British program, 115;
at Hilo, Hawaii, 372; training
for Tanganyika I Volunteers,
173

Pakistan, 205, 213
Pakorra, Indian meat cakes, 321
Pamar, Vira, 323; administrative
assistant in India program,
308, 326–28
Panama, 289
Passman, Otto (Congressman from
Louisiana): India program visit,
318–20; review of Peru
program, 305; views on Peace
Corps, 31
Payton, Dr. Carolyn: evaluating the
Peace Corps experience, 371
Peace Corps Schools, 252
Peace Corps Volunteer (newsletter),
95, 124
Peru, 52, 55–59, 288–307;
community development
program, 293; living on Lake
Titicaca, 301–3
Peters, Charles, 144, 170, 211,
294, 387, 389, 391, 401; and
Arecibo training site contract,
217; chief of evaluation,
199–218; internal politics,
204–5
Philippines, 143–44; suggested as
first program site, 31; in "The
Towering Task," 144
Po' Co': Poverty programs, 401
Point Four Agencies (of ICA), 20
Point Four Youth Corps, 7
Politics: Bisauli Workshop
harassment, 321–25; family
planning and program, 300–301;
image and groaking in Peru,
304–5; and Michelmore

Starr, Dr. John: public health physician, Peru, 296
Start-up period, 135–85
Stevens, Siaka (president of Sierra Leone), 284
Stevenson, Adlai, 8; ambassador to United Nations, 54
Stopper, William: AID, India, 313
Sullivan, Patricia, 112
Summers, Sir Spencer: Outward Bound Trust (Britain), 115; Outward Bound, Arecibo, 116
Sunrise with Seamonsters (Paul Theroux), 359
Support: Aryanayakam, Ashadevi, 141; Jeffrey, Mildred, 12–14; at Michigan, University of, 13
Swahili, language in Africa, 54, 136

Tanganyika, 54, 135–36, 173–80
Tanzania. *See* Tanganyika
Taylor, General Maxwell: on pregnancy and childbirth among Volunteers, 113
Tedesco, Salvatore (deputy Rep in Ghana), 172
Teefs, thieves, 282–83
Tej, Ethiopian drink, 161
Temne, language in Sierra Leone, 268
Thailand, 209, 213
Theroux, Paul, 359–60
Towering Task, The: paper on concept, 30–32; Philippines' place in, 144; speed of implementation, 46; as vehicle for personal advancement, 32–33
Training program: at Arecibo, Puerto Rico, 58; 216–17; results as seen in India, 317–18; routinization of,

375; setting up the Africa programs, 79
Training site: at Arecibo, Puerto Rico, for Peru, 58; at Berkeley for Ghana III, 62; at Cornell University for Peru, 58; at Ibadan, University of, 119; at Indiana, University of for Tunisia II, 62; at New York University for Somalia I, 61; at Oberlin College for Ivory Coast, 378; at San Francisco State University for Liberia III, 62; at Texas Western University for Tanganyika I, 173; at UCLA for Nigeria I, 150
Tunisia, 180–85
Twentyone Twice (Mark Harris), 387
Twi, language of Ghana, 80, 138

Uhuru, freedom in Swahili, 172, 271
University of Michigan: birth of Peace Corps, 3
Unsoeld, Willi (assistant Rep in Nepal), 85
Upp, Robertson, 389–90
USIA: in Ivory Coast, 381; in Tunisia, 183

Vanderwood, Paul (evaluator), 213
Vaughn, Jack, 46, 55–56, 130, 248, 288; appointment as ambassador, 395; director following Shriver, 403; Director of Latin America Regional Office, 55; at ICA, 395; and impact of Kennedy assassination, 392–94; on In, Up & Out policy, 130
Venezuela, 289